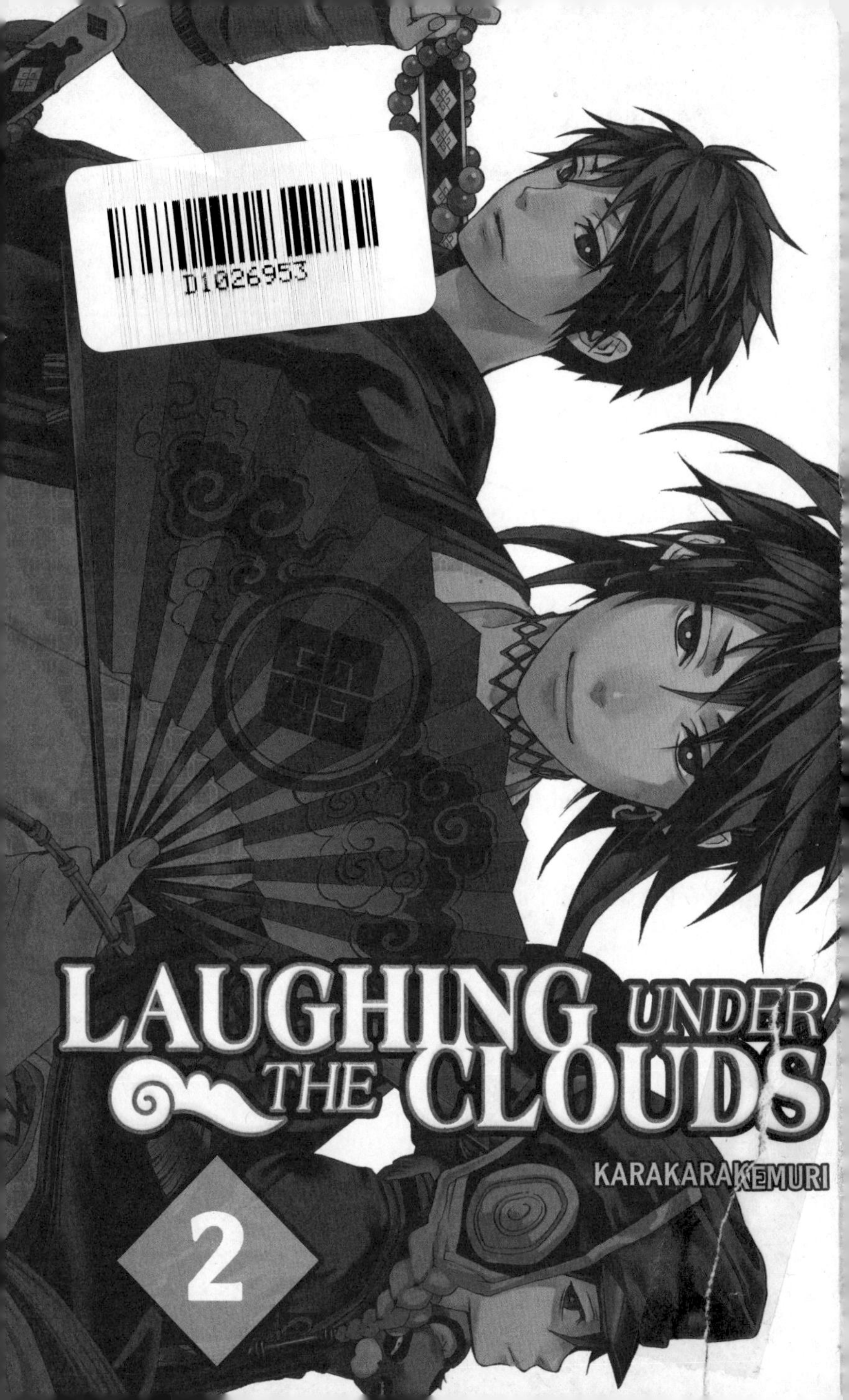
LAUGHING UNDER THE CLOUDS
KARAKARAKEMURI
2

Table of Contents

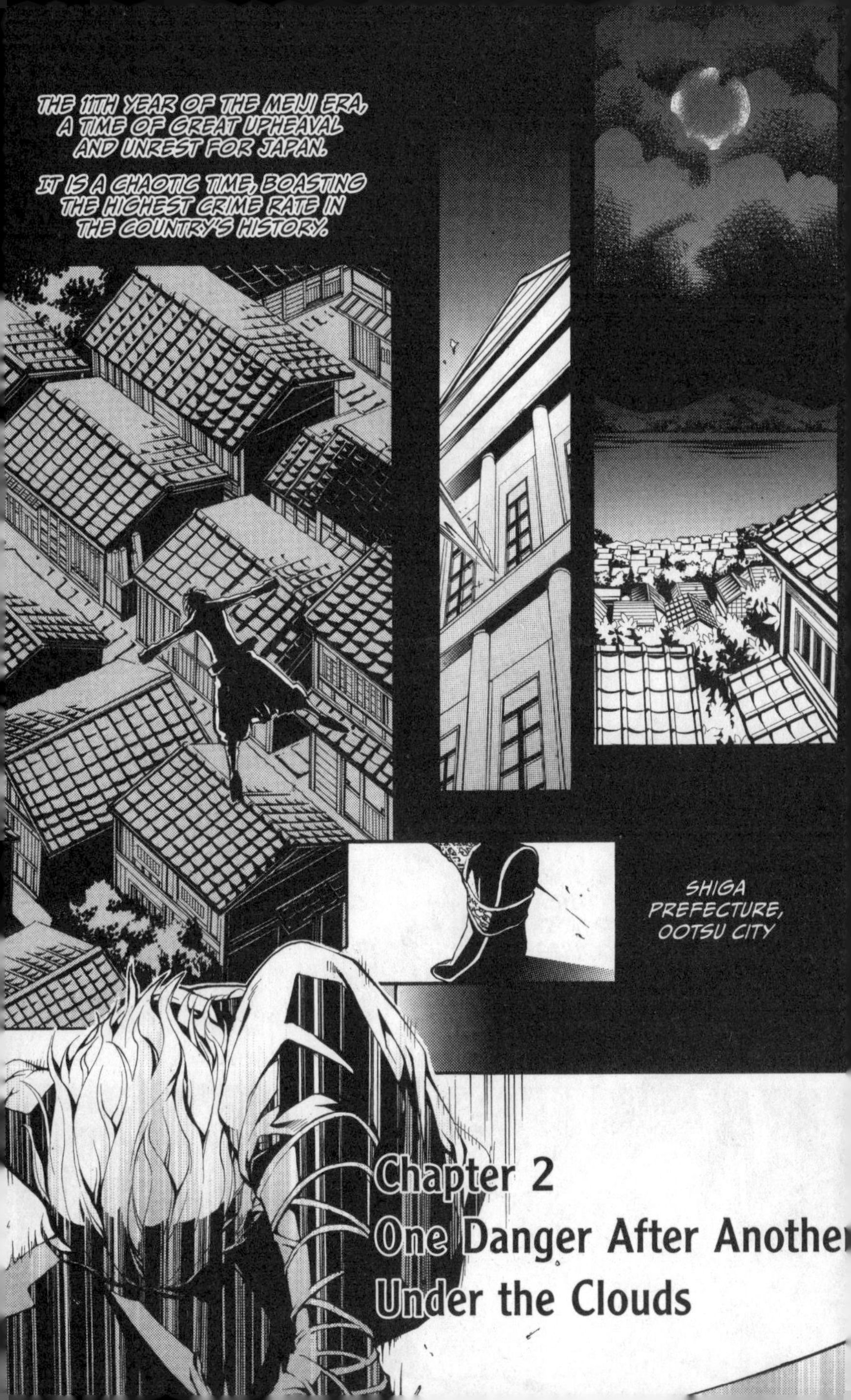
THE 11TH YEAR OF THE MEIJI ERA, A TIME OF GREAT UPHEAVAL AND UNREST FOR JAPAN.
IT IS A CHAOTIC TIME, BOASTING THE HIGHEST CRIME RATE IN THE COUNTRY'S HISTORY.
SHIGA PREFECTURE, OOTSU CITY
Chapter 2
One Danger After Another
Under the Clouds

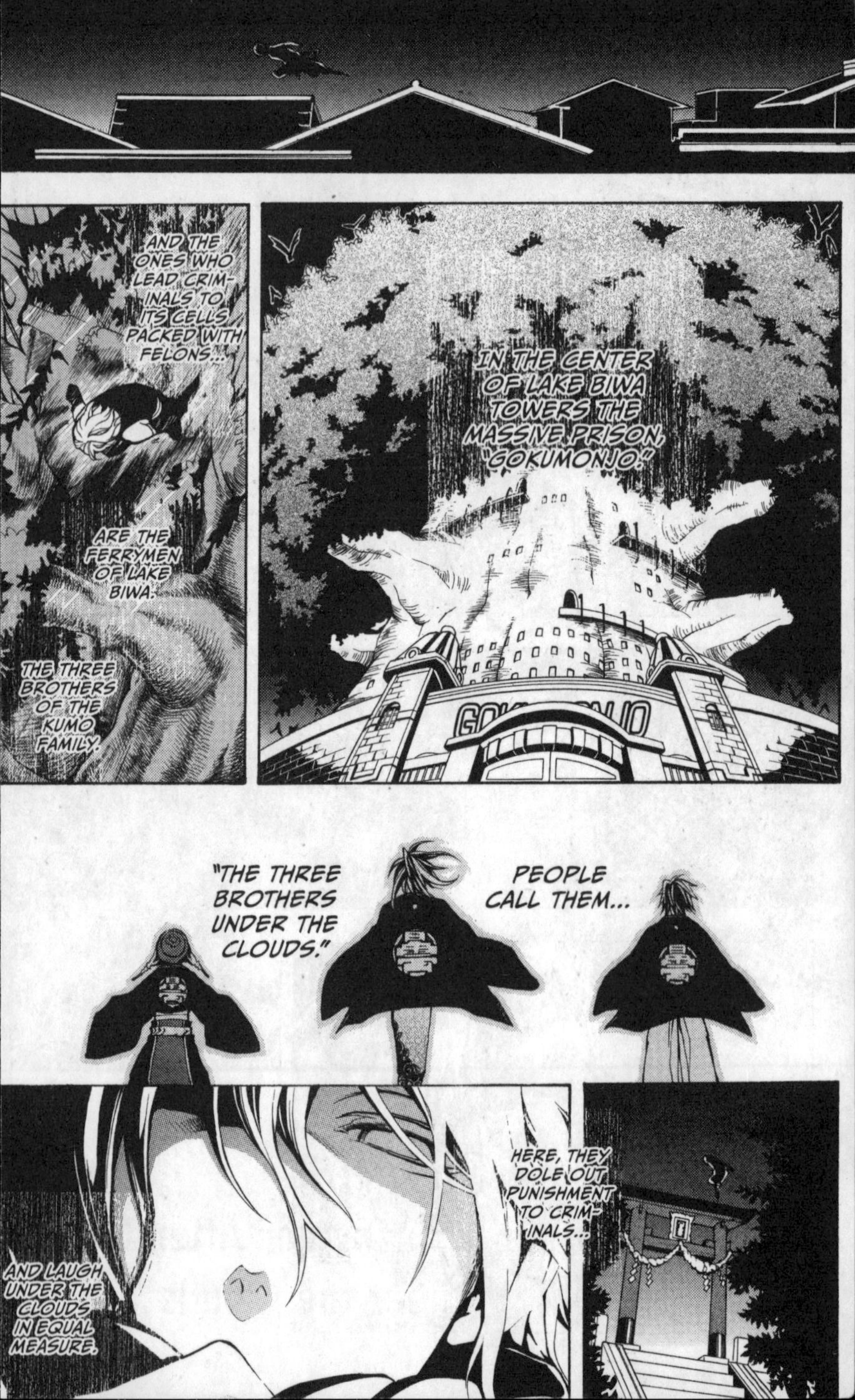
IN THE CENTER OF LAKE BIWA TOWERS THE MASSIVE PRISON, "GOKUMONJO."
AND THE ONES WHO LEAD CRIMINALS TO ITS CELLS PACKED WITH FELONS...
ARE THE FERRYMEN OF LAKE BIWA.
THE THREE BROTHERS OF THE KUMO FAMILY.
PEOPLE CALL THEM...
"THE THREE BROTHERS UNDER THE CLOUDS."
HERE, THEY DOLE OUT PUNISHMENT TO CRIMINALS...
AND LAUGH UNDER THE CLOUDS IN EQUAL MEASURE.

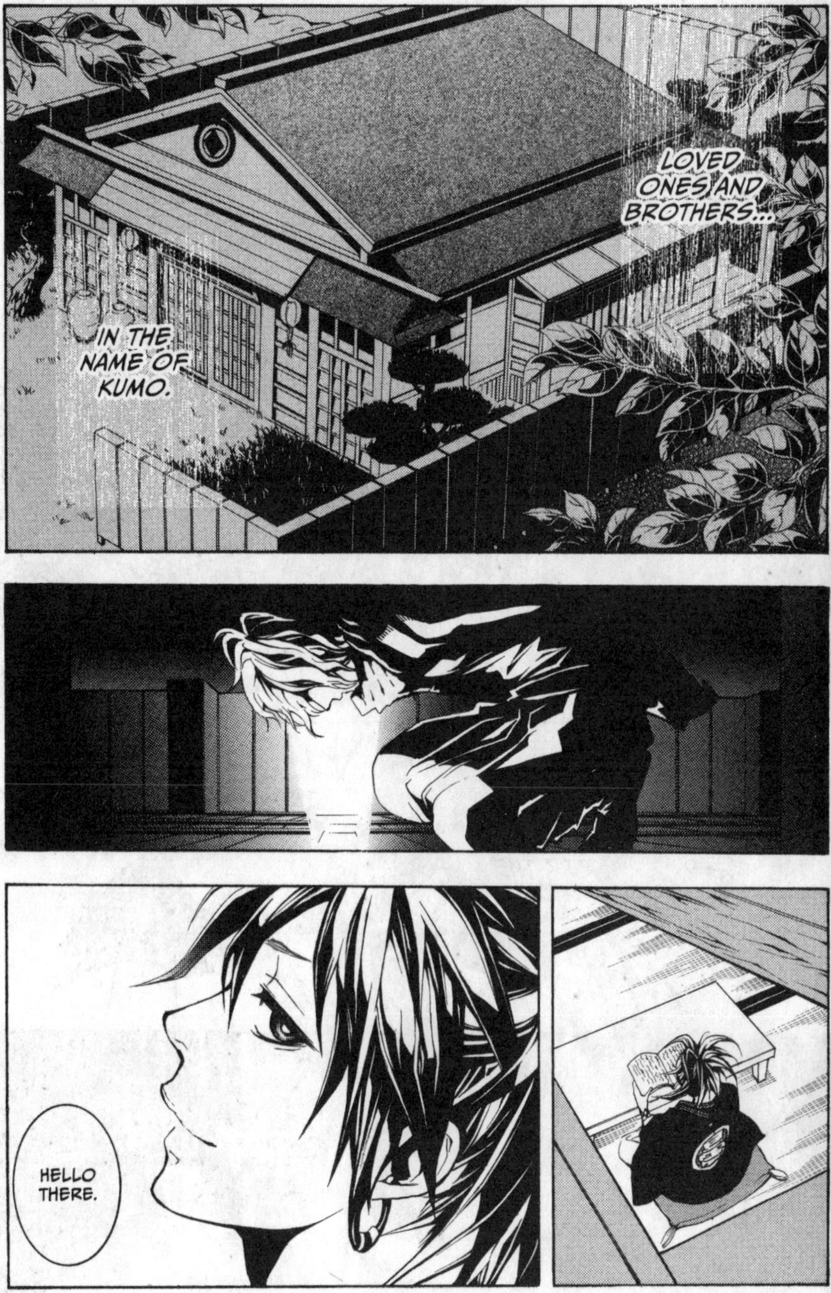
LOVED ONES AND BROTHERS...
IN THE NAME OF KUMO.
HELLO THERE.

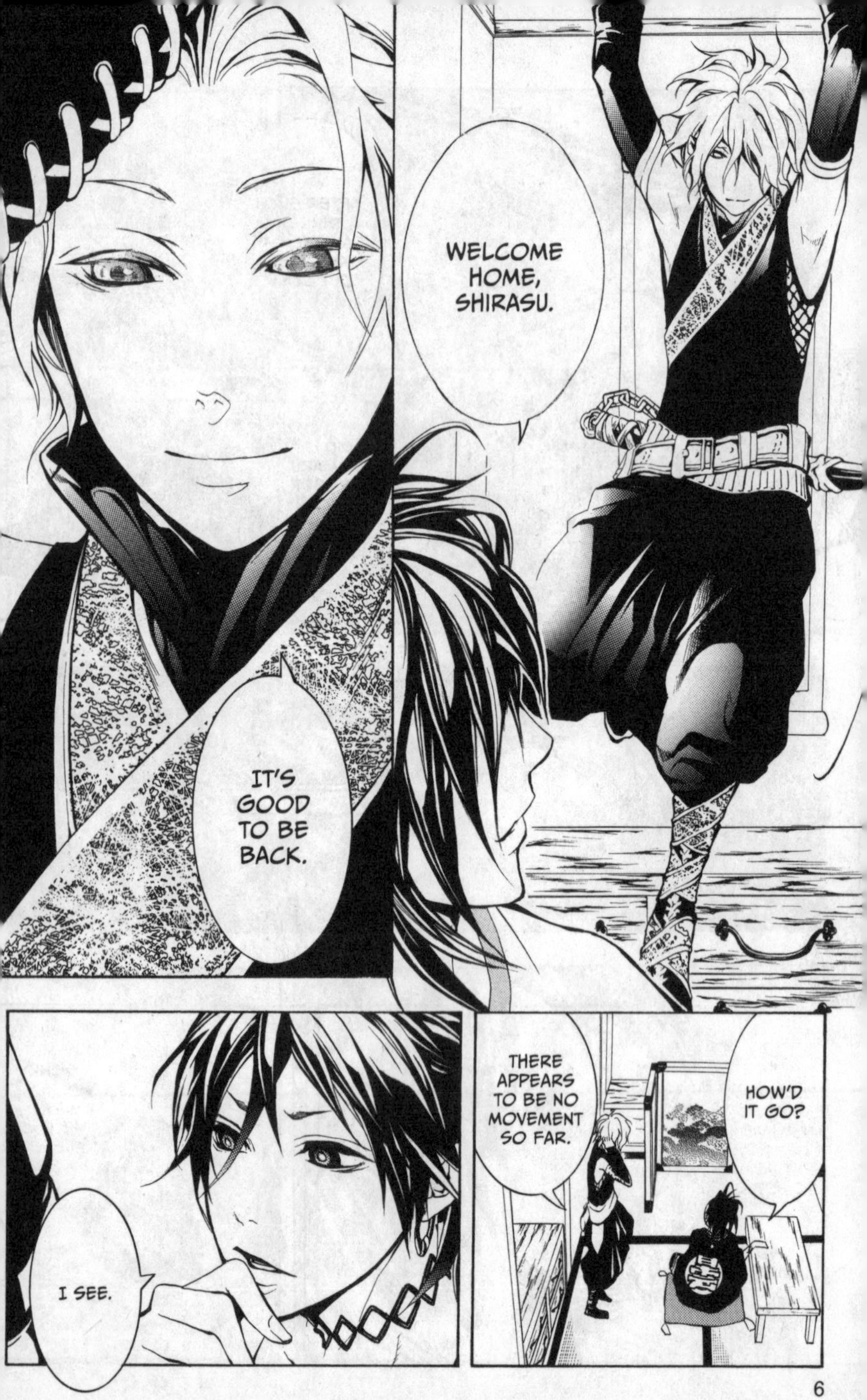
WELCOME HOME, SHIRASU.
IT'S GOOD TO BE BACK.
HOW'D IT GO?
THERE APPEARS TO BE NO MOVEMENT SO FAR.
I SEE.

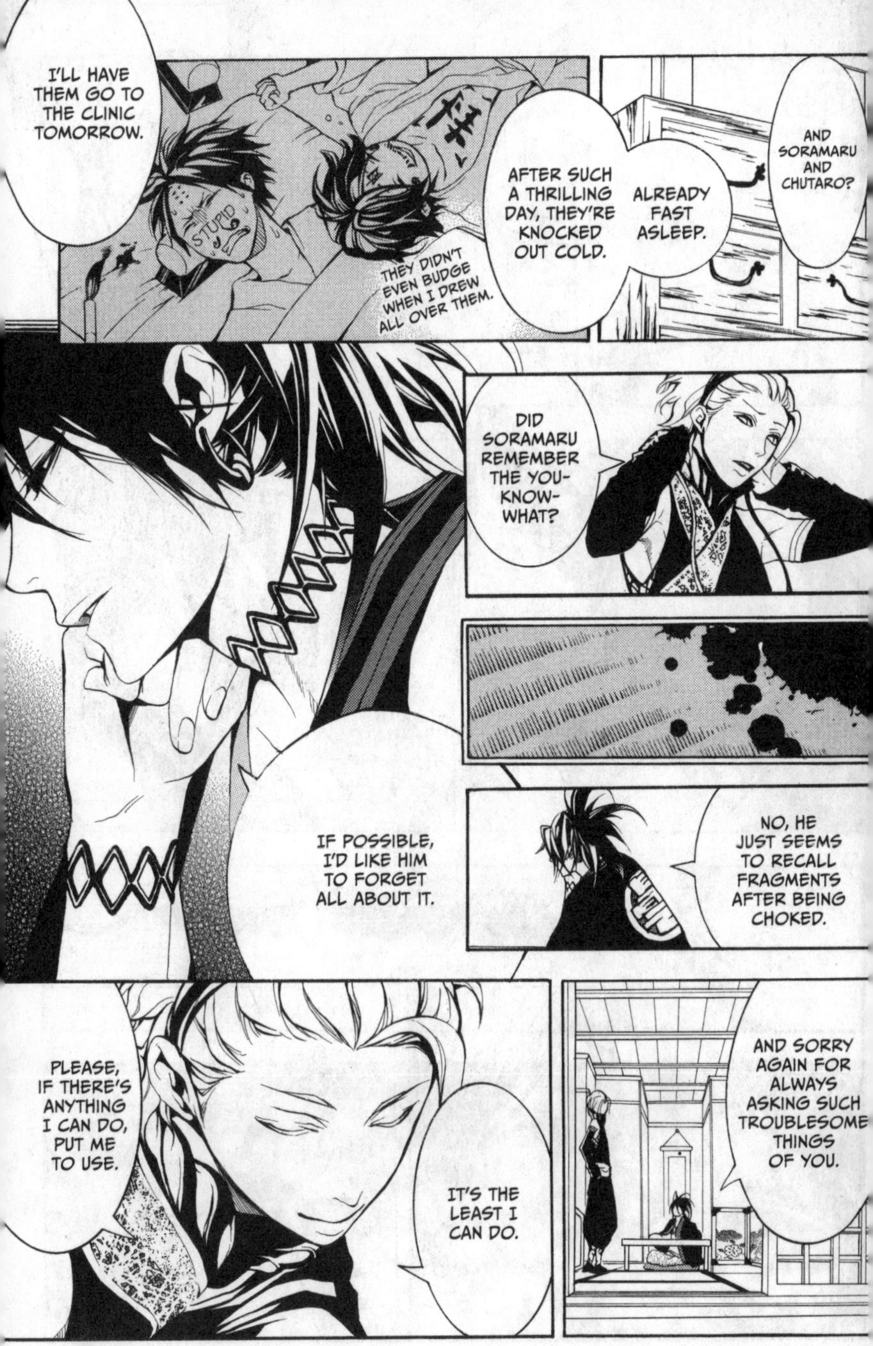
AND SORAMARU AND CHUTARO?
ALREADY FAST ASLEEP.
AFTER SUCH A THRILLING DAY, THEY'RE KNOCKED OUT COLD.
THEY DIDN'T EVEN BUDGE WHEN I DREW ALL OVER THEM.
STUPID
I'LL HAVE THEM GO TO THE CLINIC TOMORROW.
DID SORAMARU REMEMBER THE YOU-KNOW-WHAT?
NO, HE JUST SEEMS TO RECALL FRAGMENTS AFTER BEING CHOKED.
IF POSSIBLE, I'D LIKE HIM TO FORGET ALL ABOUT IT.
AND SORRY AGAIN FOR ALWAYS ASKING SUCH TROUBLESOME THINGS OF YOU.
IT'S THE LEAST I CAN DO.
PLEASE, IF THERE'S ANYTHING I CAN DO, PUT ME TO USE.

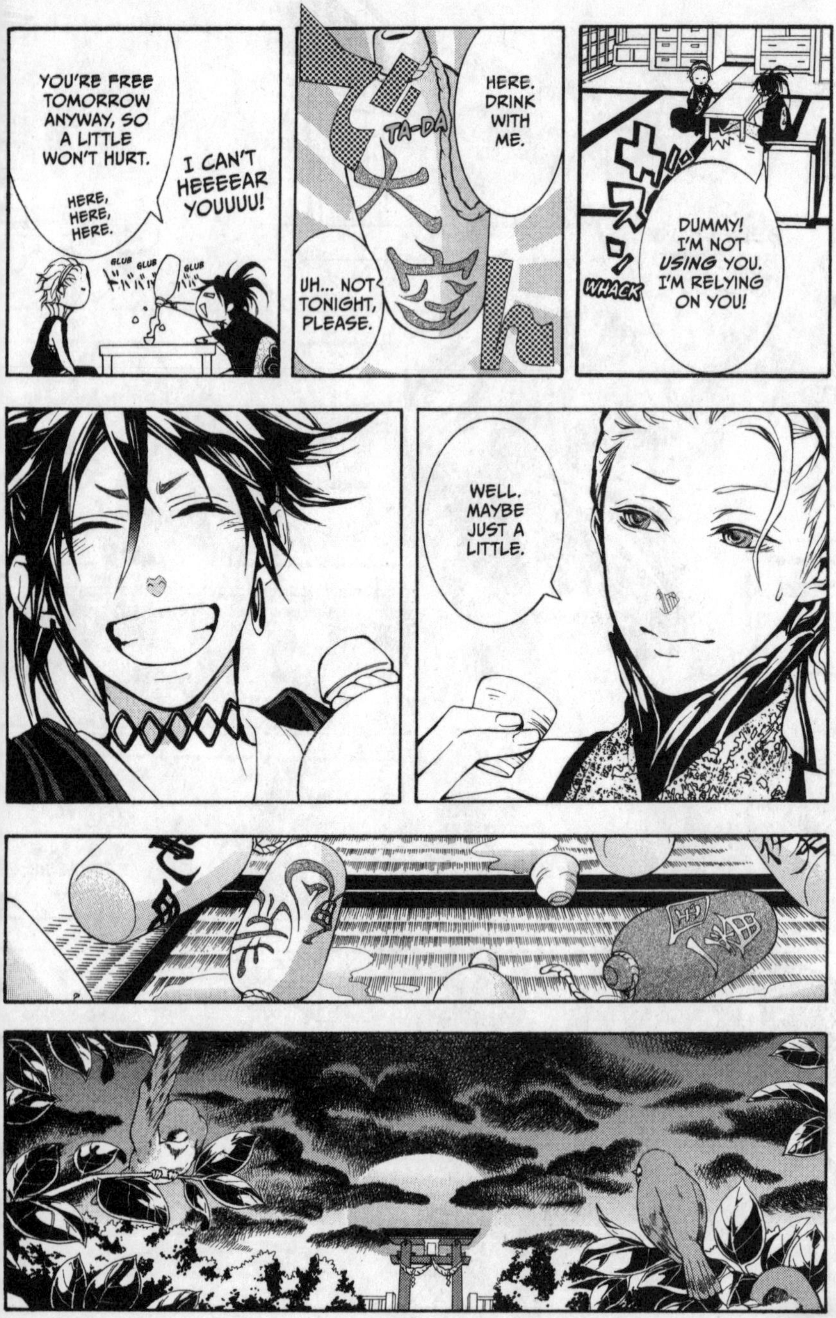
DUMMY! I'M NOT USING YOU. I'M RELYING ON YOU!
WHACK
HERE. DRINK WITH ME.
TA-DA
UH... NOT TONIGHT, PLEASE.
YOU'RE FREE TOMORROW ANYWAY, SO A LITTLE WON'T HURT.
HERE, HERE, HERE.
I CAN'T HEEEEAR YOUUUU!
GLUB GLUB GLUB
WELL. MAYBE JUST A LITTLE.

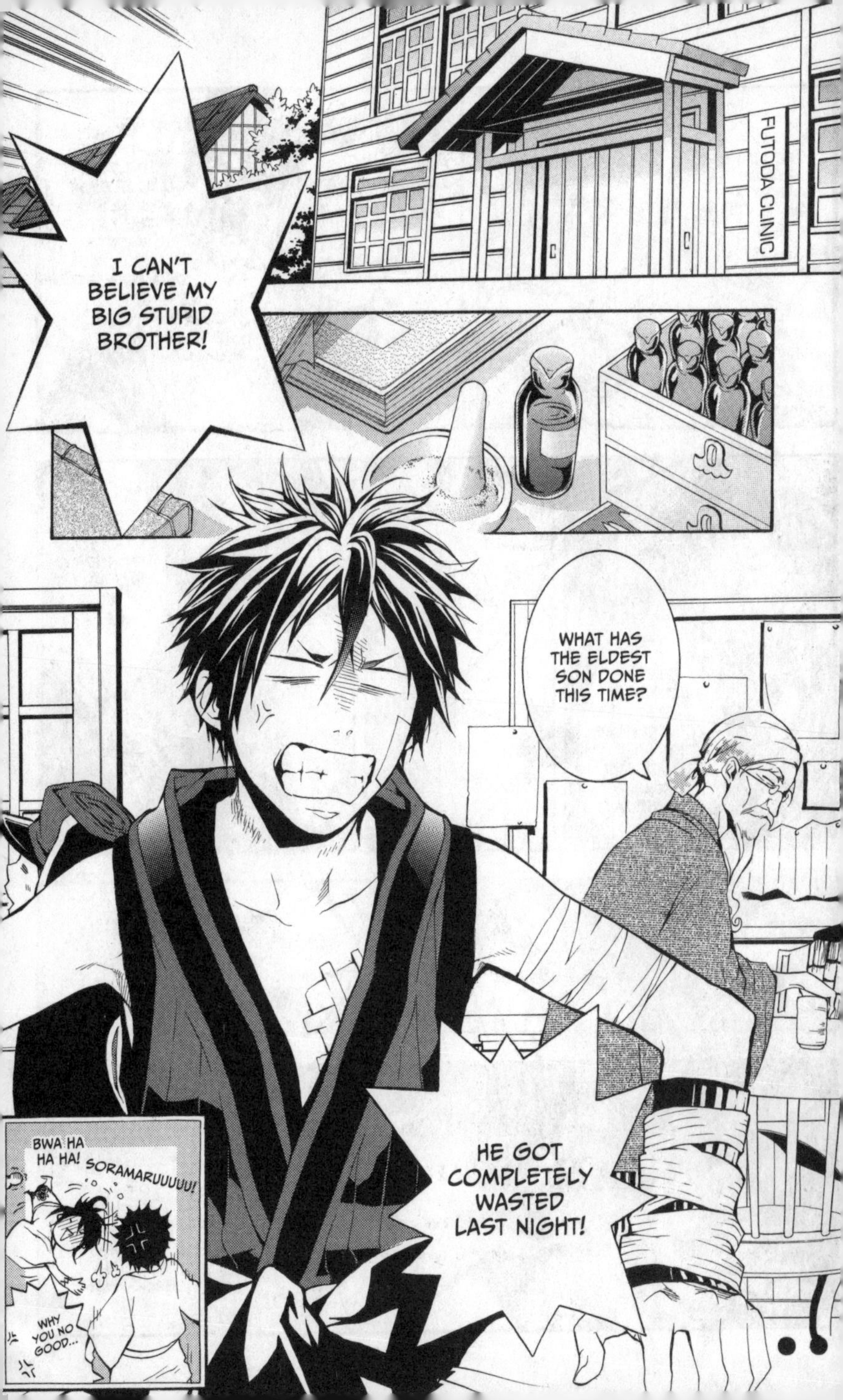
FUTODA CLINIC
I CAN'T BELIEVE MY BIG STUPID BROTHER!
WHAT HAS THE ELDEST SON DONE THIS TIME?
HE GOT COMPLETELY WASTED LAST NIGHT!
BWA HA HA HA!
SORAMARUUUUU!
WHY YOU NO GOOD...

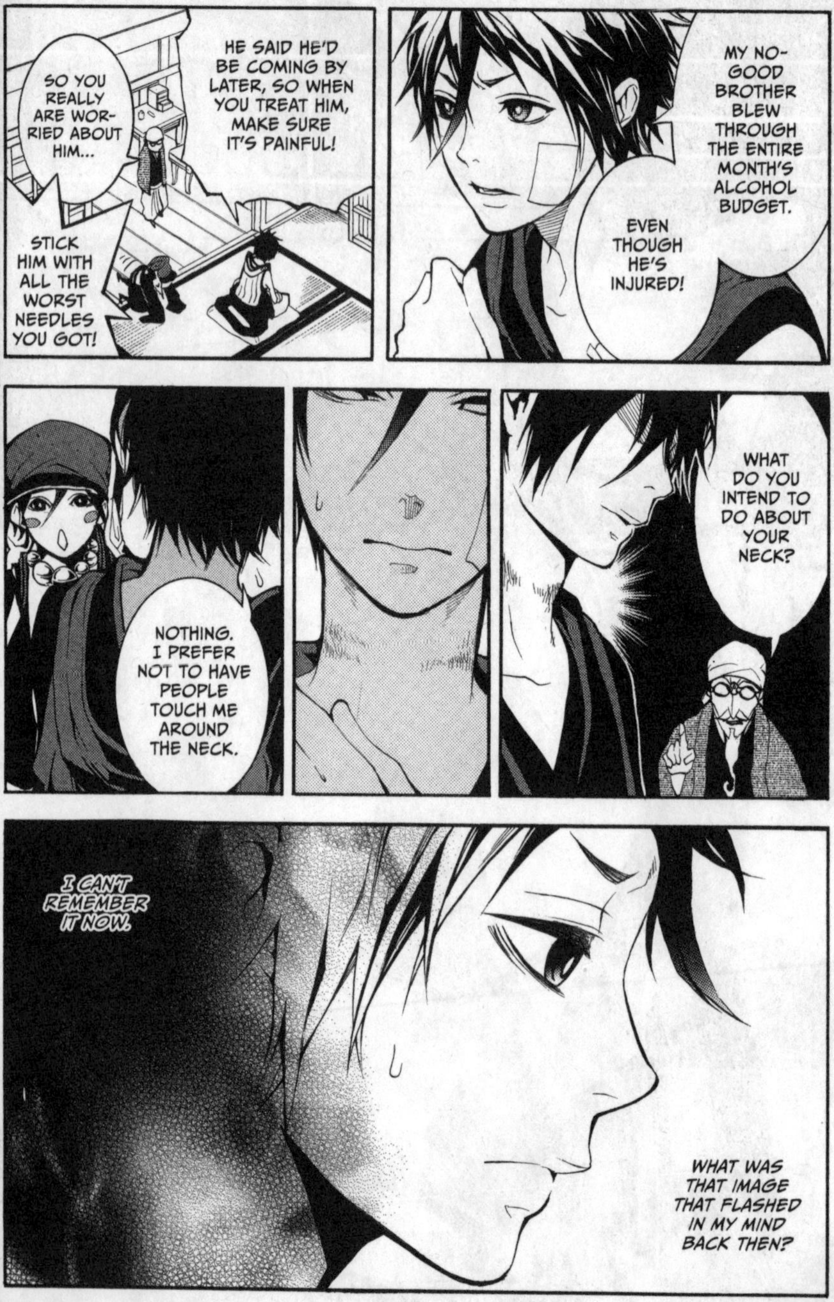
MY NO-GOOD BROTHER BLEW THROUGH THE ENTIRE MONTH'S ALCOHOL BUDGET.
EVEN THOUGH HE'S INJURED!
HE SAID HE'D BE COMING BY LATER, SO WHEN YOU TREAT HIM, MAKE SURE IT'S PAINFUL!
SO YOU REALLY ARE WORRIED ABOUT HIM...
STICK HIM WITH ALL THE WORST NEEDLES YOU GOT!
WHAT DO YOU INTEND TO DO ABOUT YOUR NECK?
NOTHING. I PREFER NOT TO HAVE PEOPLE TOUCH ME AROUND THE NECK.
WHAT WAS THAT IMAGE THAT FLASHED IN MY MIND BACK THEN?
I CAN'T REMEMBER IT NOW.

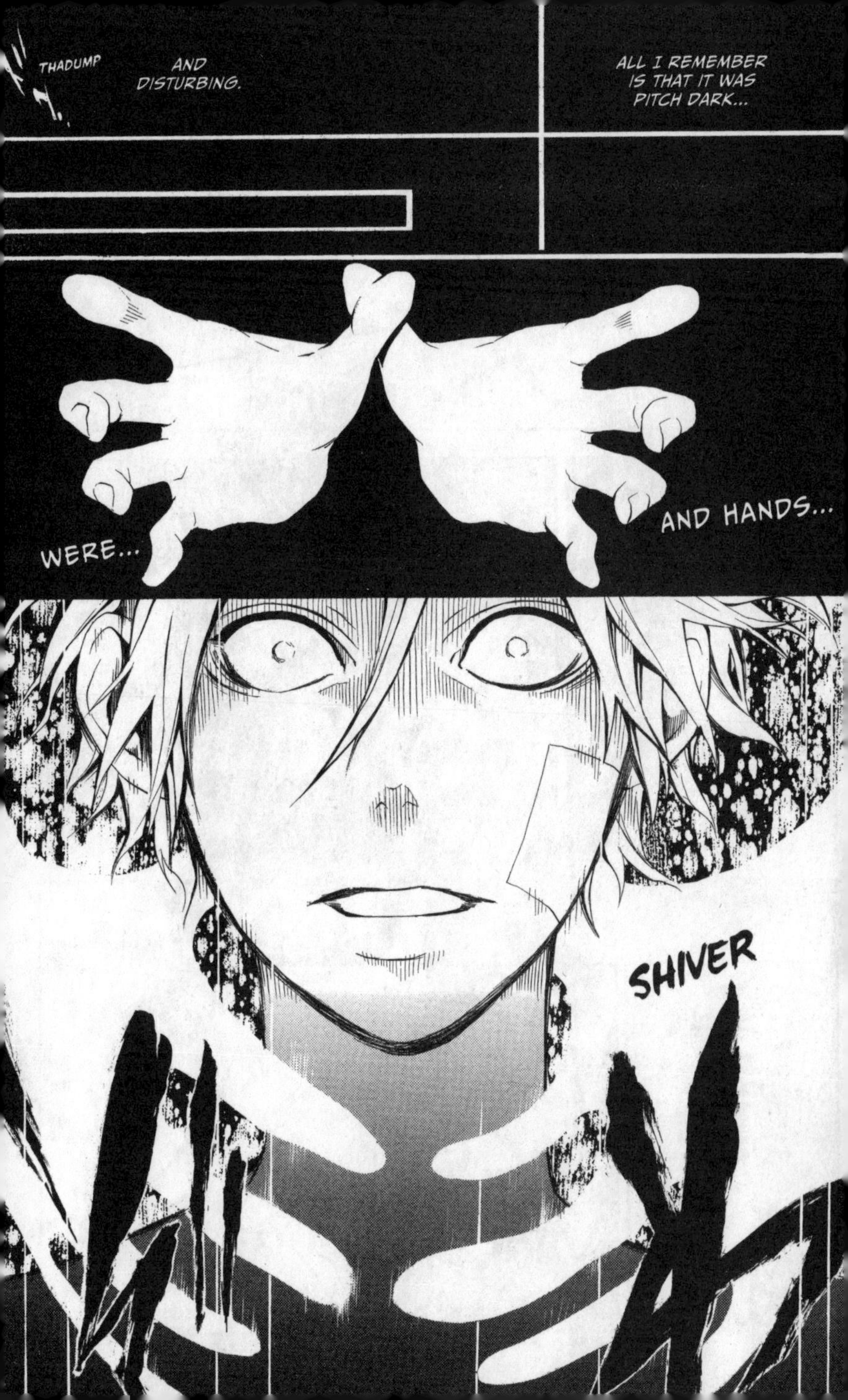
ALL I REMEMBER IS THAT IT WAS PITCH DARK...
AND DISTURBING.
THADUMP
AND HANDS...
WERE...
SHIVER

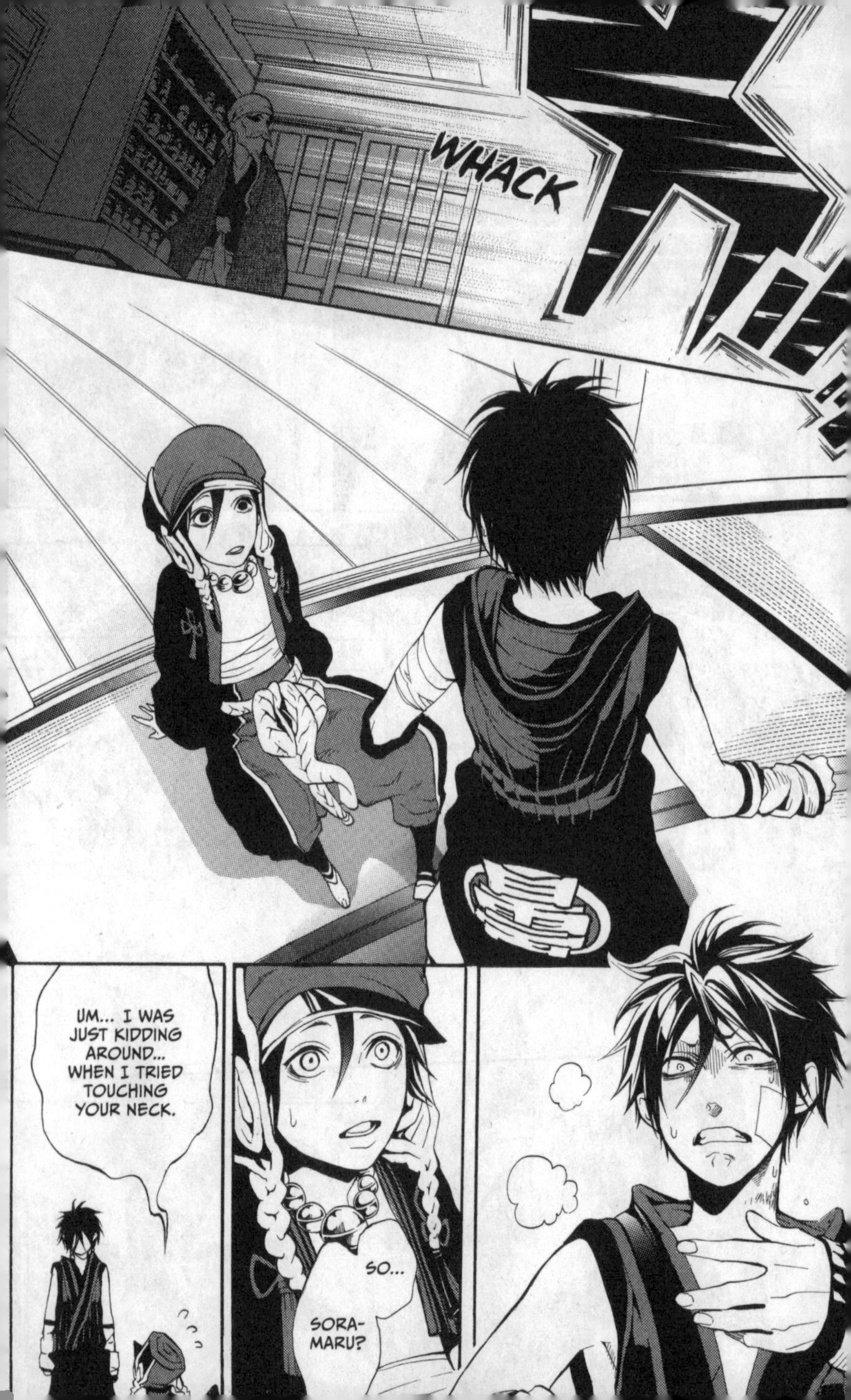
WHACK
SO...
SORA-MARU?
UM... I WAS JUST KIDDING AROUND... WHEN I TRIED TOUCHING YOUR NECK.

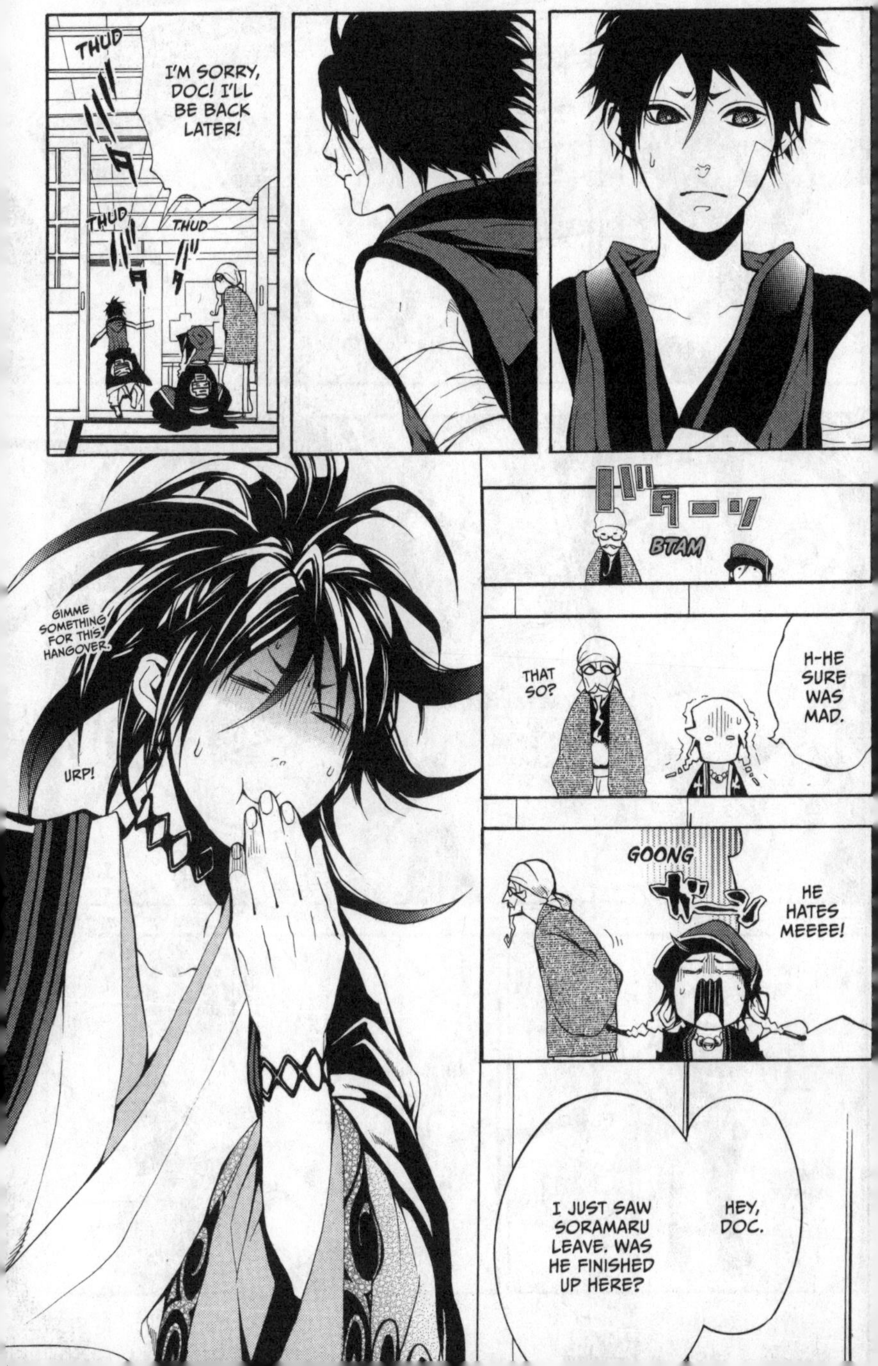
THUD
I'M SORRY, DOC! I'LL BE BACK LATER!
THUD
THUD
BTAM
H-HE SURE WAS MAD.
THAT SO?
GOONG
HE HATES MEEEE!
HEY, DOC.
I JUST SAW SORAMARU LEAVE. WAS HE FINISHED UP HERE?
GIMME SOMETHING FOR THIS HANGOVER.
URP!

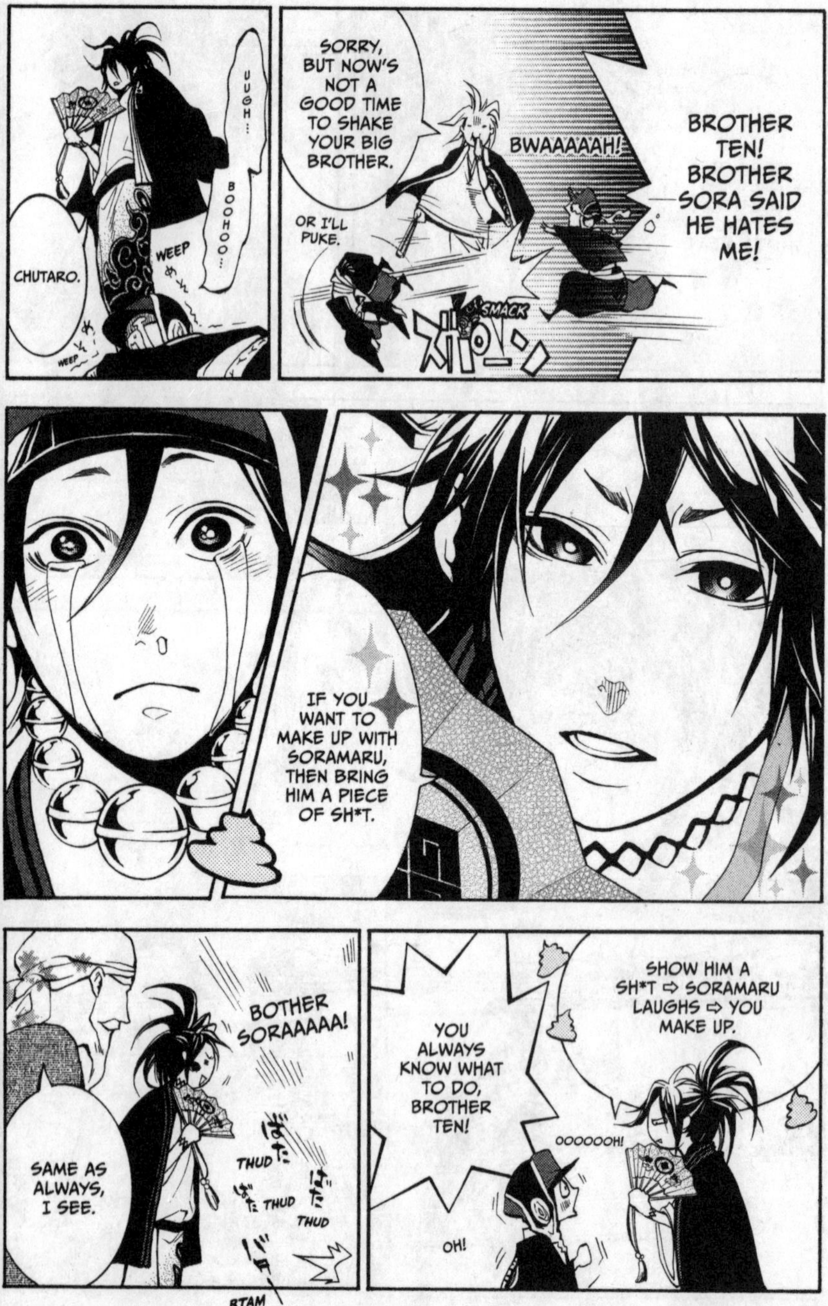
BROTHER TEN! BROTHER SORA SAID HE HATES ME!
BWAAAAAH!
SORRY, BUT NOW'S NOT A GOOD TIME TO SHAKE YOUR BIG BROTHER.
OR I'LL PUKE.
SMACK
UUGH...
BOOHOO...
WEEP
CHUTARO.
WEEP
IF YOU WANT TO MAKE UP WITH SORAMARU, THEN BRING HIM A PIECE OF SH*T.
SHOW HIM A SH*T ⇨ SORAMARU LAUGHS ⇨ YOU MAKE UP.
OOOOOOH!
YOU ALWAYS KNOW WHAT TO DO, BROTHER TEN!
OH!
BOTHER SORAAAAA!
THUD
THUD
THUD
SAME AS ALWAYS, I SEE.
BTAM

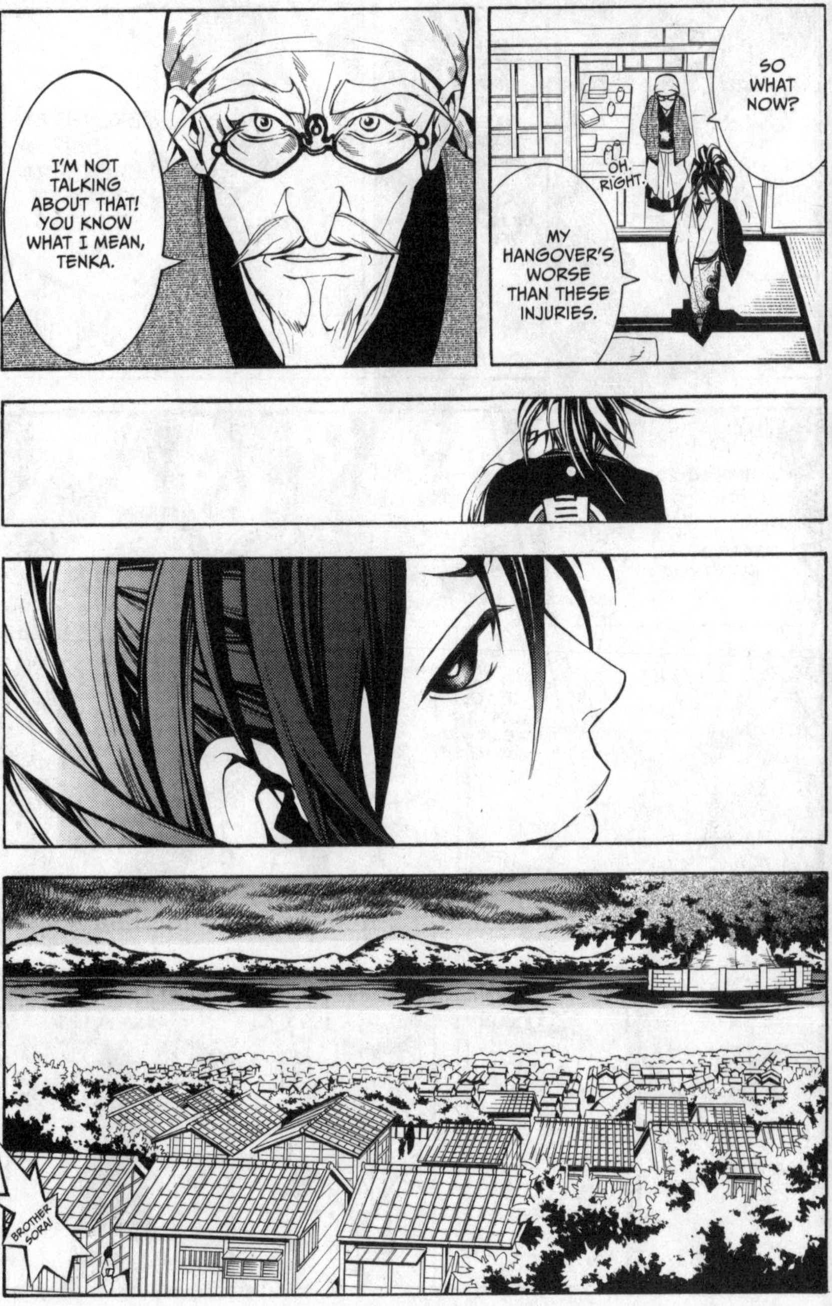
SO WHAT NOW?
OH. RIGHT.
MY HANGOVER'S WORSE THAN THESE INJURIES.
I'M NOT TALKING ABOUT THAT! YOU KNOW WHAT I MEAN, TENKA.
BROTHER SORA!

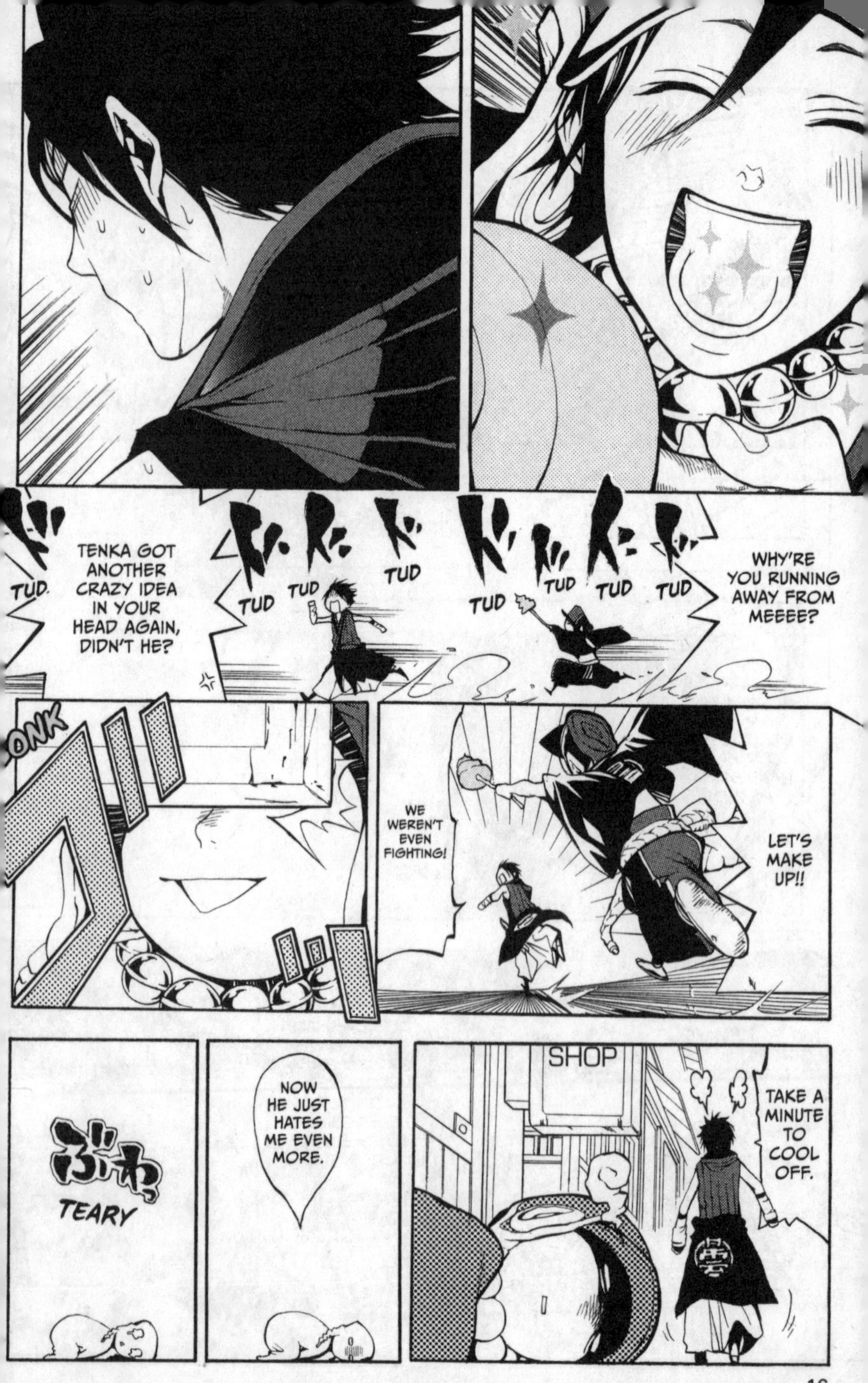
WHY'RE YOU RUNNING AWAY FROM MEEEE?
TUD
TUD
TUD
TUD
TUD
TUD
TUD
TENKA GOT ANOTHER CRAZY IDEA IN YOUR HEAD AGAIN, DIDN'T HE?
TUD
LET'S MAKE UP!!
WE WEREN'T EVEN FIGHTING!
ONK
SHOP
TAKE A MINUTE TO COOL OFF.
NOW HE JUST HATES ME EVEN MORE.
TEARY

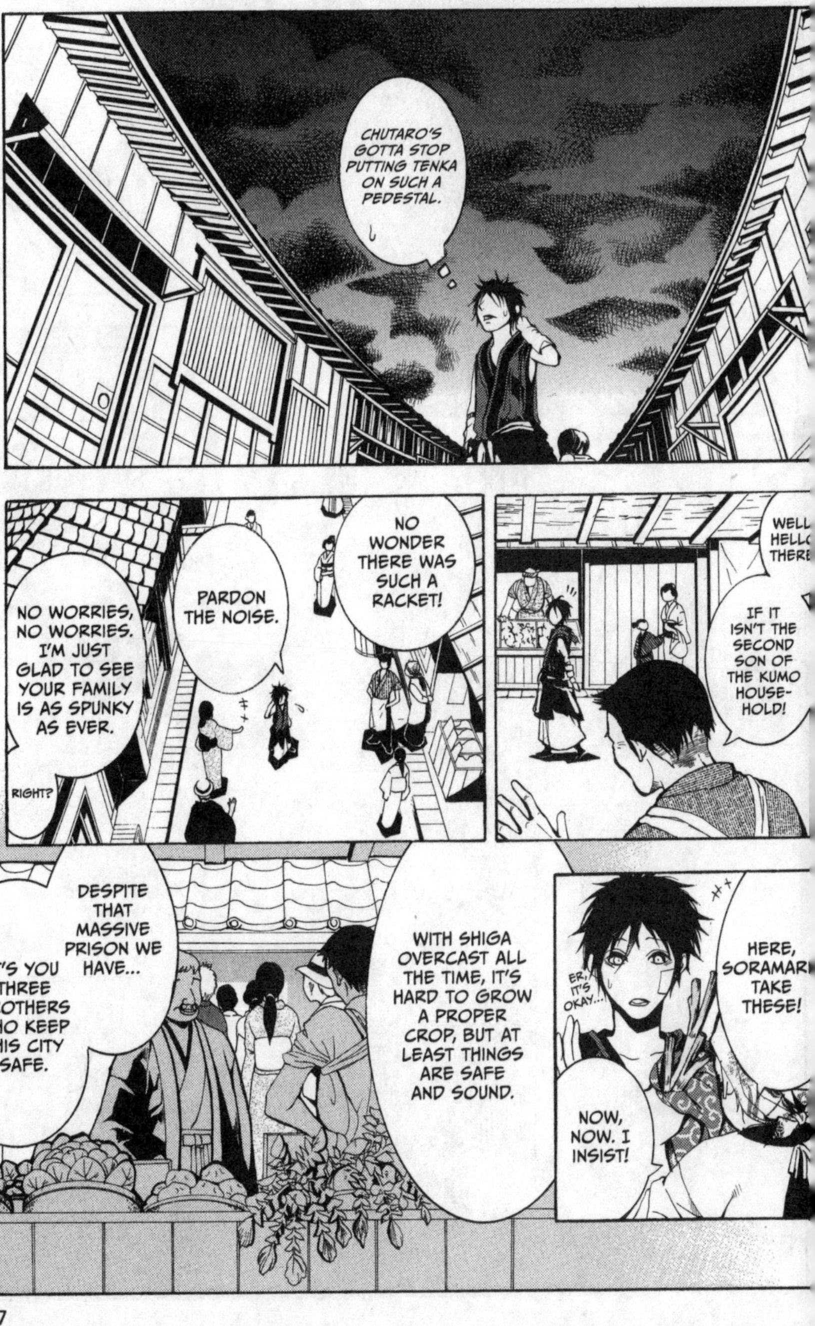
CHUTARO'S GOTTA STOP PUTTING TENKA ON SUCH A PEDESTAL.
WELL HELLO THERE
IF IT ISN'T THE SECOND SON OF THE KUMO HOUSE-HOLD!
NO WONDER THERE WAS SUCH A RACKET!
PARDON THE NOISE.
NO WORRIES, NO WORRIES. I'M JUST GLAD TO SEE YOUR FAMILY IS AS SPUNKY AS EVER.
RIGHT?
HERE, SORAMAR TAKE THESE!
ER, IT'S OKAY...
NOW, NOW. I INSIST!
WITH SHIGA OVERCAST ALL THE TIME, IT'S HARD TO GROW A PROPER CROP, BUT AT LEAST THINGS ARE SAFE AND SOUND.
DESPITE THAT MASSIVE PRISON WE HAVE...
IT'S YOU THREE BROTHERS WHO KEEP THIS CITY SAFE.

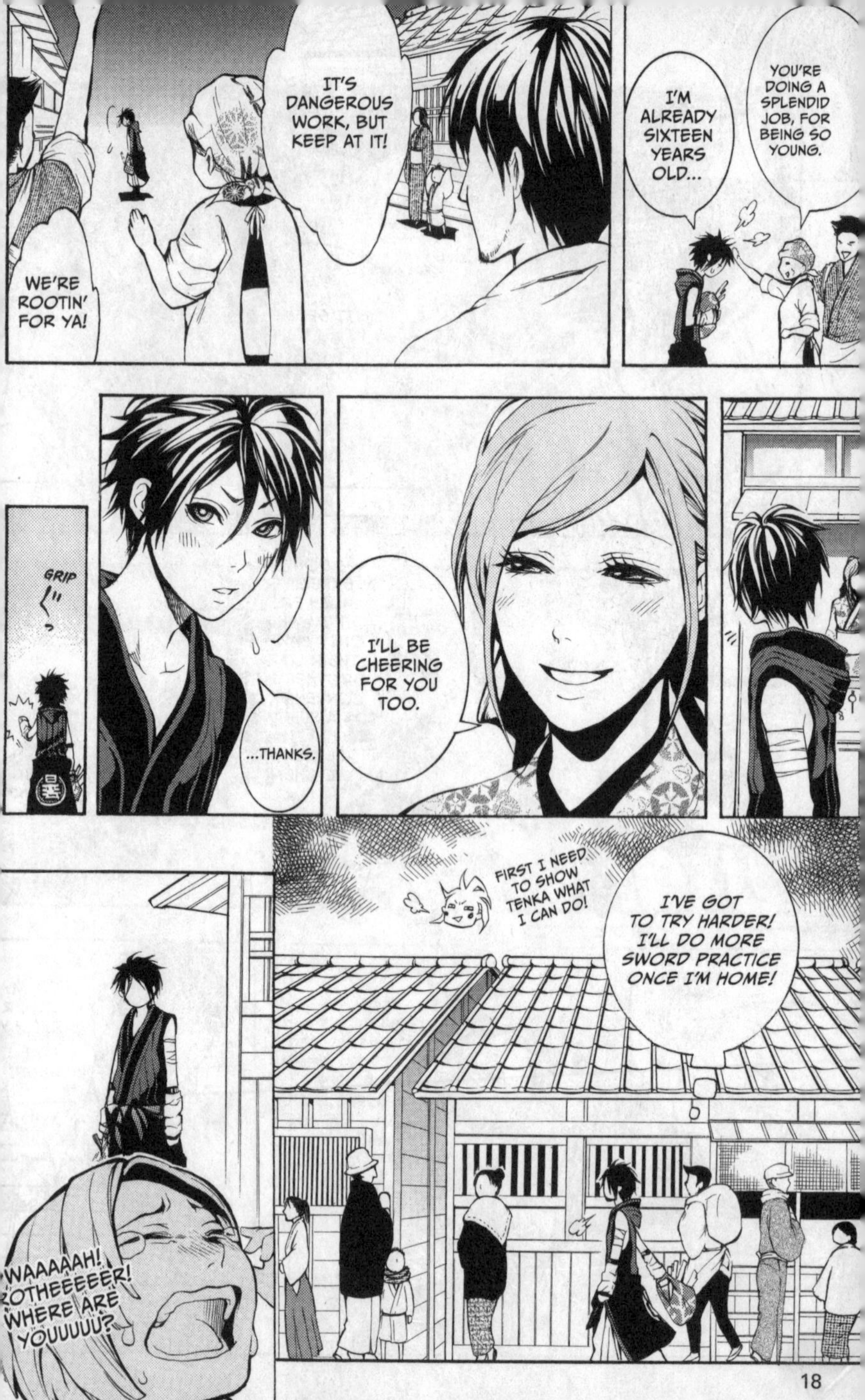
YOU'RE DOING A SPLENDID JOB, FOR BEING SO YOUNG.
I'M ALREADY SIXTEEN YEARS OLD...
IT'S DANGEROUS WORK, BUT KEEP AT IT!
WE'RE ROOTIN' FOR YA!
I'LL BE CHEERING FOR YOU TOO.
...THANKS.
GRIP
I'VE GOT TO TRY HARDER! I'LL DO MORE SWORD PRACTICE ONCE I'M HOME!
FIRST I NEED TO SHOW TENKA WHAT I CAN DO!
WAAAAAH! OTHEEEEER! WHERE ARE YOUUUUU?

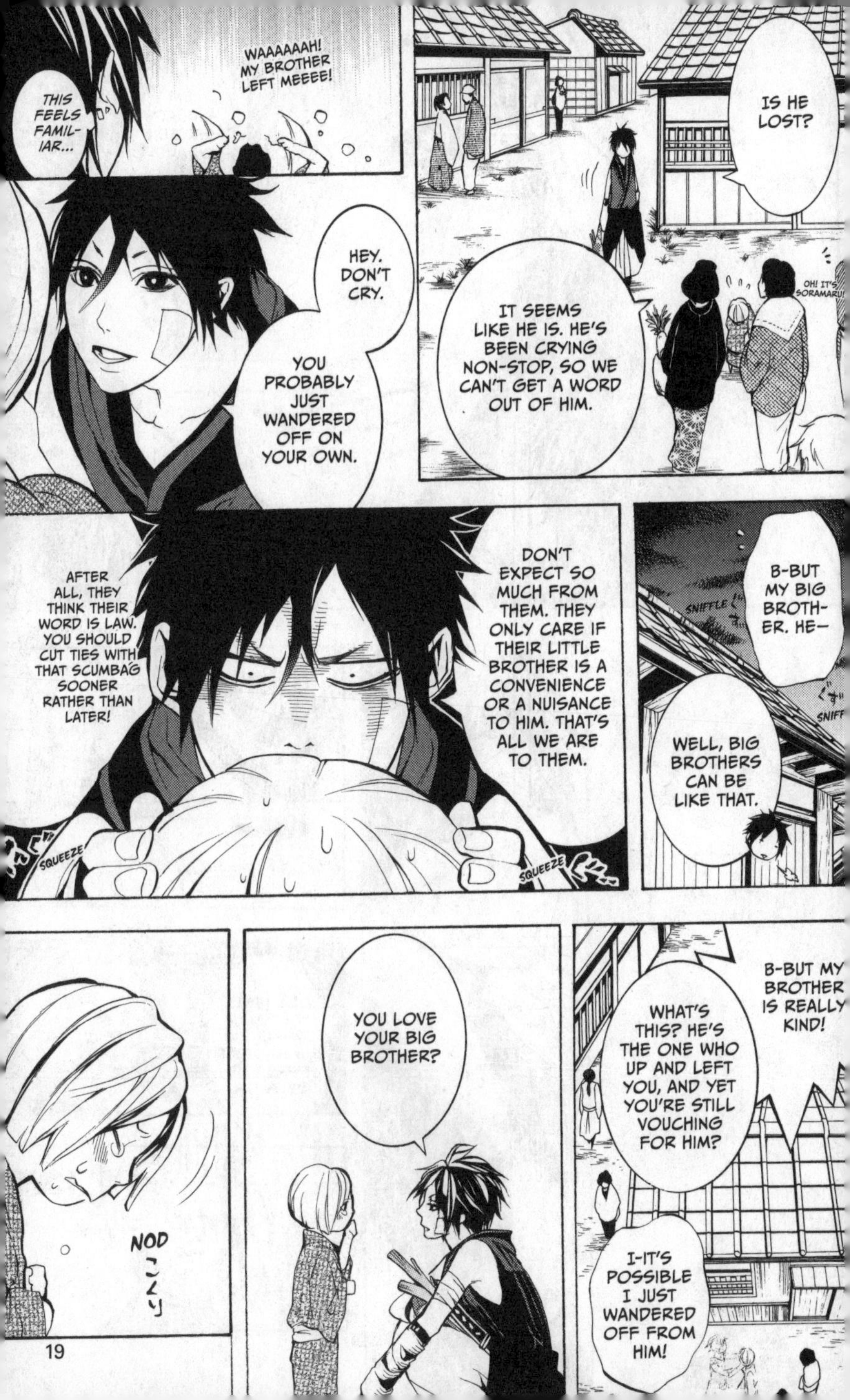
IS HE LOST?
OH! IT'S SORAMARU!
IT SEEMS LIKE HE IS. HE'S BEEN CRYING NON-STOP, SO WE CAN'T GET A WORD OUT OF HIM.
WAAAAAAH! MY BROTHER LEFT MEEEE!
THIS FEELS FAMIL-IAR...
HEY. DON'T CRY.
YOU PROBABLY JUST WANDERED OFF ON YOUR OWN.
B-BUT MY BIG BROTH-ER. HE—
SNIFFLE
SNIFF
WELL, BIG BROTHERS CAN BE LIKE THAT.
DON'T EXPECT SO MUCH FROM THEM. THEY ONLY CARE IF THEIR LITTLE BROTHER IS A CONVENIENCE OR A NUISANCE TO HIM. THAT'S ALL WE ARE TO THEM.
AFTER ALL, THEY THINK THEIR WORD IS LAW. YOU SHOULD CUT TIES WITH THAT SCUMBAG SOONER RATHER THAN LATER!
SQUEEZE
SQUEEZE
B-BUT MY BROTHER IS REALLY KIND!
WHAT'S THIS? HE'S THE ONE WHO UP AND LEFT YOU, AND YET YOU'RE STILL VOUCHING FOR HIM?
I-IT'S POSSIBLE I JUST WANDERED OFF FROM HIM!
YOU LOVE YOUR BIG BROTHER?
NOD

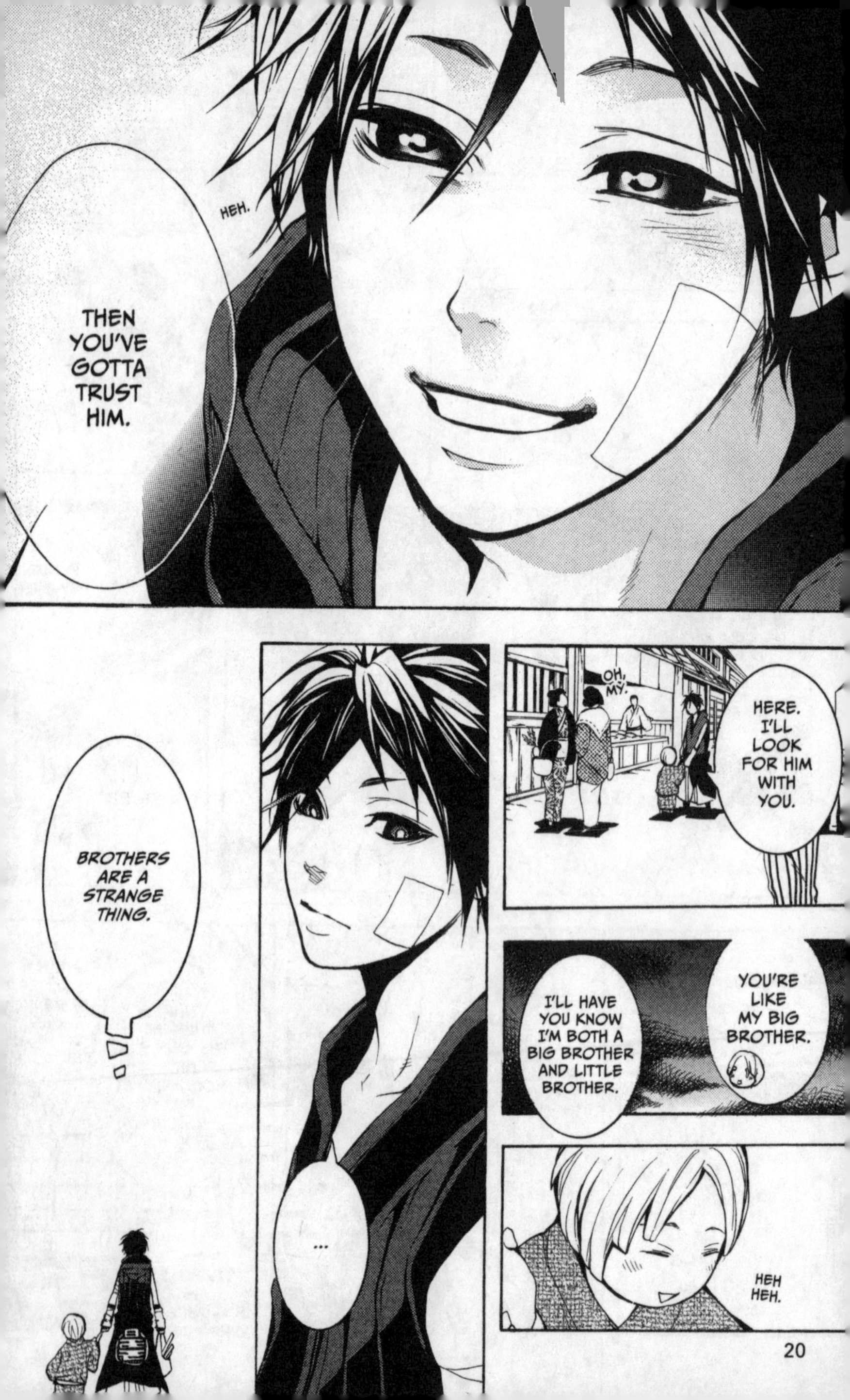
HEH.
THEN YOU'VE GOTTA TRUST HIM.
HERE. I'LL LOOK FOR HIM WITH YOU.
OH, MY.
YOU'RE LIKE MY BIG BROTHER.
I'LL HAVE YOU KNOW I'M BOTH A BIG BROTHER AND LITTLE BROTHER.
HEH HEH.
...
BROTHERS ARE A STRANGE THING.

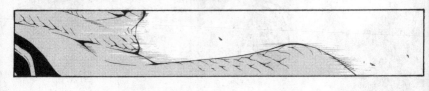

WHAT'S
HE UP
TO?

KUMO

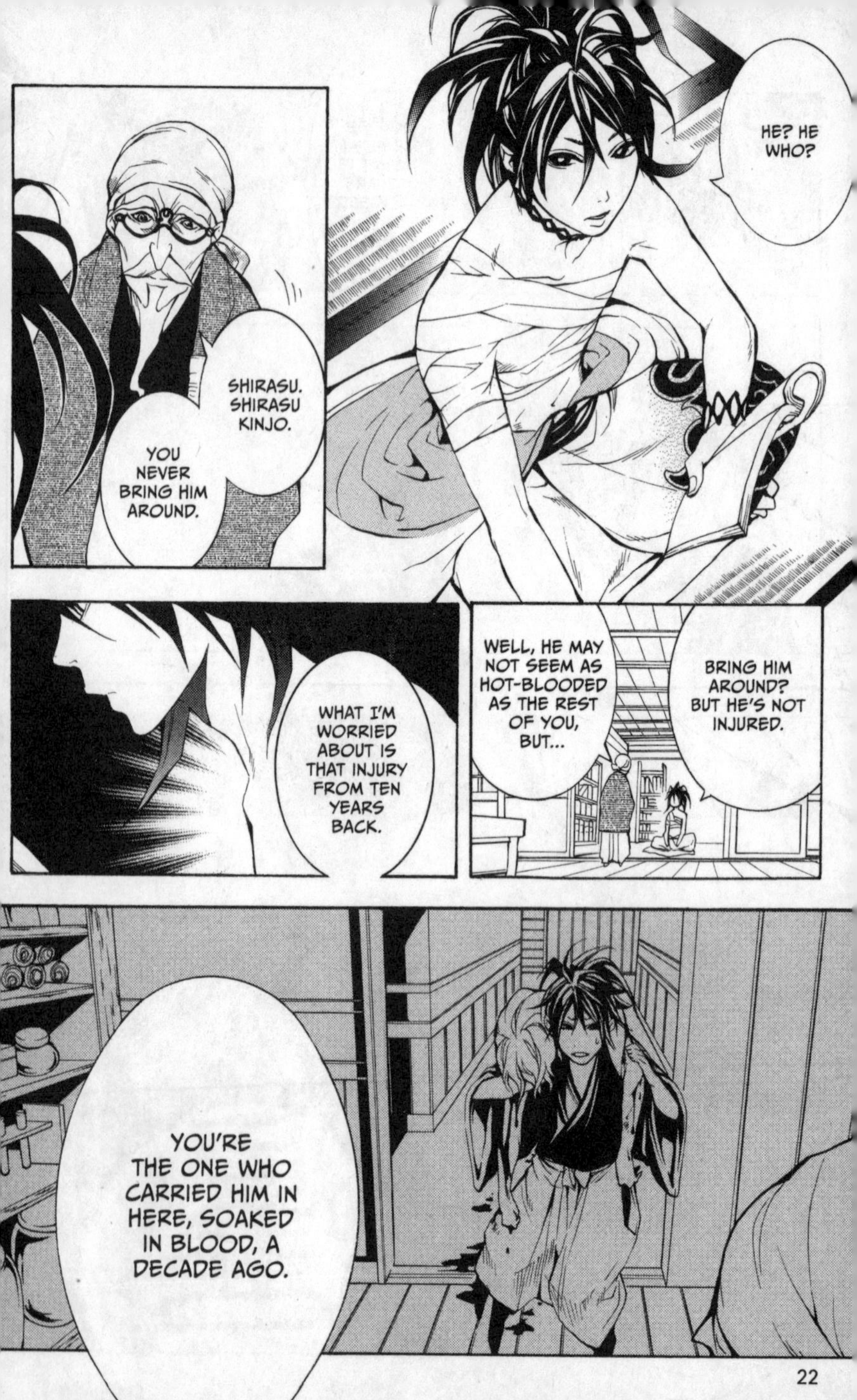
HE? HE WHO?
SHIRASU. SHIRASU KINJO.
YOU NEVER BRING HIM AROUND.
BRING HIM AROUND? BUT HE'S NOT INJURED.
WELL, HE MAY NOT SEEM AS HOT-BLOODED AS THE REST OF YOU, BUT...
WHAT I'M WORRIED ABOUT IS THAT INJURY FROM TEN YEARS BACK.
YOU'RE THE ONE WHO CARRIED HIM IN HERE, SOAKED IN BLOOD, A DECADE AGO.

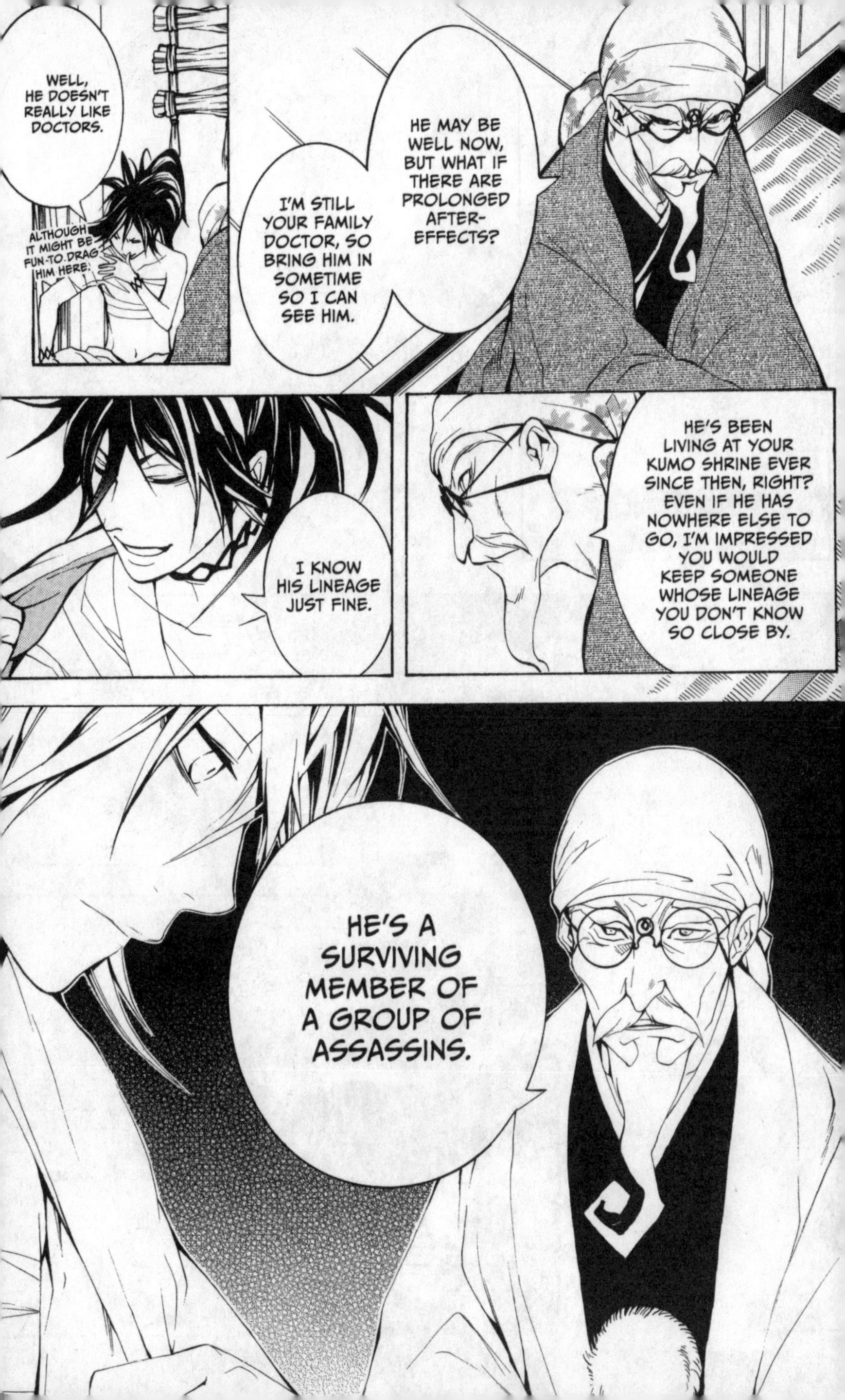
HE MAY BE WELL NOW, BUT WHAT IF THERE ARE PROLONGED AFTER-EFFECTS?
I'M STILL YOUR FAMILY DOCTOR, SO BRING HIM IN SOMETIME SO I CAN SEE HIM.
WELL, HE DOESN'T REALLY LIKE DOCTORS.
ALTHOUGH IT MIGHT BE FUN TO DRAG HIM HERE.
HE'S BEEN LIVING AT YOUR KUMO SHRINE EVER SINCE THEN, RIGHT? EVEN IF HE HAS NOWHERE ELSE TO GO, I'M IMPRESSED YOU WOULD KEEP SOMEONE WHOSE LINEAGE YOU DON'T KNOW SO CLOSE BY.
I KNOW HIS LINEAGE JUST FINE.
HE'S A SURVIVING MEMBER OF A GROUP OF ASSASSINS.

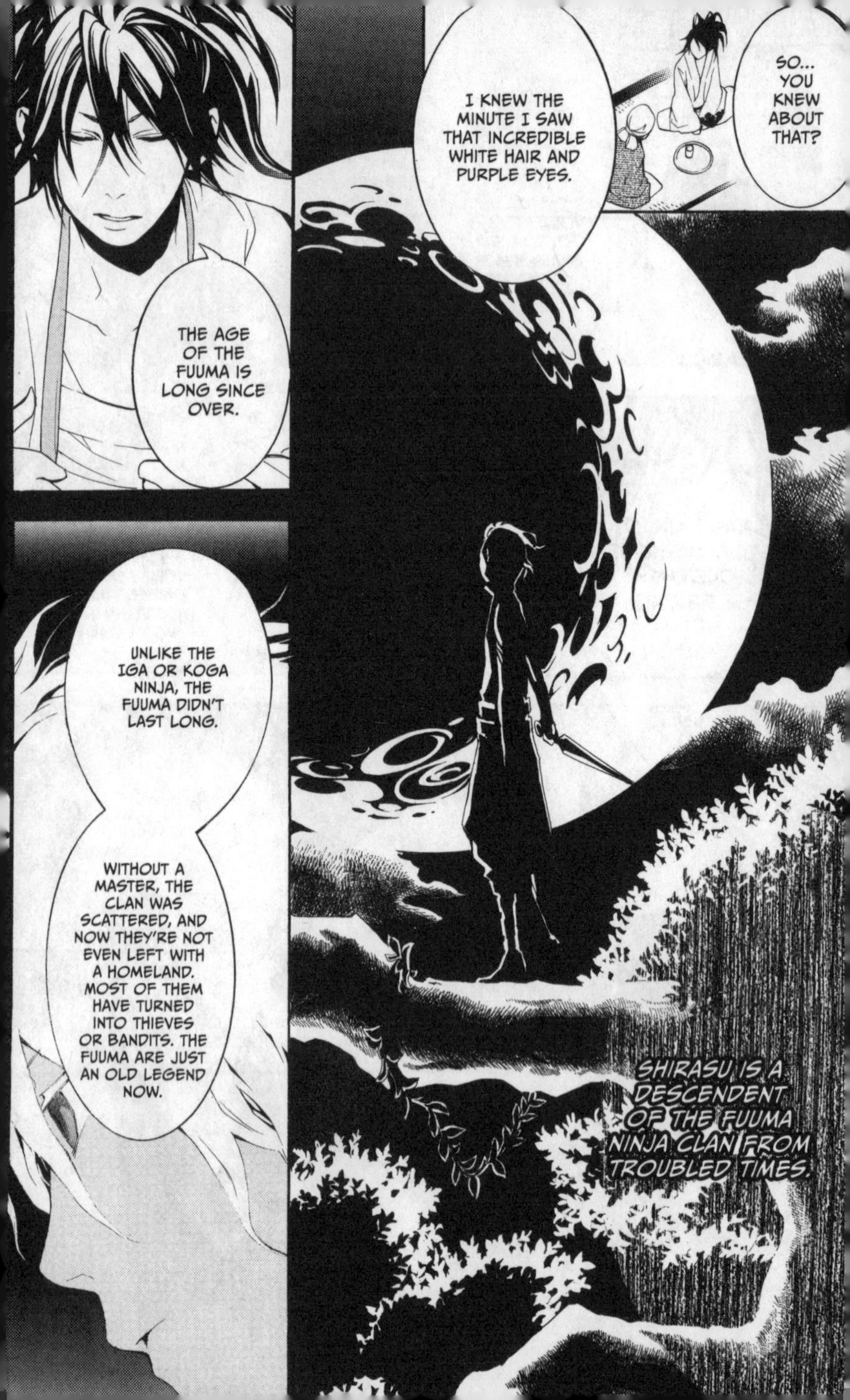
SO... YOU KNEW ABOUT THAT?
I KNEW THE MINUTE I SAW THAT INCREDIBLE WHITE HAIR AND PURPLE EYES.
SHIRASU IS A DESCENDENT OF THE FUUMA NINJA CLAN FROM TROUBLED TIMES.
THE AGE OF THE FUUMA IS LONG SINCE OVER.
UNLIKE THE IGA OR KOGA NINJA, THE FUUMA DIDN'T LAST LONG.
WITHOUT A MASTER, THE CLAN WAS SCATTERED, AND NOW THEY'RE NOT EVEN LEFT WITH A HOMELAND. MOST OF THEM HAVE TURNED INTO THIEVES OR BANDITS. THE FUUMA ARE JUST AN OLD LEGEND NOW.

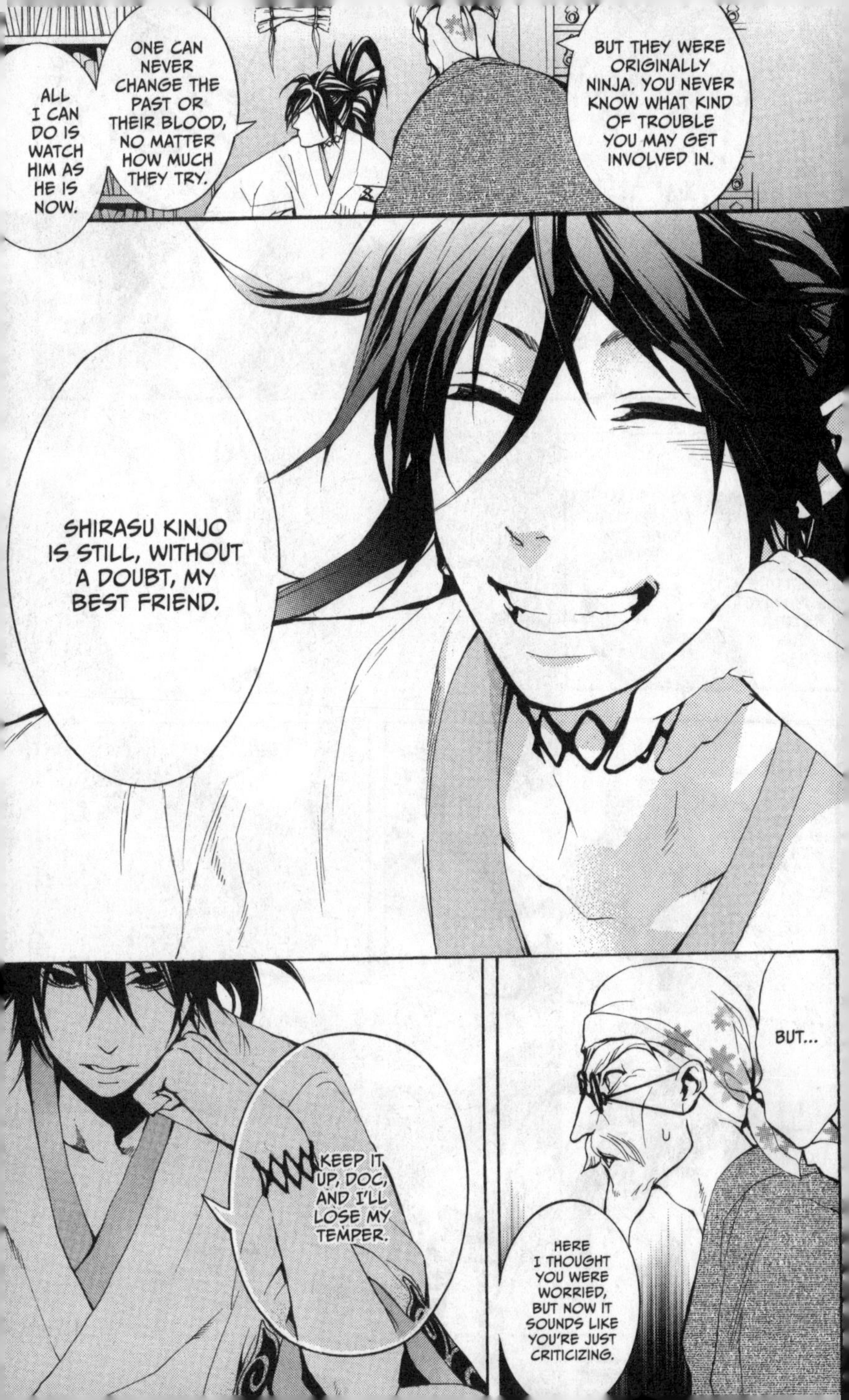
BUT THEY WERE ORIGINALLY NINJA. YOU NEVER KNOW WHAT KIND OF TROUBLE YOU MAY GET INVOLVED IN.
ONE CAN NEVER CHANGE THE PAST OR THEIR BLOOD, NO MATTER HOW MUCH THEY TRY.
ALL I CAN DO IS WATCH HIM AS HE IS NOW.
SHIRASU KINJO IS STILL, WITHOUT A DOUBT, MY BEST FRIEND.
BUT...
HERE I THOUGHT YOU WERE WORRIED, BUT NOW IT SOUNDS LIKE YOU'RE JUST CRITICIZING.
KEEP IT UP, DOC, AND I'LL LOSE MY TEMPER.

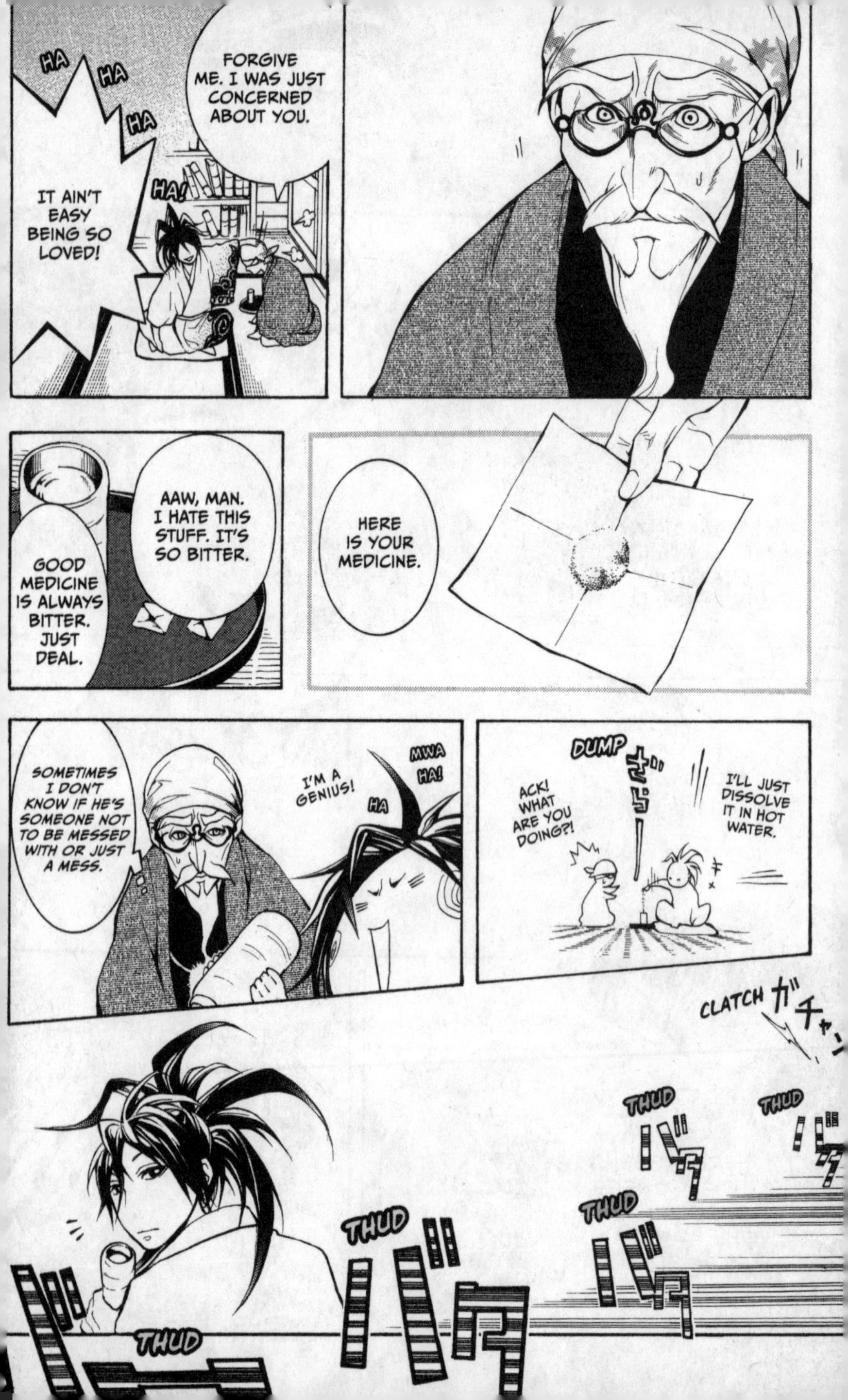
FORGIVE ME. I WAS JUST CONCERNED ABOUT YOU.
HA HA HA HA!
IT AIN'T EASY BEING SO LOVED!
HERE IS YOUR MEDICINE.
AAW, MAN. I HATE THIS STUFF. IT'S SO BITTER.
GOOD MEDICINE IS ALWAYS BITTER. JUST DEAL.
DUMP
I'LL JUST DISSOLVE IT IN HOT WATER.
ACK! WHAT ARE YOU DOING?!
MWA HA! HA
I'M A GENIUS!
SOMETIMES I DON'T KNOW IF HE'S SOMEONE NOT TO BE MESSED WITH OR JUST A MESS.
CLATCH
THUD
THUD
THUD
THUD
THUD

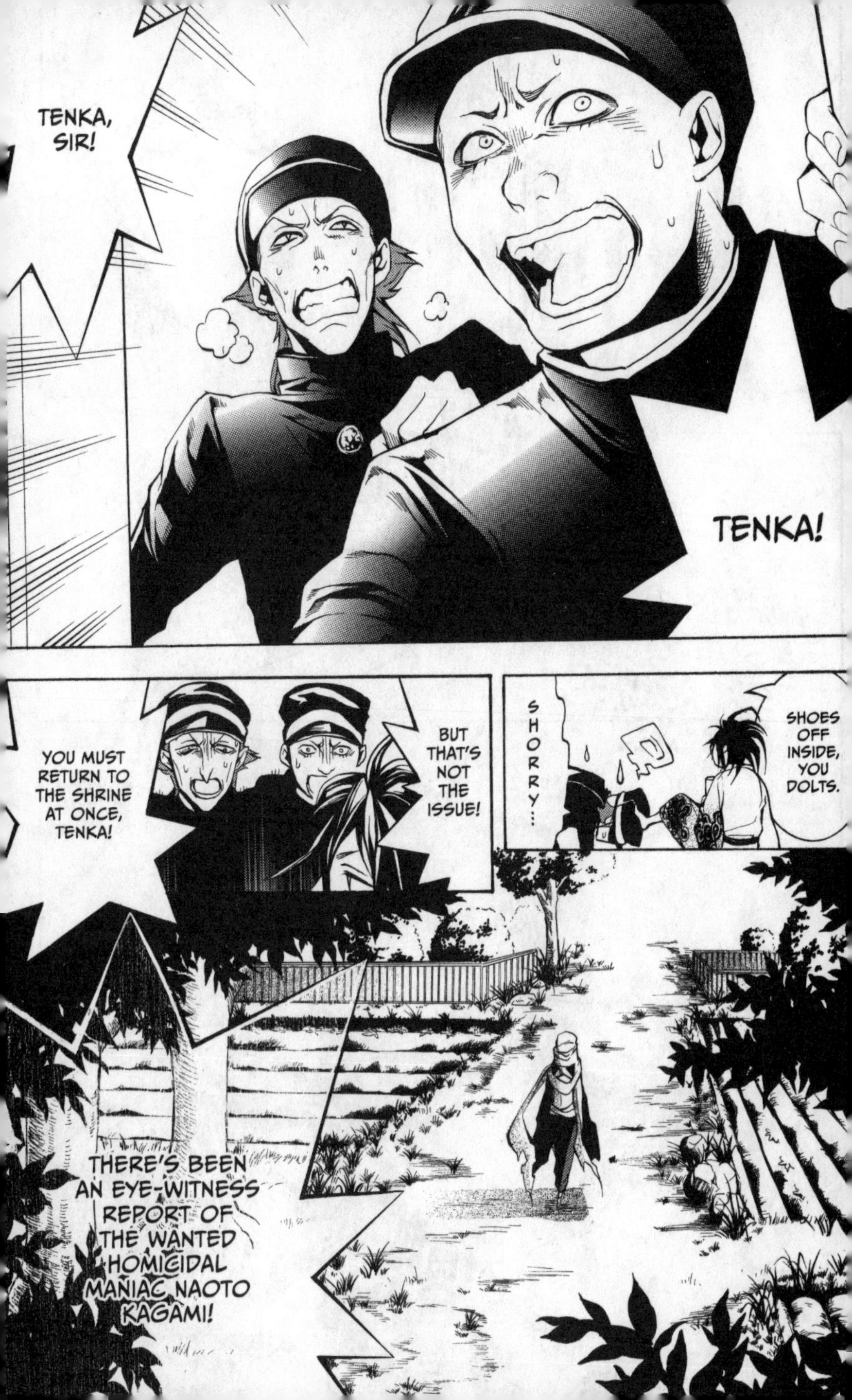
TENKA!
TENKA, SIR!
SHOES OFF INSIDE, YOU DOLTS.
SHORRY...
BUT THAT'S NOT THE ISSUE!
YOU MUST RETURN TO THE SHRINE AT ONCE, TENKA!
THERE'S BEEN AN EYE-WITNESS REPORT OF THE WANTED HOMICIDAL MANIAC NAOTO KAGAMI!

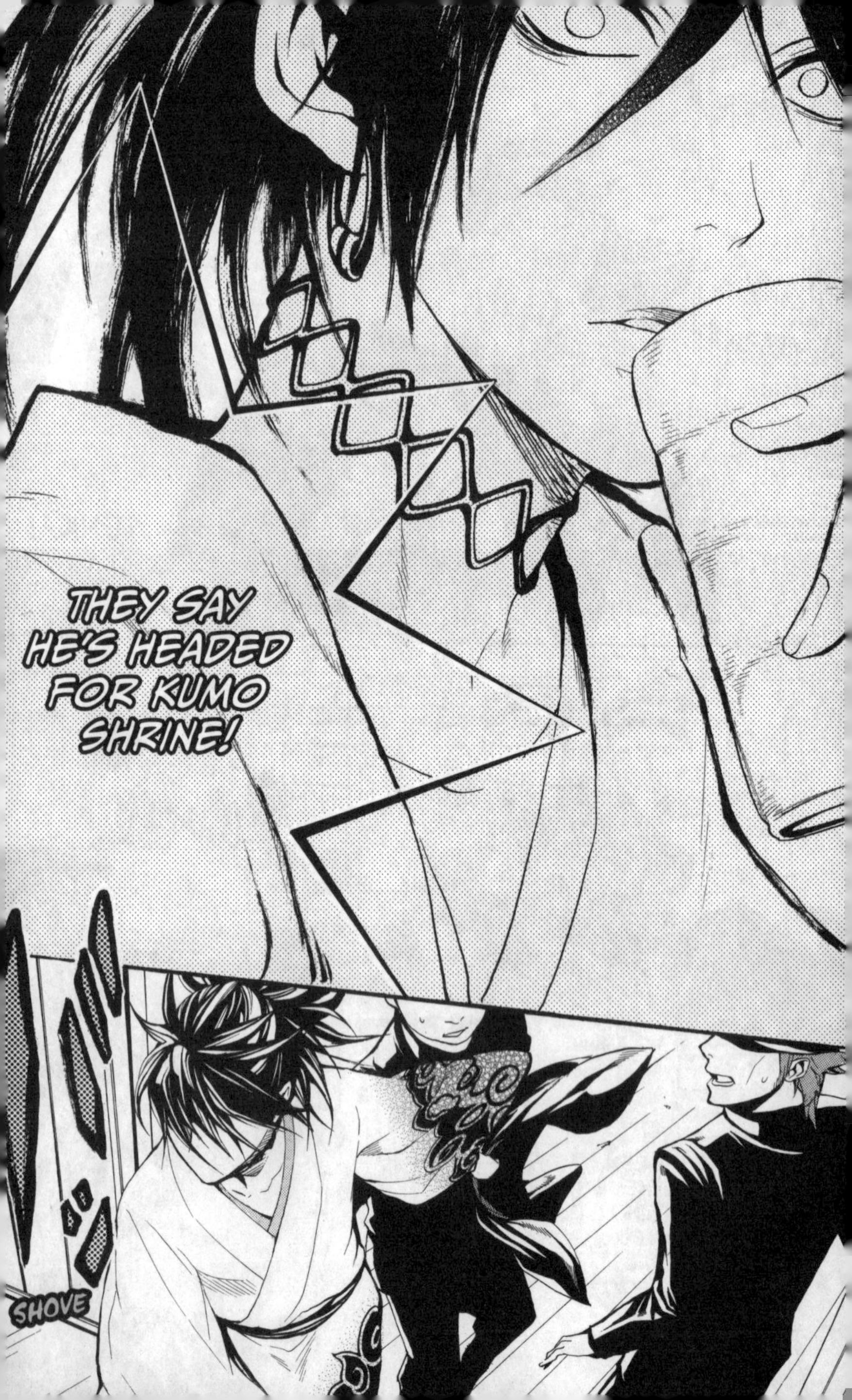
THEY SAY HE'S HEADED FOR KUMO SHRINE!
SHOVE

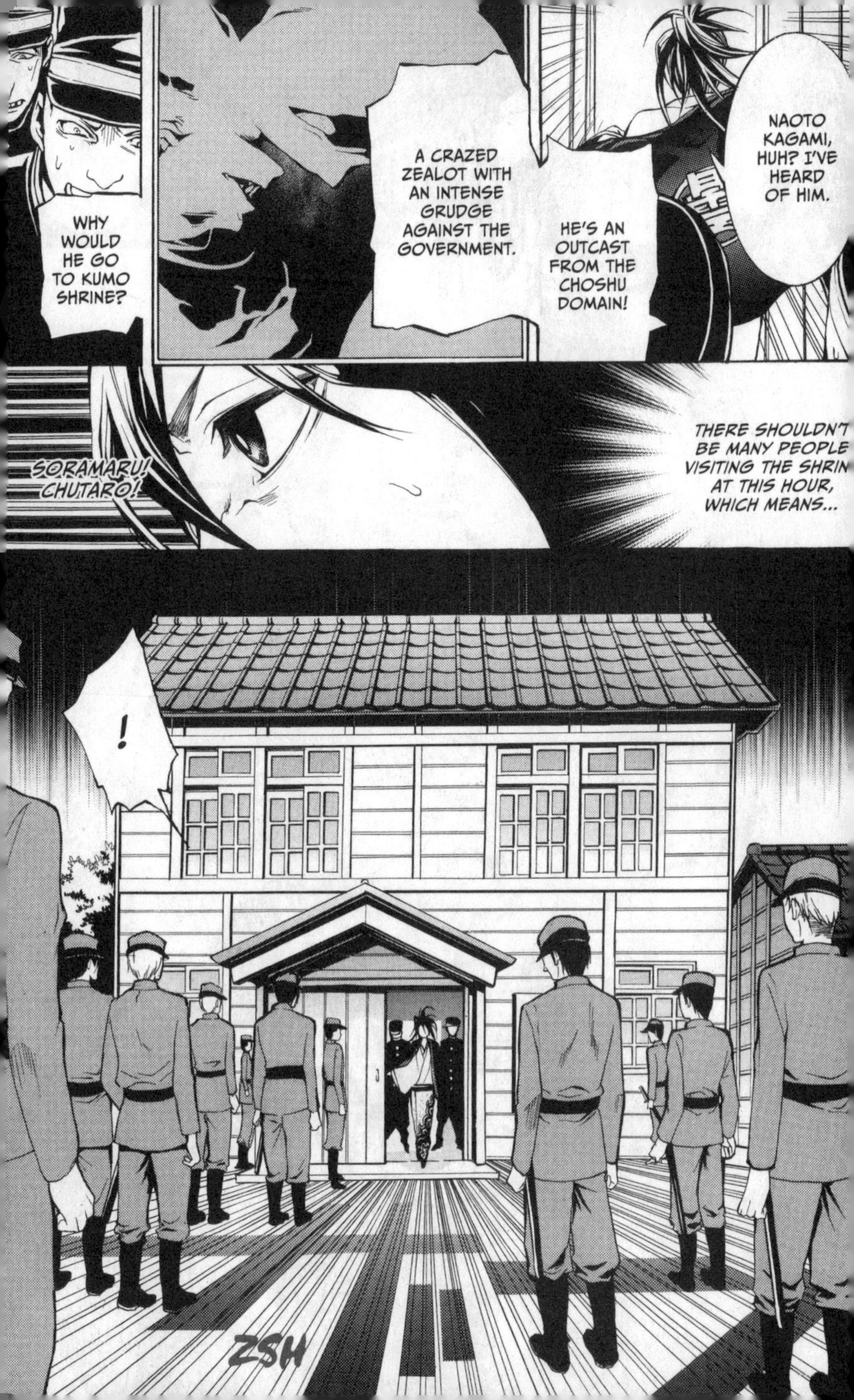

NAOTO KAGAMI, HUH? I'VE HEARD OF HIM.
HE'S AN OUTCAST FROM THE CHOSHU DOMAIN!
A CRAZED ZEALOT WITH AN INTENSE GRUDGE AGAINST THE GOVERNMENT.
WHY WOULD HE GO TO KUMO SHRINE?
THERE SHOULDN'T BE MANY PEOPLE VISITING THE SHRIN AT THIS HOUR, WHICH MEANS...
SORAMARU! CHUTARO!
!
ZSH

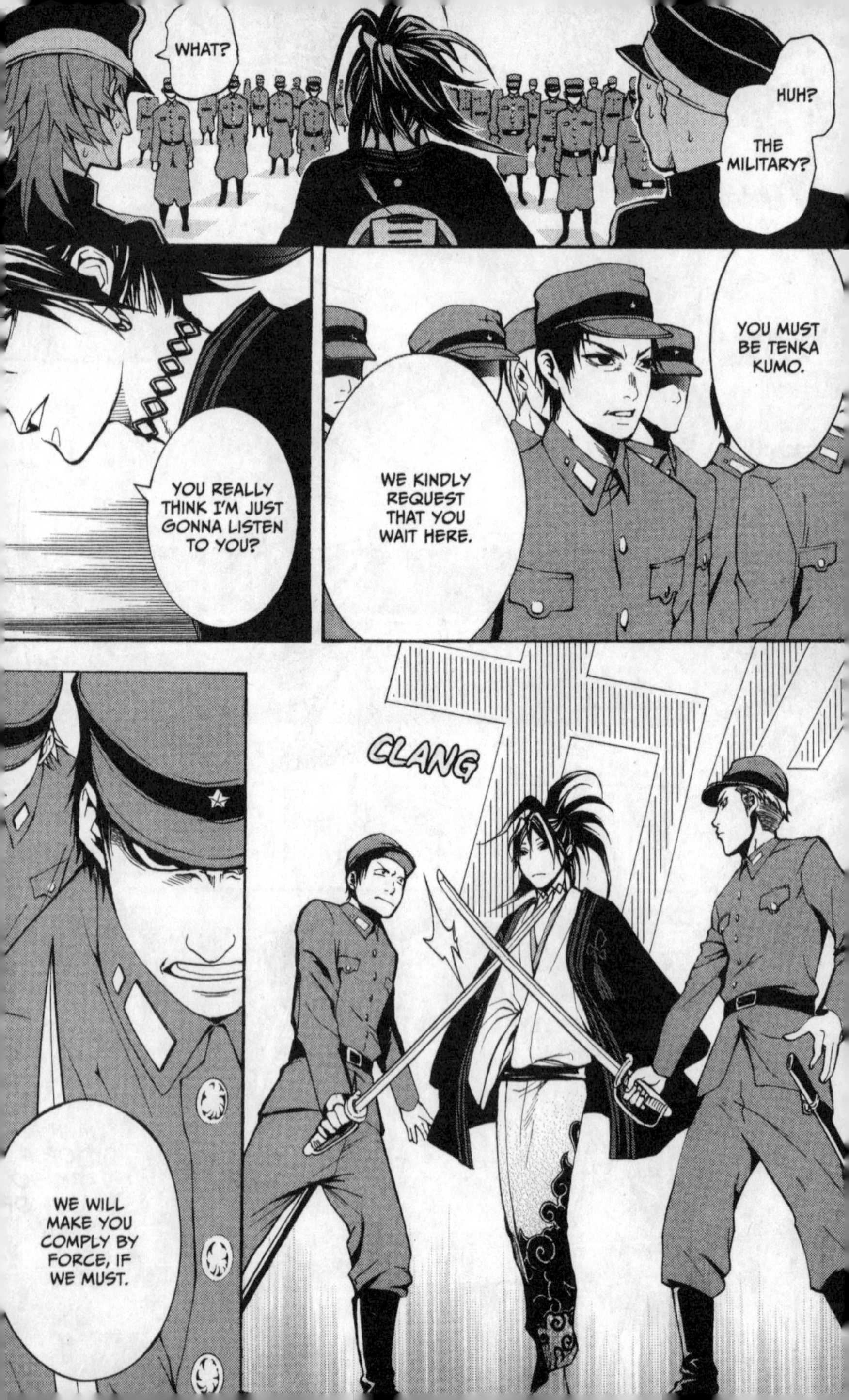
HUH?
THE MILITARY?
WHAT?
YOU MUST BE TENKA KUMO.
WE KINDLY REQUEST THAT YOU WAIT HERE.
YOU REALLY THINK I'M JUST GONNA LISTEN TO YOU?
CLANG
WE WILL MAKE YOU COMPLY BY FORCE, IF WE MUST.

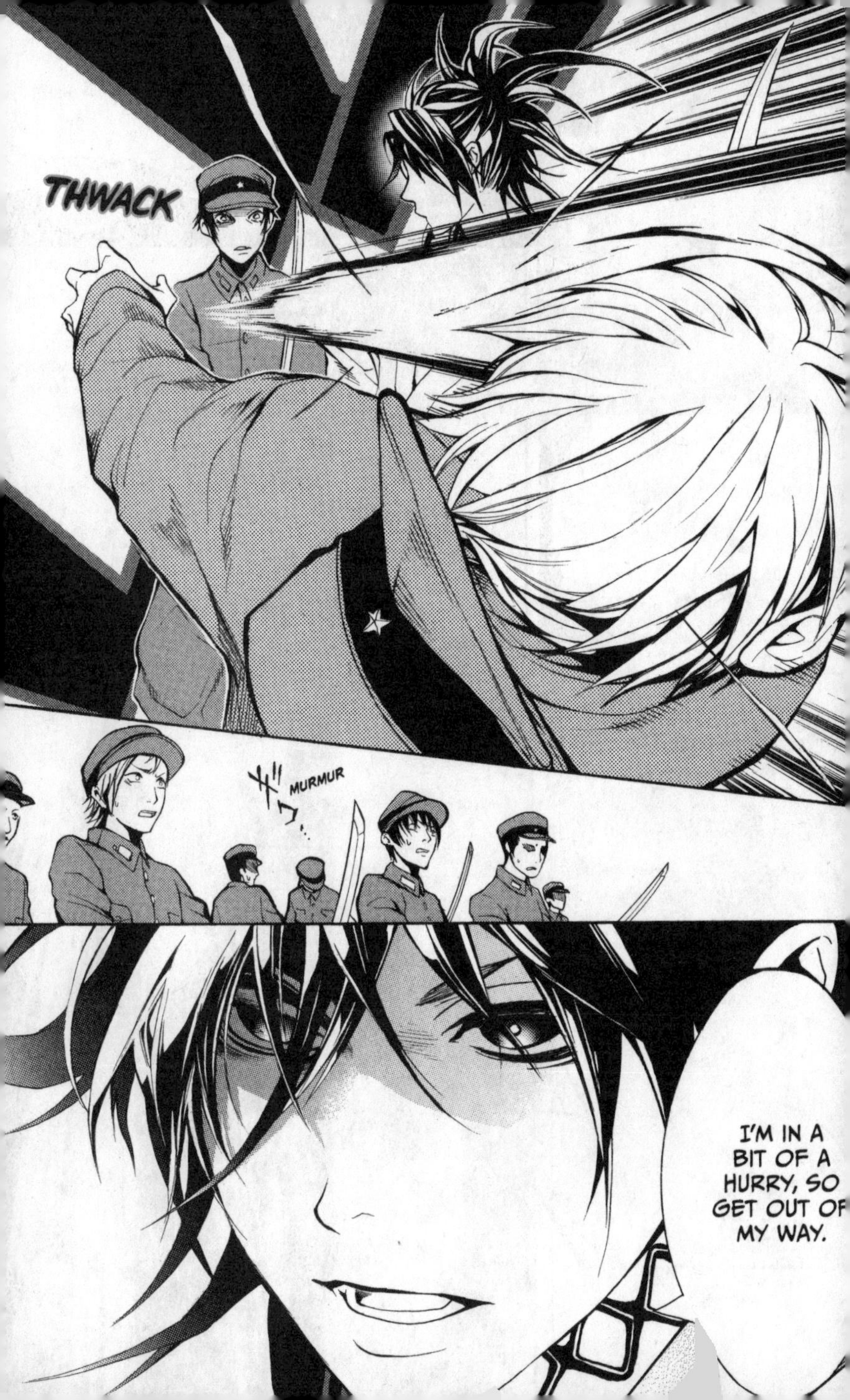
THWACK
ザワ MURMUR
I'M IN A BIT OF A HURRY, SO GET OUT OF MY WAY.

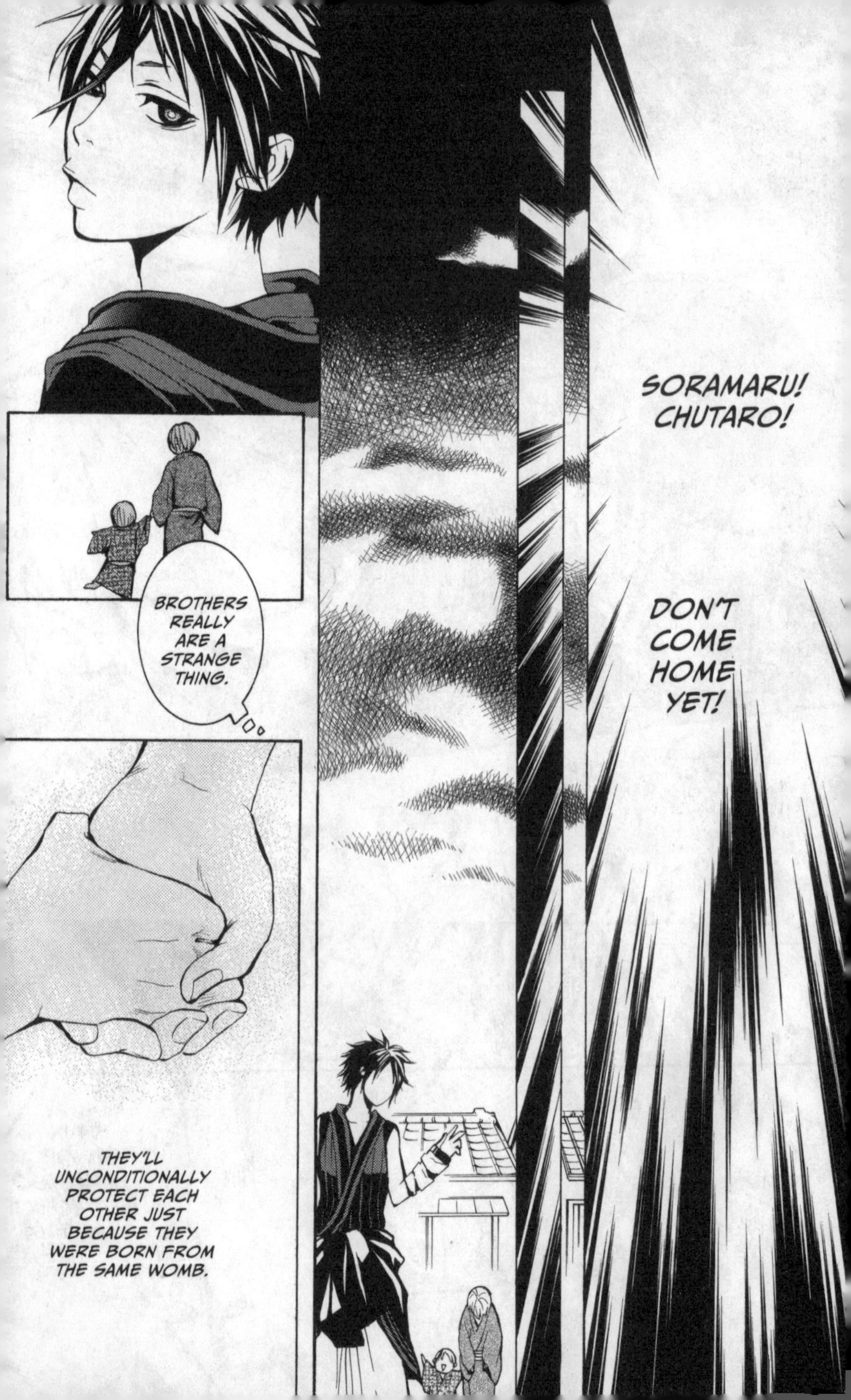
SORAMARU! CHUTARO!
DON'T COME HOME YET!
BROTHERS REALLY ARE A STRANGE THING.
THEY'LL UNCONDITIONALLY PROTECT EACH OTHER JUST BECAUSE THEY WERE BORN FROM THE SAME WOMB.

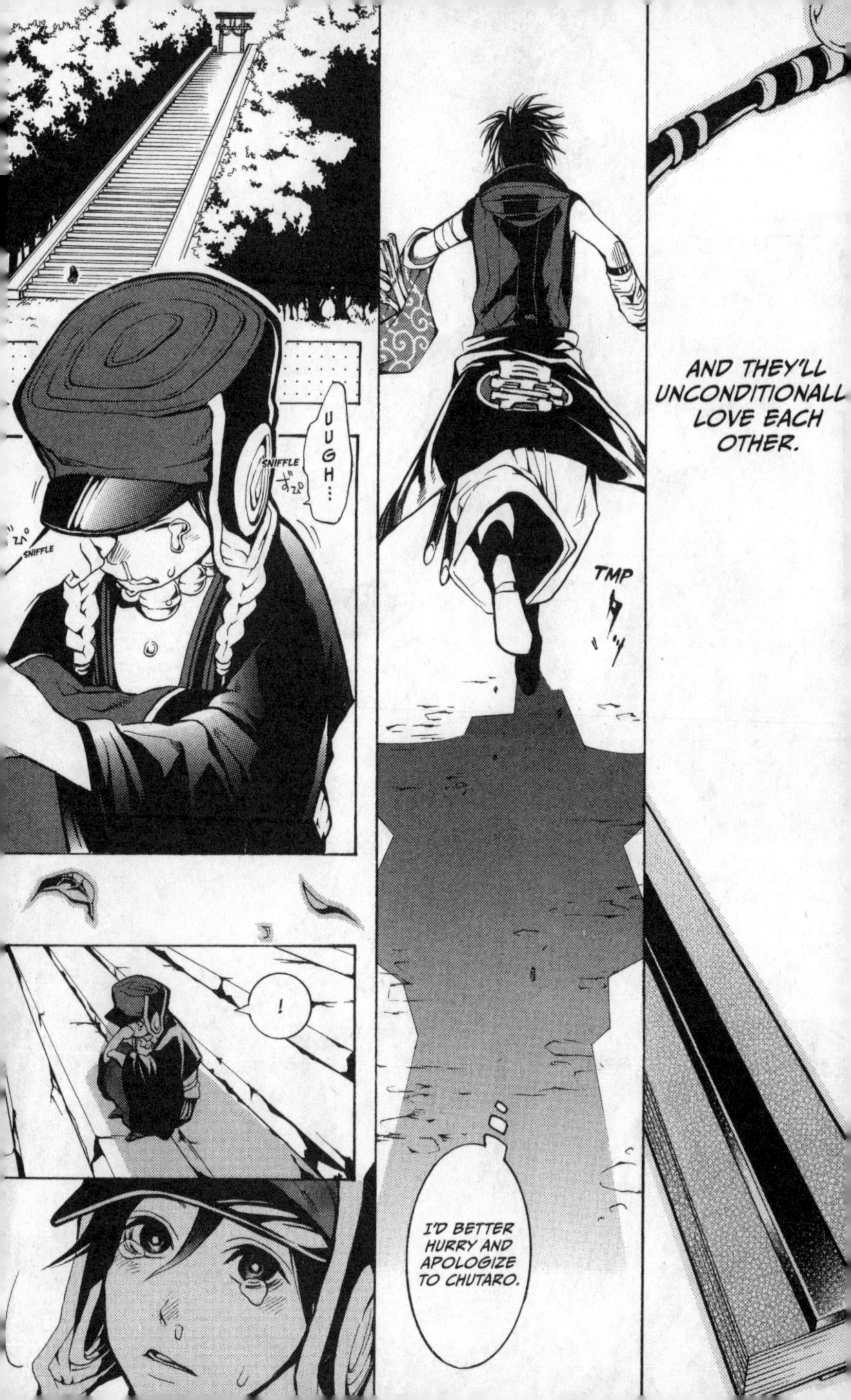
AND THEY'LL UNCONDITIONALL LOVE EACH OTHER.
TMP
I'D BETTER HURRY AND APOLOGIZE TO CHUTARO.
UUGH...
SNIFFLE
SNIFFLE
!

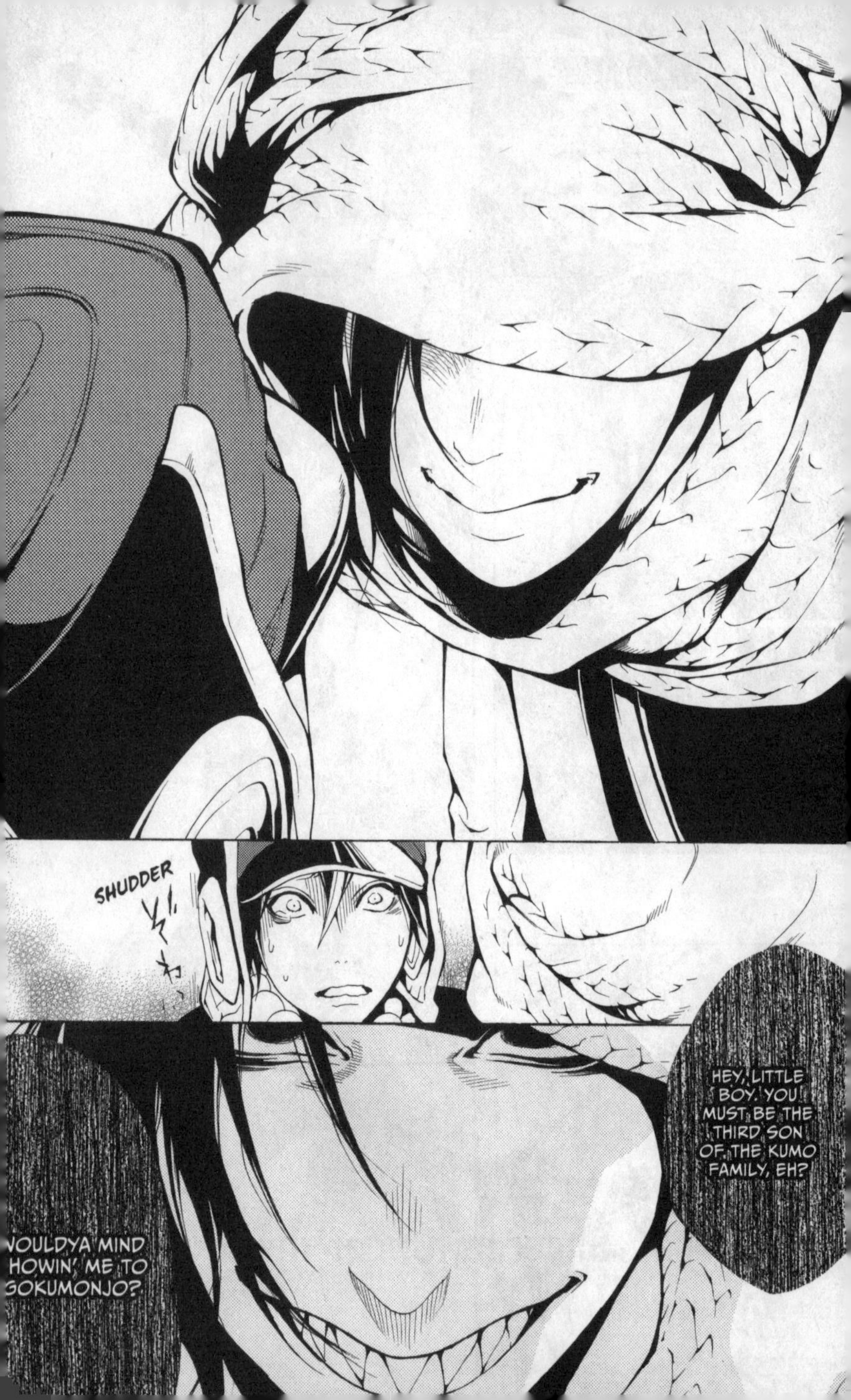
SHUDDER
HEY, LITTLE BOY. YOU MUST BE THE THIRD SON OF THE KUMO FAMILY, EH?
WOULDYA MIND HOWIN' ME TO GOKUMONJO?

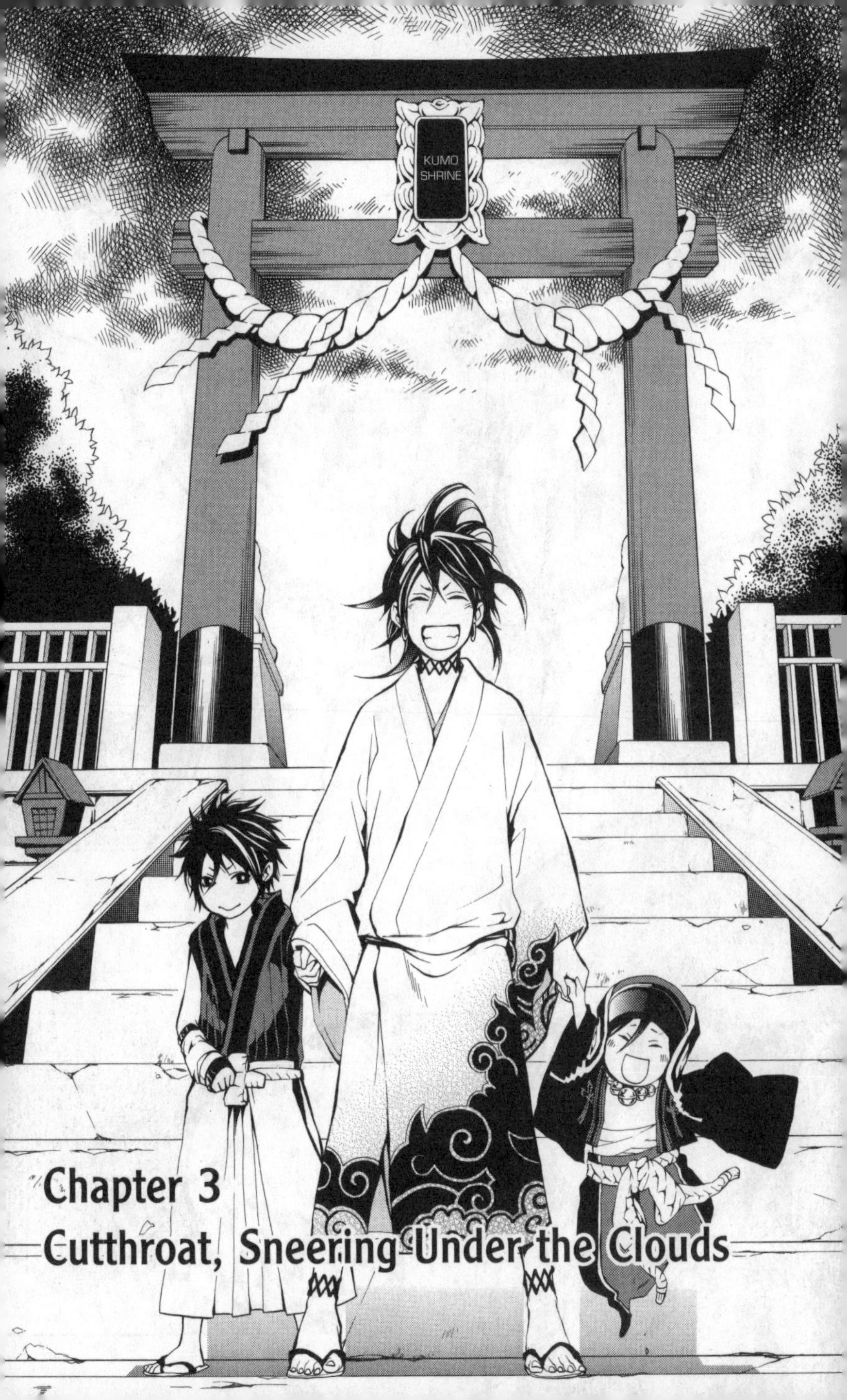
KUMO SHRINE

Chapter 3
Cutthroat, Sneering Under the Clouds

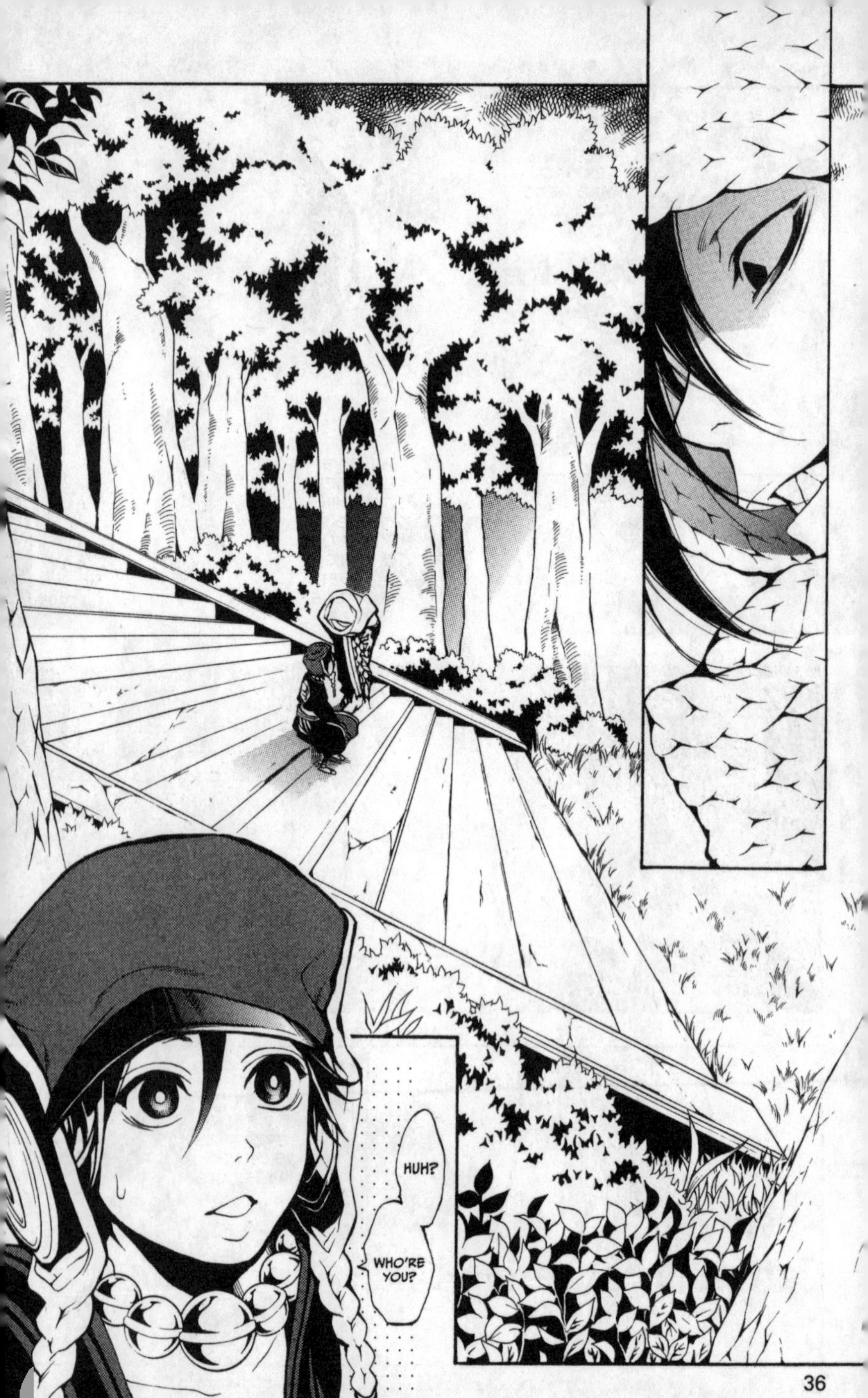
HUH?
WHO'RE YOU?

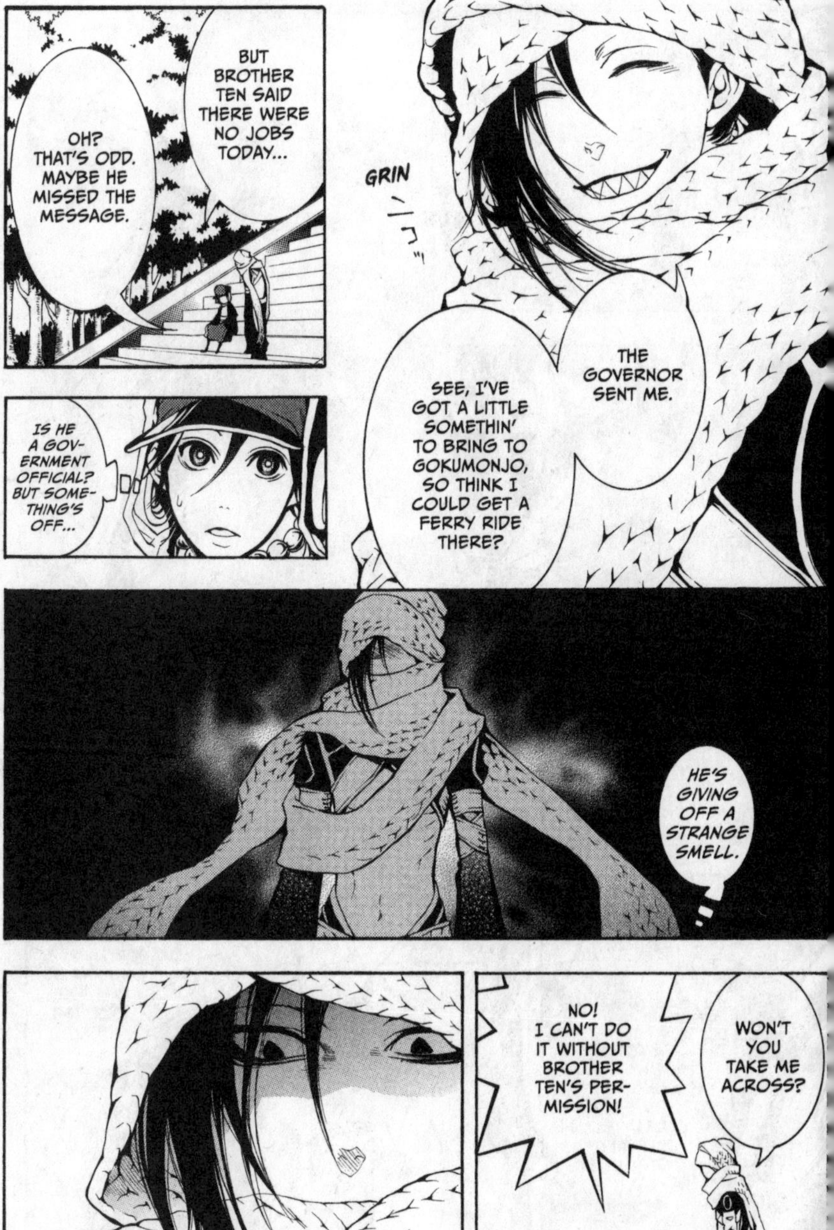
GRIN
THE GOVERNOR SENT ME.
SEE, I'VE GOT A LITTLE SOMETHIN' TO BRING TO GOKUMONJO, SO THINK I COULD GET A FERRY RIDE THERE?
BUT BROTHER TEN SAID THERE WERE NO JOBS TODAY...
OH? THAT'S ODD. MAYBE HE MISSED THE MESSAGE.
IS HE A GOVERNMENT OFFICIAL? BUT SOMETHING'S OFF...
HE'S GIVING OFF A STRANGE SMELL.
WON'T YOU TAKE ME ACROSS?
NO! I CAN'T DO IT WITHOUT BROTHER TEN'S PERMISSION!
FWIP

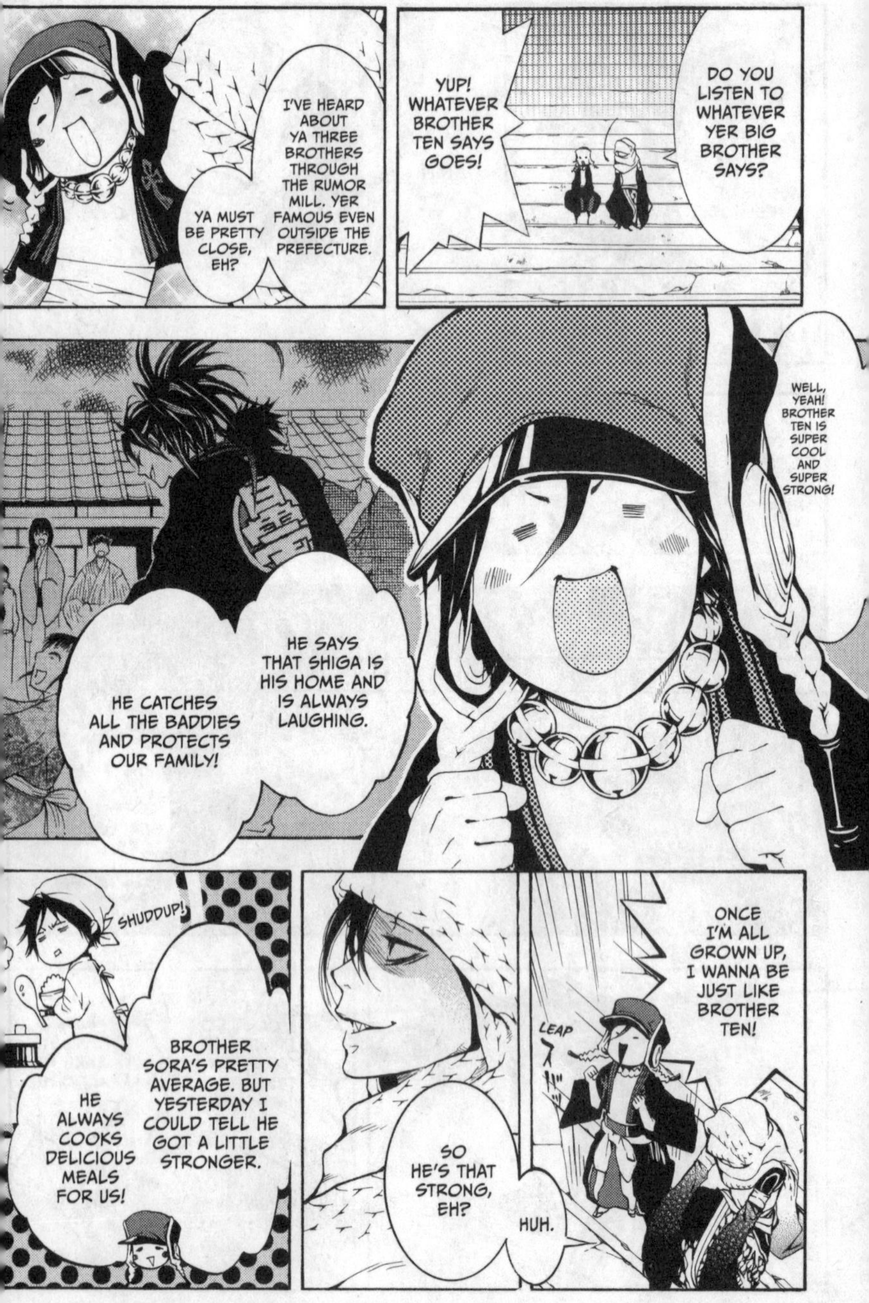
DO YOU LISTEN TO WHATEVER YER BIG BROTHER SAYS?
YUP! WHATEVER BROTHER TEN SAYS GOES!
I'VE HEARD ABOUT YA THREE BROTHERS THROUGH THE RUMOR MILL. YER FAMOUS EVEN OUTSIDE THE PREFECTURE.
YA MUST BE PRETTY CLOSE, EH?
WELL, YEAH! BROTHER TEN IS SUPER COOL AND SUPER STRONG!
HE SAYS THAT SHIGA IS HIS HOME AND IS ALWAYS LAUGHING.
HE CATCHES ALL THE BADDIES AND PROTECTS OUR FAMILY!
ONCE I'M ALL GROWN UP, I WANNA BE JUST LIKE BROTHER TEN!
LEAP
HUH.
SO HE'S THAT STRONG, EH?
SHUDDUP!
BROTHER SORA'S PRETTY AVERAGE. BUT YESTERDAY I COULD TELL HE GOT A LITTLE STRONGER.
HE ALWAYS COOKS DELICIOUS MEALS FOR US!

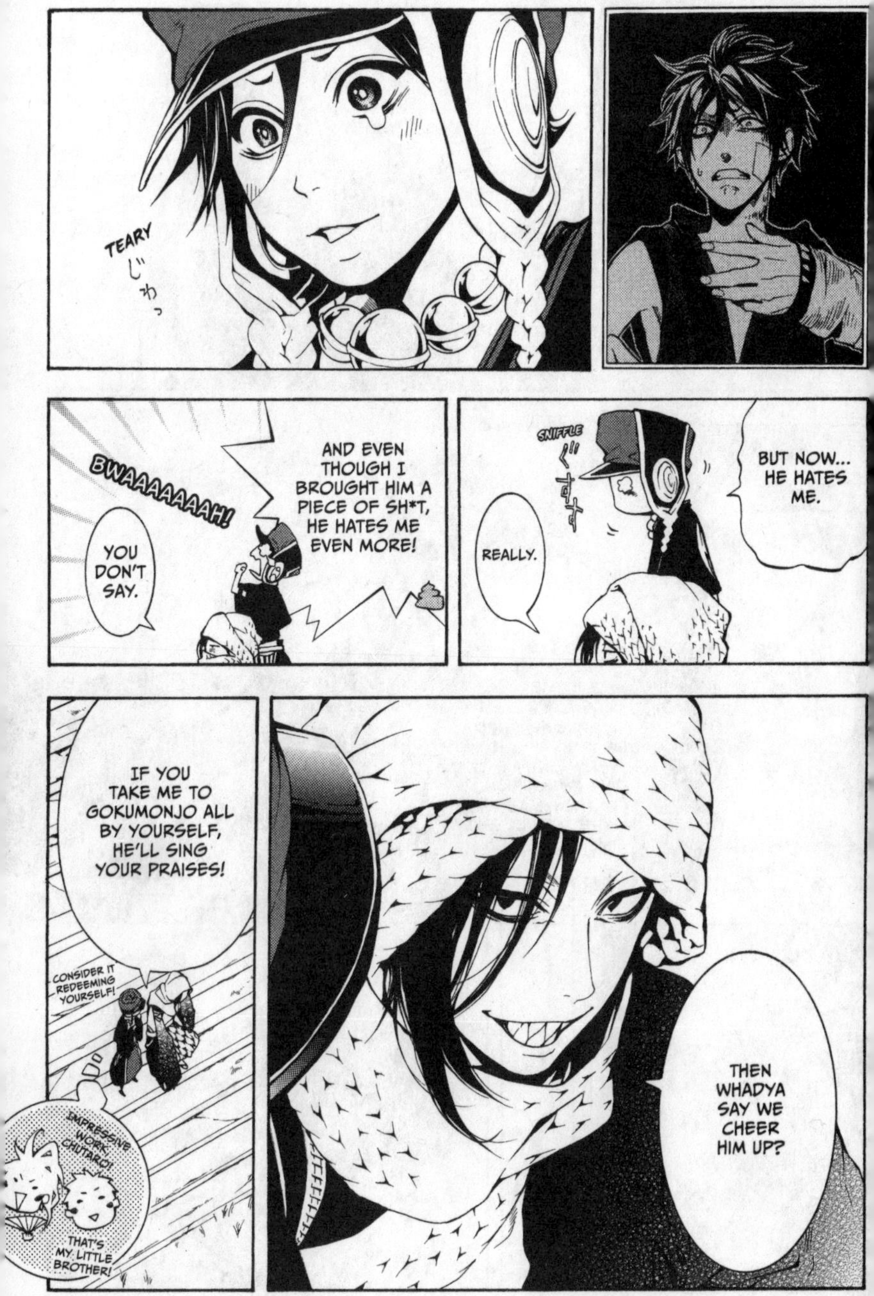
TEARY
じわっ
BUT NOW... HE HATES ME.
SNIFFLE
REALLY.
AND EVEN THOUGH I BROUGHT HIM A PIECE OF SH*T, HE HATES ME EVEN MORE!
BWAAAAAAAH!
YOU DON'T SAY.
THEN WHADYA SAY WE CHEER HIM UP?
IF YOU TAKE ME TO GOKUMONJO ALL BY YOURSELF, HE'LL SING YOUR PRAISES!
CONSIDER IT REDEEMING YOURSELF!
IMPRESSIVE WORK, CHUTARO!
THAT'S MY LITTLE BROTHER!

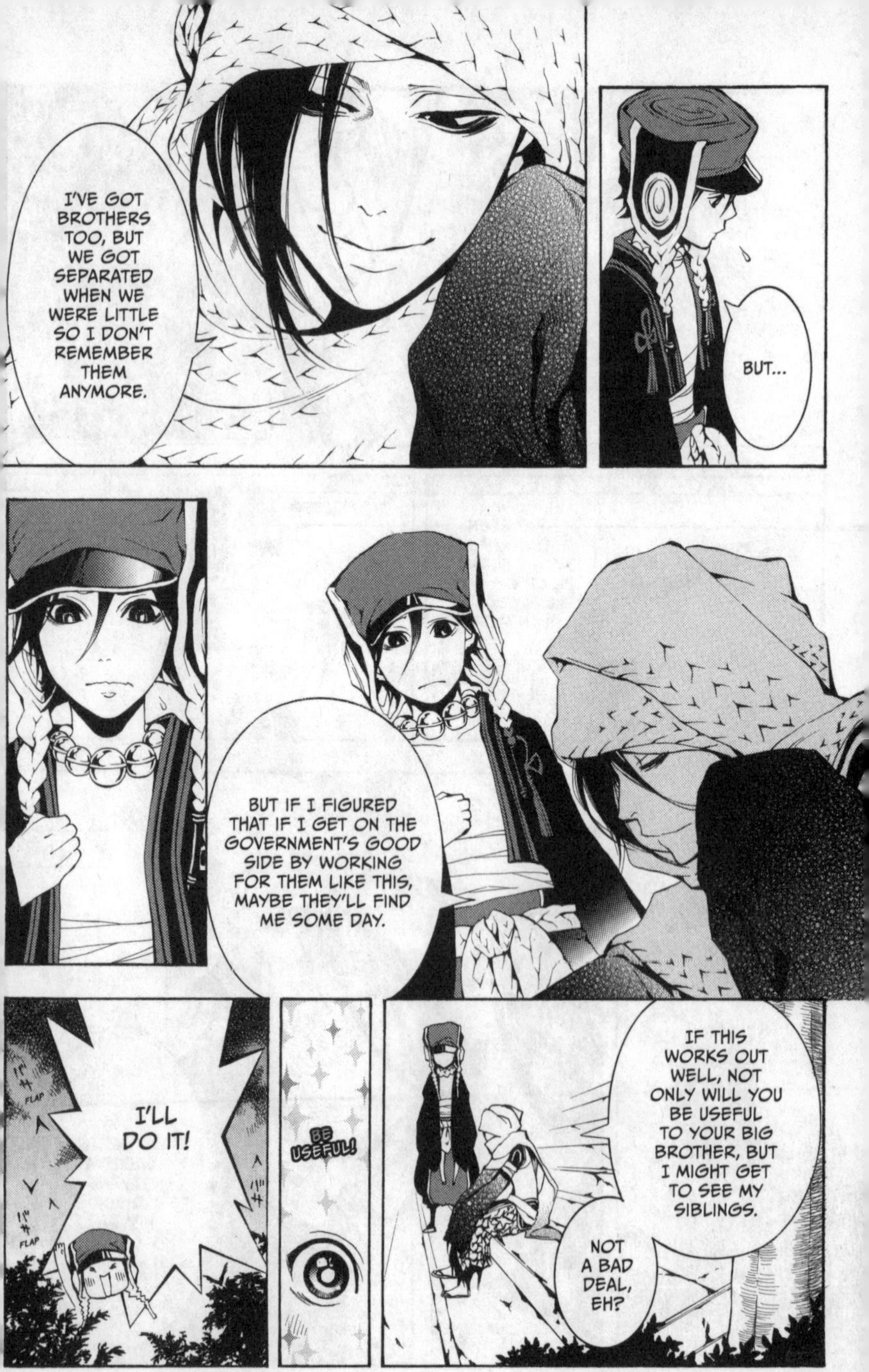
BUT...
I'VE GOT BROTHERS TOO, BUT WE GOT SEPARATED WHEN WE WERE LITTLE SO I DON'T REMEMBER THEM ANYMORE.
BUT IF I FIGURED THAT IF I GET ON THE GOVERNMENT'S GOOD SIDE BY WORKING FOR THEM LIKE THIS, MAYBE THEY'LL FIND ME SOME DAY.
IF THIS WORKS OUT WELL, NOT ONLY WILL YOU BE USEFUL TO YOUR BIG BROTHER, BUT I MIGHT GET TO SEE MY SIBLINGS.
NOT A BAD DEAL, EH?
BE USEFUL!
FLAP
FLAP
I'LL DO IT!

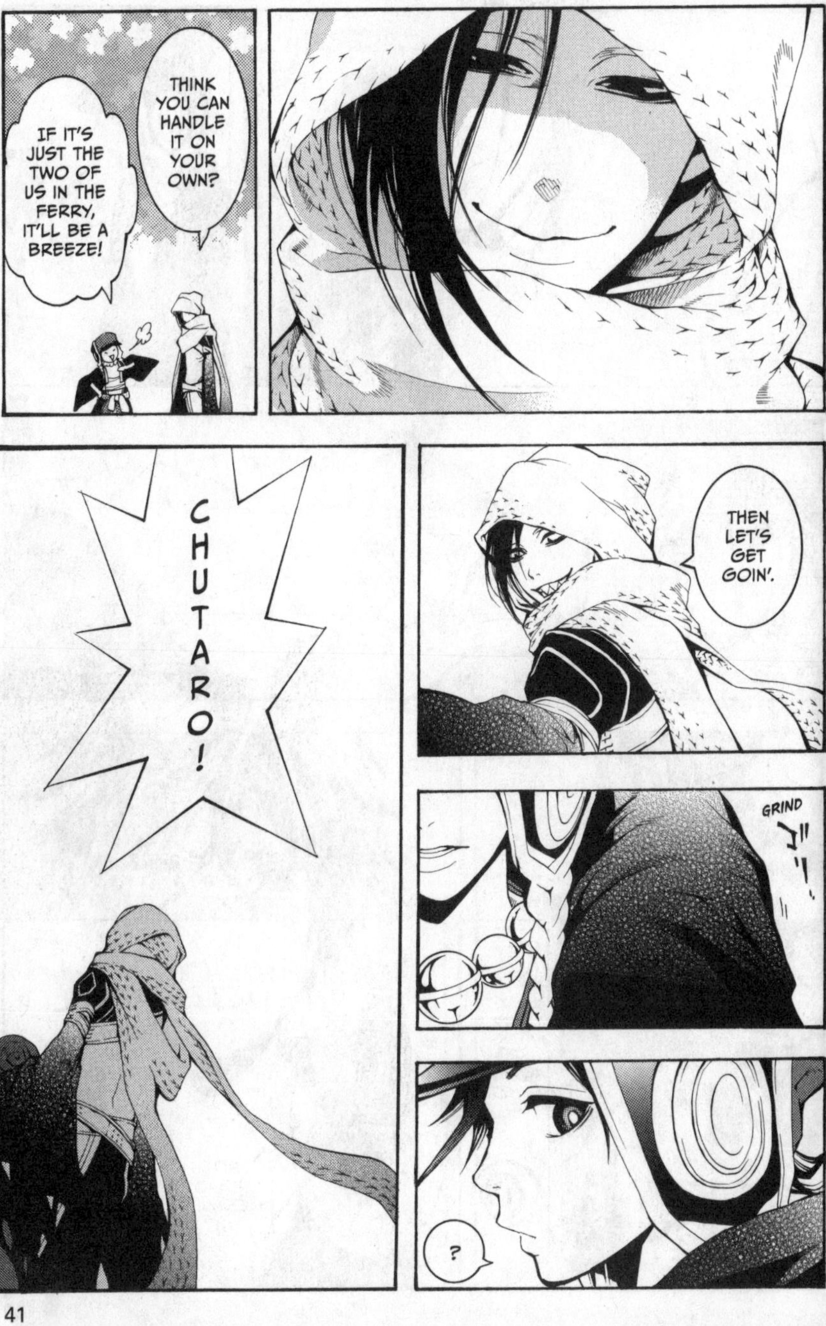
THINK YOU CAN HANDLE IT ON YOUR OWN?
IF IT'S JUST THE TWO OF US IN THE FERRY, IT'LL BE A BREEZE!
THEN LET'S GET GOIN'.
GRIND
?
CHUTARO!

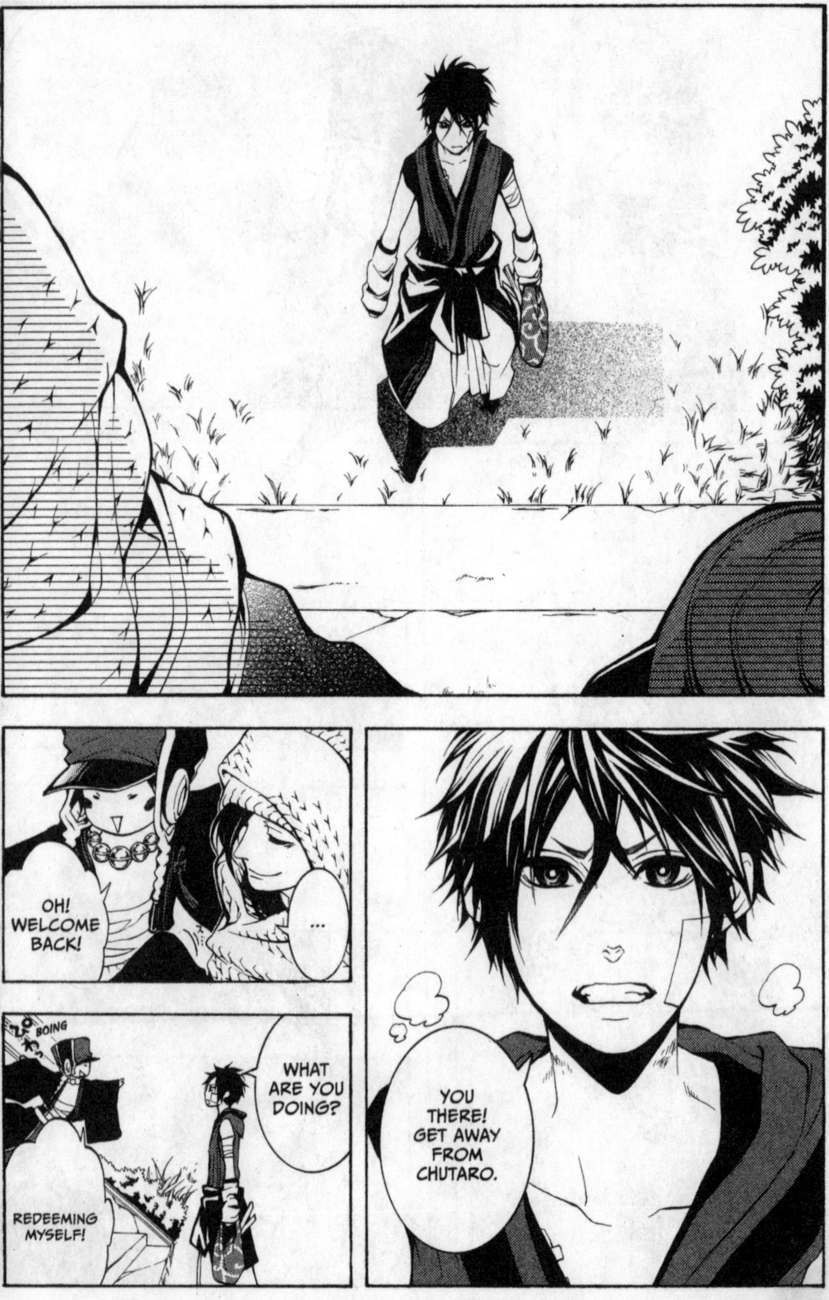
YOU THERE! GET AWAY FROM CHUTARO.
...
OH! WELCOME BACK!
WHAT ARE YOU DOING?
BOING
REDEEMING MYSELF!

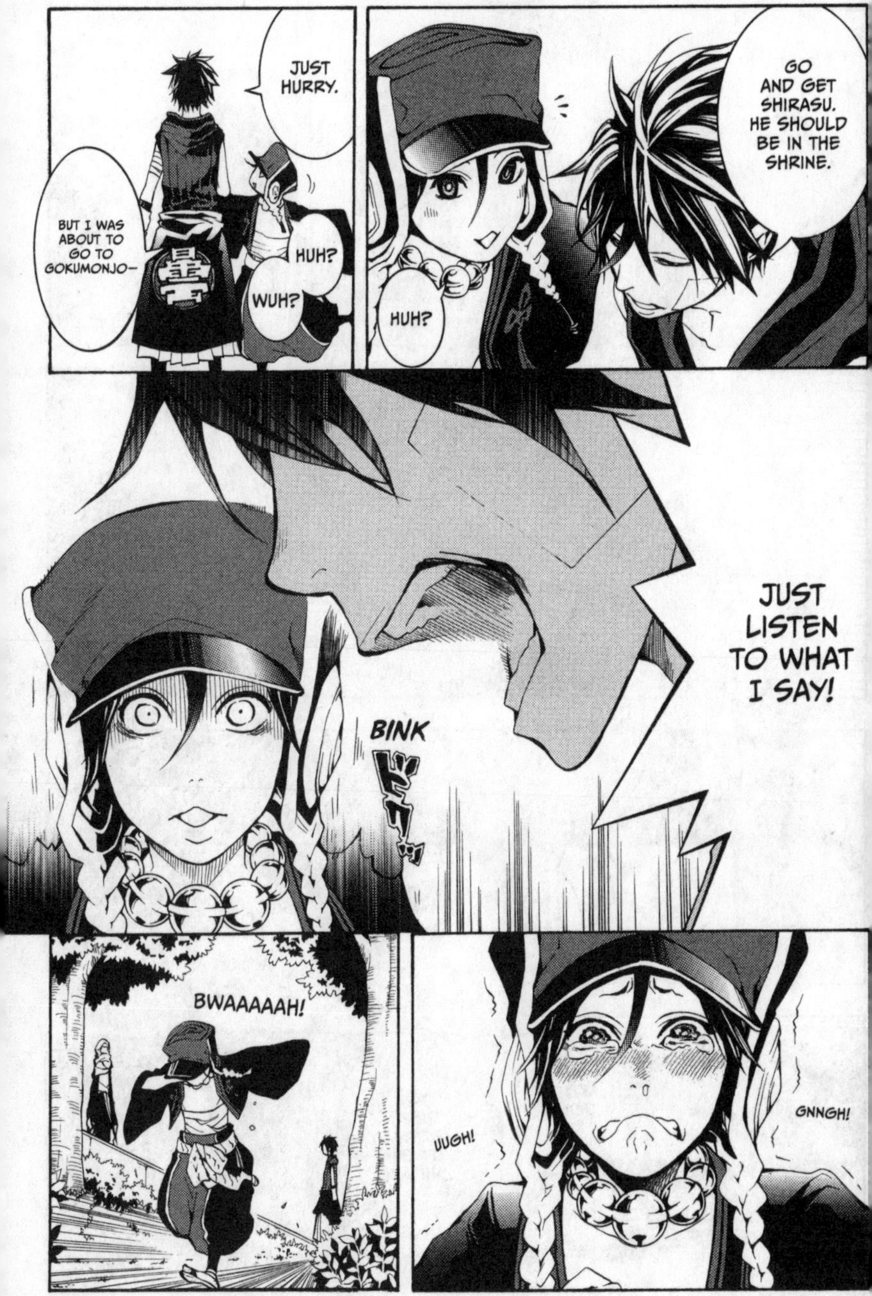
GO AND GET SHIRASU. HE SHOULD BE IN THE SHRINE.
HUH?
JUST HURRY.
HUH?
WUH?
BUT I WAS ABOUT TO GO TO GOKUMONJO—
JUST LISTEN TO WHAT I SAY!
BINK
GNNGH!
UUGH!
BWAAAAAH!

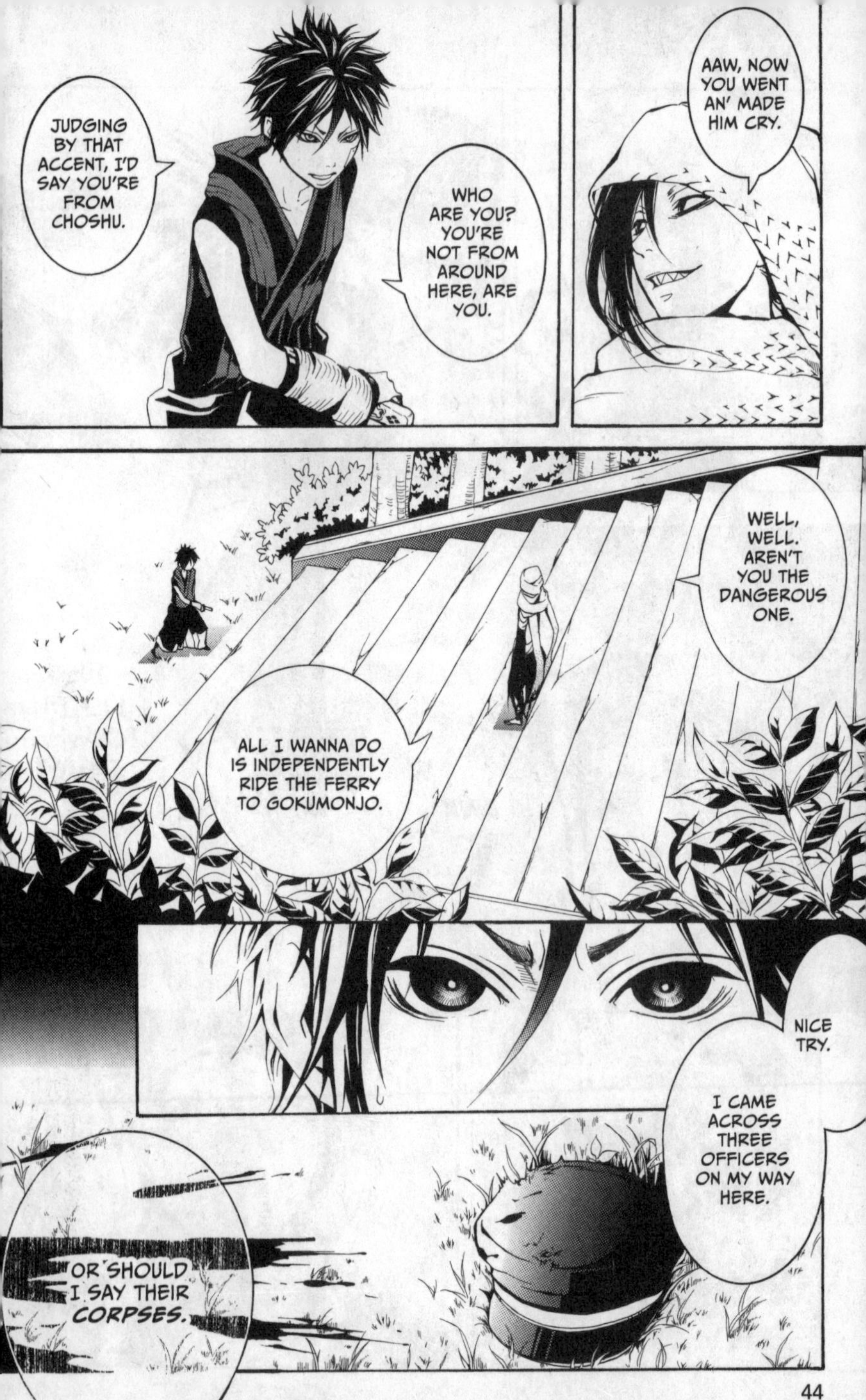
AAW, NOW YOU WENT AN' MADE HIM CRY.
WHO ARE YOU? YOU'RE NOT FROM AROUND HERE, ARE YOU.
JUDGING BY THAT ACCENT, I'D SAY YOU'RE FROM CHOSHU.
WELL, WELL. AREN'T YOU THE DANGEROUS ONE.
ALL I WANNA DO IS INDEPENDENTLY RIDE THE FERRY TO GOKUMONJO.
NICE TRY.
I CAME ACROSS THREE OFFICERS ON MY WAY HERE.
OR SHOULD I SAY THEIR *CORPSES.*

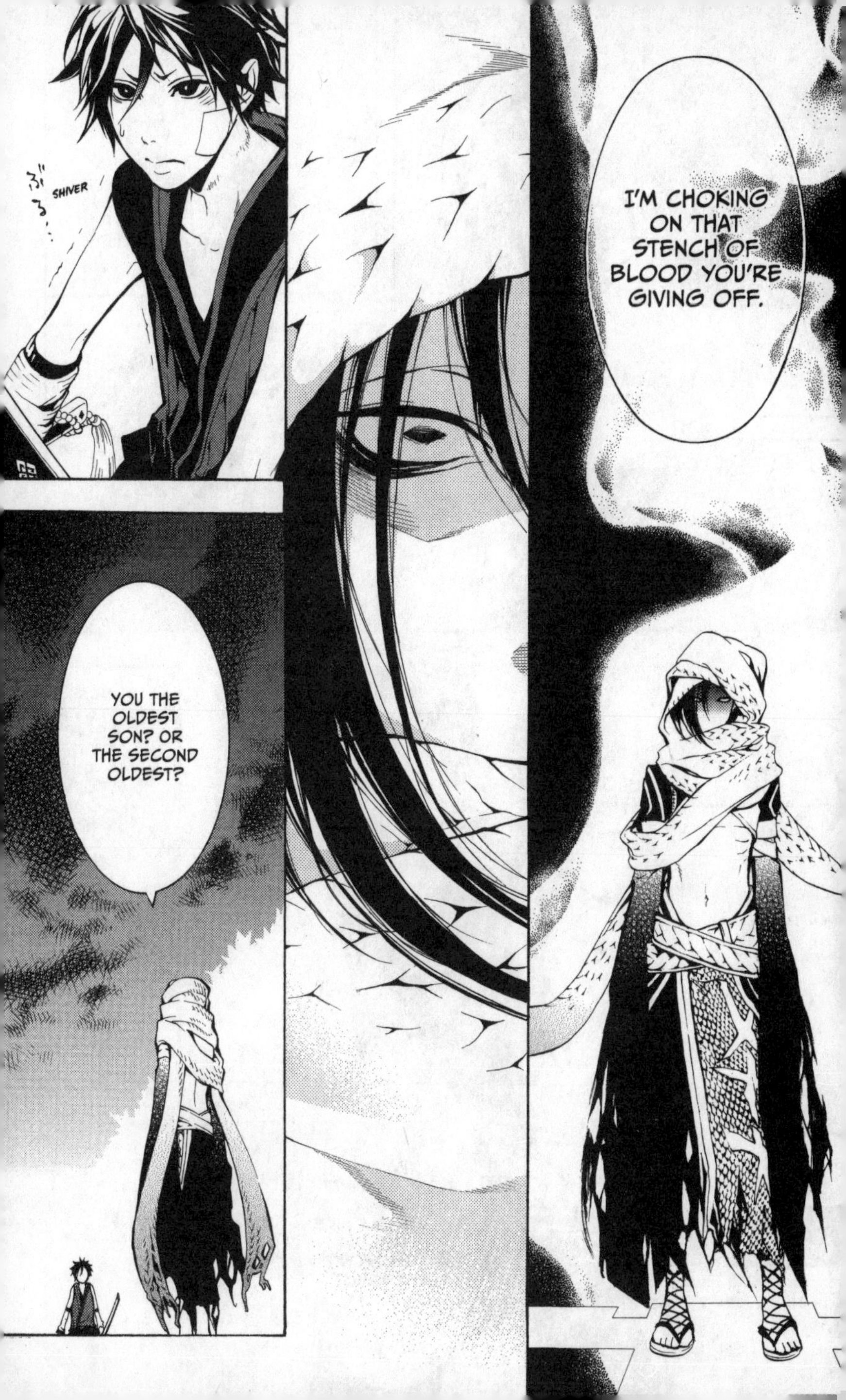
I'M CHOKING ON THAT STENCH OF BLOOD YOU'RE GIVING OFF.
ぶる…
SHIVER
YOU THE OLDEST SON? OR THE SECOND OLDEST?

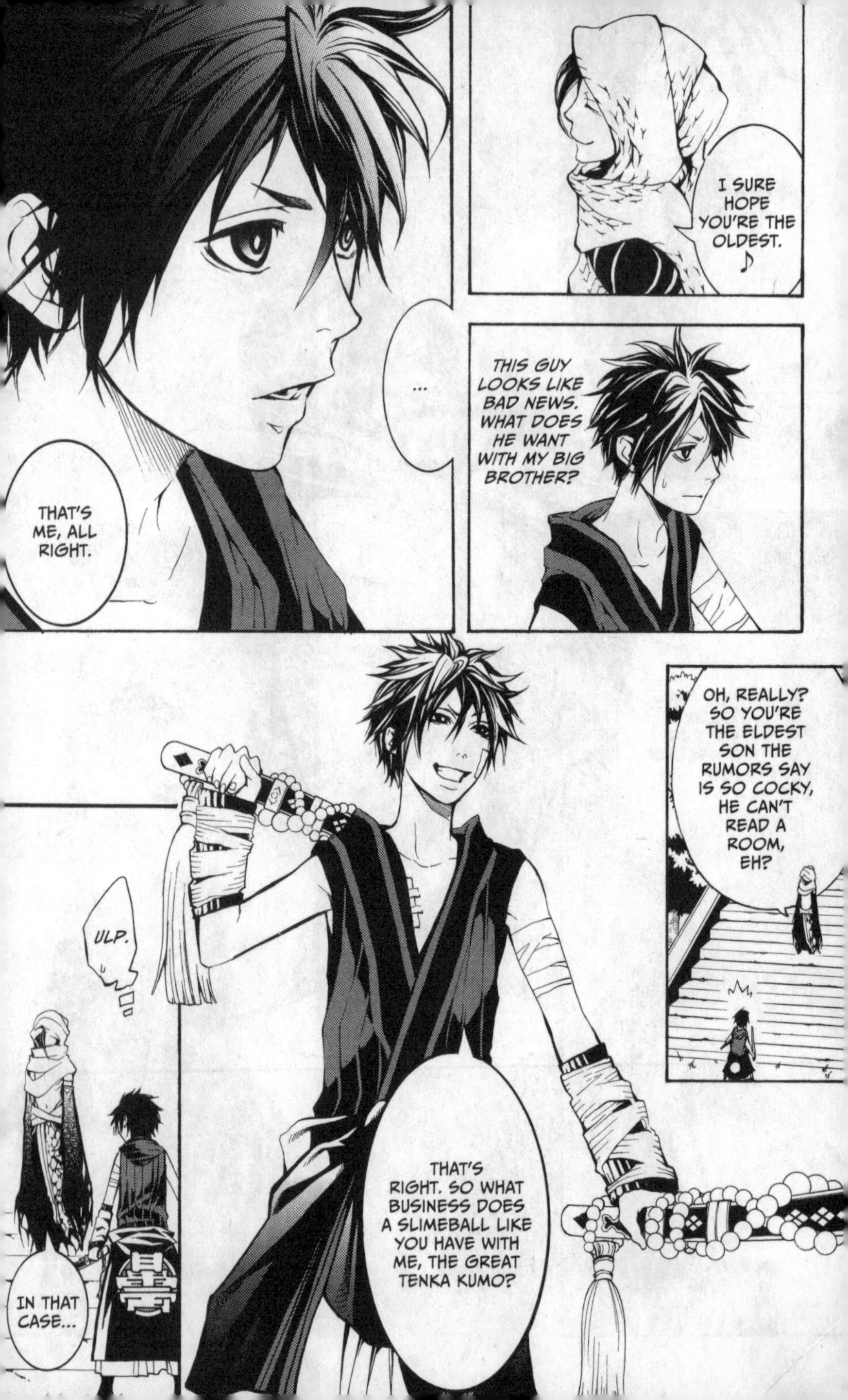
I SURE HOPE YOU'RE THE OLDEST. ♪
THIS GUY LOOKS LIKE BAD NEWS. WHAT DOES HE WANT WITH MY BIG BROTHER?
...
THAT'S ME, ALL RIGHT.
OH, REALLY? SO YOU'RE THE ELDEST SON THE RUMORS SAY IS SO COCKY, HE CAN'T READ A ROOM, EH?
THAT'S RIGHT. SO WHAT BUSINESS DOES A SLIMEBALL LIKE YOU HAVE WITH ME, THE GREAT TENKA KUMO?
ULP.
IN THAT CASE...

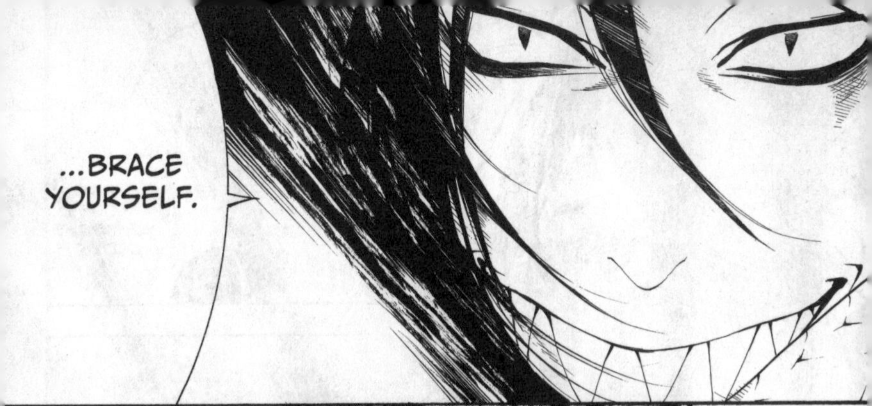
...BRACE YOURSELF.

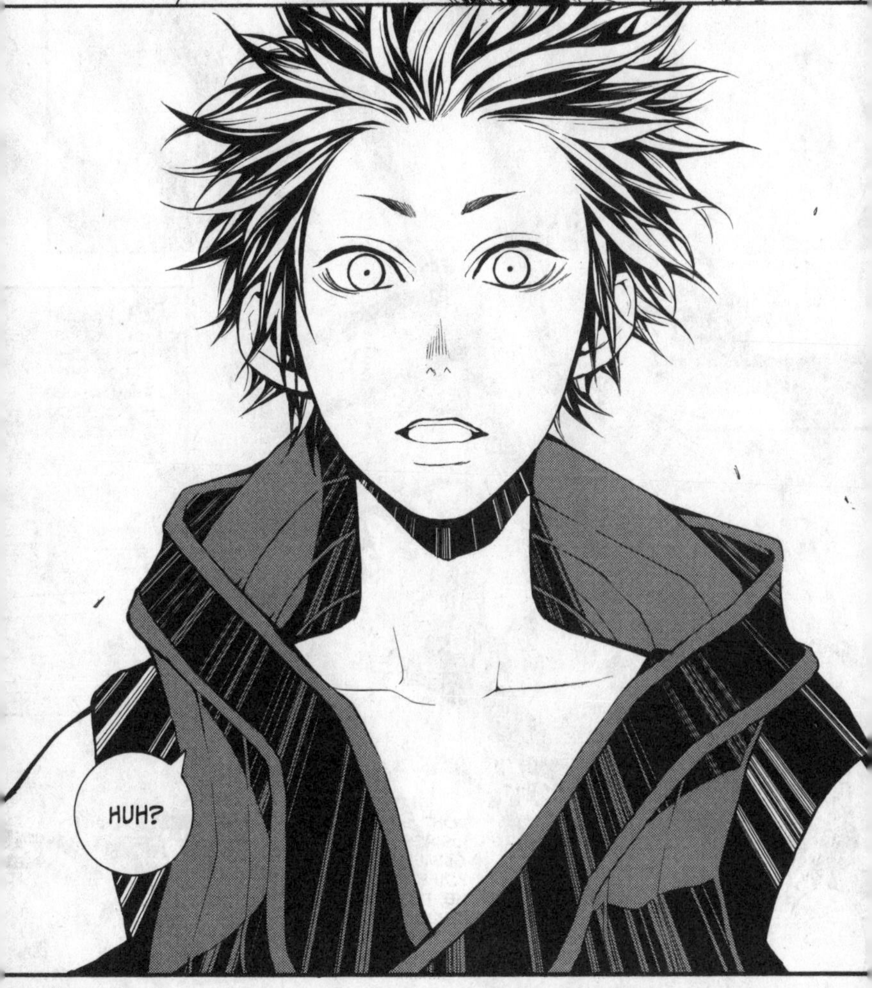
HUH?

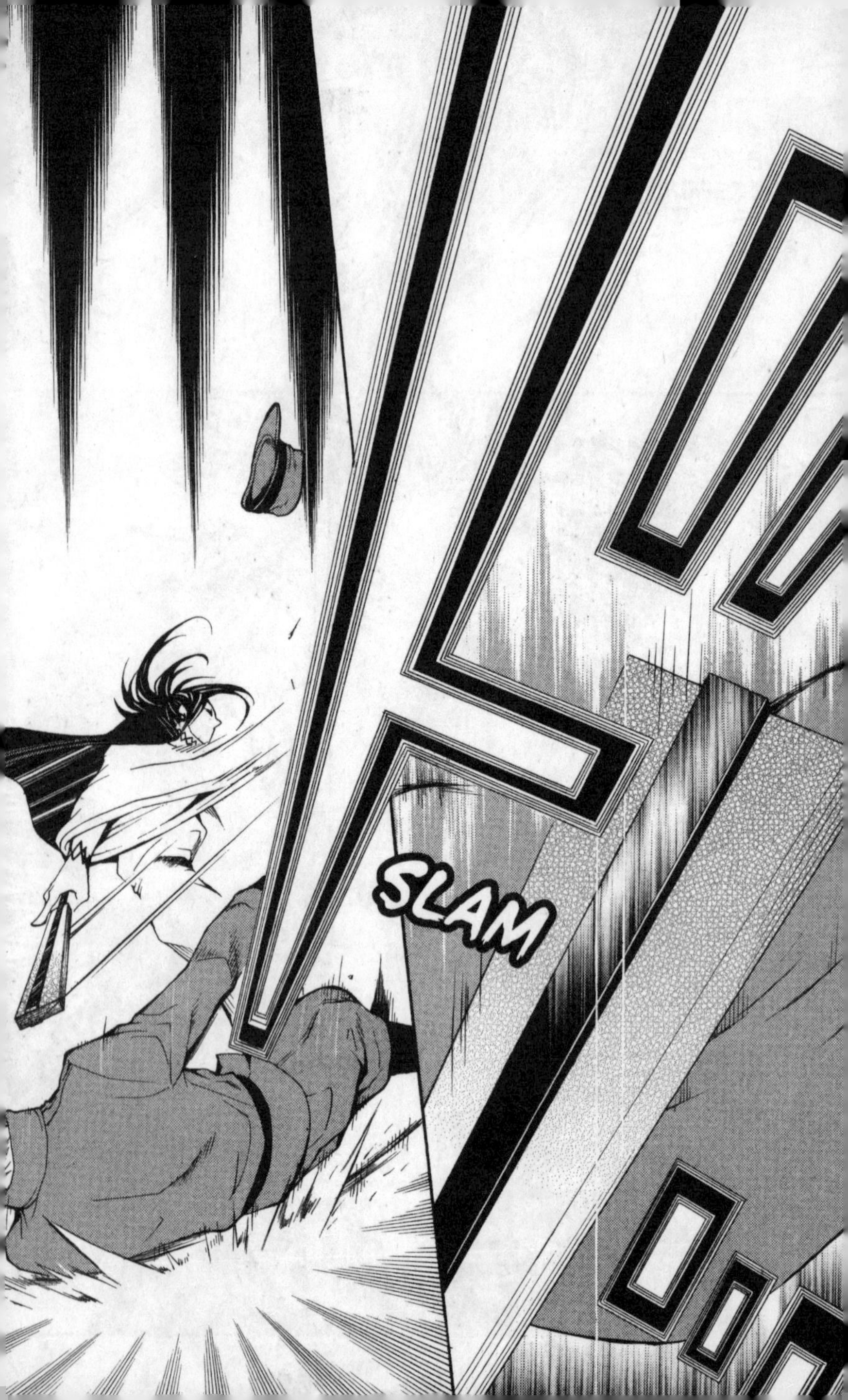
SLAM

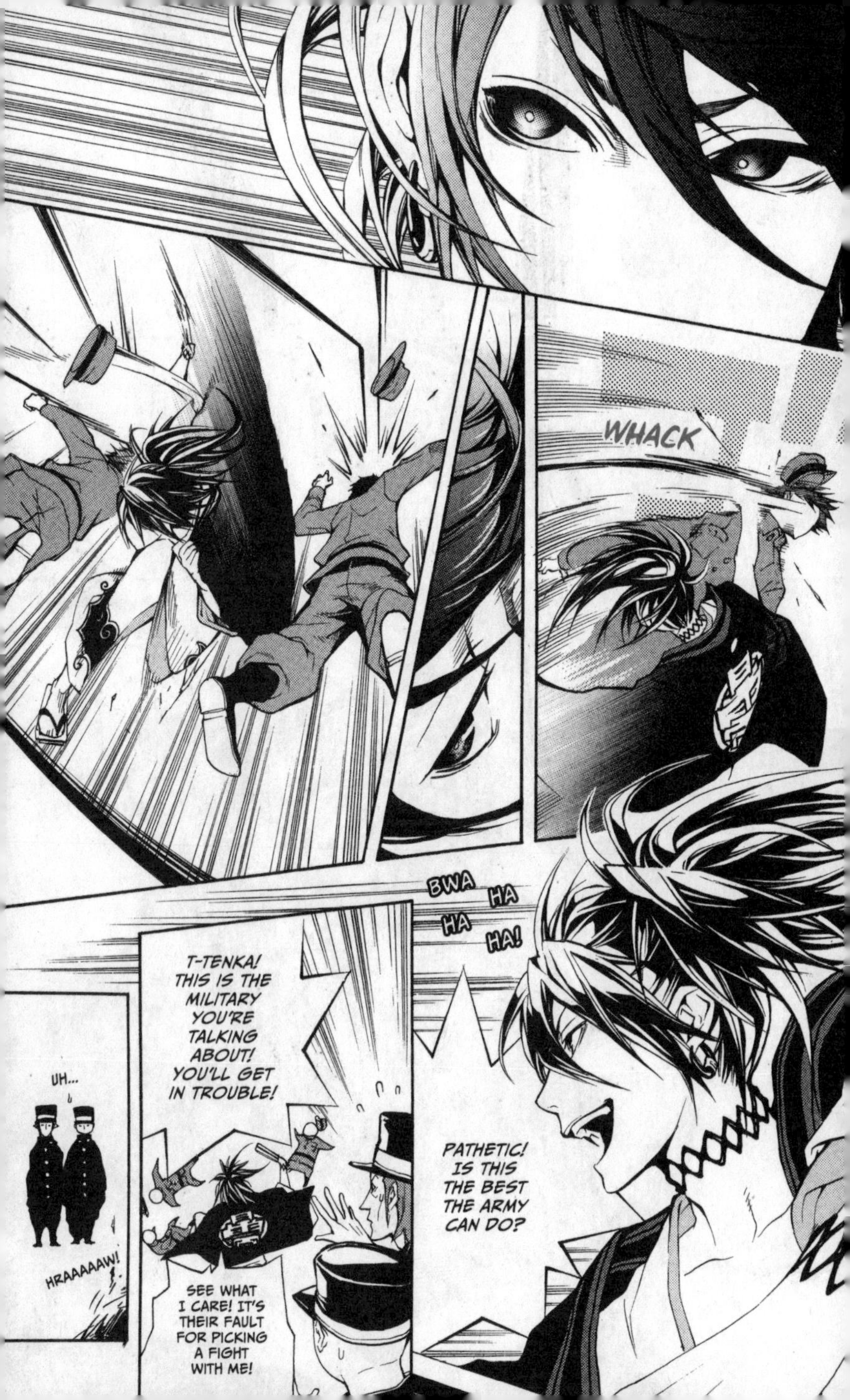
WHACK
BWA HA HA HA!
PATHETIC! IS THIS THE BEST THE ARMY CAN DO?
T-TENKA! THIS IS THE MILITARY YOU'RE TALKING ABOUT! YOU'LL GET IN TROUBLE!
SEE WHAT I CARE! IT'S THEIR FAULT FOR PICKING A FIGHT WITH ME!
UH...
HRAAAAAW!

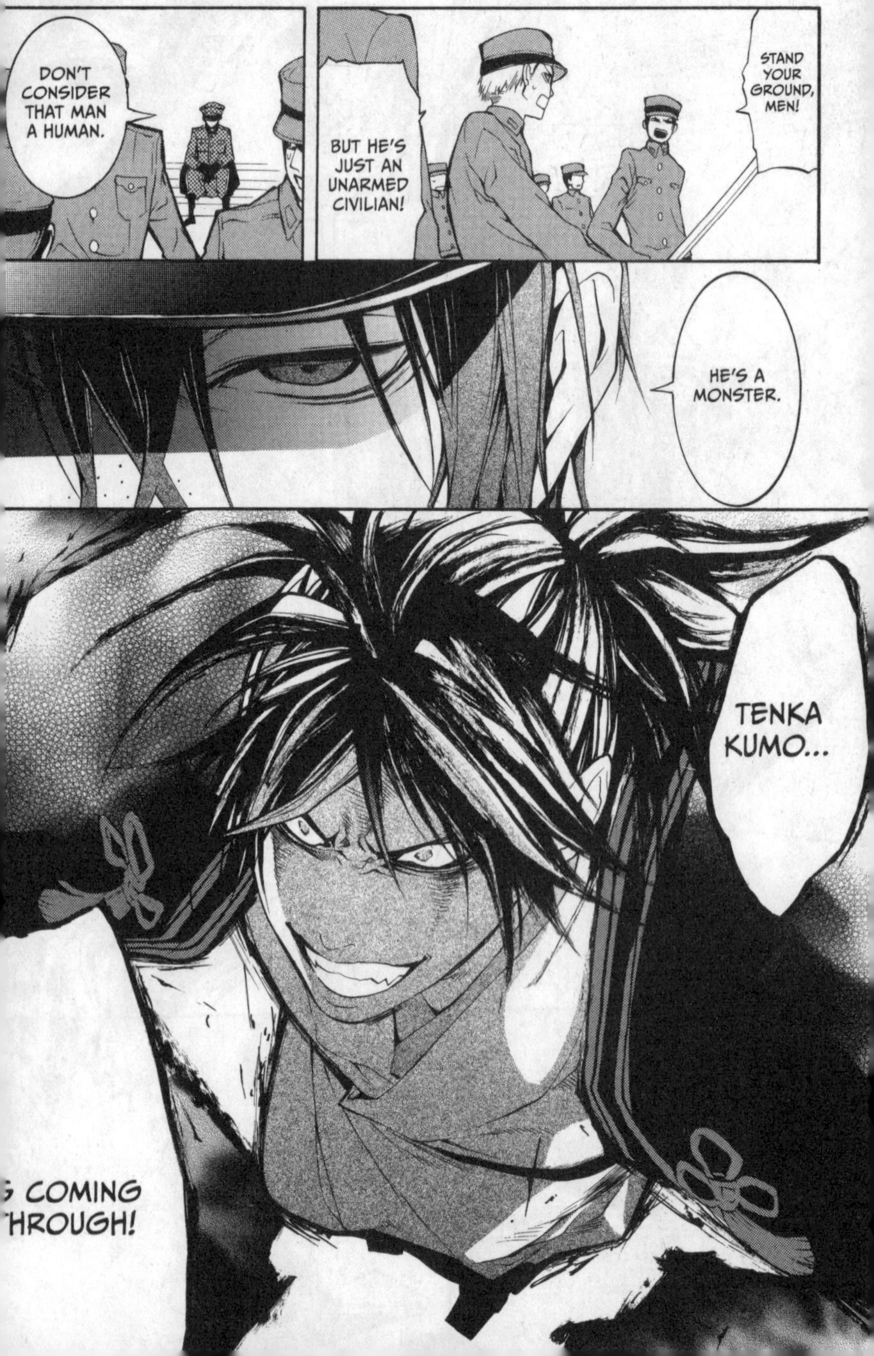
STAND YOUR GROUND, MEN!
BUT HE'S JUST AN UNARMED CIVILIAN!
DON'T CONSIDER THAT MAN A HUMAN.
HE'S A MONSTER.
TENKA KUMO...
COMING THROUGH!

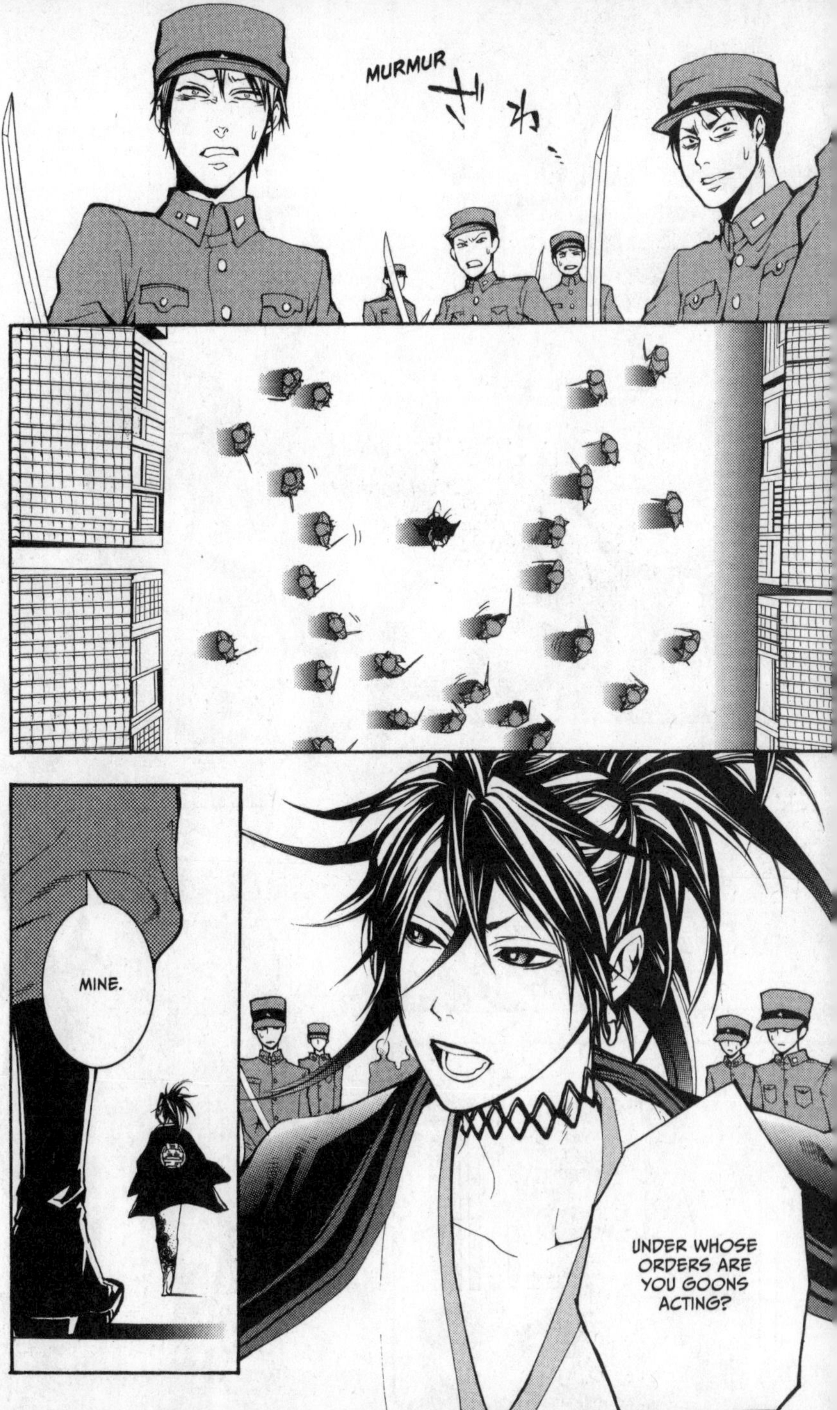
MURMUR
ざわ…
UNDER WHOSE ORDERS ARE YOU GOONS ACTING?
MINE.

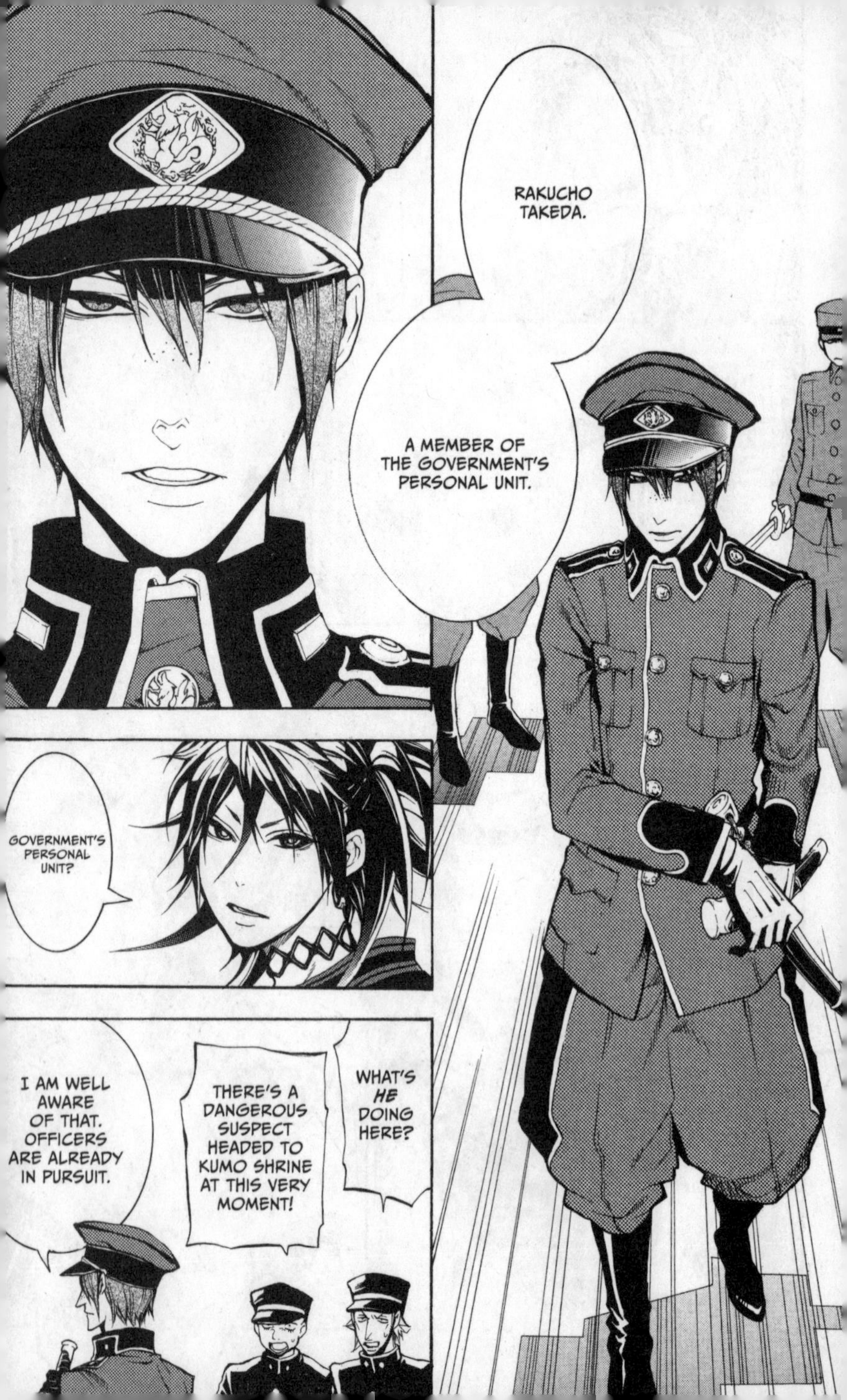
RAKUCHO TAKEDA.
A MEMBER OF THE GOVERNMENT'S PERSONAL UNIT.
GOVERNMENT'S PERSONAL UNIT?
WHAT'S *HE* DOING HERE?
THERE'S A DANGEROUS SUSPECT HEADED TO KUMO SHRINE AT THIS VERY MOMENT!
I AM WELL AWARE OF THAT. OFFICERS ARE ALREADY IN PURSUIT.

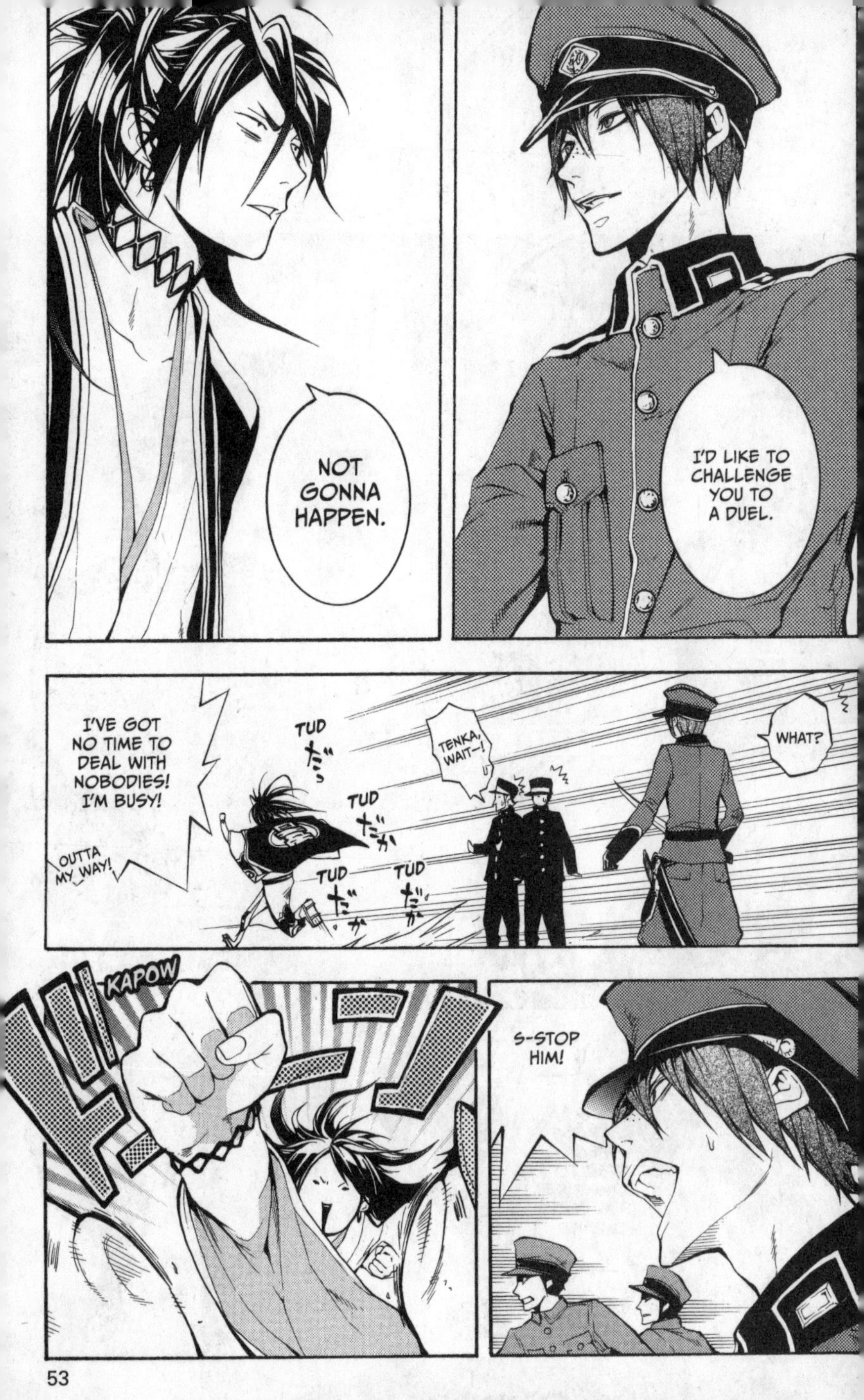
I'D LIKE TO CHALLENGE YOU TO A DUEL.
NOT GONNA HAPPEN.
WHAT?
TENKA, WAIT—!
TUD
TUD
TUD
TUD
I'VE GOT NO TIME TO DEAL WITH NOBODIES! I'M BUSY!
OUTTA MY WAY!
S-STOP HIM!
KAPOW

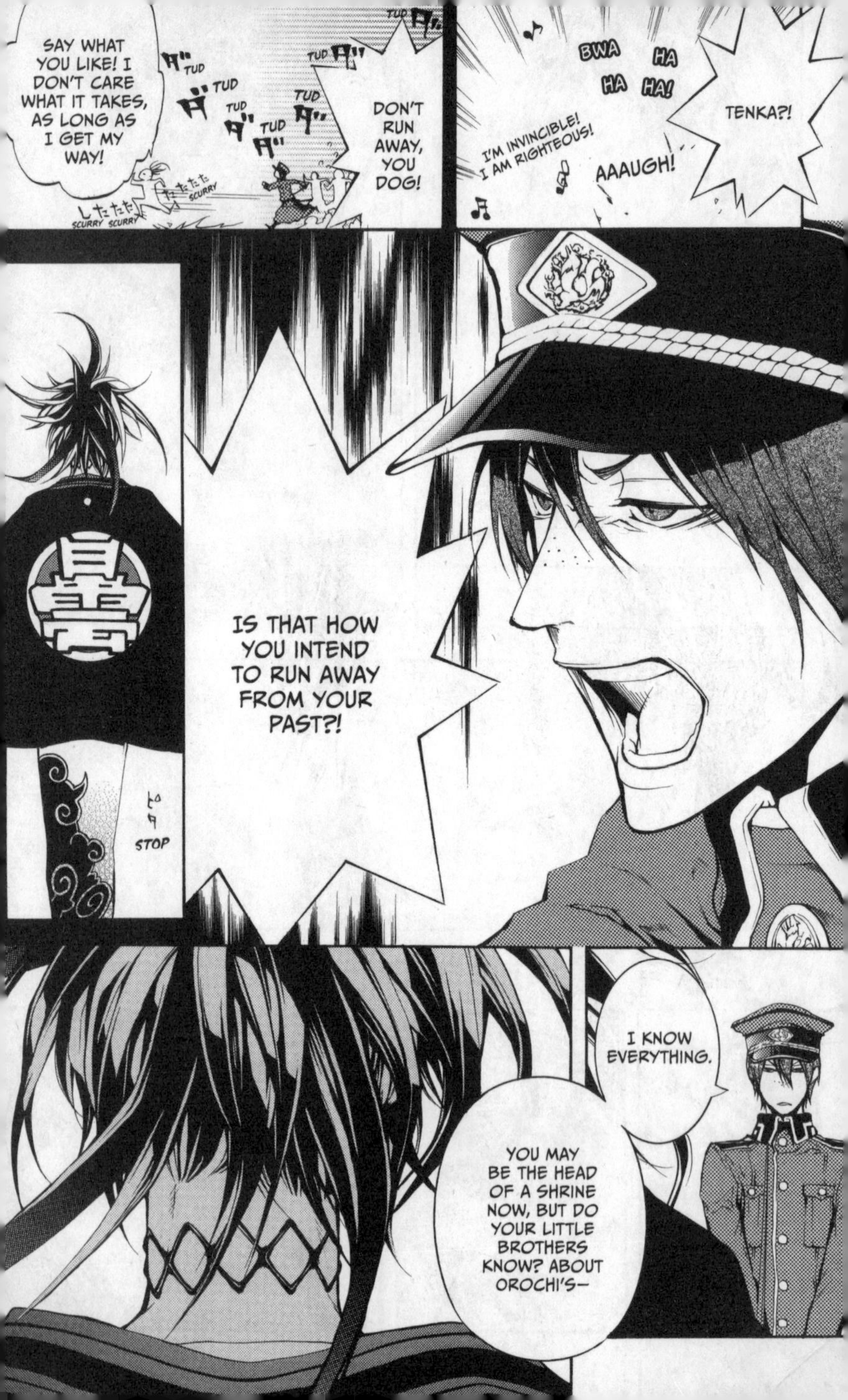
TENKA?!
BWA HA HA HA!
I'M INVINCIBLE! I AM RIGHTEOUS!
AAAUGH!
TUD TUD TUD TUD TUD TUD
DON'T RUN AWAY, YOU DOG!
SAY WHAT YOU LIKE! I DON'T CARE WHAT IT TAKES, AS LONG AS I GET MY WAY!
SCURRY SCURRY SCURRY
IS THAT HOW YOU INTEND TO RUN AWAY FROM YOUR PAST?!
STOP
I KNOW EVERYTHING.
YOU MAY BE THE HEAD OF A SHRINE NOW, BUT DO YOUR LITTLE BROTHERS KNOW? ABOUT OROCHI'S—

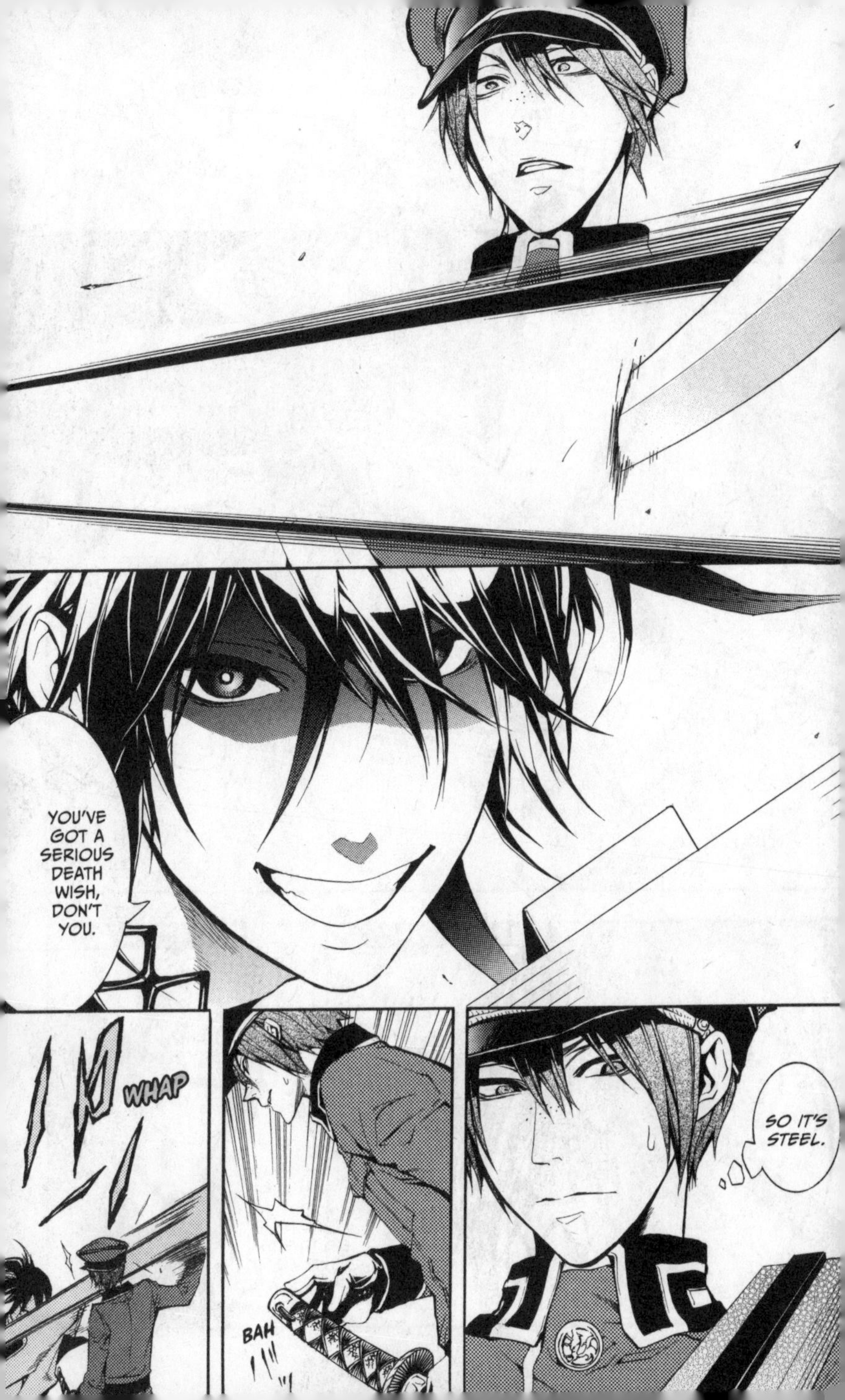
YOU'VE GOT A SERIOUS DEATH WISH, DON'T YOU.
SO IT'S STEEL.
BAH
WHAP

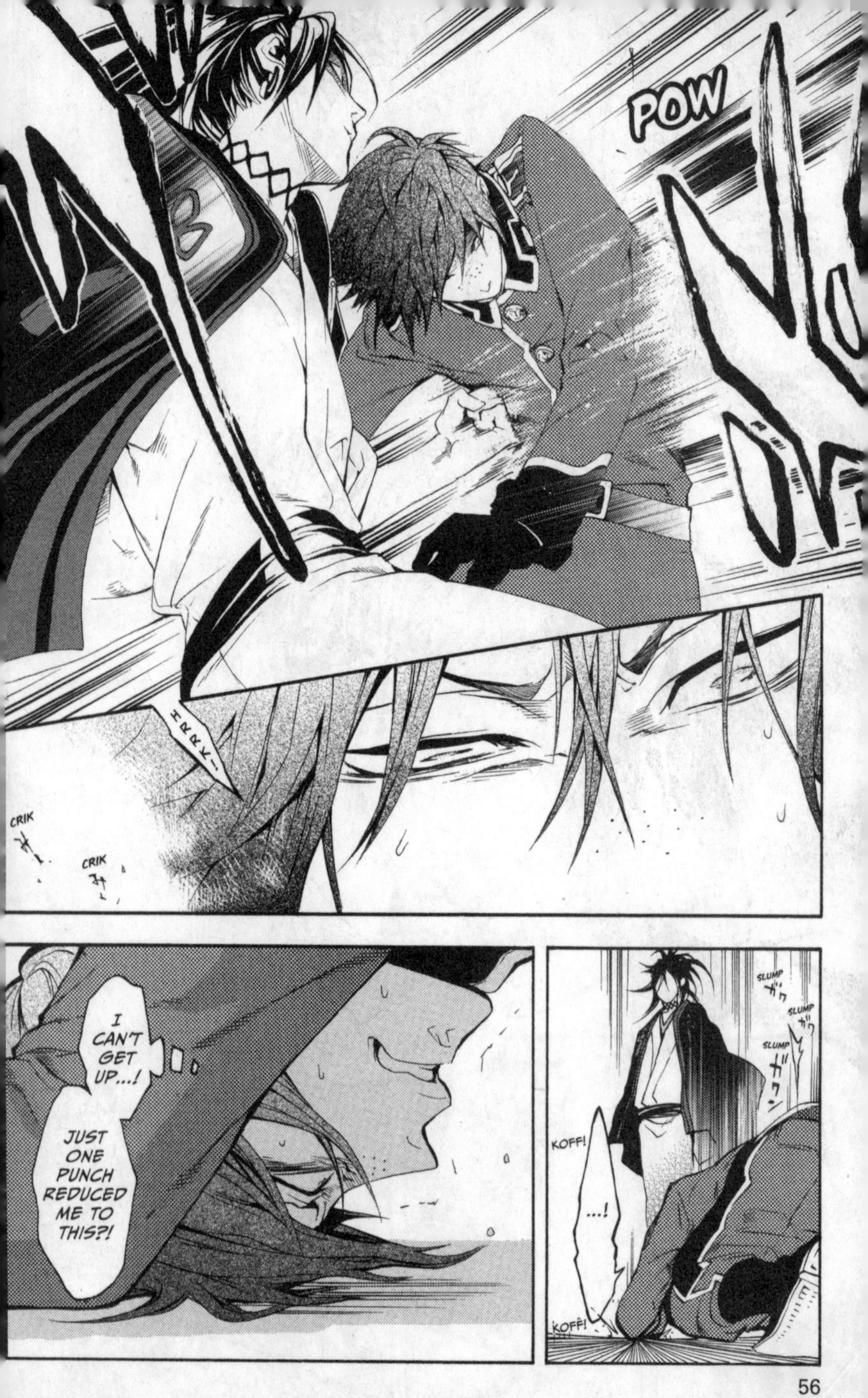
POW
HRRK!
CRIK
CRIK
SLUMP
SLUMP
SLUMP
KOFF!
...!
KOFF!
I CAN'T GET UP...!
JUST ONE PUNCH REDUCED ME TO THIS?!

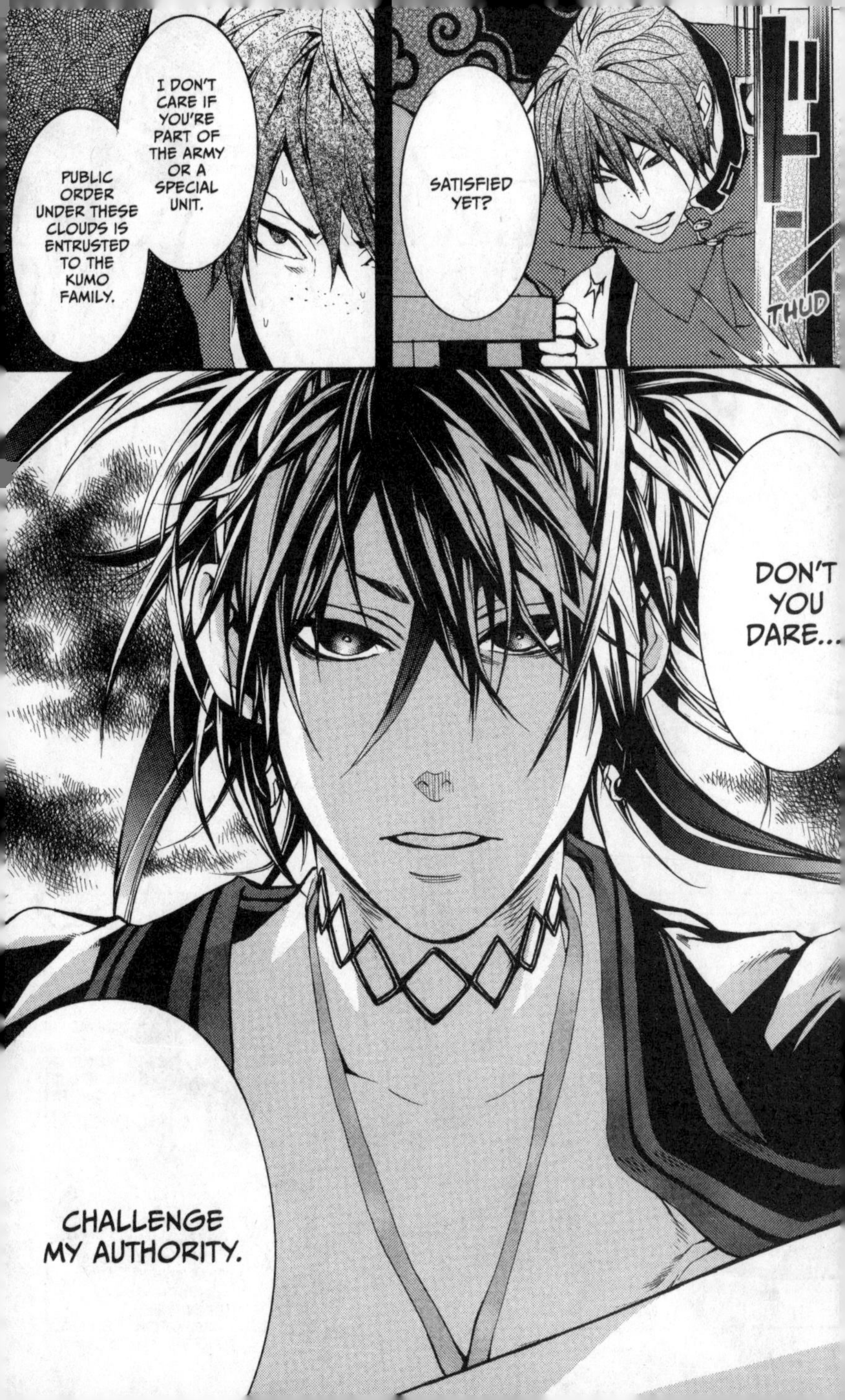
THUD
SATISFIED YET?
I DON'T CARE IF YOU'RE PART OF THE ARMY OR A SPECIAL UNIT.
PUBLIC ORDER UNDER THESE CLOUDS IS ENTRUSTED TO THE KUMO FAMILY.
DON'T YOU DARE...
CHALLENGE MY AUTHORITY.

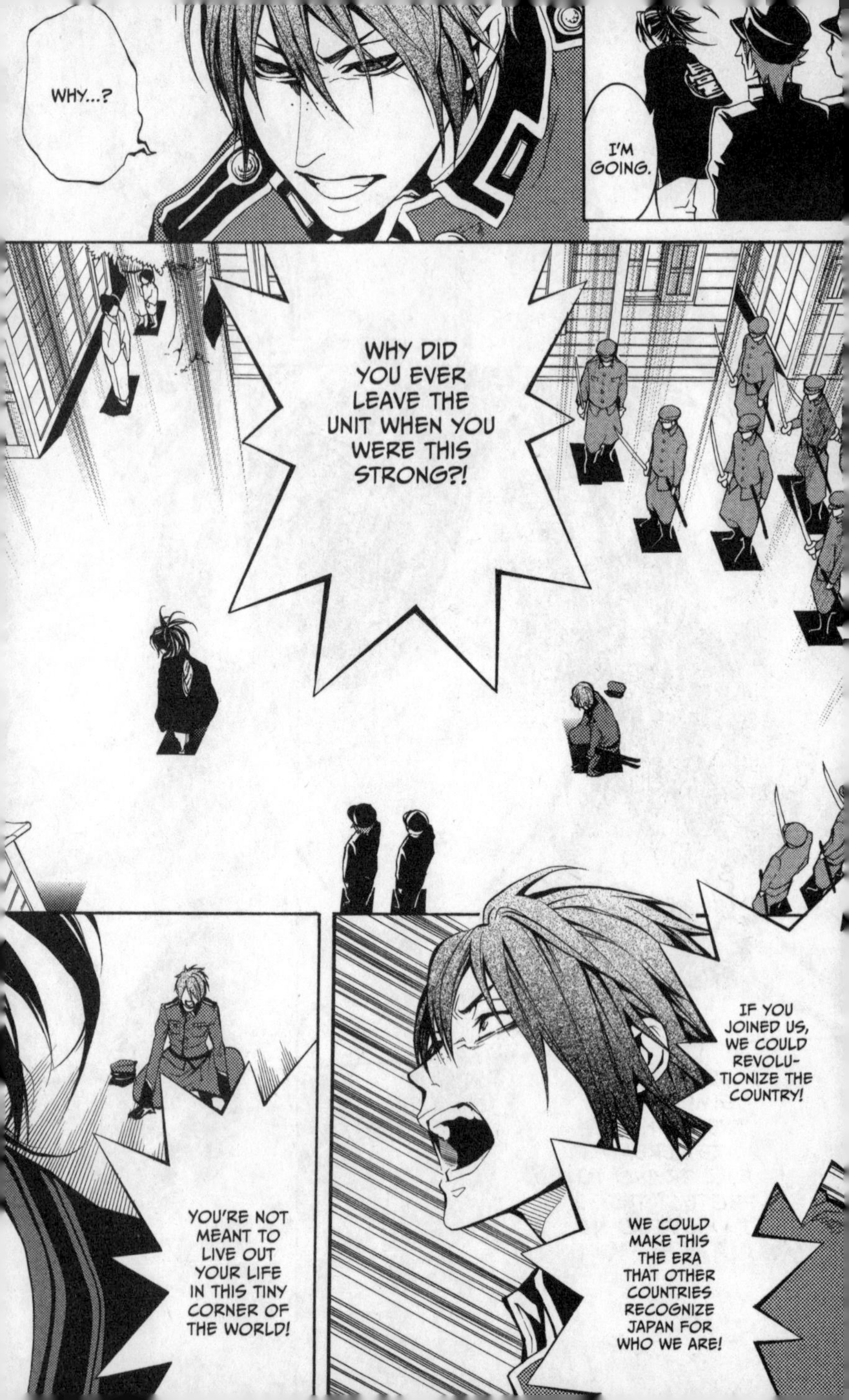
I'M GOING.
WHY...?
WHY DID YOU EVER LEAVE THE UNIT WHEN YOU WERE THIS STRONG?!
IF YOU JOINED US, WE COULD REVOLUTIONIZE THE COUNTRY!
WE COULD MAKE THIS THE ERA THAT OTHER COUNTRIES RECOGNIZE JAPAN FOR WHO WE ARE!
YOU'RE NOT MEANT TO LIVE OUT YOUR LIFE IN THIS TINY CORNER OF THE WORLD!

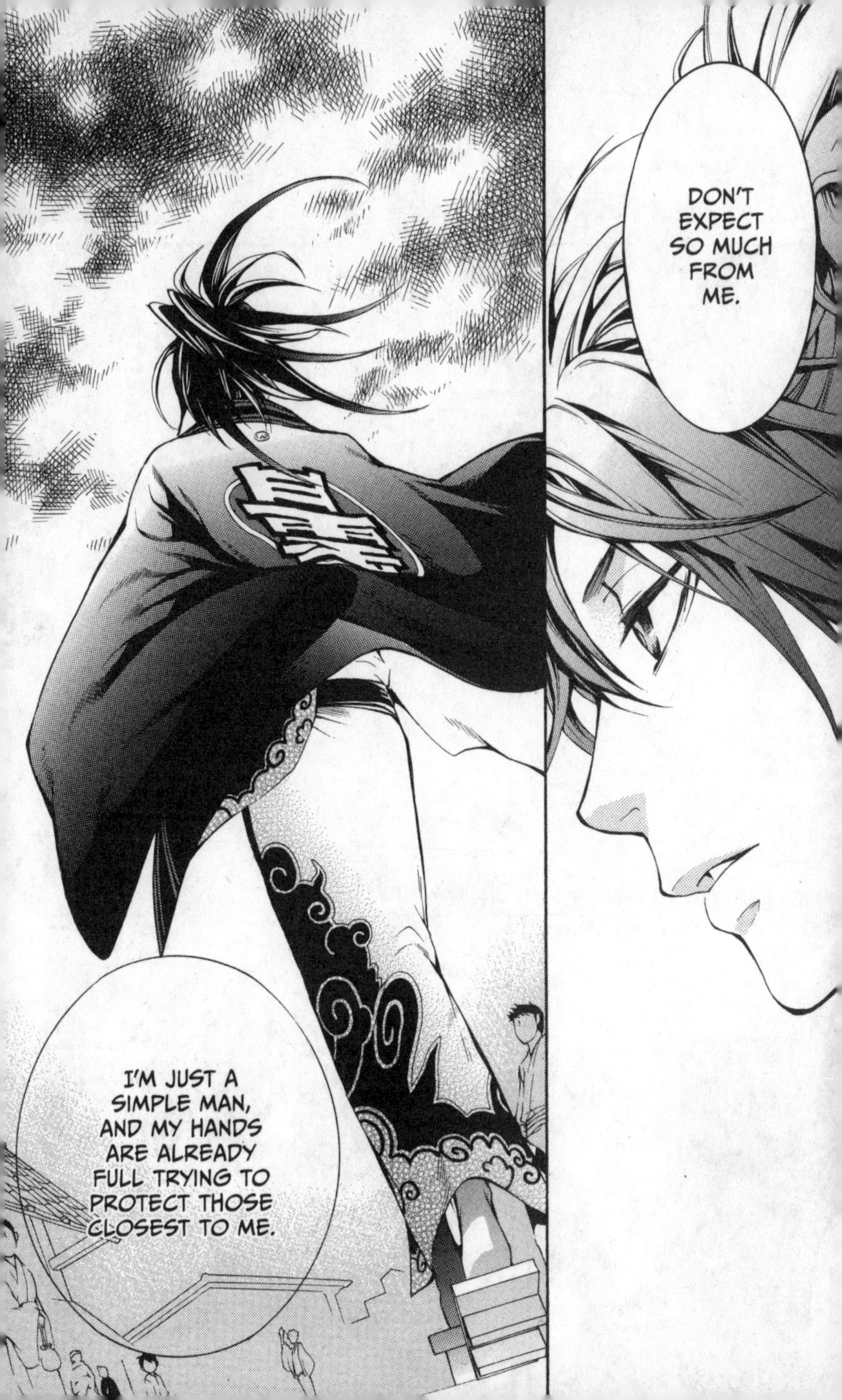
DON'T EXPECT SO MUCH FROM ME.
I'M JUST A SIMPLE MAN, AND MY HANDS ARE ALREADY FULL TRYING TO PROTECT THOSE CLOSEST TO ME.

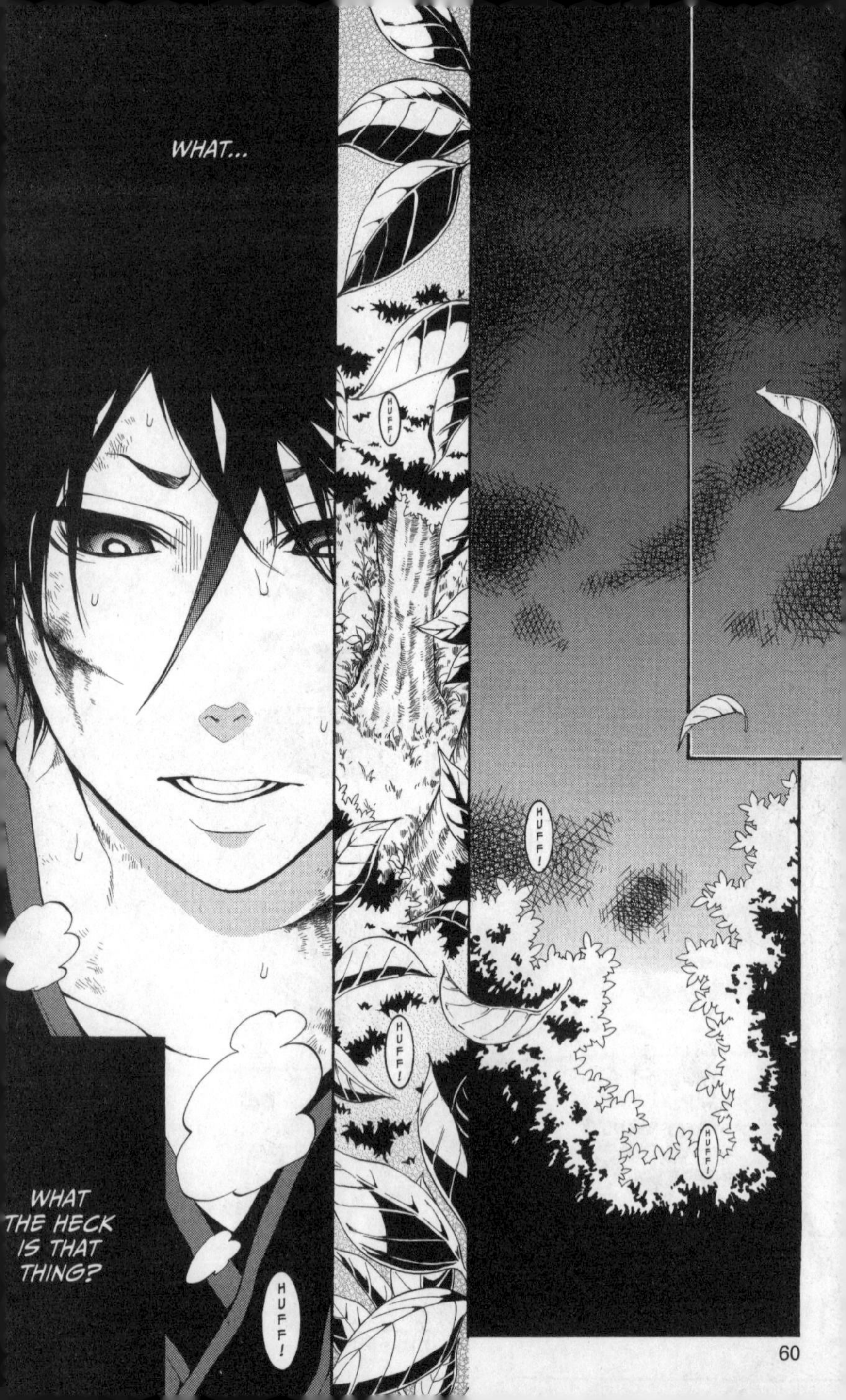
HUFF!
HUFF!
HUFF!
HUFF!
WHAT...
WHAT THE HECK IS THAT THING?
HUFF!

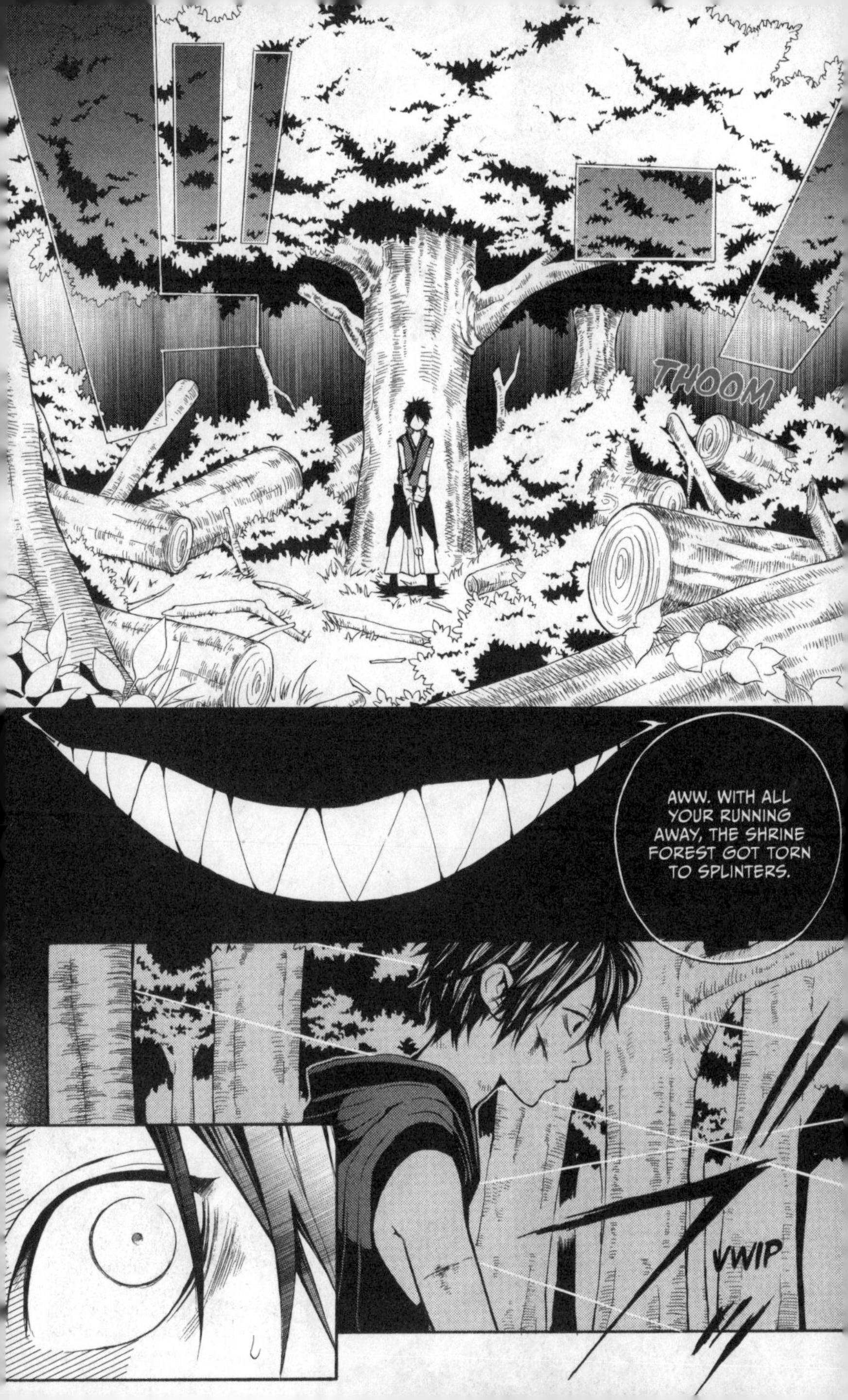
THOOM
AWW. WITH ALL YOUR RUNNING AWAY, THE SHRINE FOREST GOT TORN TO SPLINTERS.
VWIP

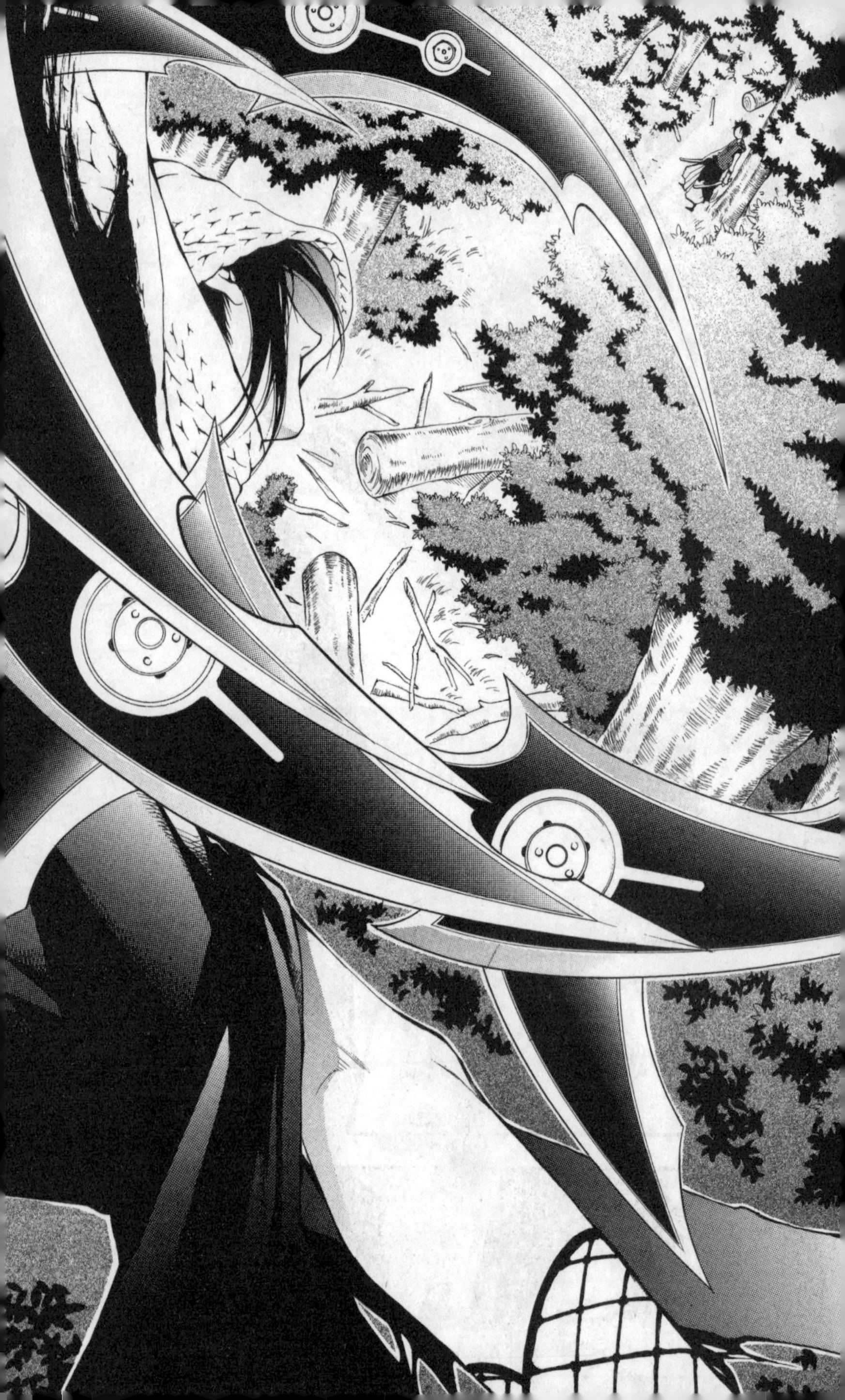

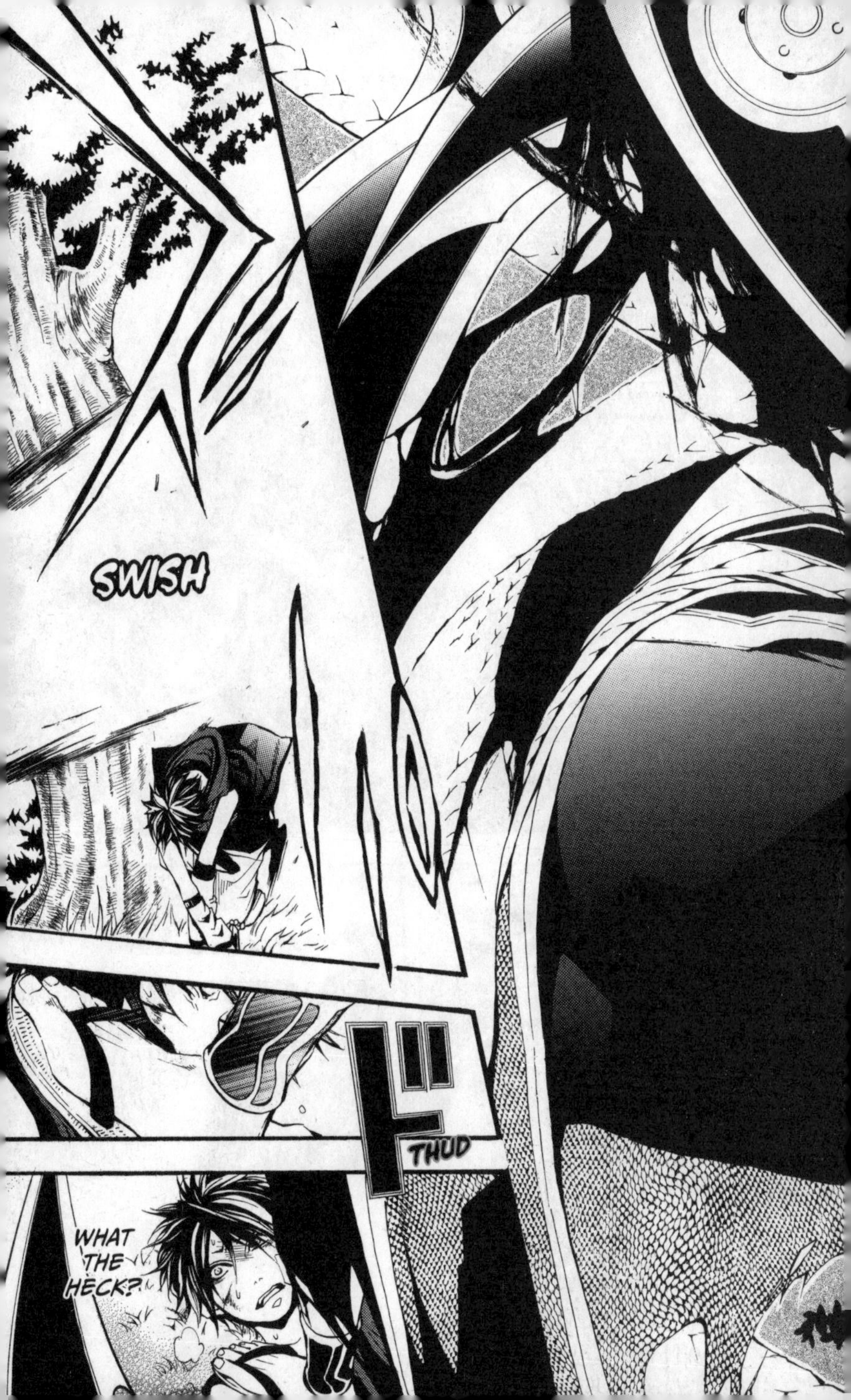
SWISH
THUD
WHAT THE HECK?

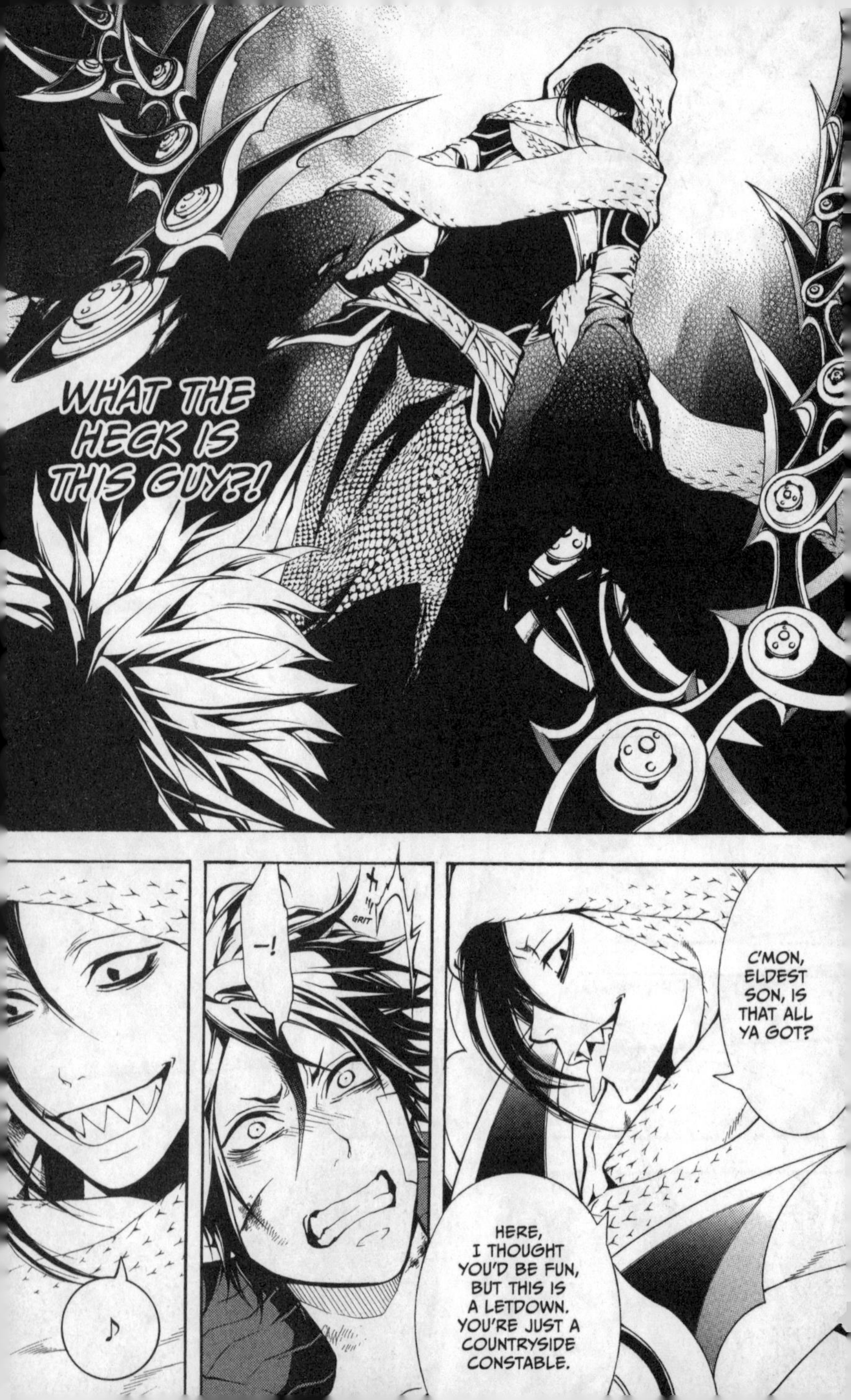
WHAT THE HECK IS THIS GUY?!
C'MON, ELDEST SON, IS THAT ALL YA GOT?
HERE, I THOUGHT YOU'D BE FUN, BUT THIS IS A LETDOWN. YOU'RE JUST A COUNTRYSIDE CONSTABLE.
GRIT
—!
♪

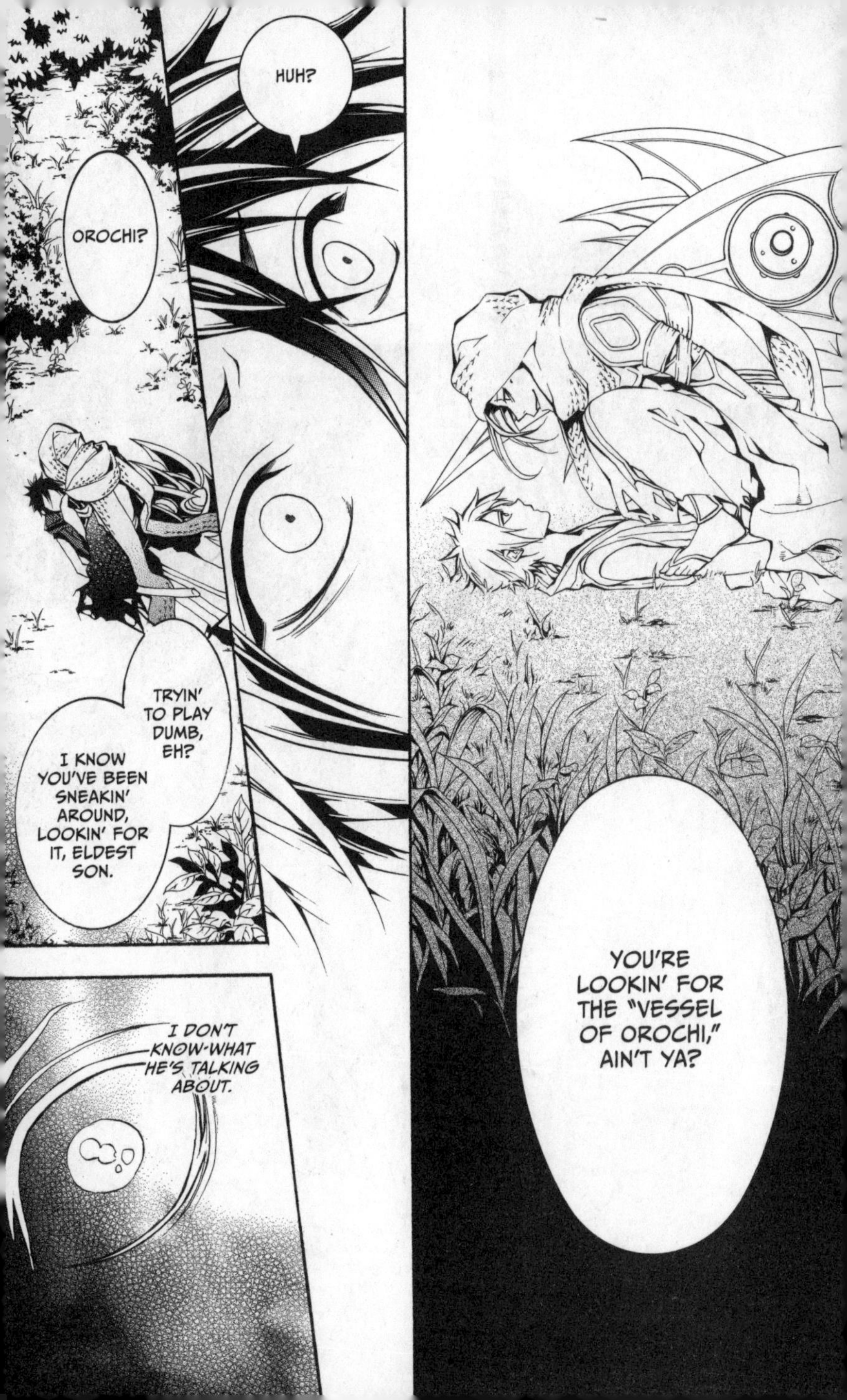
YOU'RE LOOKIN' FOR THE "VESSEL OF OROCHI," AIN'T YA?
HUH?
OROCHI?
TRYIN' TO PLAY DUMB, EH?
I KNOW YOU'VE BEEN SNEAKIN' AROUND, LOOKIN' FOR IT, ELDEST SON.
I DON'T KNOW WHAT HE'S TALKING ABOUT.

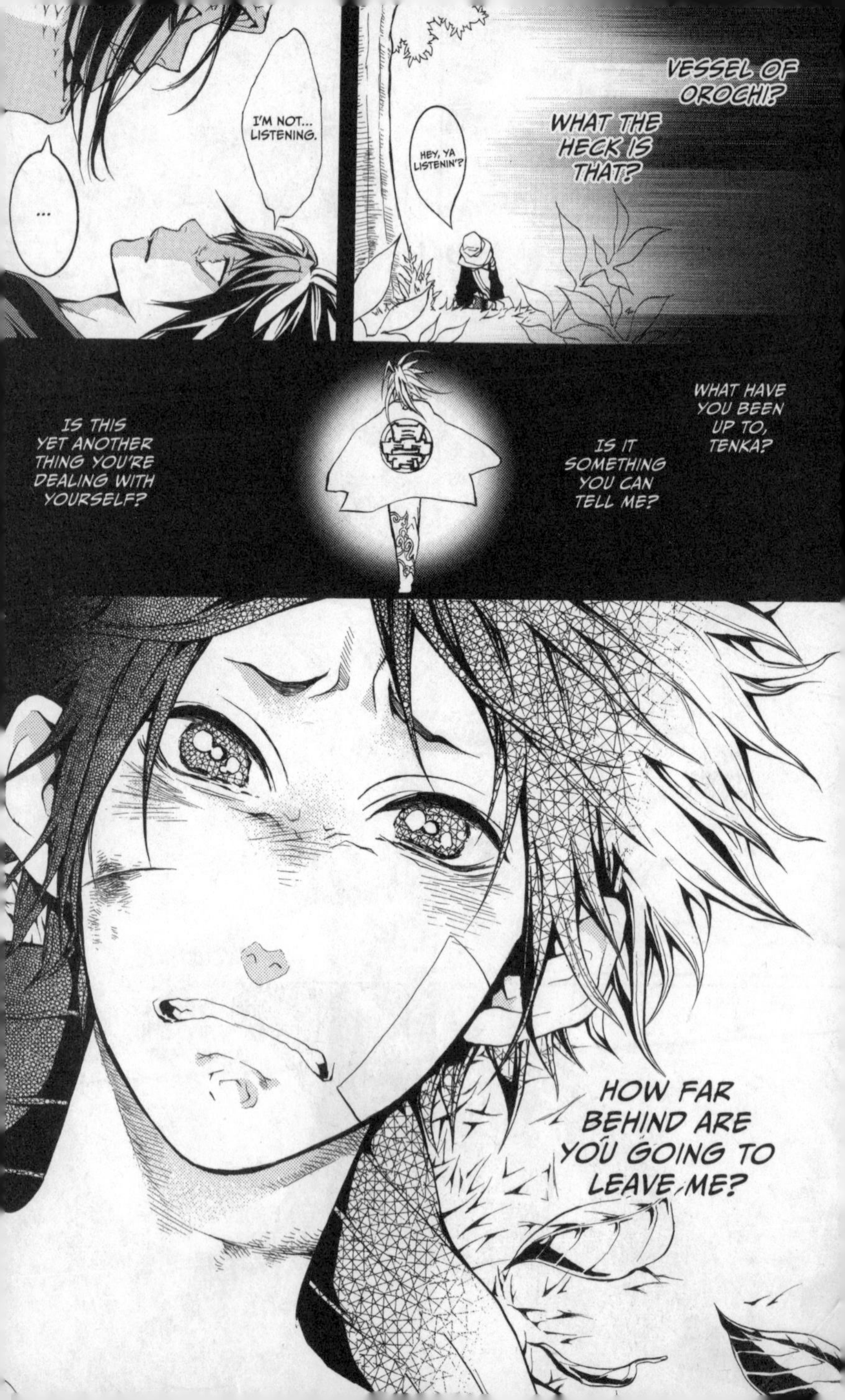
VESSEL OF OROCHI?
WHAT THE HECK IS THAT?
HEY, YA LISTENIN'?
I'M NOT... LISTENING.
...
WHAT HAVE YOU BEEN UP TO, TENKA?
IS IT SOMETHING YOU CAN TELL ME?
IS THIS YET ANOTHER THING YOU'RE DEALING WITH YOURSELF?
HOW FAR BEHIND ARE YOU GOING TO LEAVE ME?

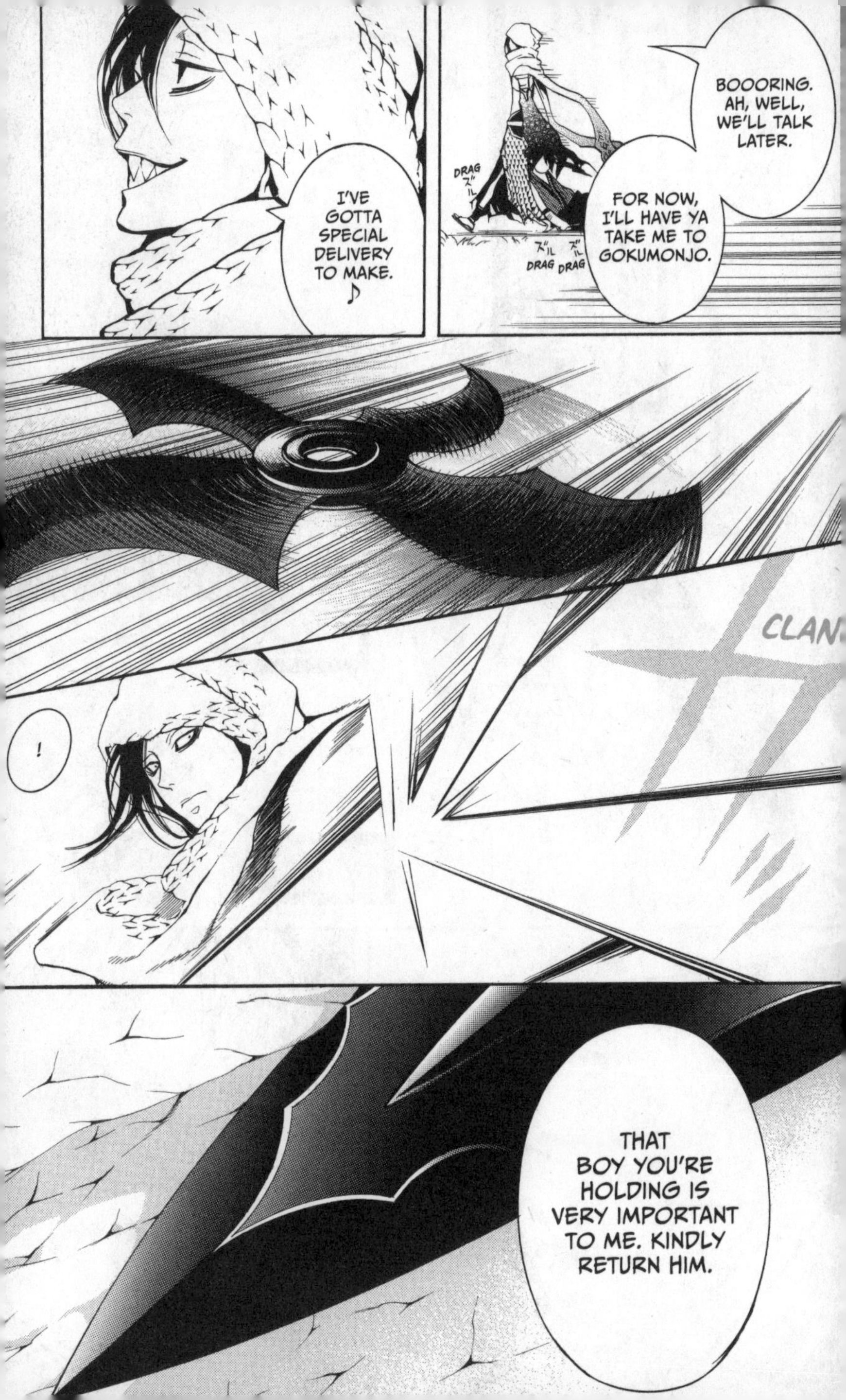
BOOORING. AH, WELL, WE'LL TALK LATER.
FOR NOW, I'LL HAVE YA TAKE ME TO GOKUMONJO.
DRAG
DRAG DRAG
I'VE GOTTA SPECIAL DELIVERY TO MAKE. ♪
CLAN
!
THAT BOY YOU'RE HOLDING IS VERY IMPORTANT TO ME. KINDLY RETURN HIM.

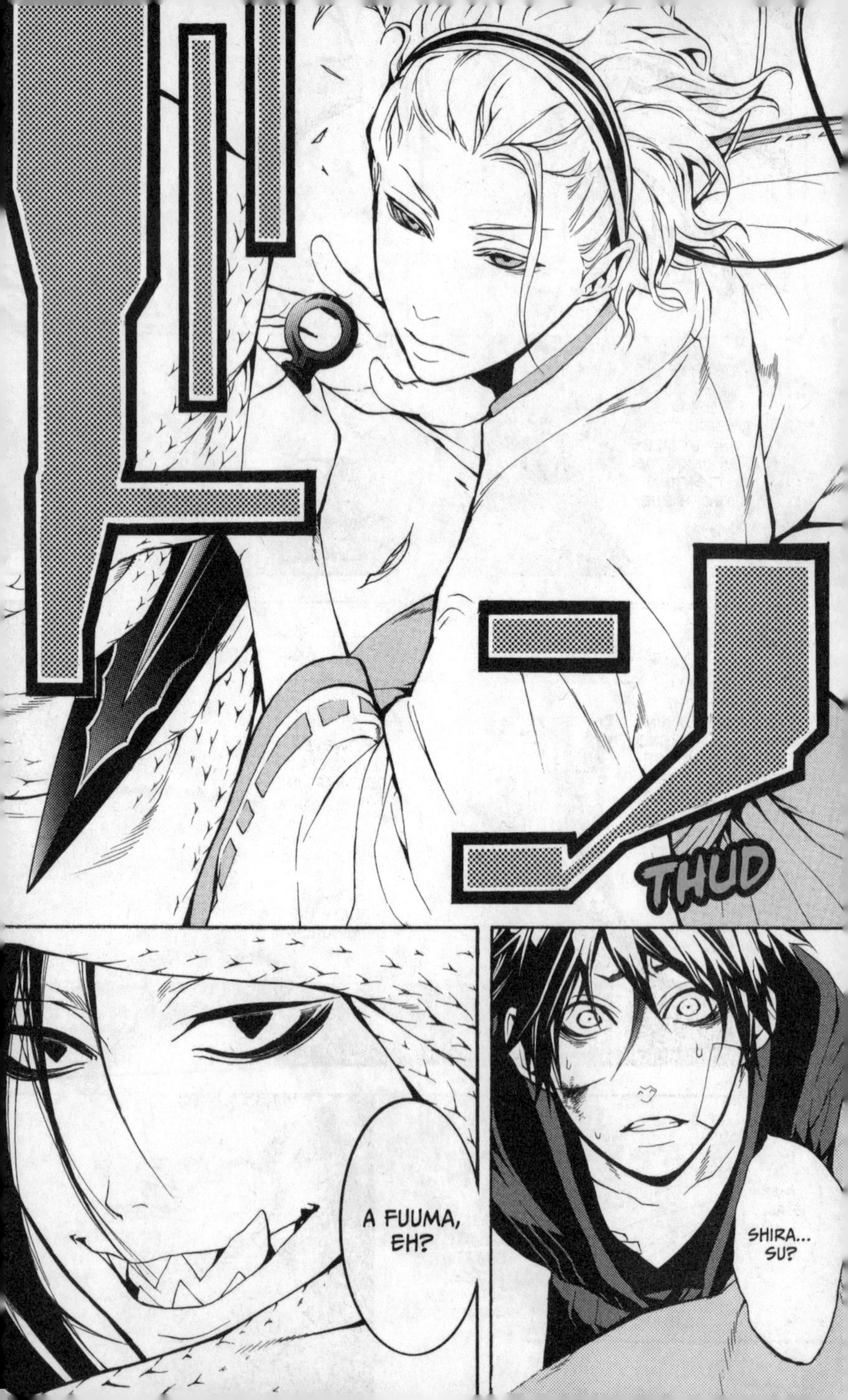
THUD
SHIRA... SU?
A FUUMA, EH?

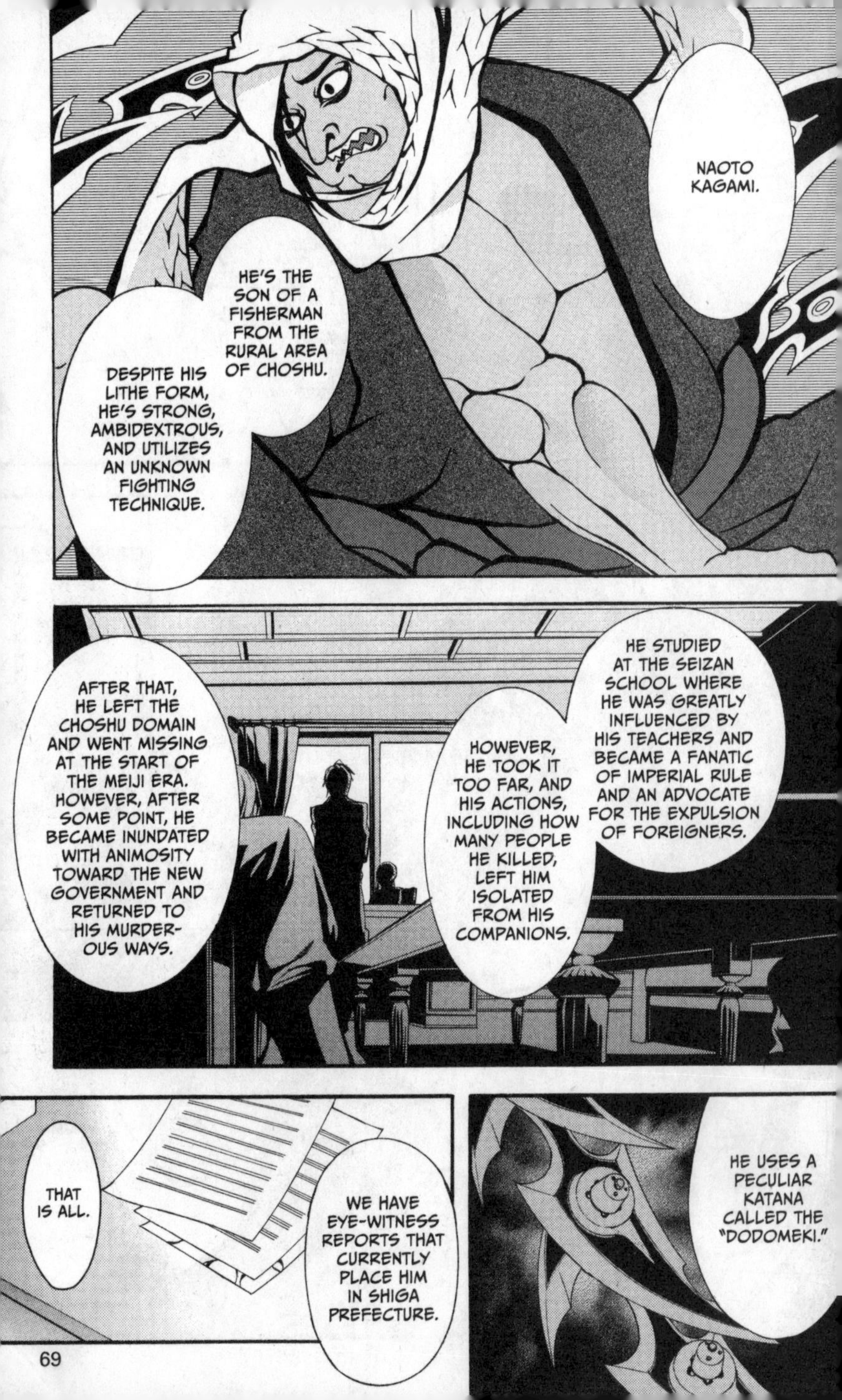
NAOTO KAGAMI.
HE'S THE SON OF A FISHERMAN FROM THE RURAL AREA OF CHOSHU.
DESPITE HIS LITHE FORM, HE'S STRONG, AMBIDEXTROUS, AND UTILIZES AN UNKNOWN FIGHTING TECHNIQUE.
HE STUDIED AT THE SEIZAN SCHOOL WHERE HE WAS GREATLY INFLUENCED BY HIS TEACHERS AND BECAME A FANATIC OF IMPERIAL RULE AND AN ADVOCATE FOR THE EXPULSION OF FOREIGNERS.
HOWEVER, HE TOOK IT TOO FAR, AND HIS ACTIONS, INCLUDING HOW MANY PEOPLE HE KILLED, LEFT HIM ISOLATED FROM HIS COMPANIONS.
AFTER THAT, HE LEFT THE CHOSHU DOMAIN AND WENT MISSING AT THE START OF THE MEIJI ERA. HOWEVER, AFTER SOME POINT, HE BECAME INUNDATED WITH ANIMOSITY TOWARD THE NEW GOVERNMENT AND RETURNED TO HIS MURDER-OUS WAYS.
HE USES A PECULIAR KATANA CALLED THE "DODOMEKI."
WE HAVE EYE-WITNESS REPORTS THAT CURRENTLY PLACE HIM IN SHIGA PREFECTURE.
THAT IS ALL.

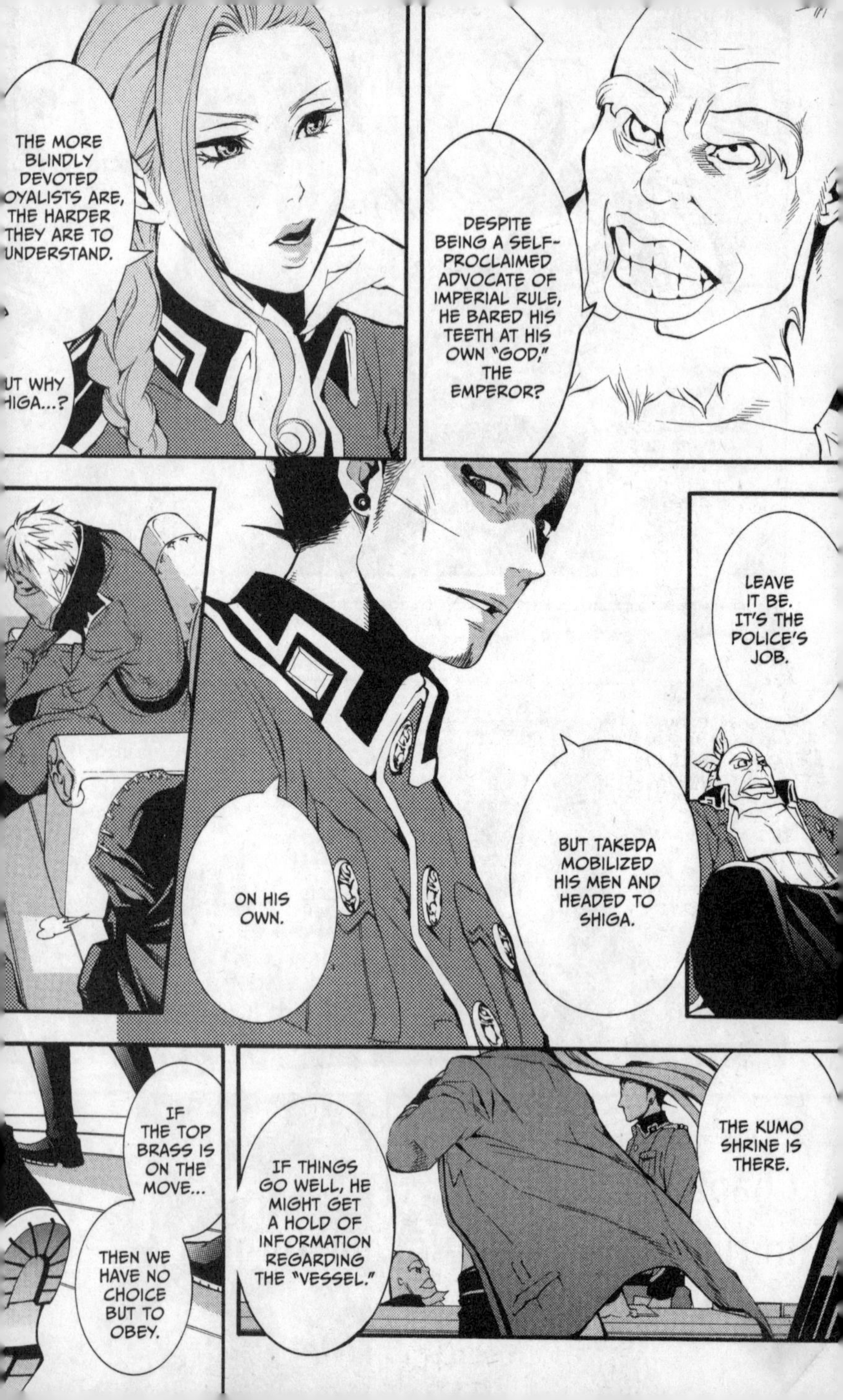
DESPITE BEING A SELF-PROCLAIMED ADVOCATE OF IMPERIAL RULE, HE BARED HIS TEETH AT HIS OWN "GOD," THE EMPEROR?
THE MORE BLINDLY DEVOTED OYALISTS ARE, THE HARDER THEY ARE TO UNDERSTAND.
UT WHY HIGA...?
LEAVE IT BE. IT'S THE POLICE'S JOB.
BUT TAKEDA MOBILIZED HIS MEN AND HEADED TO SHIGA.
ON HIS OWN.
THE KUMO SHRINE IS THERE.
IF THINGS GO WELL, HE MIGHT GET A HOLD OF INFORMATION REGARDING THE "VESSEL."
IF THE TOP BRASS IS ON THE MOVE...
THEN WE HAVE NO CHOICE BUT TO OBEY.

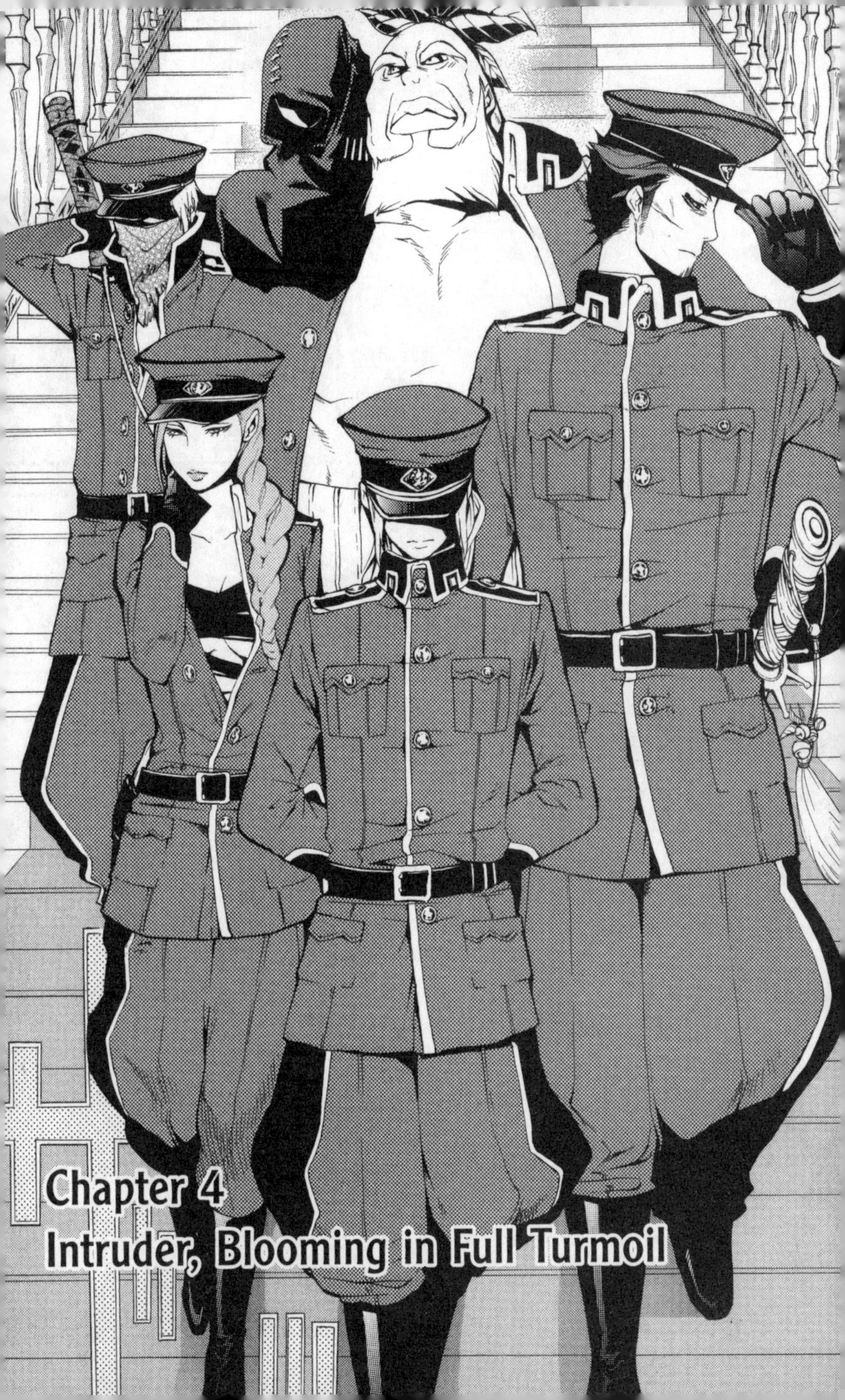
Chapter 4
Intruder, Blooming in Full Turmoil

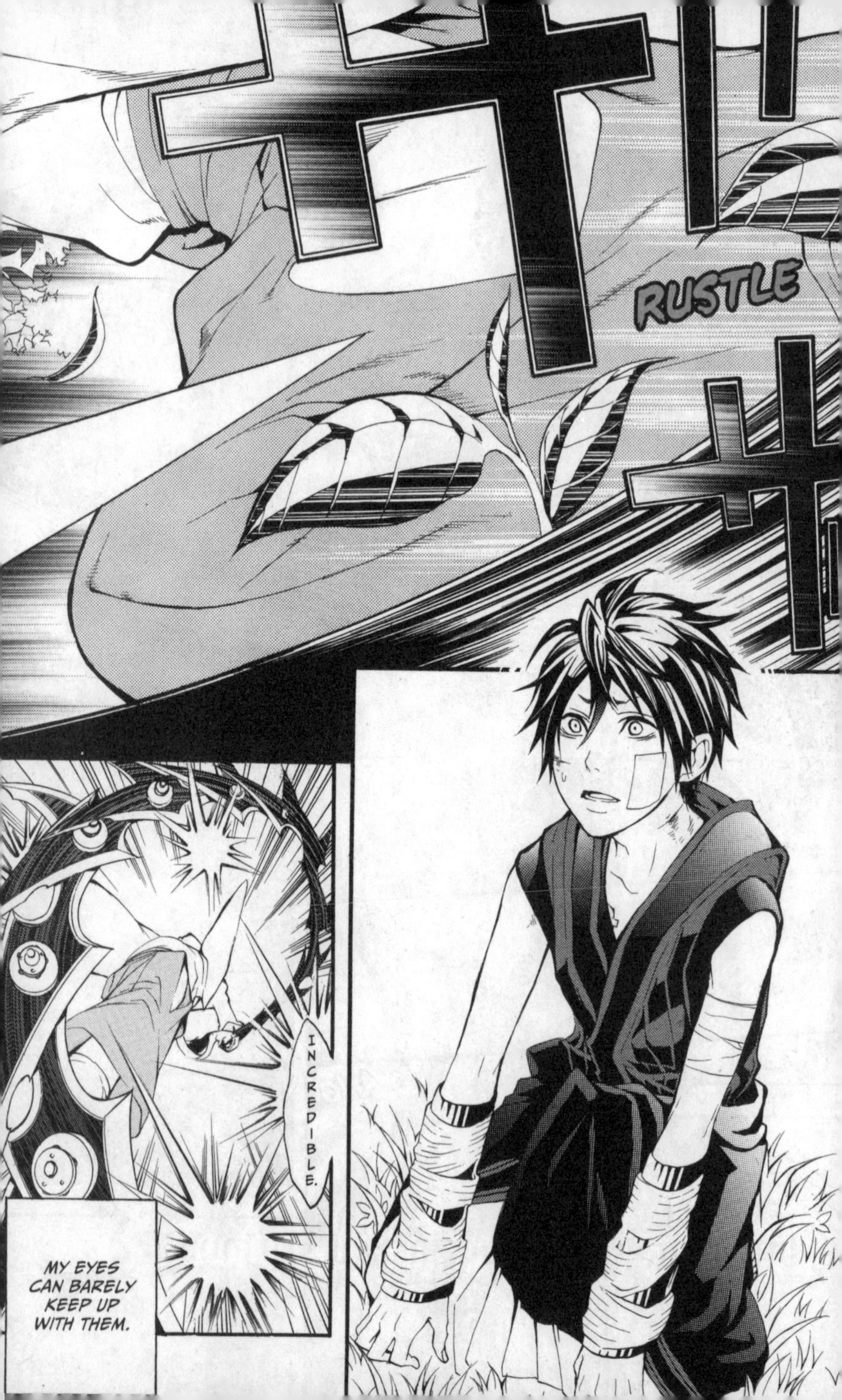
RUSTLE
INCREDIBLE.
MY EYES CAN BARELY KEEP UP WITH THEM.

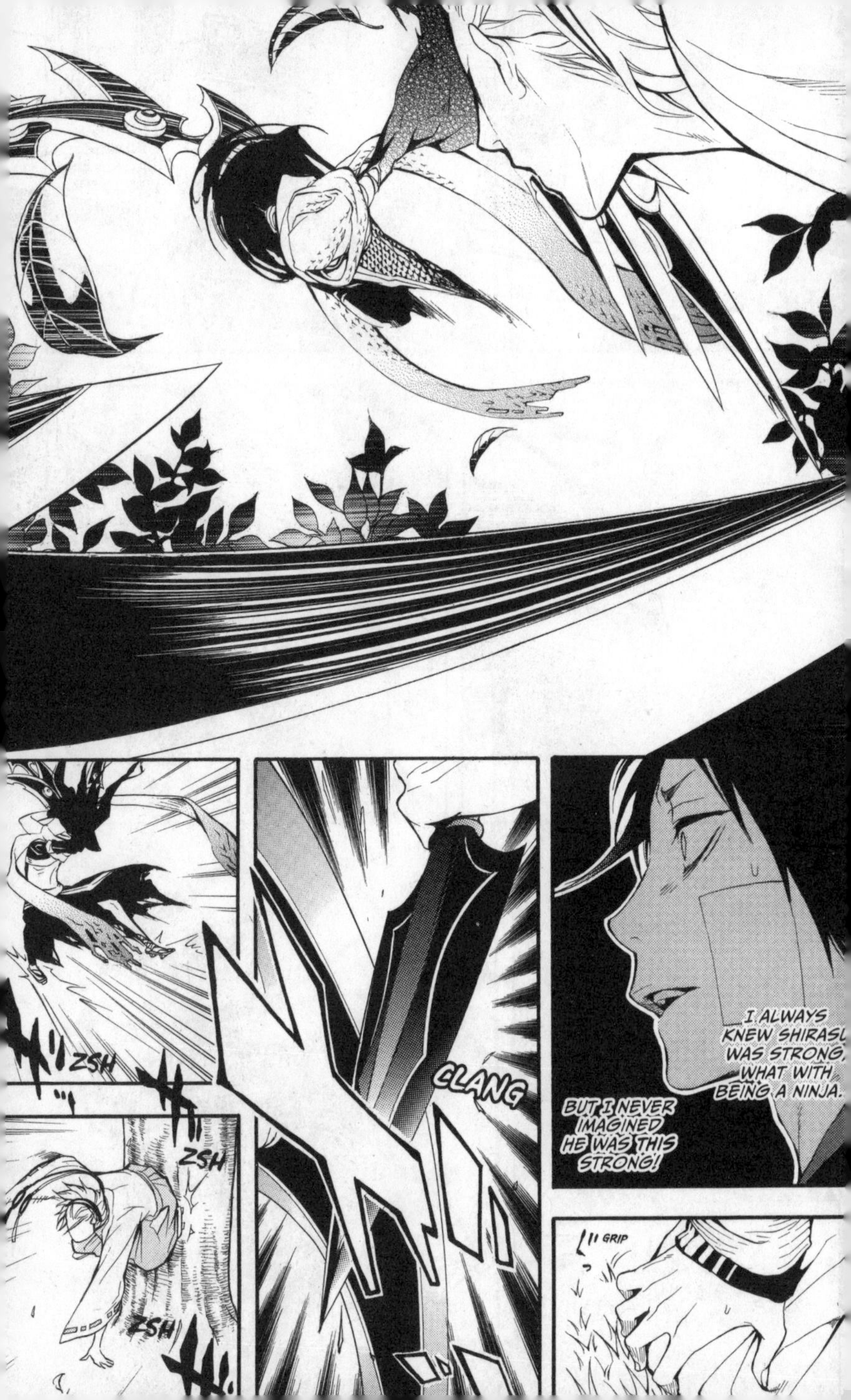
I ALWAYS KNEW SHIRASU WAS STRONG, WHAT WITH BEING A NINJA.
BUT I NEVER IMAGINED HE WAS THIS STRONG!
GRIP
CLANG
ZSH
ZSH
ZSH

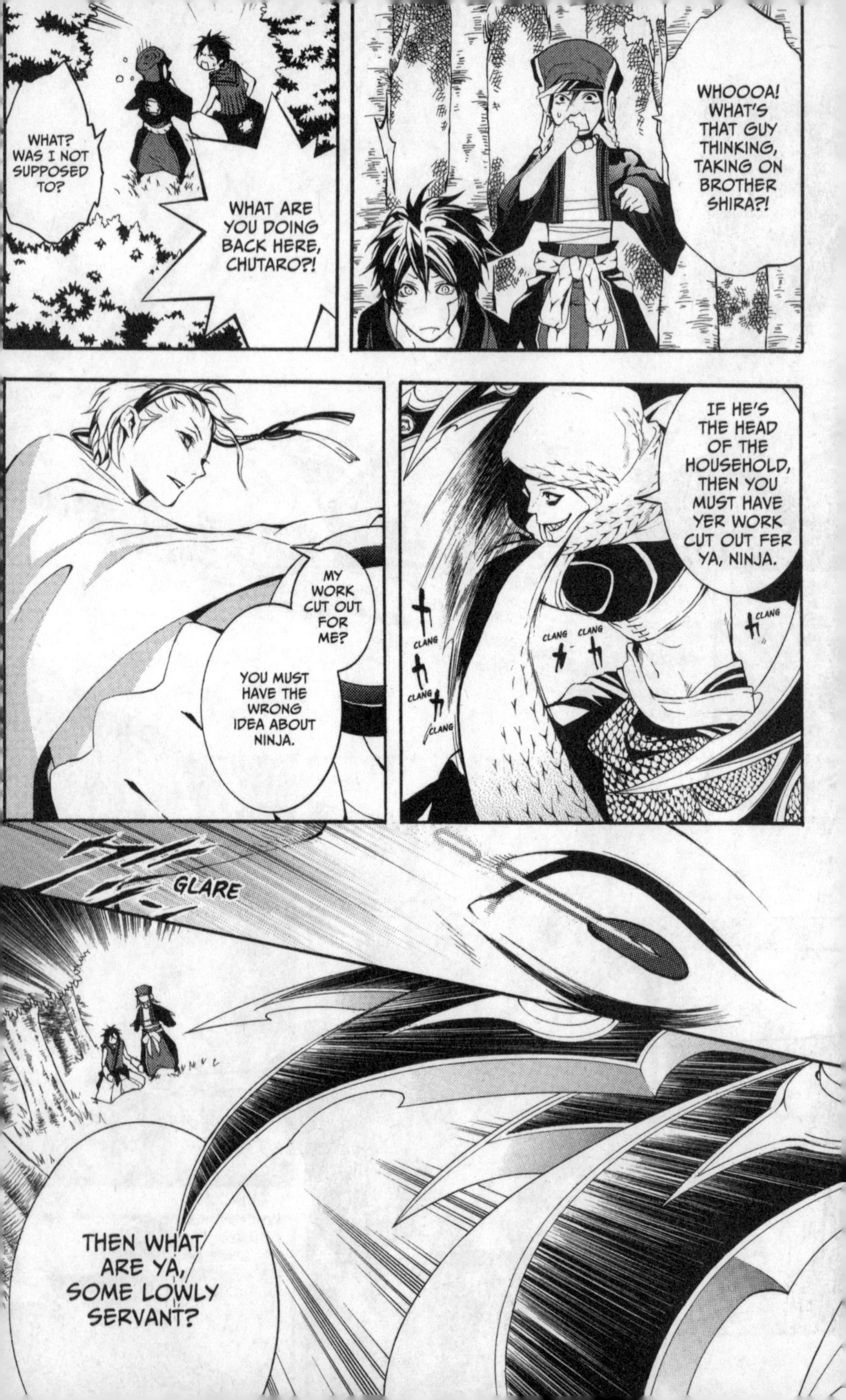
WHOOOA! WHAT'S THAT GUY THINKING, TAKING ON BROTHER SHIRA?!
WHAT ARE YOU DOING BACK HERE, CHUTARO?!
WHAT? WAS I NOT SUPPOSED TO?
IF HE'S THE HEAD OF THE HOUSEHOLD, THEN YOU MUST HAVE YER WORK CUT OUT FER YA, NINJA.
CLANG
CLANG CLANG
CLANG
CLANG
CLANG
MY WORK CUT OUT FOR ME?
YOU MUST HAVE THE WRONG IDEA ABOUT NINJA.
GLARE
THEN WHAT ARE YA, SOME LOWLY SERVANT?

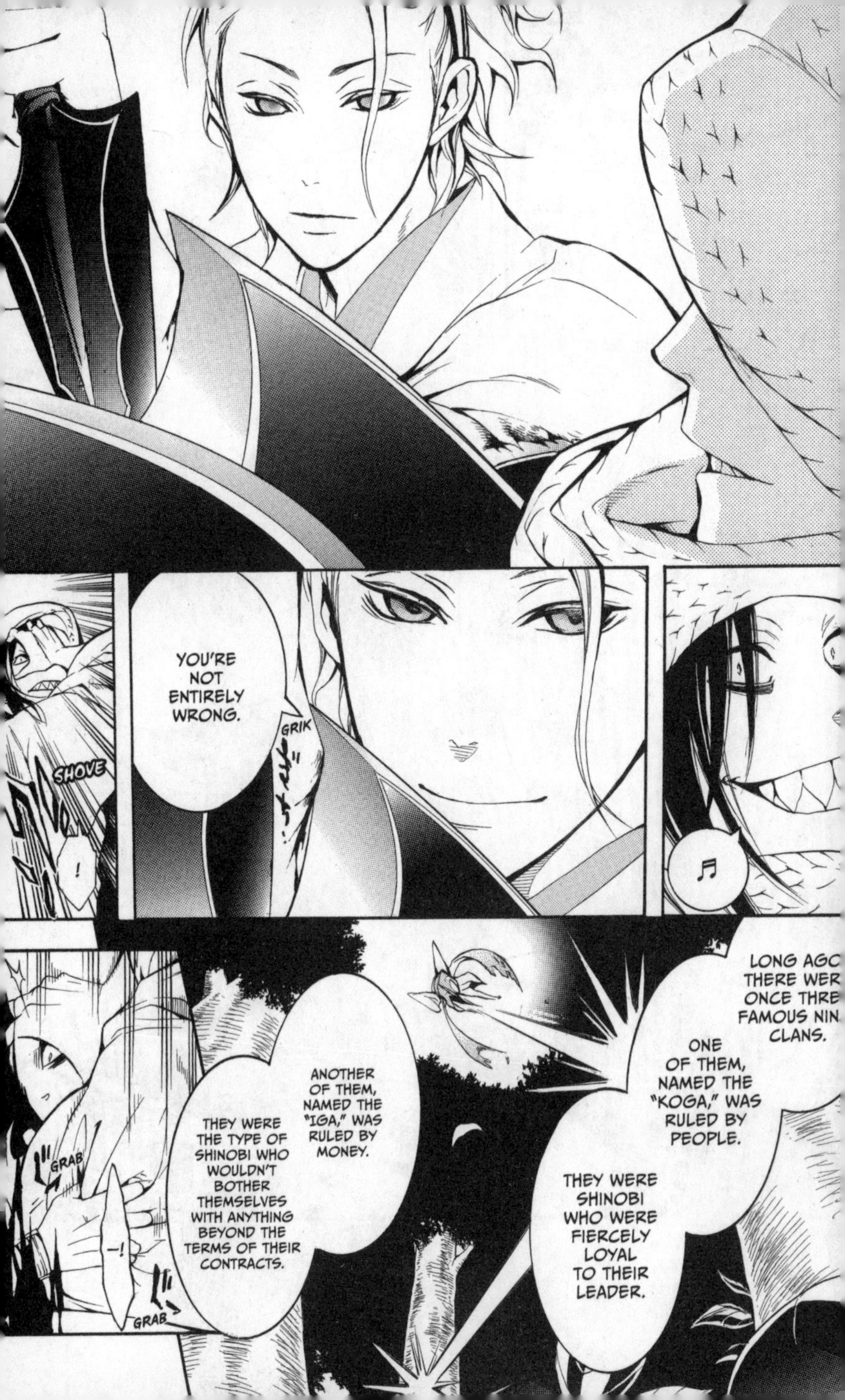
♪
YOU'RE NOT ENTIRELY WRONG.
GRIK
SHOVE
!
LONG AGO THERE WER ONCE THRE FAMOUS NIN CLANS.
ONE OF THEM, NAMED THE "KOGA," WAS RULED BY PEOPLE.
THEY WERE SHINOBI WHO WERE FIERCELY LOYAL TO THEIR LEADER.
ANOTHER OF THEM, NAMED THE "IGA," WAS RULED BY MONEY.
THEY WERE THE TYPE OF SHINOBI WHO WOULDN'T BOTHER THEMSELVES WITH ANYTHING BEYOND THE TERMS OF THEIR CONTRACTS.
GRAB
–!
GRAB

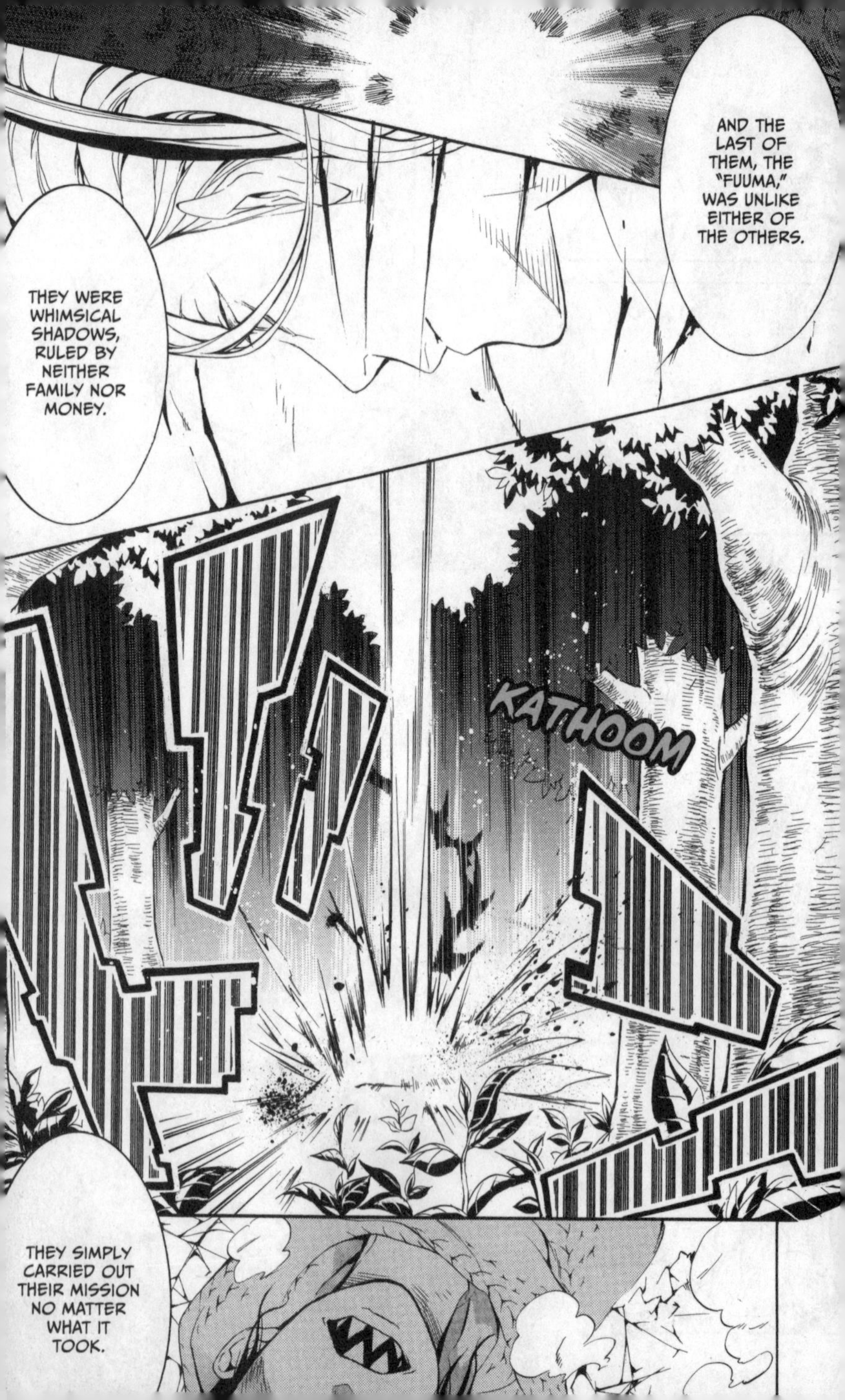
AND THE LAST OF THEM, THE "FUUMA," WAS UNLIKE EITHER OF THE OTHERS.
THEY WERE WHIMSICAL SHADOWS, RULED BY NEITHER FAMILY NOR MONEY.
KATHOOM
THEY SIMPLY CARRIED OUT THEIR MISSION NO MATTER WHAT IT TOOK.

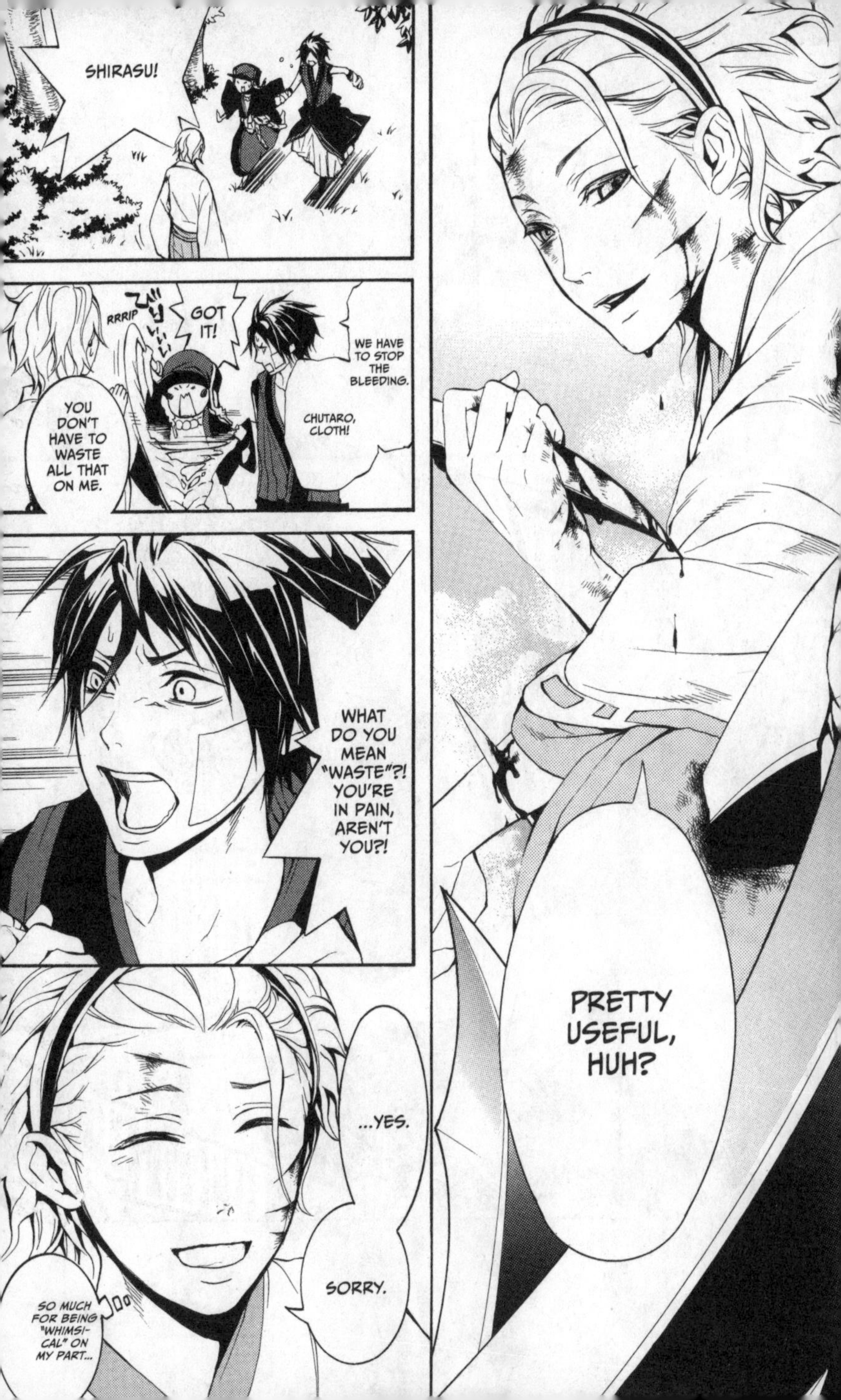
PRETTY USEFUL, HUH?
SHIRASU!
WE HAVE TO STOP THE BLEEDING.
CHUTARO, CLOTH!
GOT IT!
RRRIP
YOU DON'T HAVE TO WASTE ALL THAT ON ME.
WHAT DO YOU MEAN "WASTE"?! YOU'RE IN PAIN, AREN'T YOU?!
...YES.
SORRY.
SO MUCH FOR BEING "WHIMSICAL" ON MY PART...

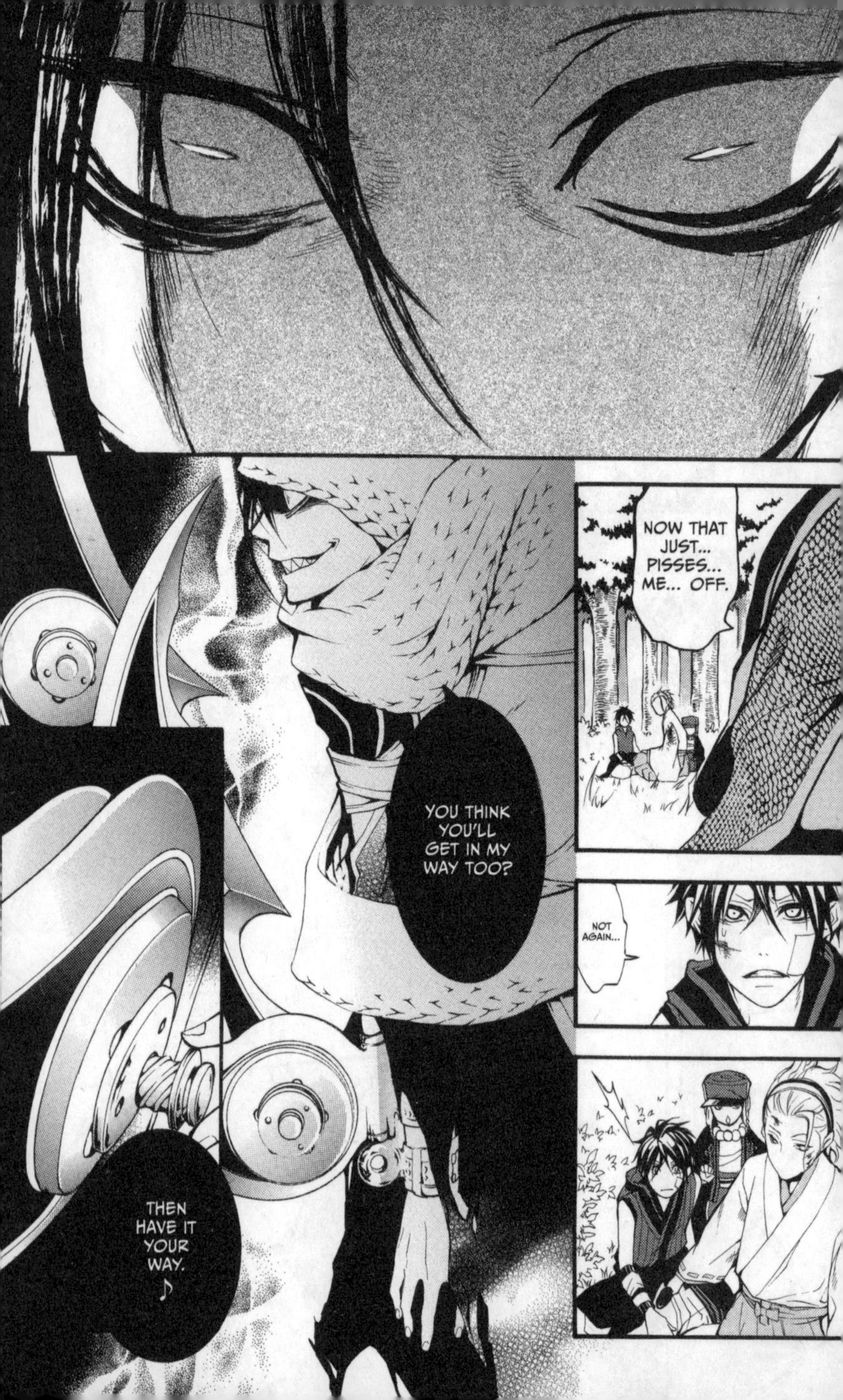
NOW THAT JUST... PISSES... ME... OFF.
NOT AGAIN...
YOU THINK YOU'LL GET IN MY WAY TOO?
THEN HAVE IT YOUR WAY. ♪

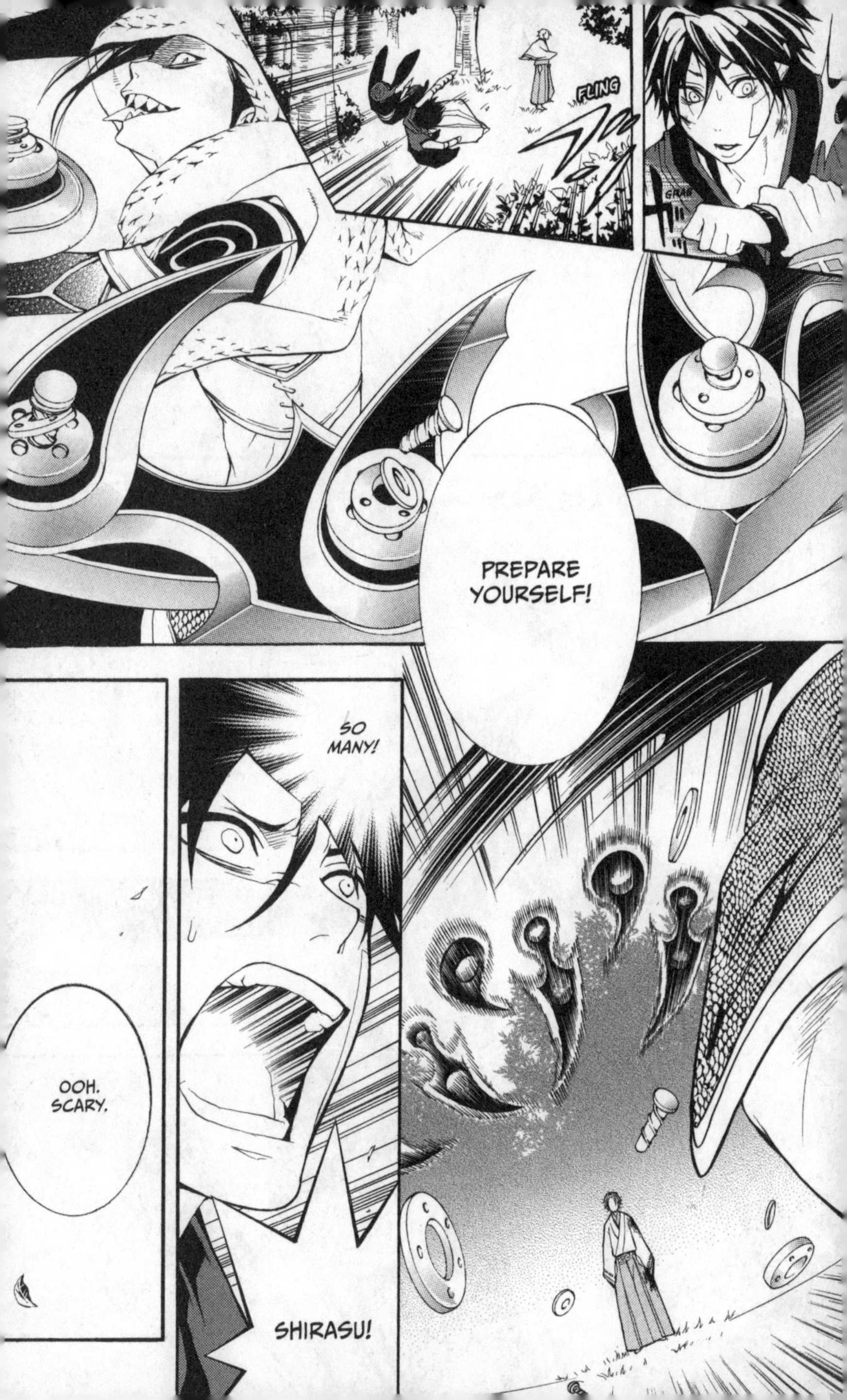
GRAB
FLING
PREPARE YOURSELF!
SO MANY!
SHIRASU!
OOH. SCARY.

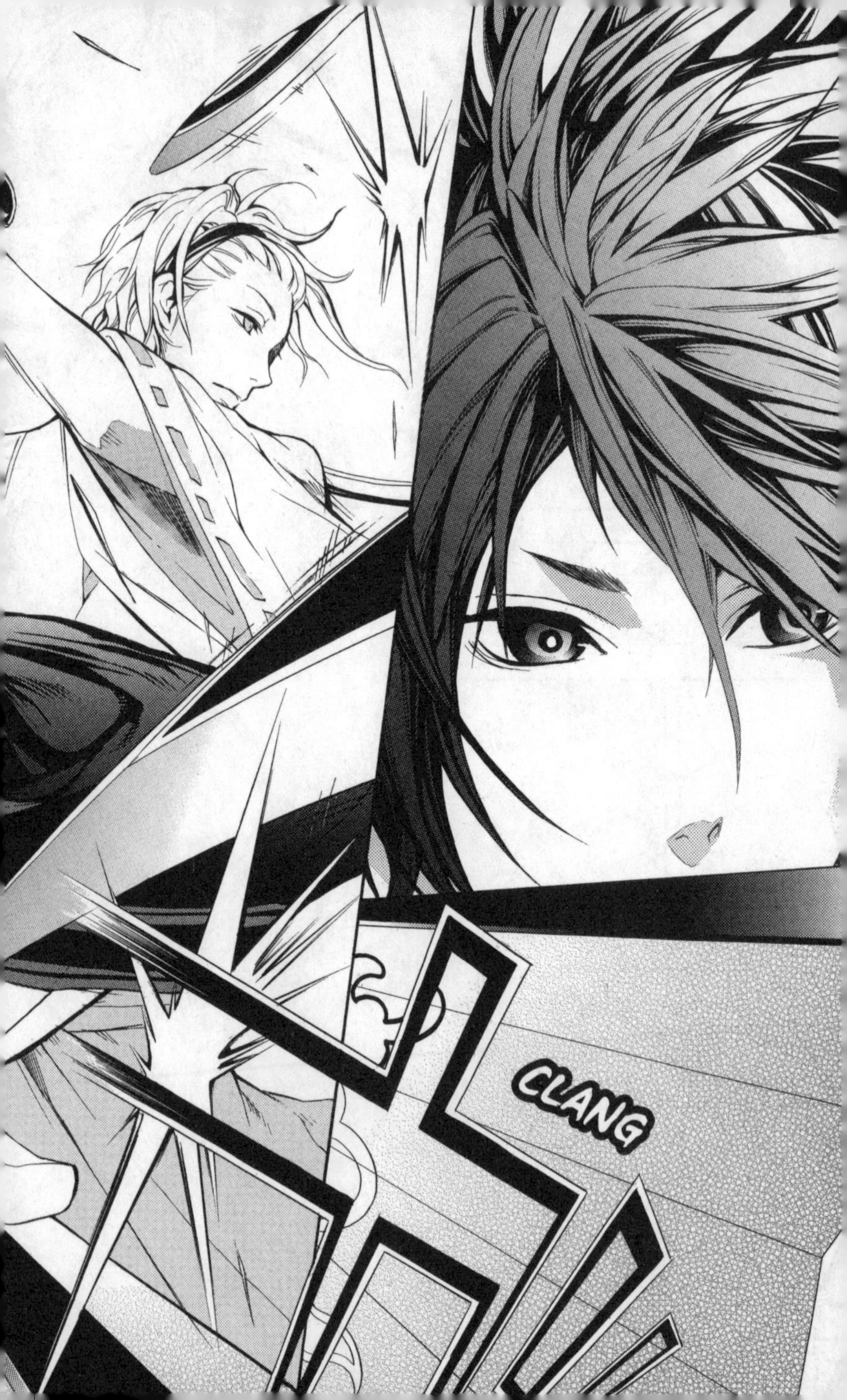
CLANG

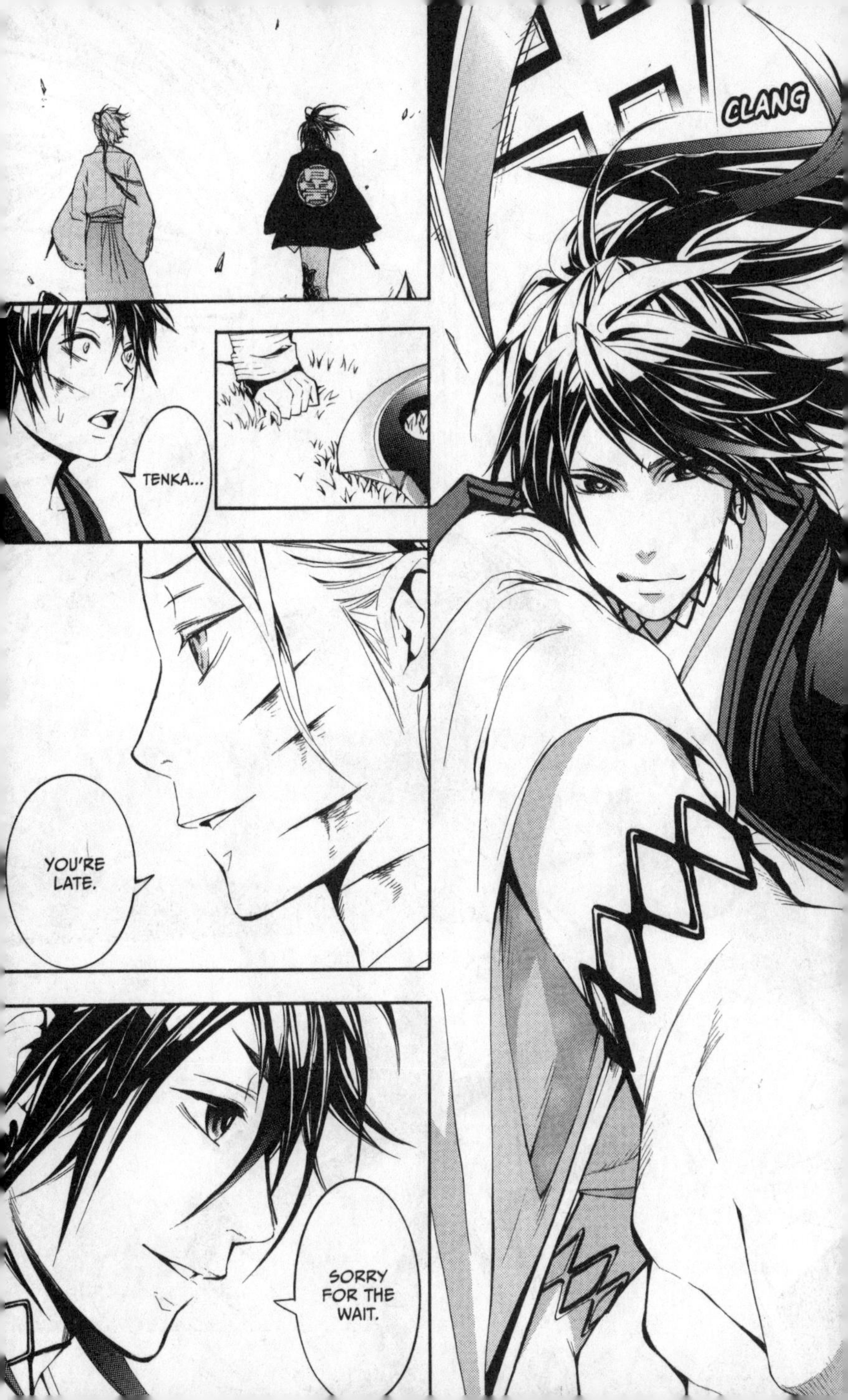
CLANG
TENKA...
YOU'RE LATE.
SORRY FOR THE WAIT.

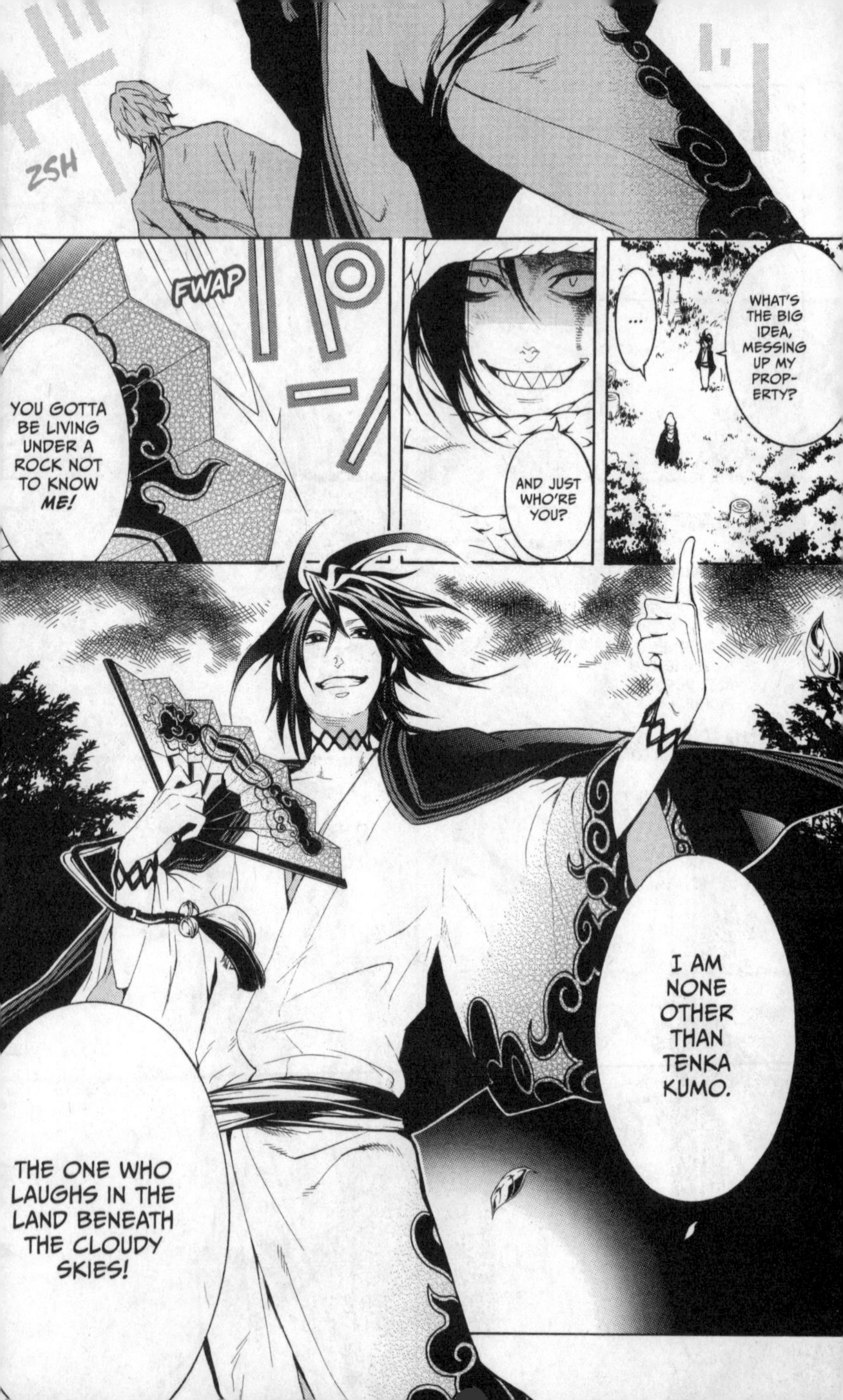
ZSH
WHAT'S THE BIG IDEA, MESSING UP MY PROPERTY?
...
AND JUST WHO'RE YOU?
FWAP
YOU GOTTA BE LIVING UNDER A ROCK NOT TO KNOW *ME!*
I AM NONE OTHER THAN TENKA KUMO.
THE ONE WHO LAUGHS IN THE LAND BENEATH THE CLOUDY SKIES!

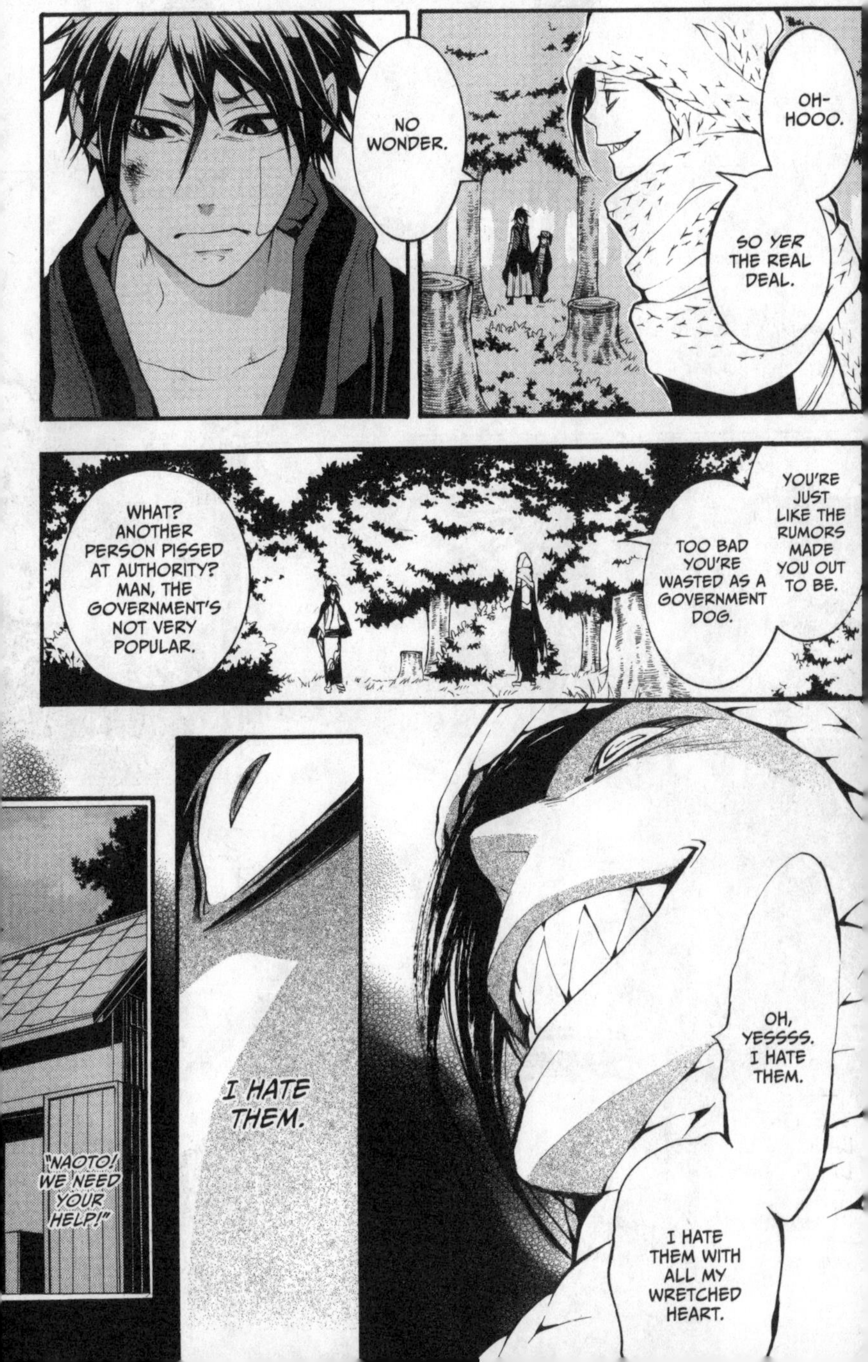
OH-HOOO.
SO YER THE REAL DEAL.
NO WONDER.
YOU'RE JUST LIKE THE RUMORS MADE YOU OUT TO BE.
TOO BAD YOU'RE WASTED AS A GOVERNMENT DOG.
WHAT? ANOTHER PERSON PISSED AT AUTHORITY? MAN, THE GOVERNMENT'S NOT VERY POPULAR.
OH, YESSSS. I HATE THEM.
I HATE THEM WITH ALL MY WRETCHED HEART.
I HATE THEM.
"NAOTO! WE NEED YOUR HELP!"

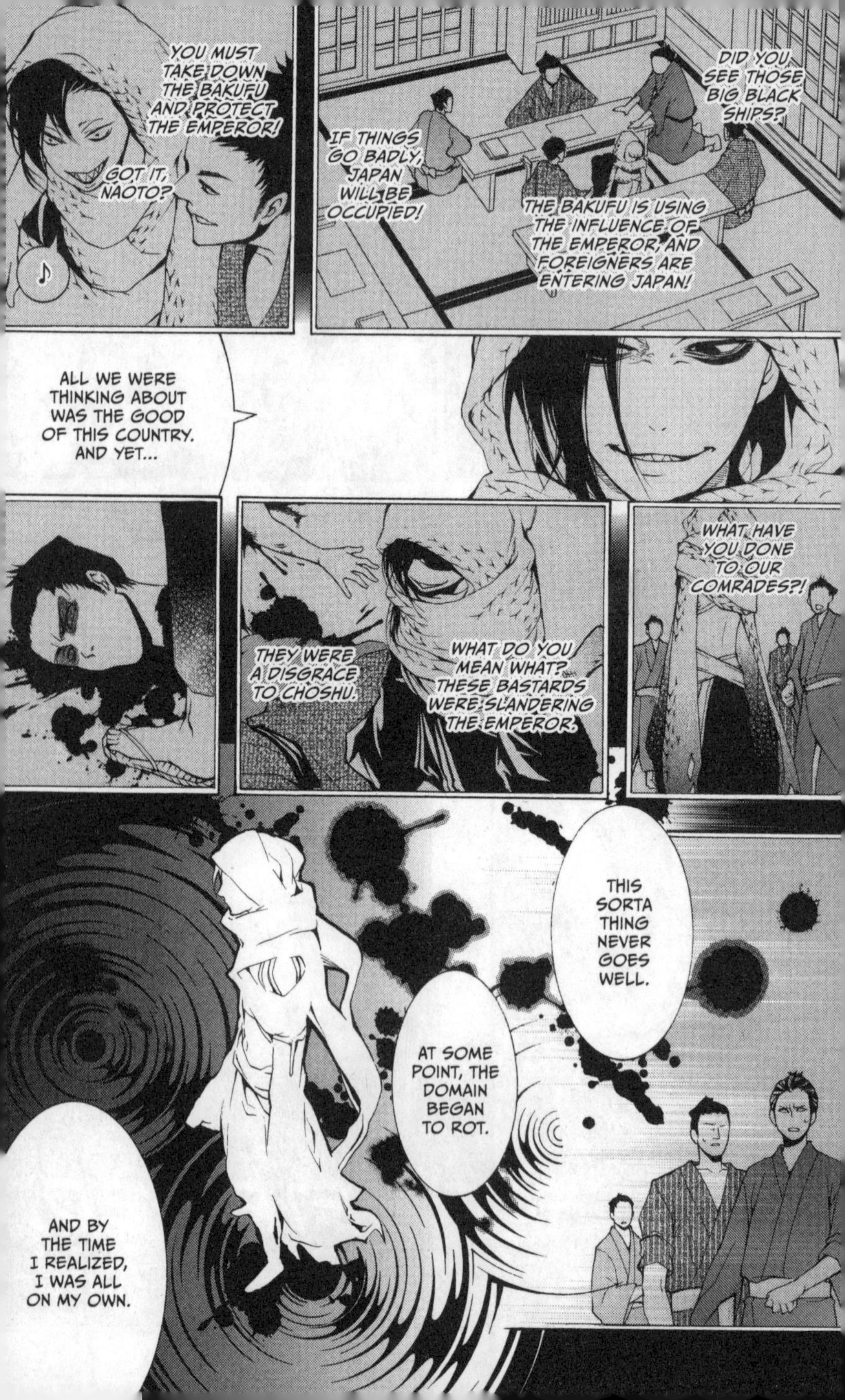
DID YOU SEE THOSE BIG BLACK SHIPS?
IF THINGS GO BADLY, JAPAN WILL BE OCCUPIED!
THE BAKUFU IS USING THE INFLUENCE OF THE EMPEROR, AND FOREIGNERS ARE ENTERING JAPAN!
YOU MUST TAKE DOWN THE BAKUFU AND PROTECT THE EMPEROR!
GOT IT, NAOTO?
♪
ALL WE WERE THINKING ABOUT WAS THE GOOD OF THIS COUNTRY. AND YET...
WHAT HAVE YOU DONE TO OUR COMRADES?!
WHAT DO YOU MEAN WHAT? THESE BASTARDS WERE SLANDERING THE EMPEROR.
THEY WERE A DISGRACE TO CHOSHU.
THIS SORTA THING NEVER GOES WELL.
AT SOME POINT, THE DOMAIN BEGAN TO ROT.
AND BY THE TIME I REALIZED, I WAS ALL ON MY OWN.

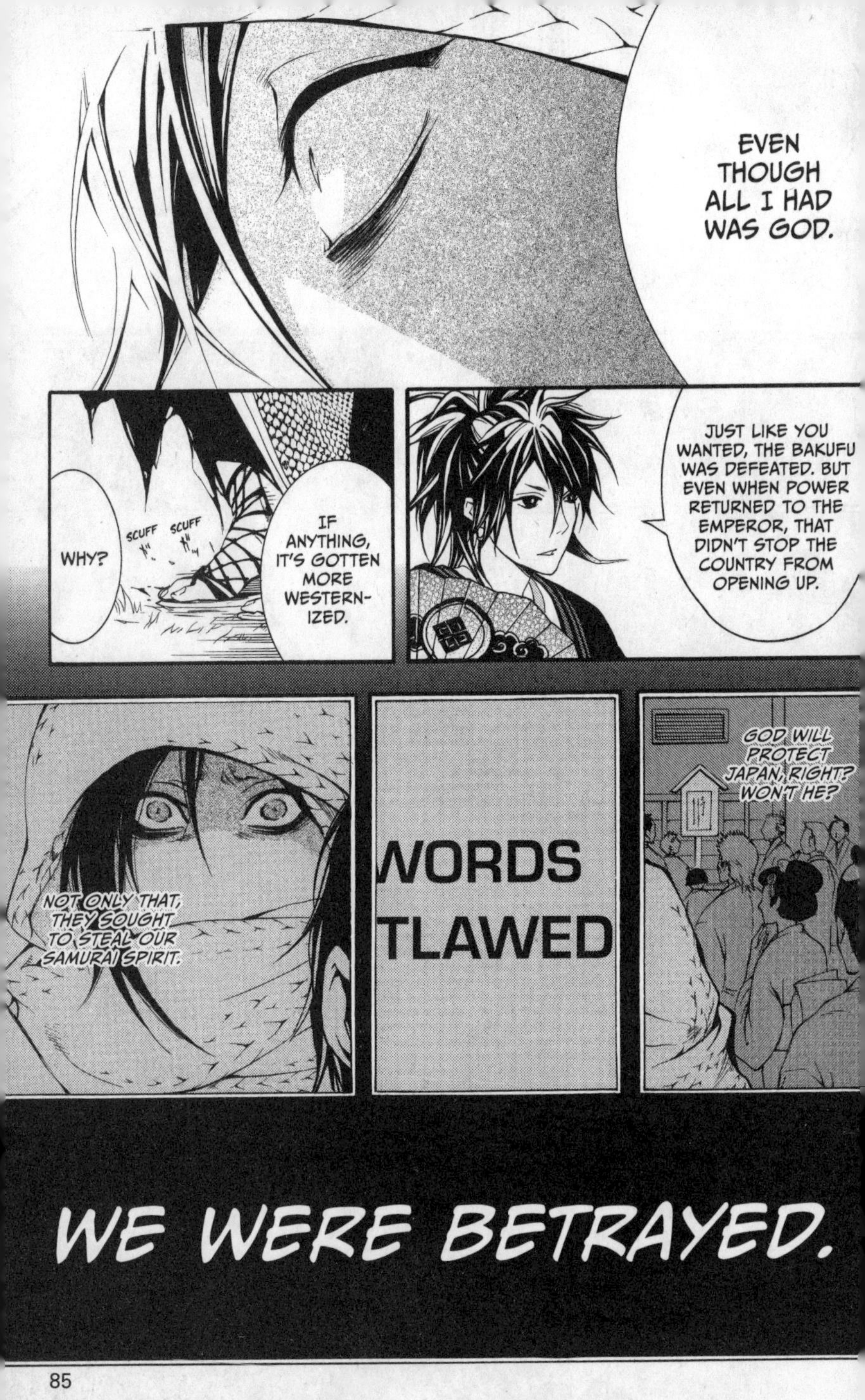
EVEN THOUGH ALL I HAD WAS GOD.
JUST LIKE YOU WANTED, THE BAKUFU WAS DEFEATED. BUT EVEN WHEN POWER RETURNED TO THE EMPEROR, THAT DIDN'T STOP THE COUNTRY FROM OPENING UP.
IF ANYTHING, IT'S GOTTEN MORE WESTERN-IZED.
SCUFF SCUFF
WHY?
GOD WILL PROTECT JAPAN, RIGHT? WON'T HE?
WORDS
TLAWED
NOT ONLY THAT, THEY SOUGHT TO STEAL OUR SAMURAI SPIRIT.
WE WERE BETRAYED.

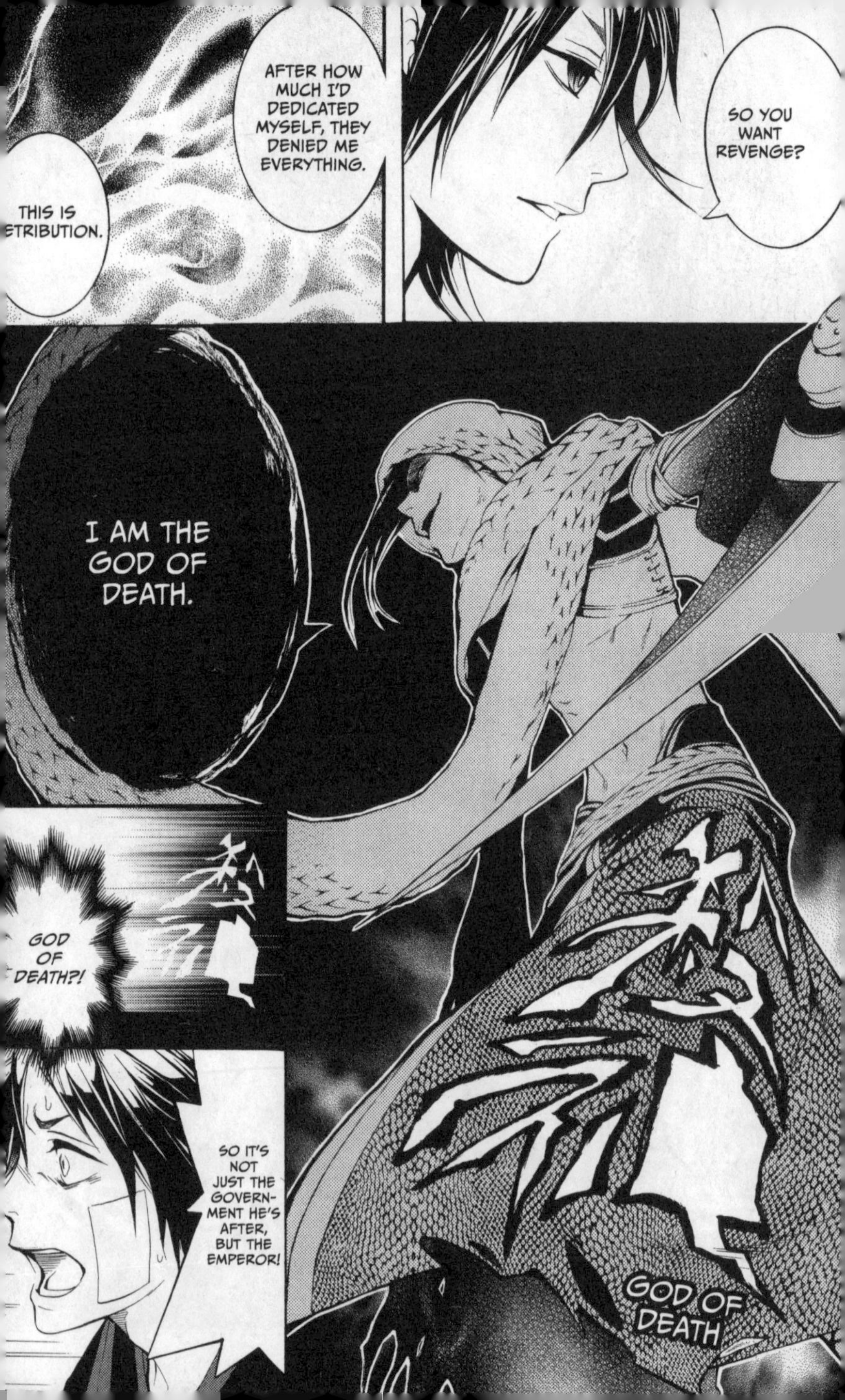
SO YOU WANT REVENGE?
AFTER HOW MUCH I'D DEDICATED MYSELF, THEY DENIED ME EVERYTHING.
THIS IS ETRIBUTION.
I AM THE GOD OF DEATH.
GOD OF DEATH
GOD OF DEATH?!
SO IT'S NOT JUST THE GOVERN-MENT HE'S AFTER, BUT THE EMPEROR!

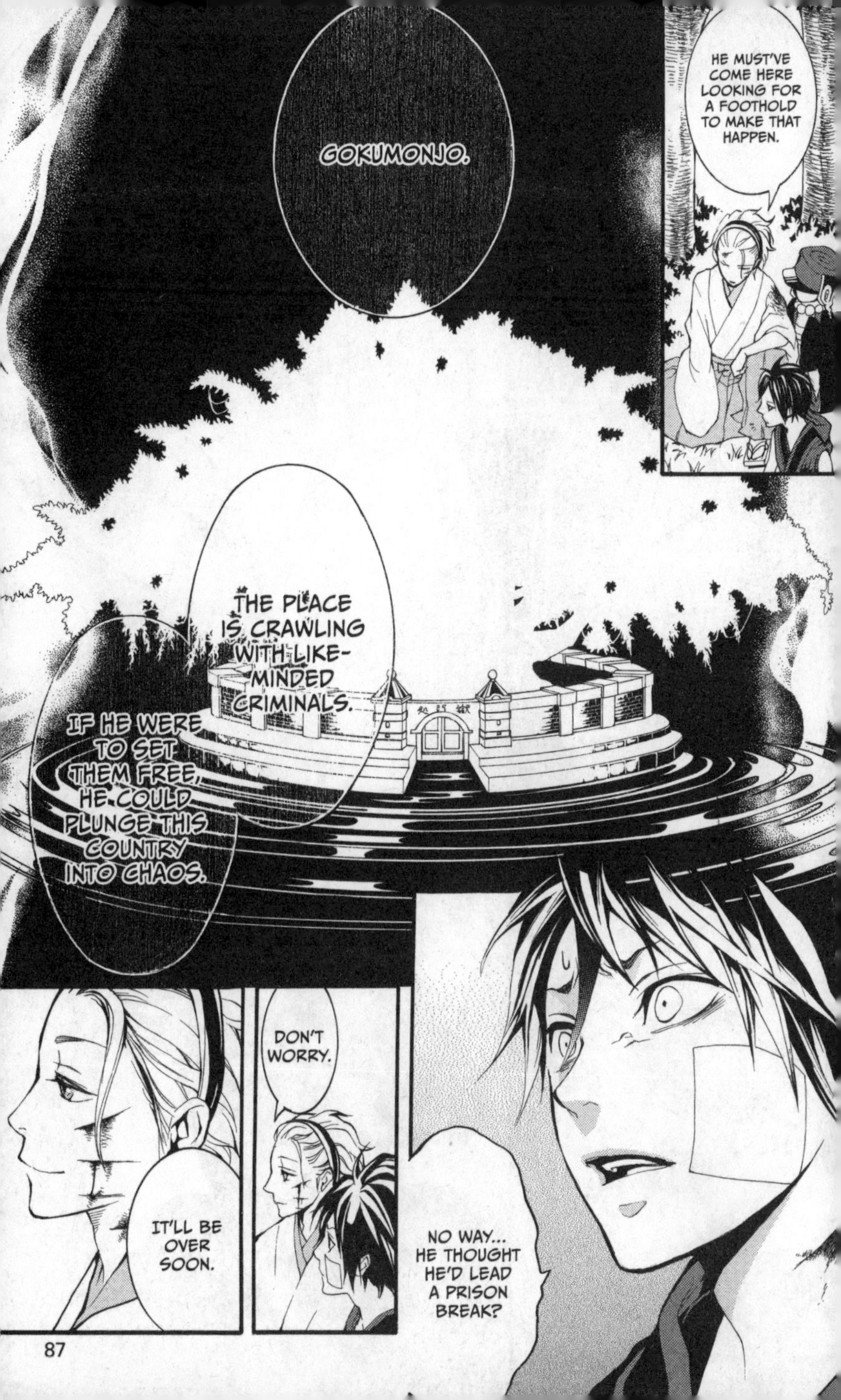
HE MUST'VE COME HERE LOOKING FOR A FOOTHOLD TO MAKE THAT HAPPEN.
GOKUMONJO.
THE PLACE IS CRAWLING WITH LIKE-MINDED CRIMINALS.
IF HE WERE TO SET THEM FREE, HE COULD PLUNGE THIS COUNTRY INTO CHAOS.
NO WAY... HE THOUGHT HE'D LEAD A PRISON BREAK?
DON'T WORRY.
IT'LL BE OVER SOON.

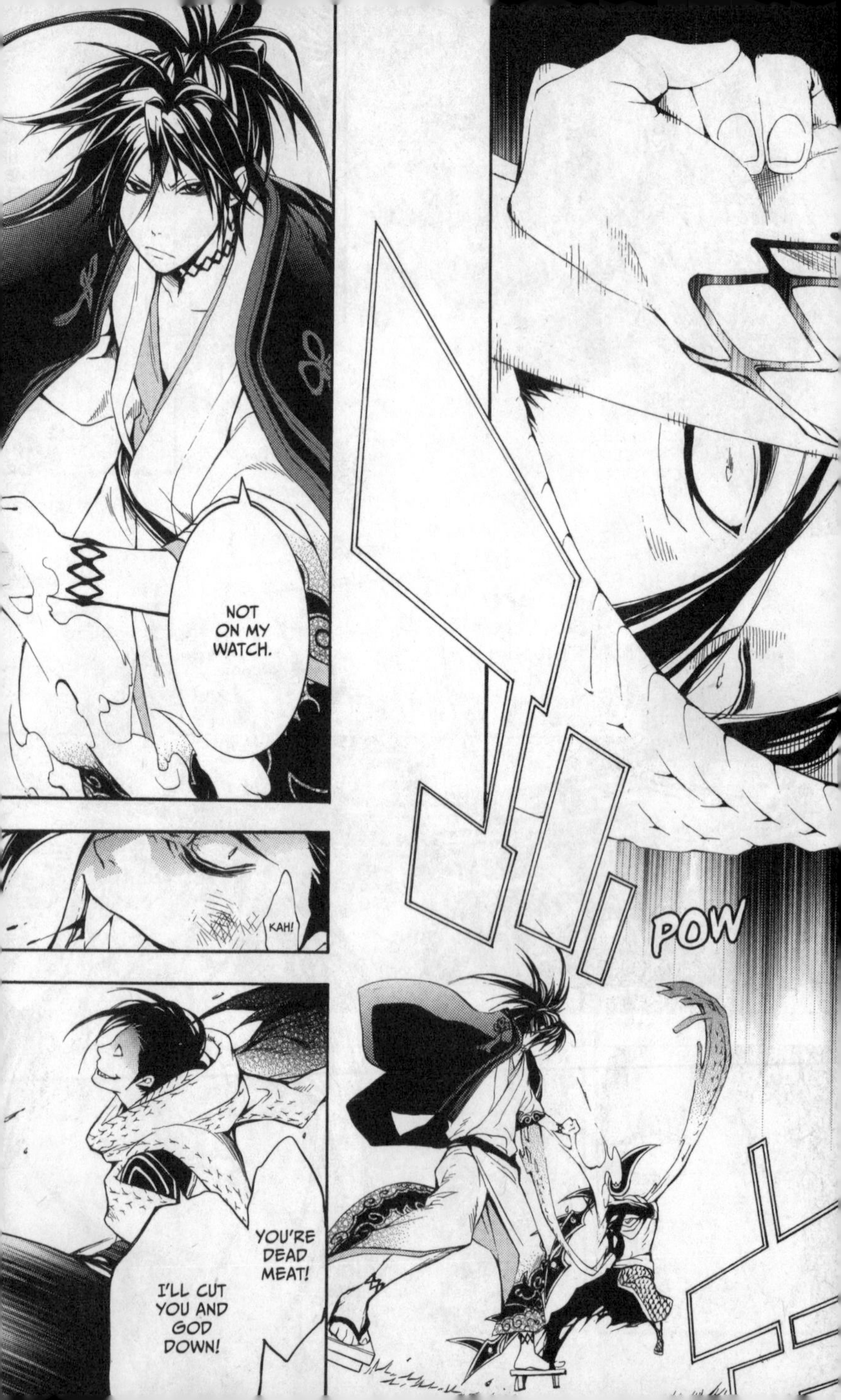
POW
NOT ON MY WATCH.
KAH!
YOU'RE DEAD MEAT!
I'LL CUT YOU AND GOD DOWN!

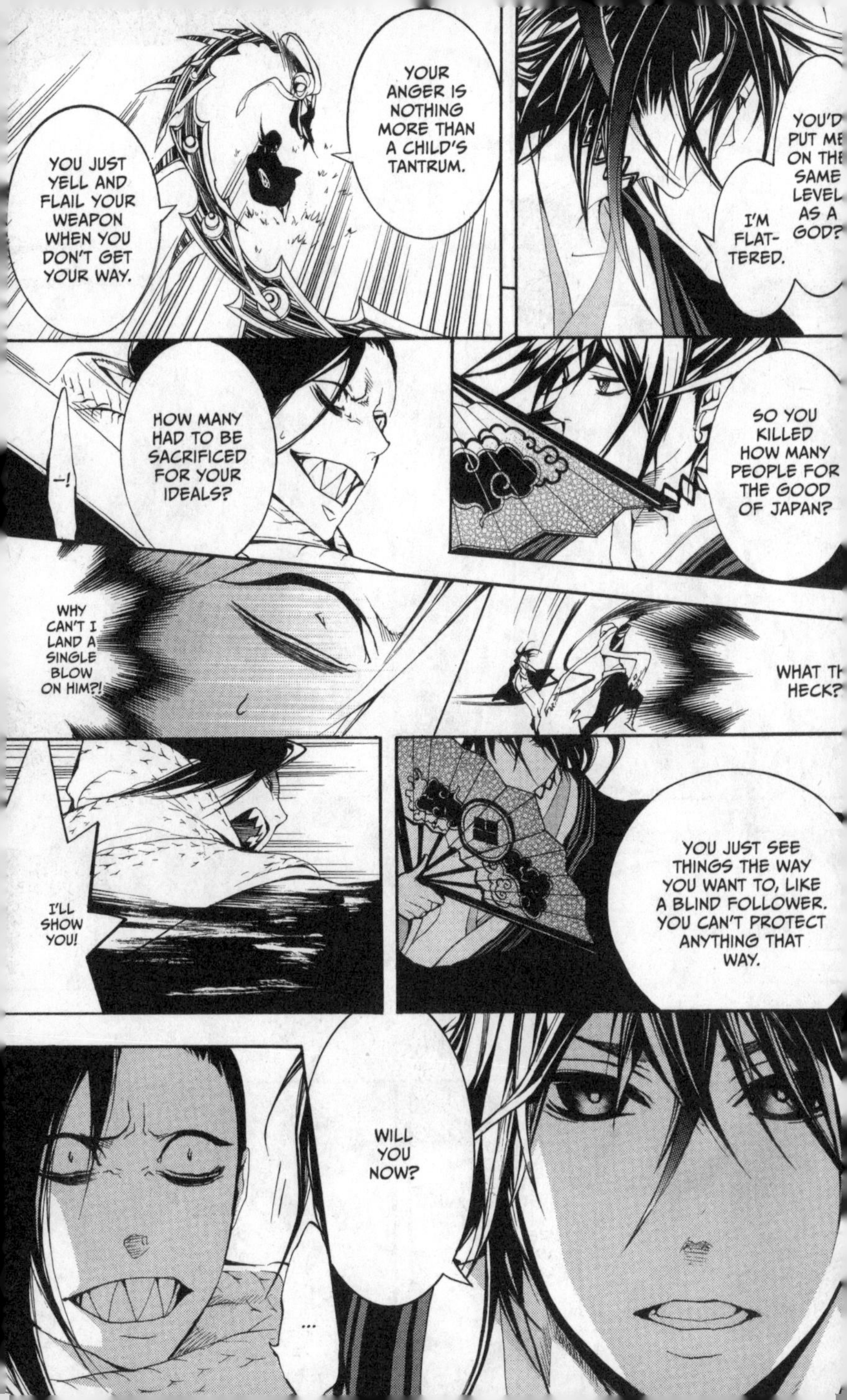
YOU'D PUT ME ON THE SAME LEVEL AS A GOD?
I'M FLAT-TERED.
YOUR ANGER IS NOTHING MORE THAN A CHILD'S TANTRUM.
YOU JUST YELL AND FLAIL YOUR WEAPON WHEN YOU DON'T GET YOUR WAY.
SO YOU KILLED HOW MANY PEOPLE FOR THE GOOD OF JAPAN?
HOW MANY HAD TO BE SACRIFICED FOR YOUR IDEALS?
—!
WHAT TH HECK?
WHY CAN'T I LAND A SINGLE BLOW ON HIM?!
YOU JUST SEE THINGS THE WAY YOU WANT TO, LIKE A BLIND FOLLOWER. YOU CAN'T PROTECT ANYTHING THAT WAY.
I'LL SHOW YOU!
WILL YOU NOW?
...

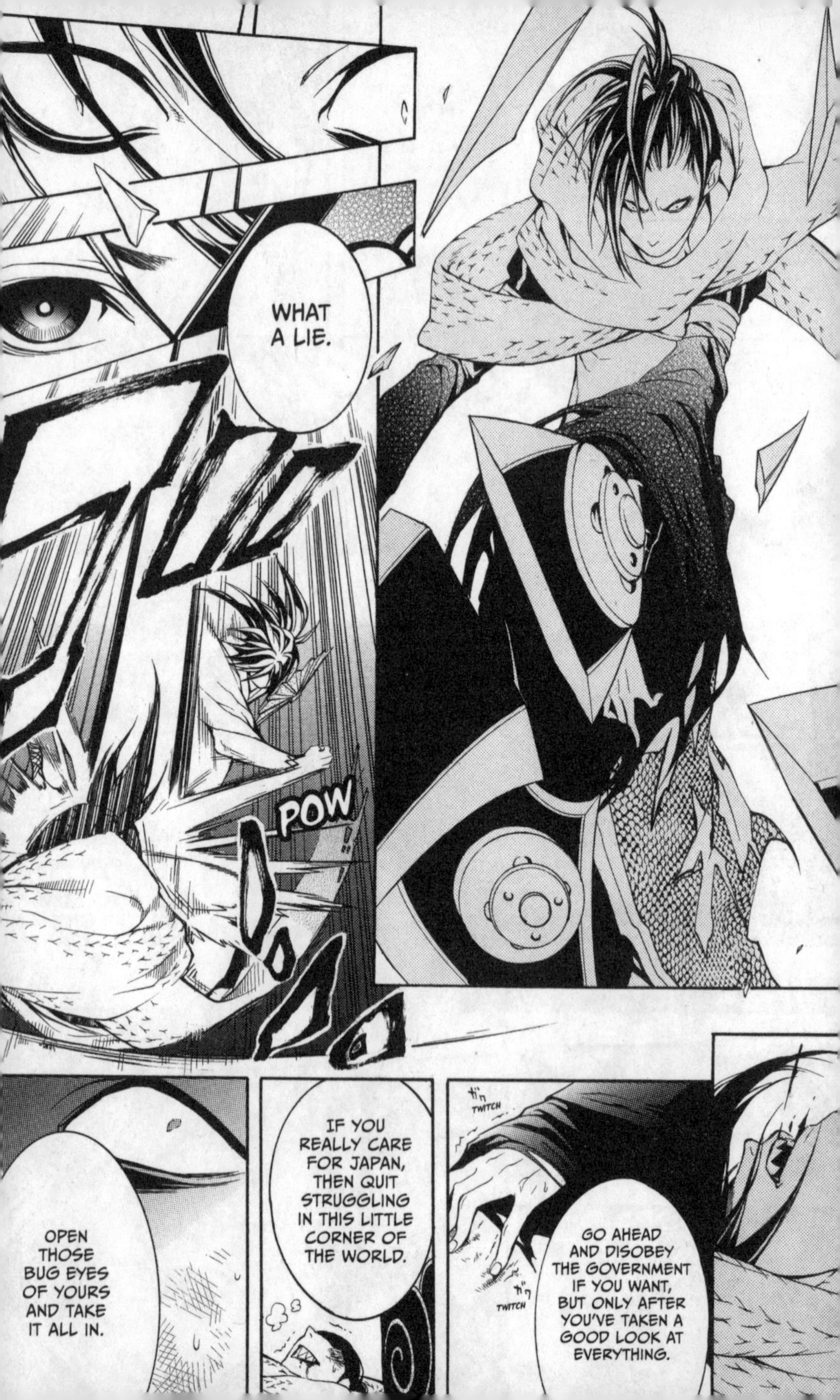
WHAT A LIE.
POW
TWITCH
GO AHEAD AND DISOBEY THE GOVERNMENT IF YOU WANT, BUT ONLY AFTER YOU'VE TAKEN A GOOD LOOK AT EVERYTHING.
TWITCH
IF YOU REALLY CARE FOR JAPAN, THEN QUIT STRUGGLING IN THIS LITTLE CORNER OF THE WORLD.
OPEN THOSE BUG EYES OF YOURS AND TAKE IT ALL IN.

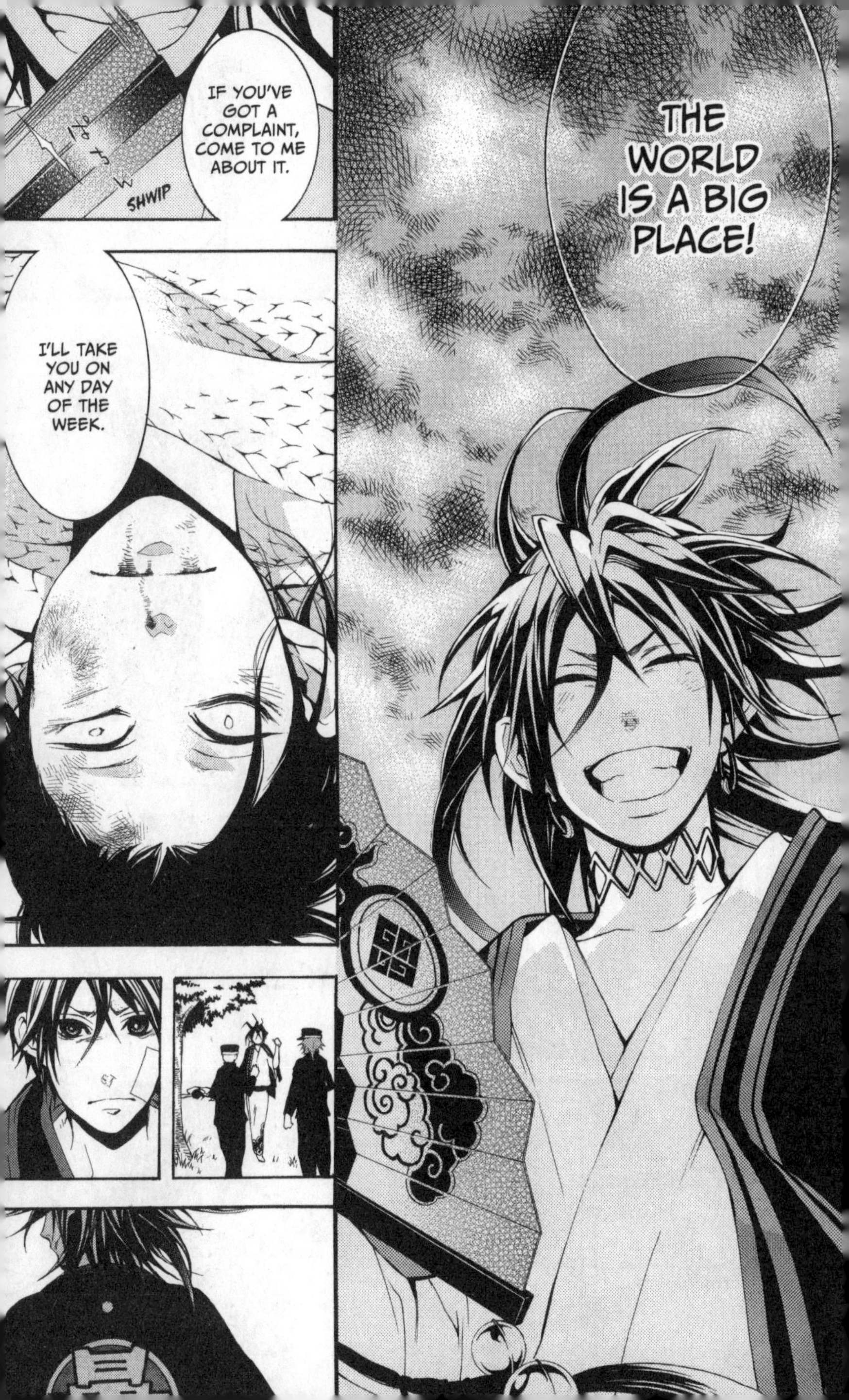
THE WORLD IS A BIG PLACE!
IF YOU'VE GOT A COMPLAINT, COME TO ME ABOUT IT.
SHWIP
I'LL TAKE YOU ON ANY DAY OF THE WEEK.

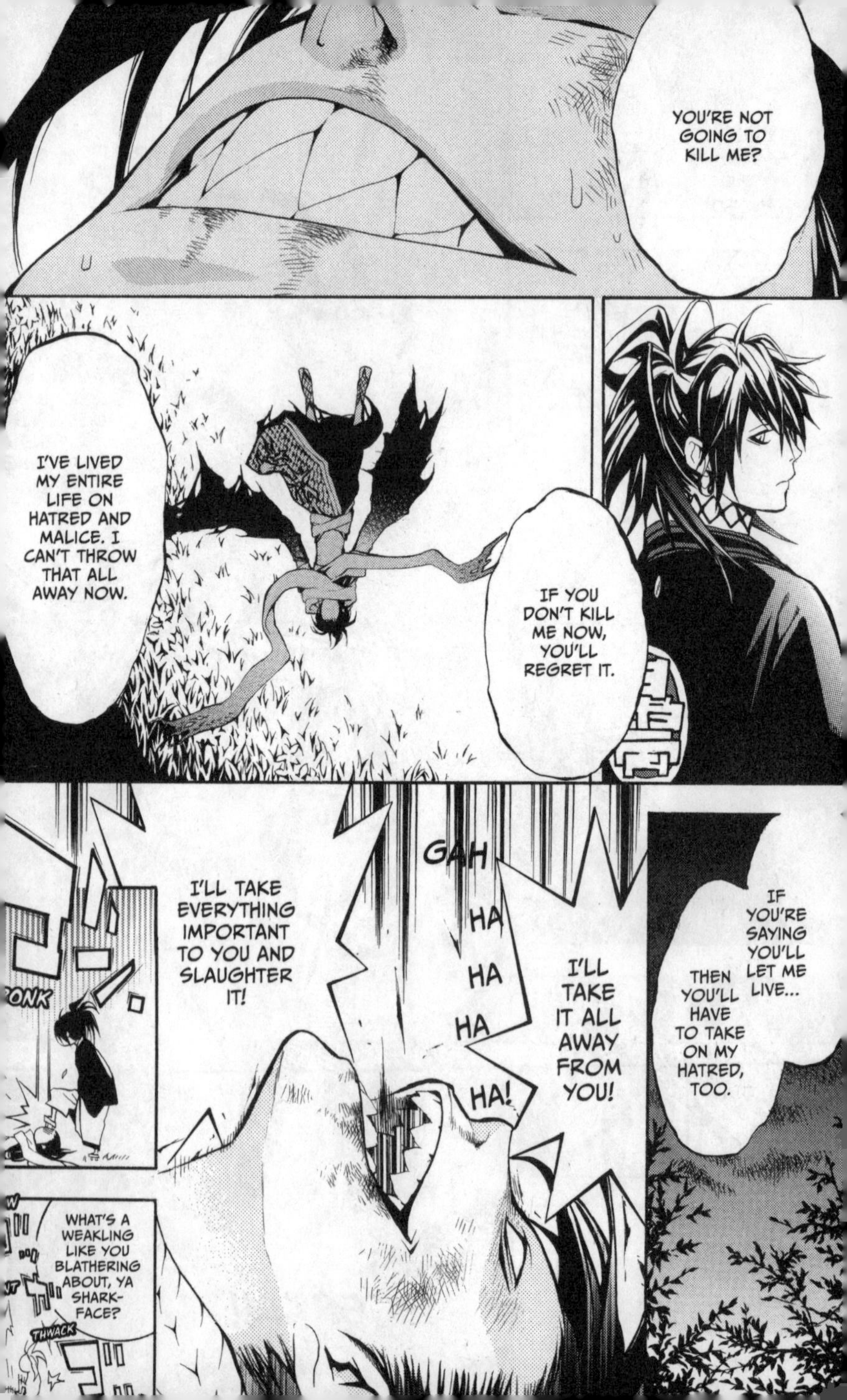
YOU'RE NOT GOING TO KILL ME?
IF YOU DON'T KILL ME NOW, YOU'LL REGRET IT.
I'VE LIVED MY ENTIRE LIFE ON HATRED AND MALICE. I CAN'T THROW THAT ALL AWAY NOW.
IF YOU'RE SAYING YOU'LL LET ME LIVE...
THEN YOU'LL HAVE TO TAKE ON MY HATRED, TOO.
I'LL TAKE IT ALL AWAY FROM YOU!
GAH HA HA HA HA!
I'LL TAKE EVERYTHING IMPORTANT TO YOU AND SLAUGHTER IT!
WHAT'S A WEAKLING LIKE YOU BLATHERING ABOUT, YA SHARK-FACE?
THWACK

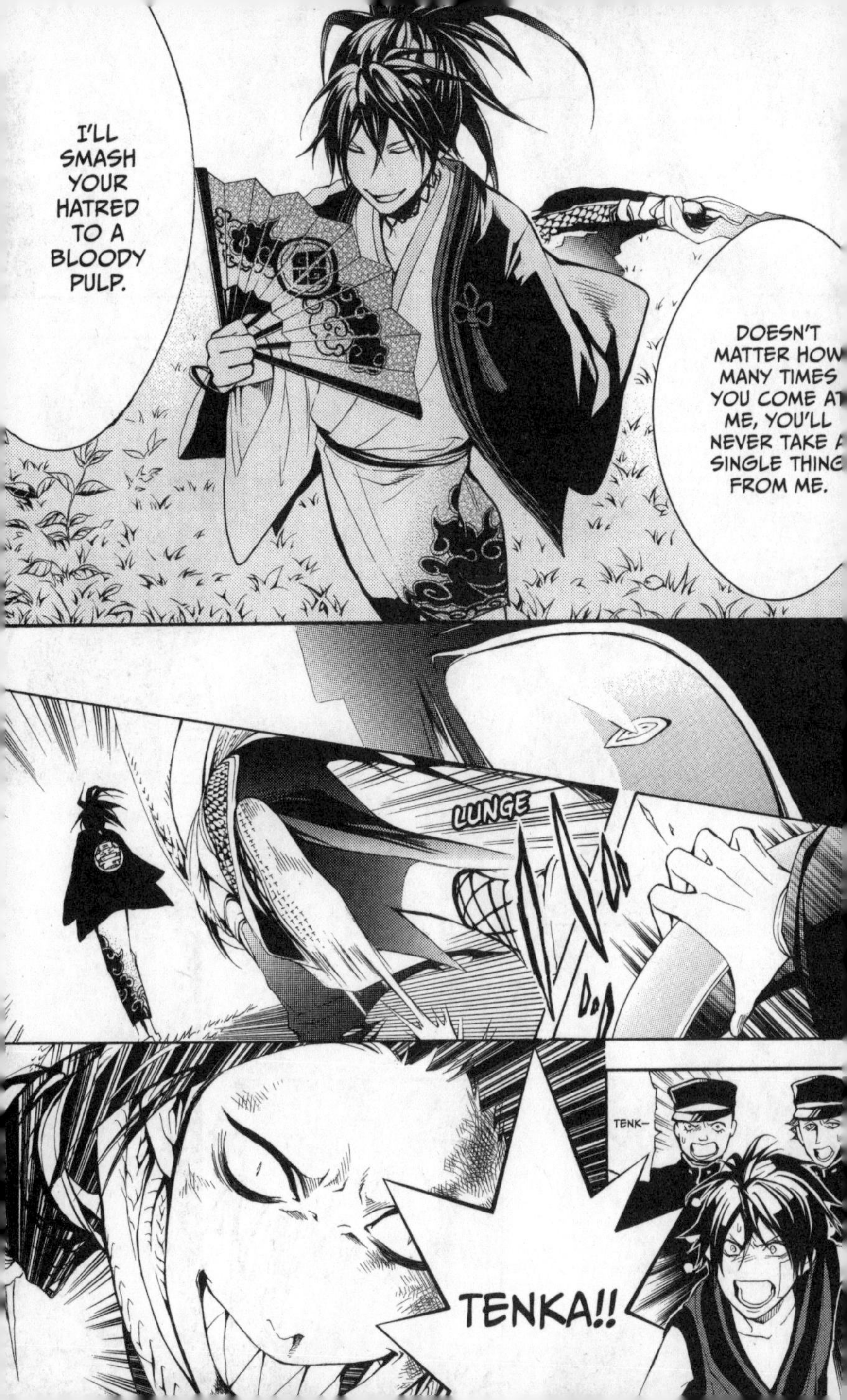
DOESN'T MATTER HOW MANY TIMES YOU COME AT ME, YOU'LL NEVER TAKE A SINGLE THING FROM ME.
I'LL SMASH YOUR HATRED TO A BLOODY PULP.
LUNGE
TENK–
TENKA!!

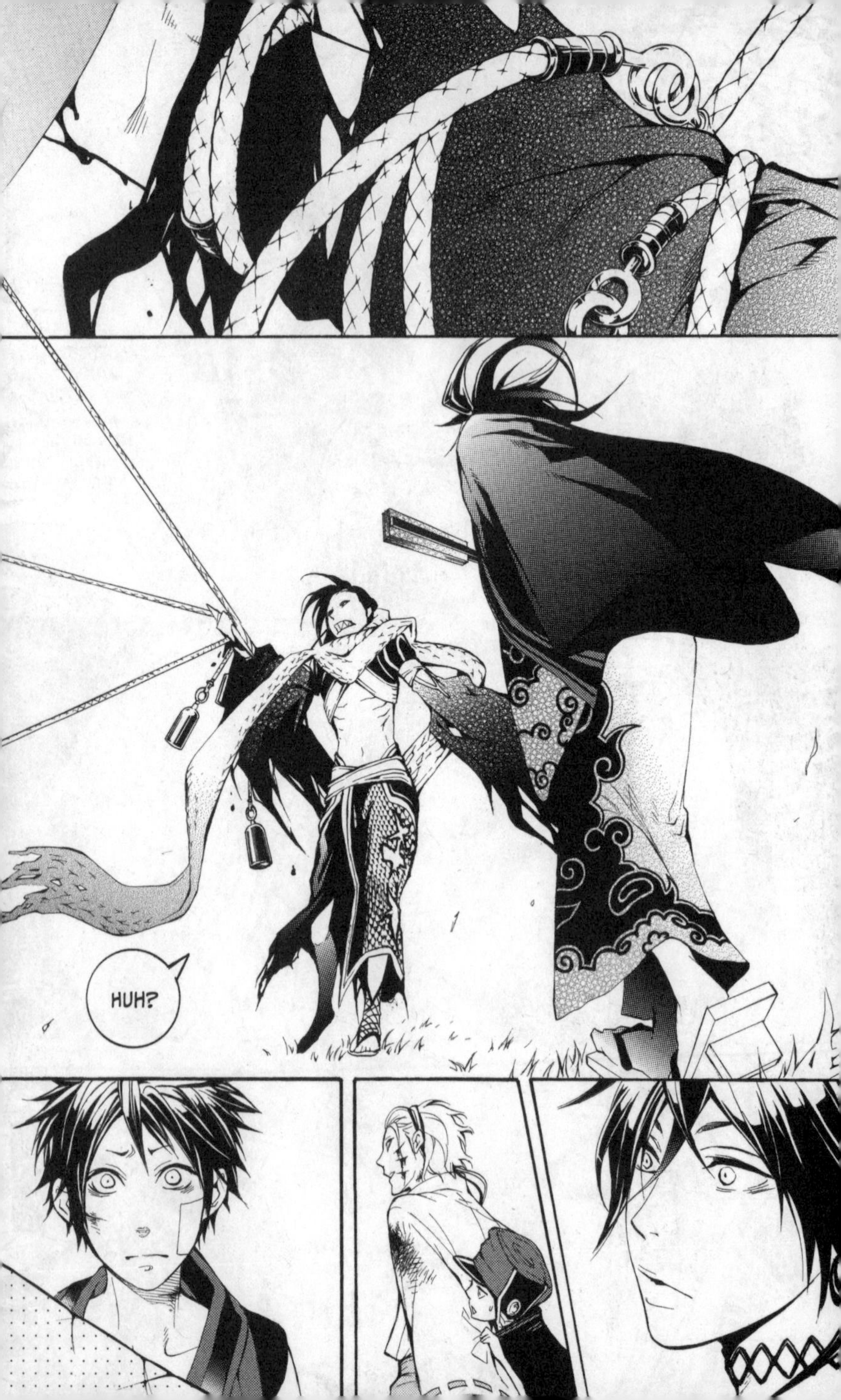
HUH?

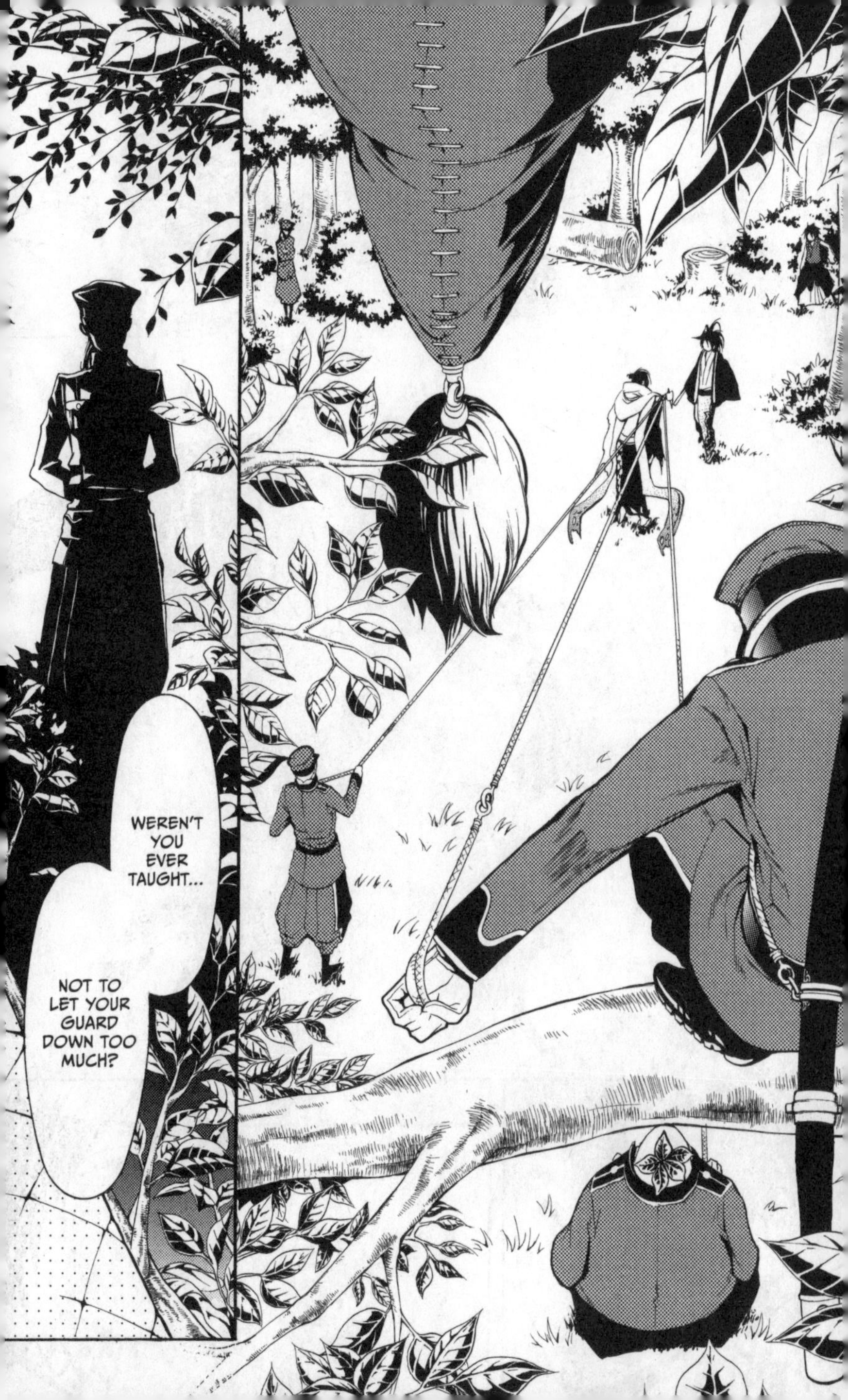
WEREN'T YOU EVER TAUGHT...
NOT TO LET YOUR GUARD DOWN TOO MUCH?

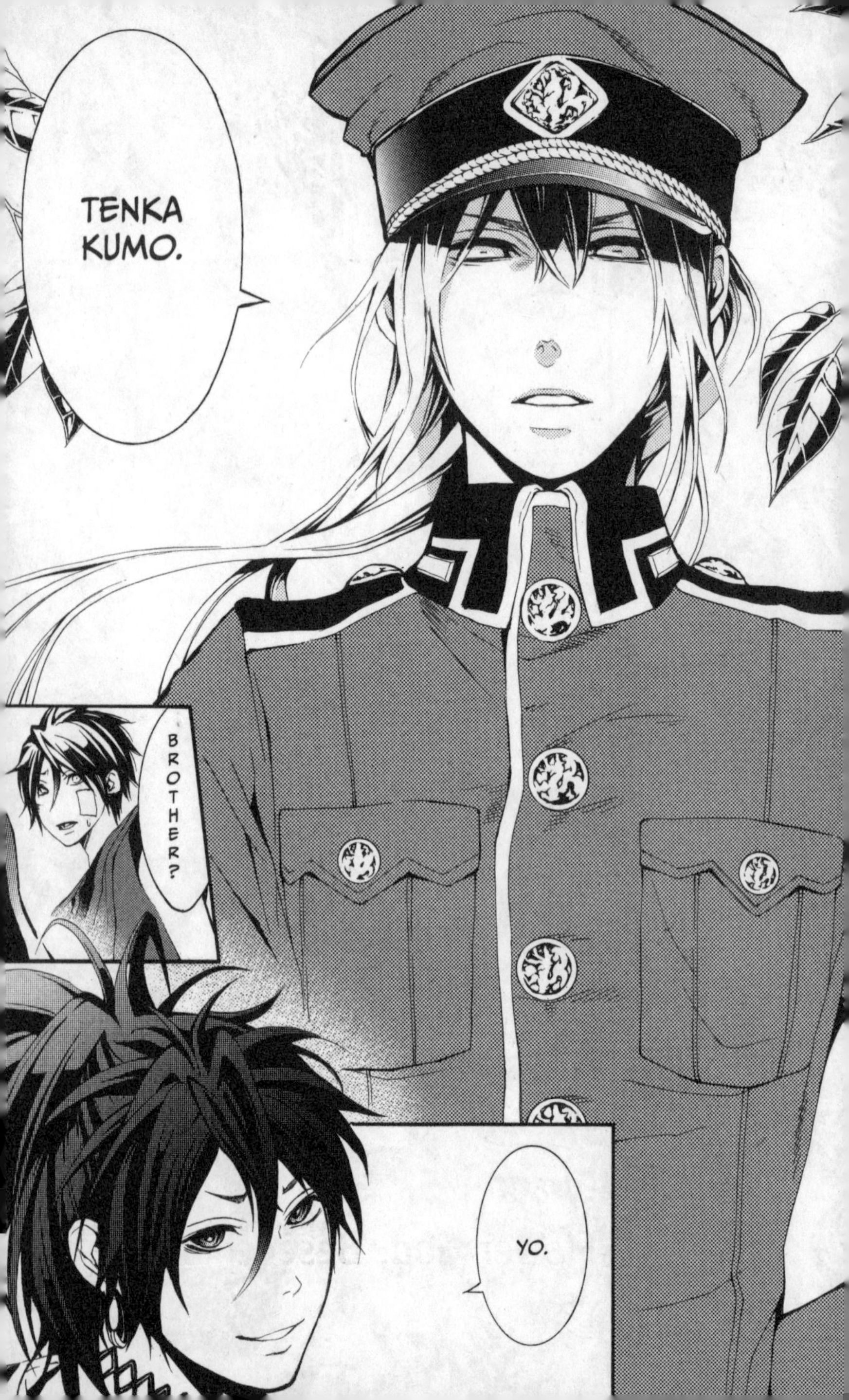
TENKA KUMO.
BROTHER?
YO.

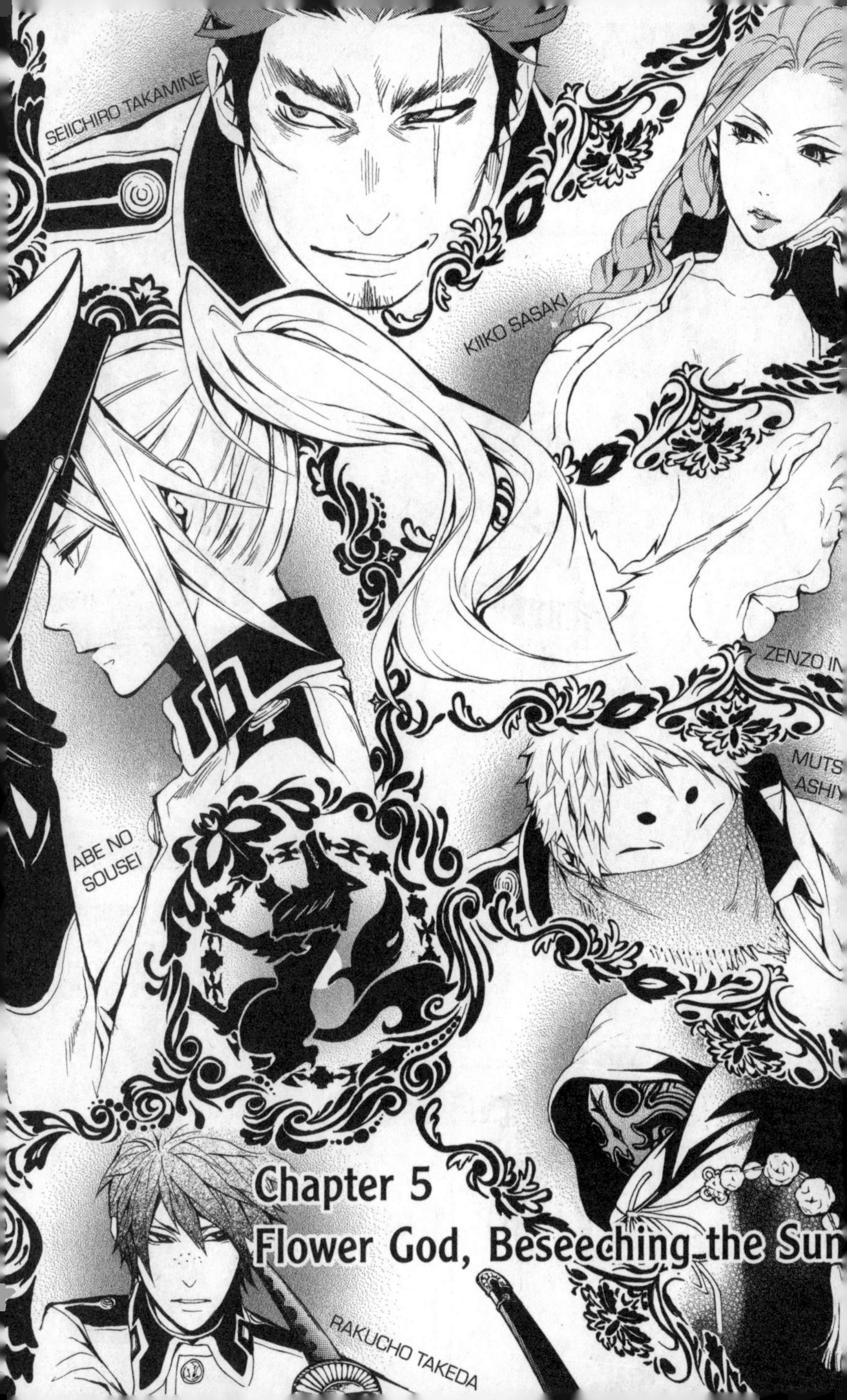
KIIKO SASAKI
SEIICHIRO TAKAMINE
ZENZO IN
MUTS
ASHIY
ABE NO SOUSEI
RAKUCHO TAKEDA

Chapter 5
Flower God, Beseeching the Sun

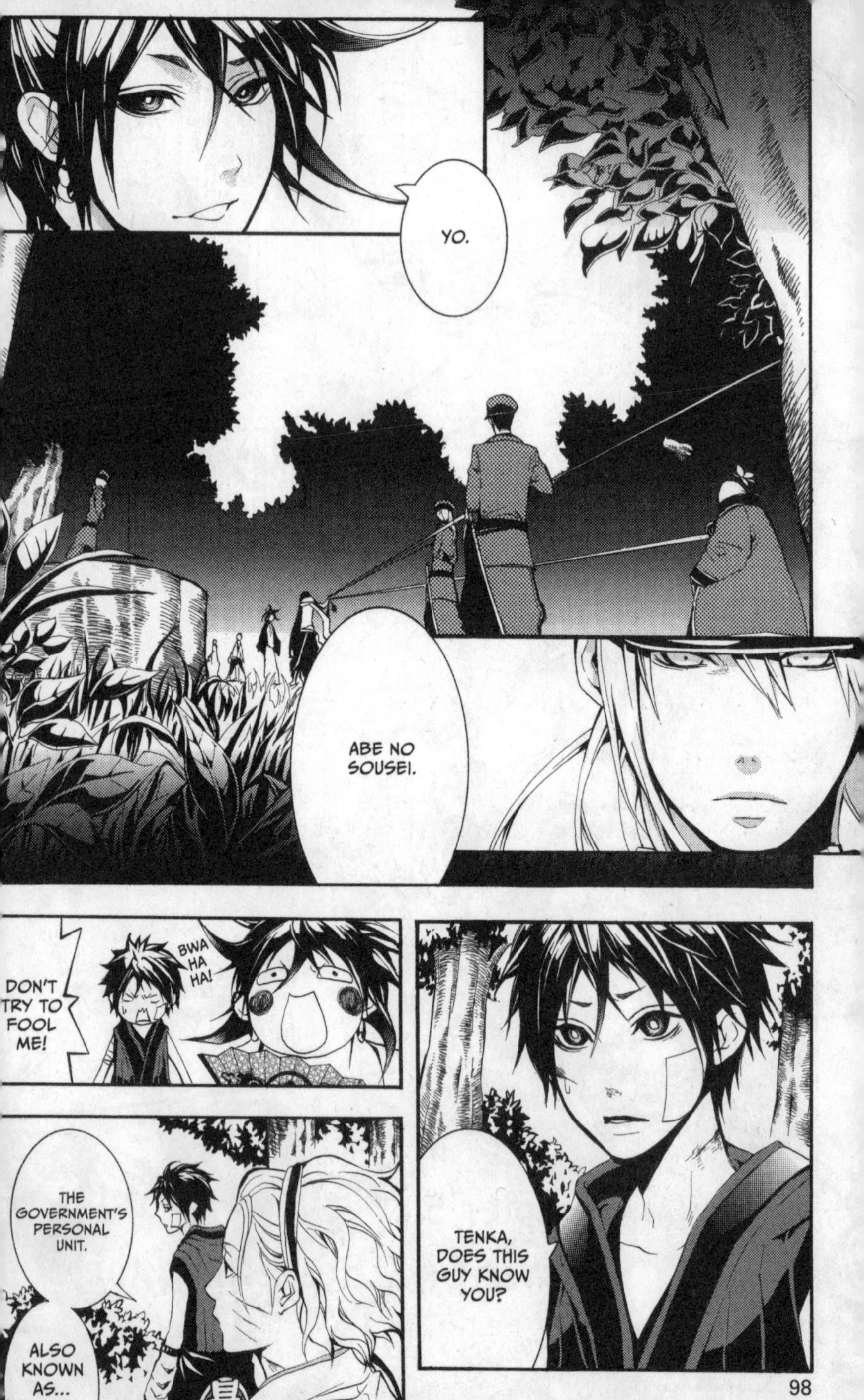
YO.
ABE NO SOUSEI.
TENKA, DOES THIS GUY KNOW YOU?
BWA HA HA!
DON'T TRY TO FOOL ME!
THE GOVERNMENT'S PERSONAL UNIT.
ALSO KNOWN AS...

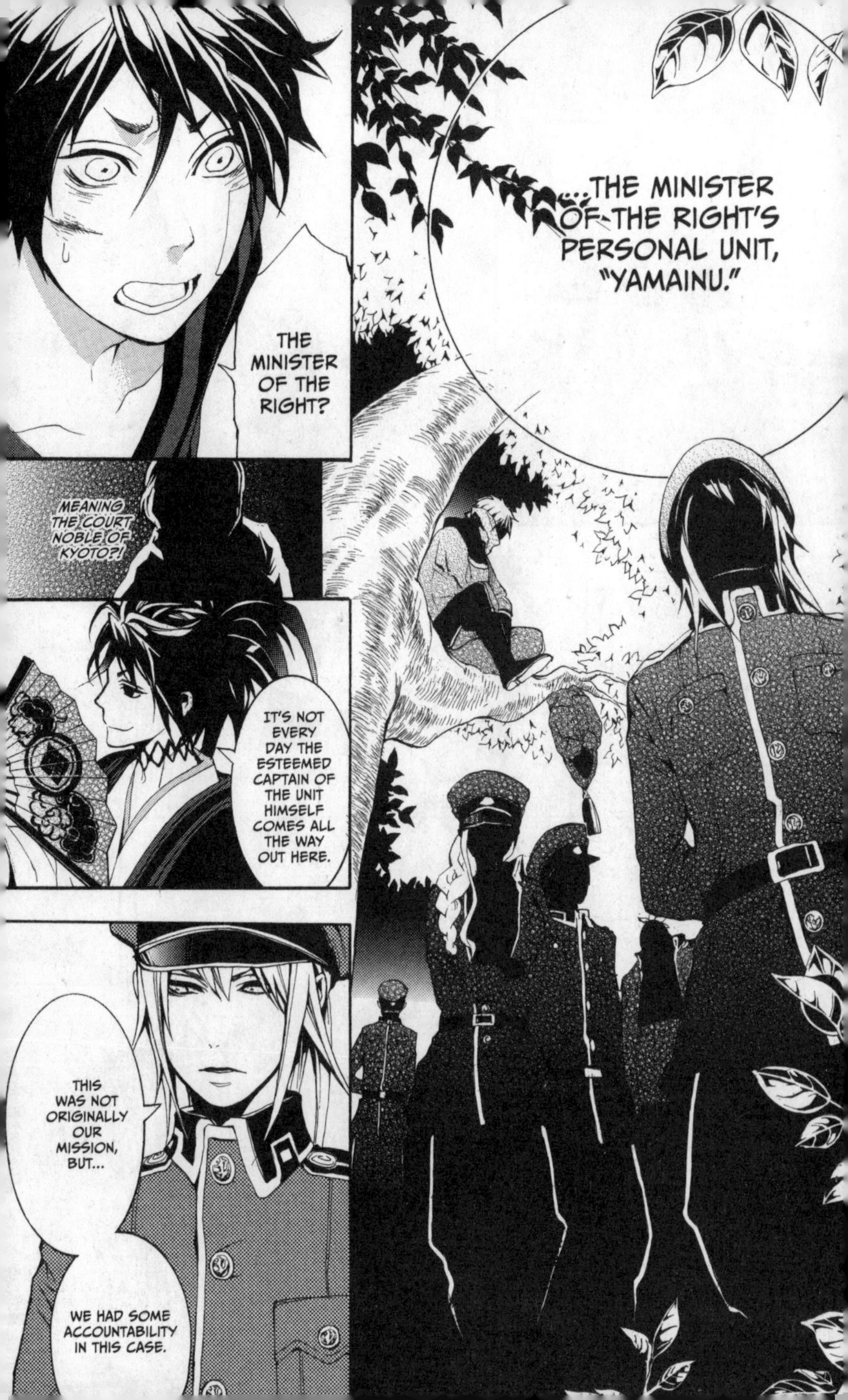

...THE MINISTER OF THE RIGHT'S PERSONAL UNIT, "YAMAINU."
THE MINISTER OF THE RIGHT?
MEANING THE COURT NOBLE OF KYOTO?!
IT'S NOT EVERY DAY THE ESTEEMED CAPTAIN OF THE UNIT HIMSELF COMES ALL THE WAY OUT HERE.
THIS WAS NOT ORIGINALLY OUR MISSION, BUT...
WE HAD SOME ACCOUNTABILITY IN THIS CASE.

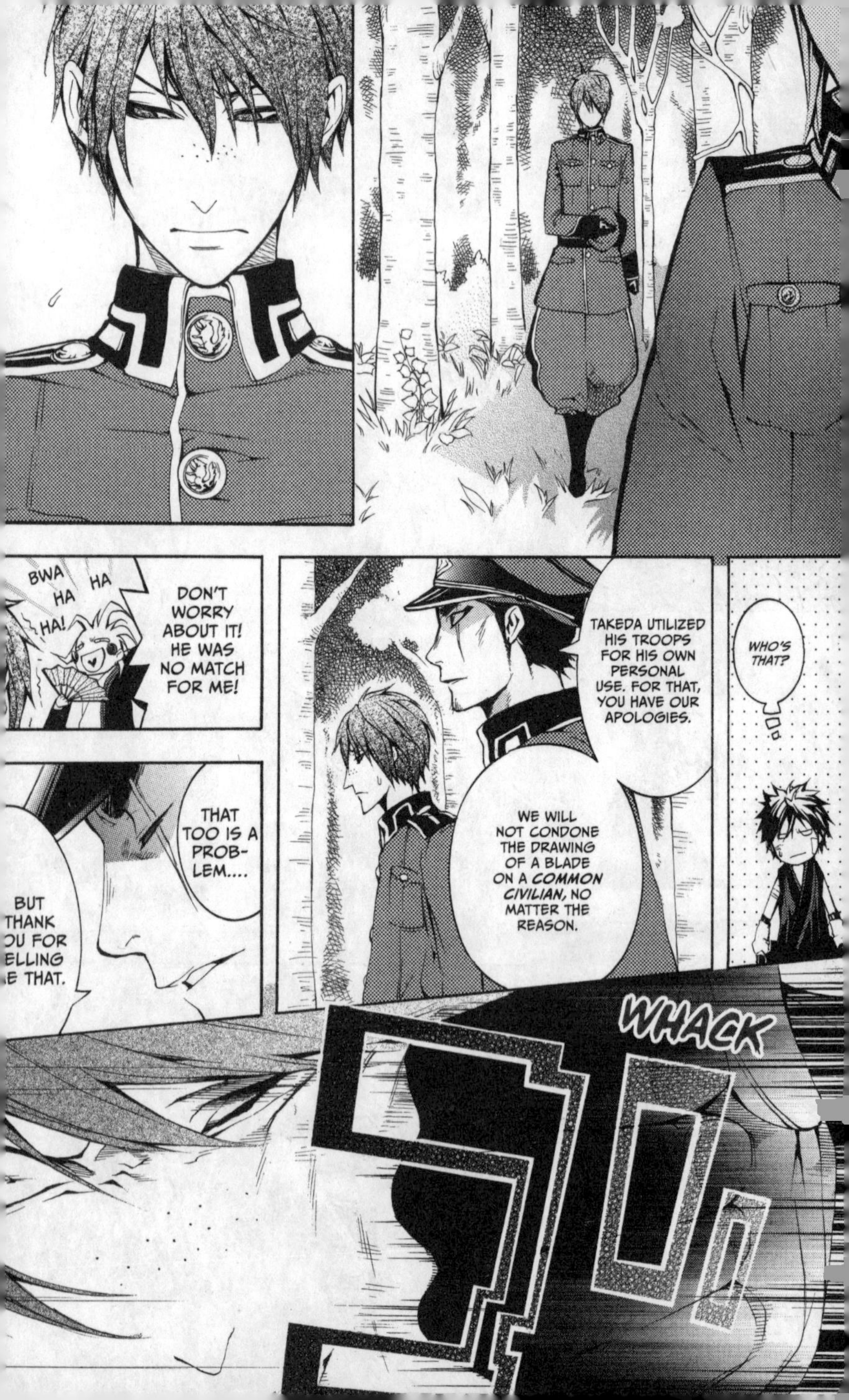
WHO'S THAT?
TAKEDA UTILIZED HIS TROOPS FOR HIS OWN PERSONAL USE. FOR THAT, YOU HAVE OUR APOLOGIES.
WE WILL NOT CONDONE THE DRAWING OF A BLADE ON A *COMMON CIVILIAN,* NO MATTER THE REASON.
BWA HA HA HA!
DON'T WORRY ABOUT IT! HE WAS NO MATCH FOR ME!
THAT TOO IS A PROB-LEM....
BUT THANK OU FOR ELLING E THAT.
WHACK

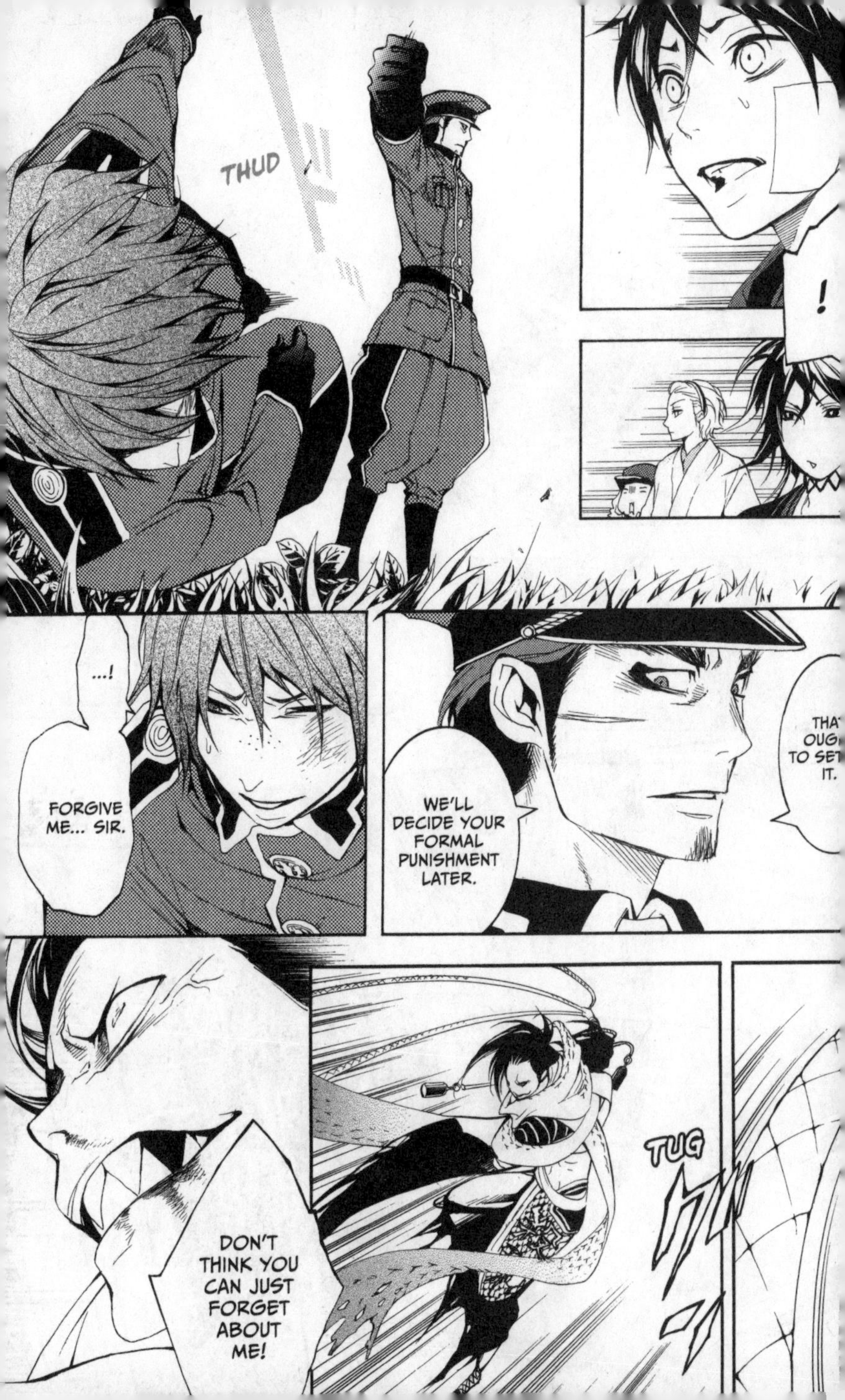
!
THUD
THA
OUG
TO SET
IT.
WE'LL DECIDE YOUR FORMAL PUNISHMENT LATER.
...!
FORGIVE ME... SIR.
TUG
DON'T THINK YOU CAN JUST FORGET ABOUT ME!

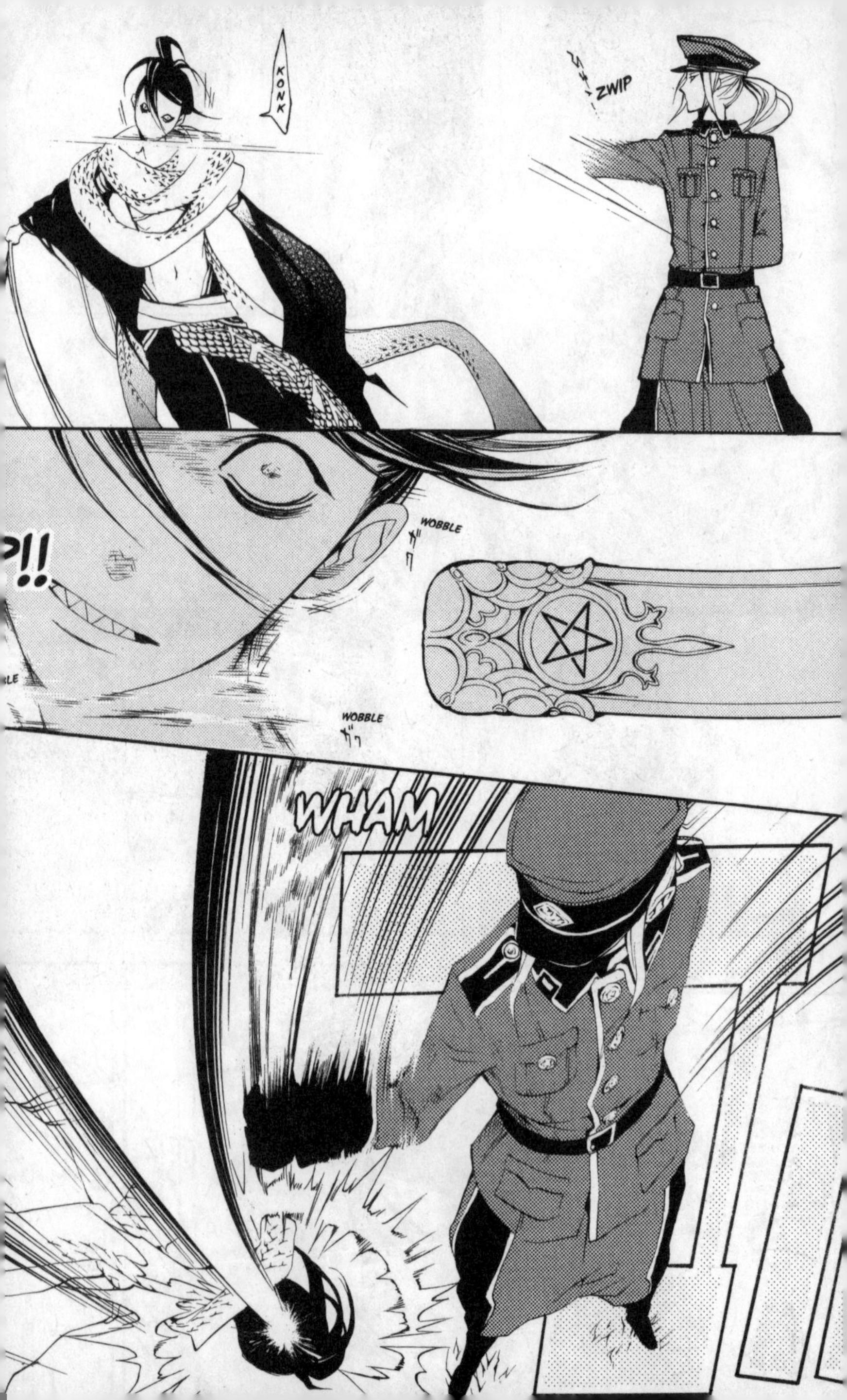
ZWIP
KONK
WOBBLE
WOBBLE
WHAM

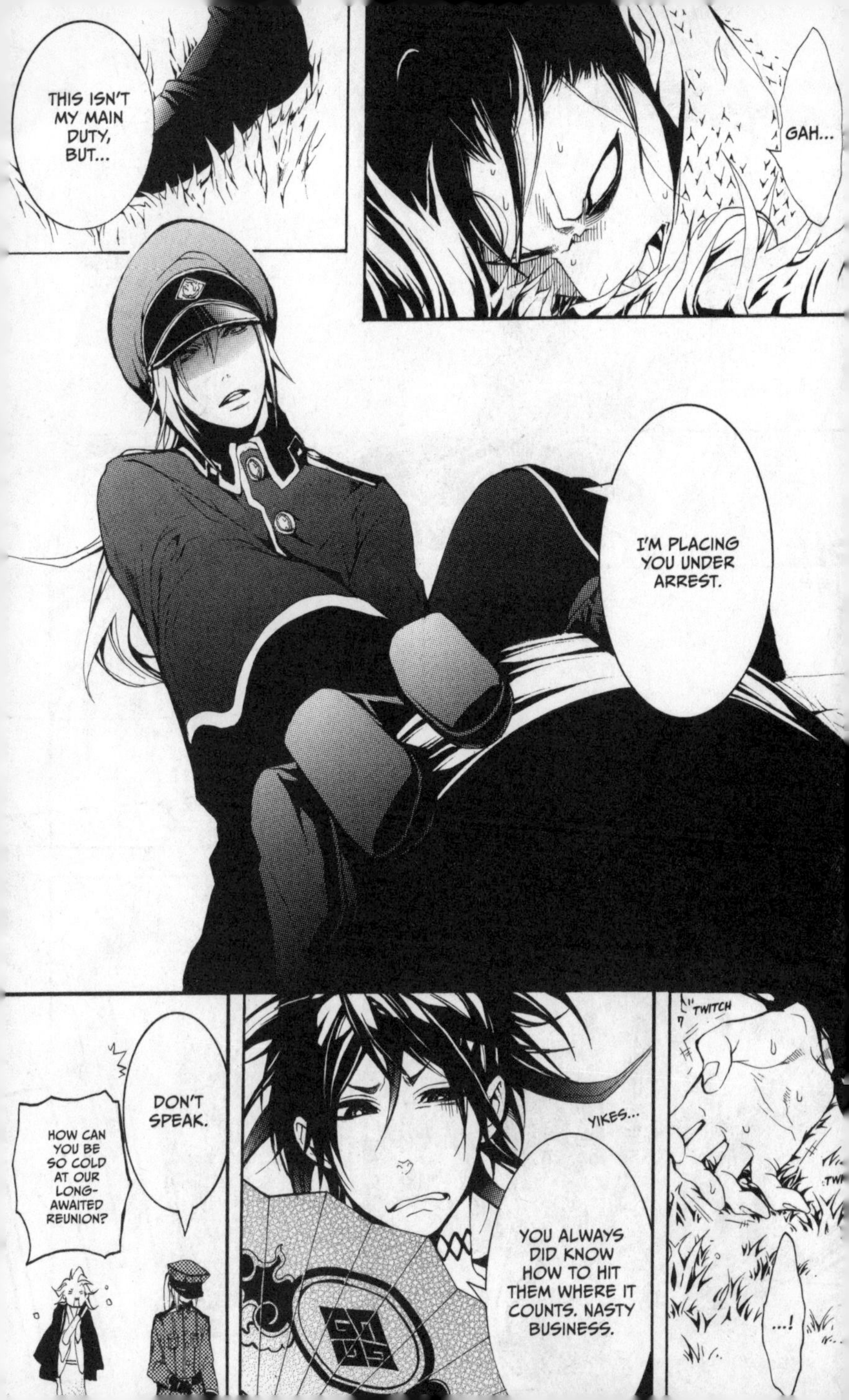
GAH...
THIS ISN'T MY MAIN DUTY, BUT...
I'M PLACING YOU UNDER ARREST.
TWITCH
...!
YIKES...
YOU ALWAYS DID KNOW HOW TO HIT THEM WHERE IT COUNTS. NASTY BUSINESS.
DON'T SPEAK.
HOW CAN YOU BE SO COLD AT OUR LONG-AWAITED REUNION?

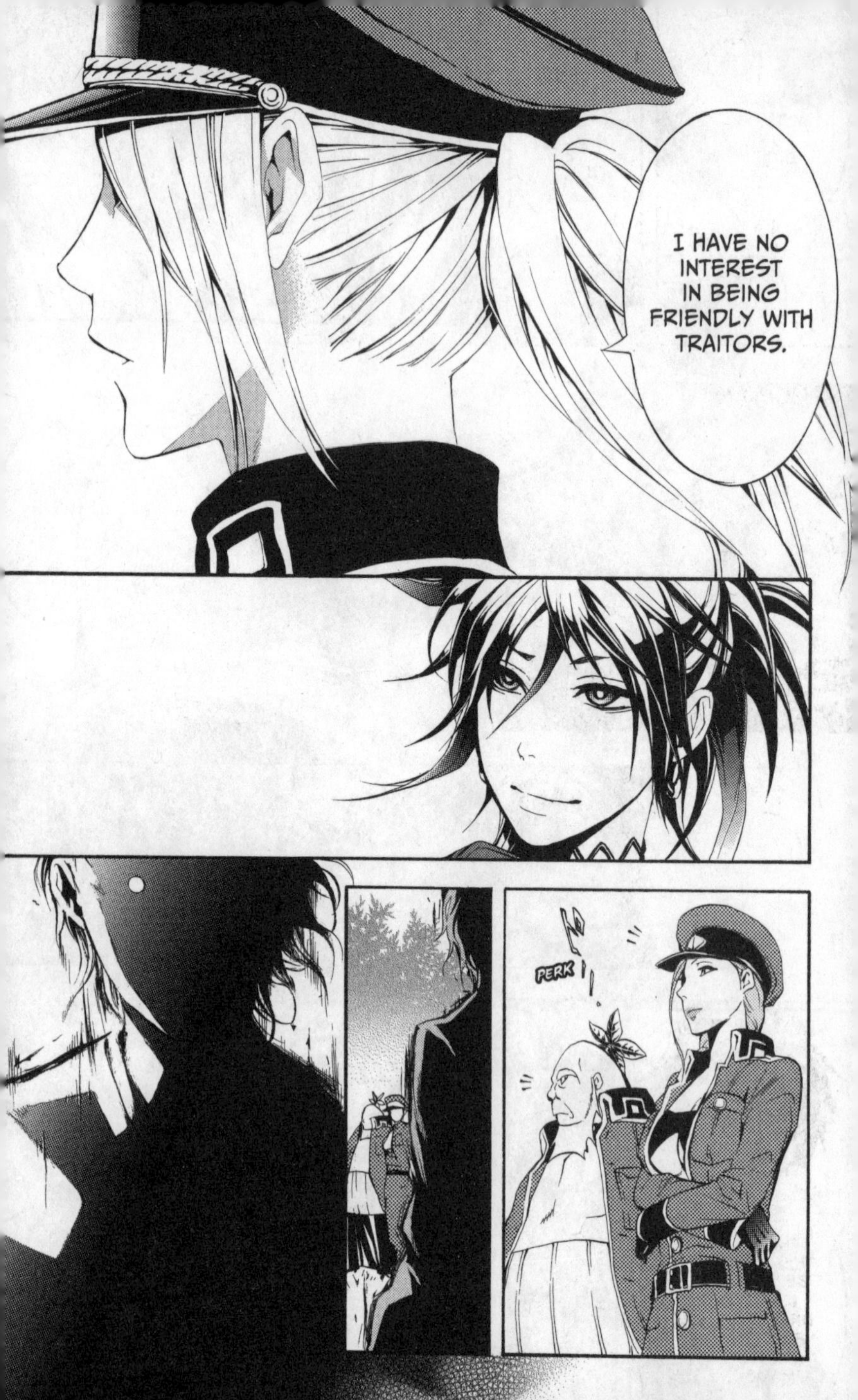
I HAVE NO INTEREST IN BEING FRIENDLY WITH TRAITORS.
PERK

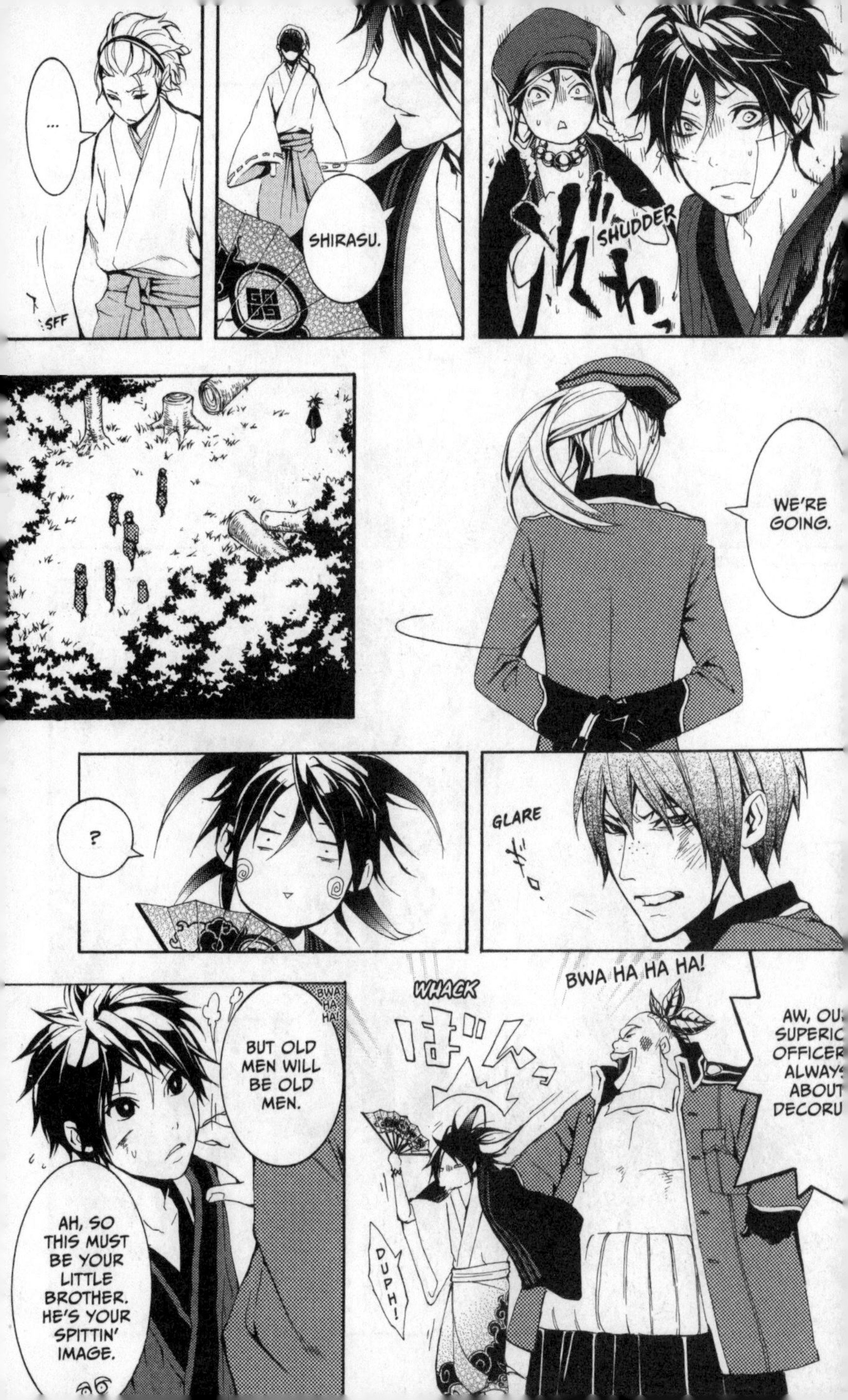
SHUDDER
SHIRASU.
...
SFF
WE'RE GOING.
GLARE
?
AW, OU SUPERIC OFFICER ALWAY ABOUT DECORU
BWA HA HA HA!
WHACK
DUPH!
BWA HA HA!
BUT OLD MEN WILL BE OLD MEN.
AH, SO THIS MUST BE YOUR LITTLE BROTHER. HE'S YOUR SPITTIN' IMAGE.

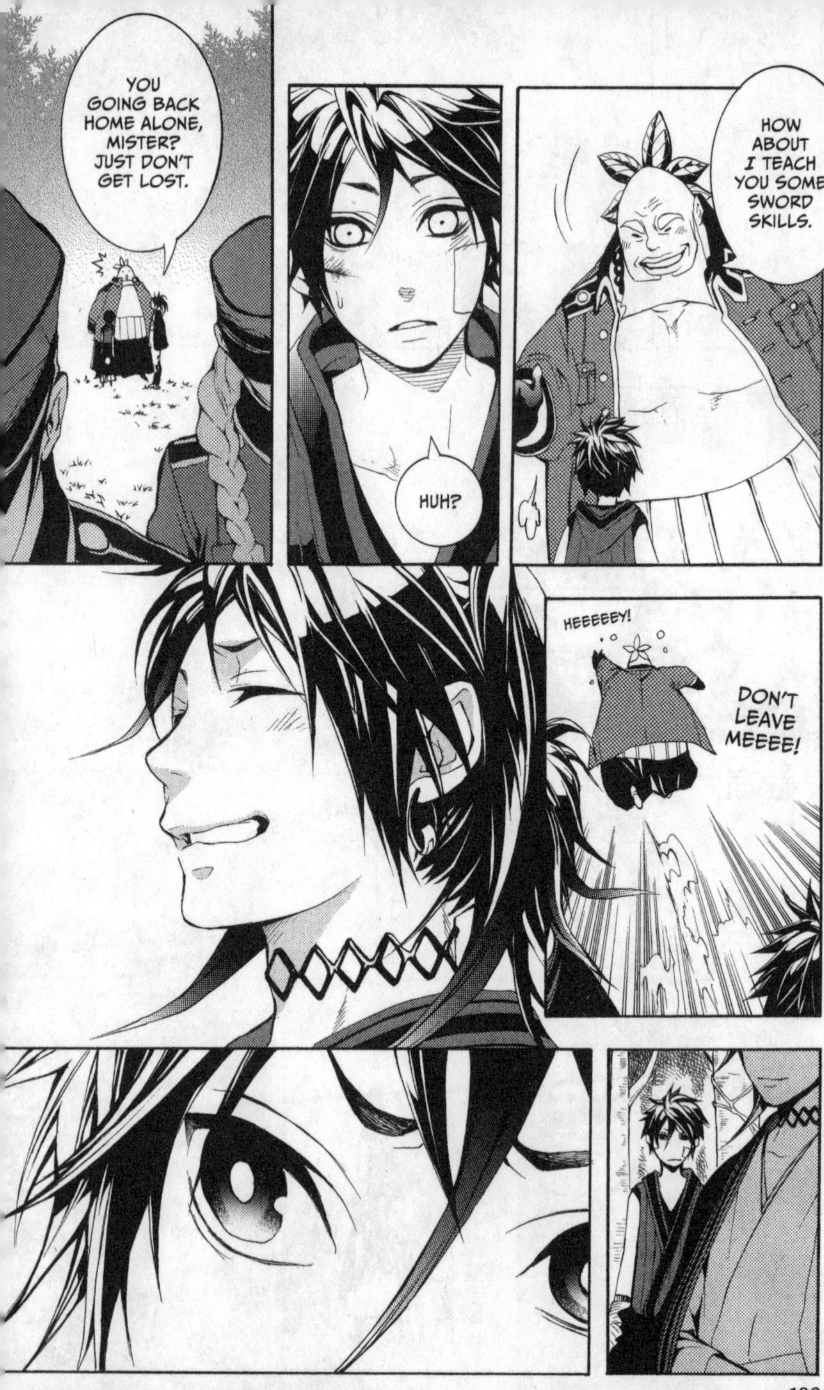
HOW ABOUT I TEACH YOU SOME SWORD SKILLS.
HUH?
YOU GOING BACK HOME ALONE, MISTER? JUST DON'T GET LOST.
HEEEEEY!
DON'T LEAVE MEEEE!

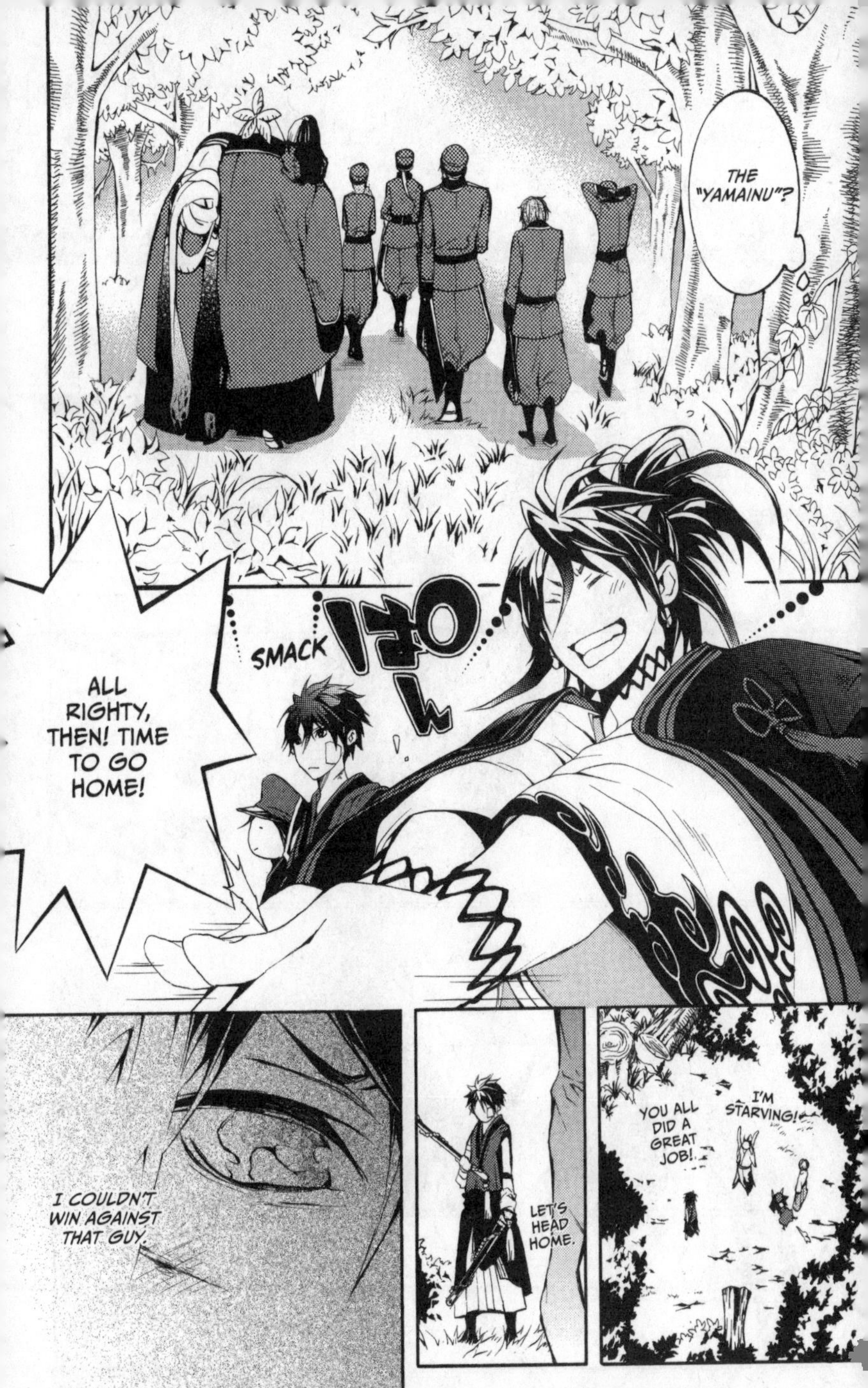
THE "YAMAINU"?
OW!
SMACK
ALL RIGHTY, THEN! TIME TO GO HOME!
I'M STARVING!
YOU ALL DID A GREAT JOB!
LET'S HEAD HOME.
I COULDN'T WIN AGAINST THAT GUY.

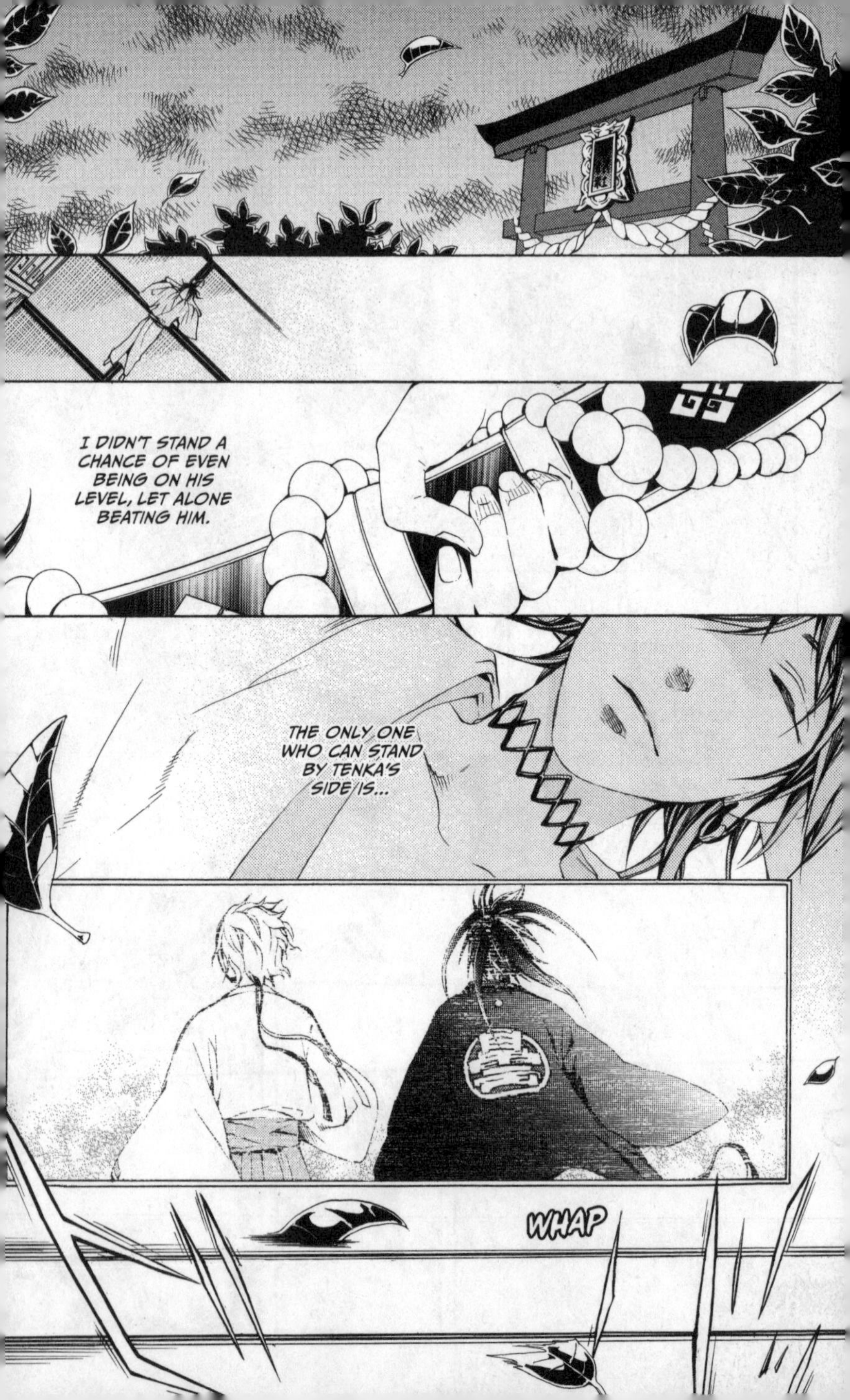
I DIDN'T STAND A CHANCE OF EVEN BEING ON HIS LEVEL, LET ALONE BEATING HIM.
THE ONLY ONE WHO CAN STAND BY TENKA'S SIDE IS...
WHAP

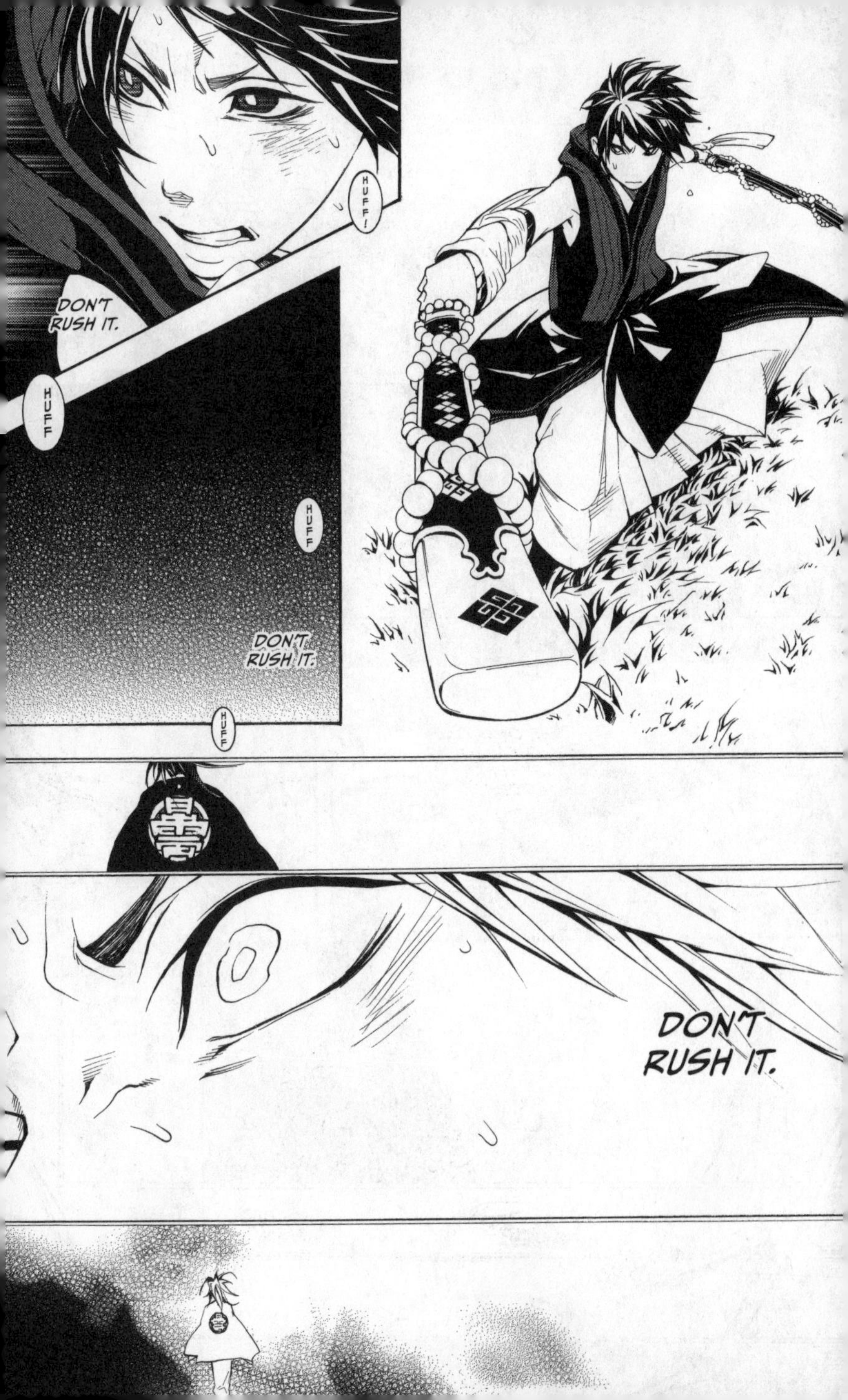
HUFF!
DON'T RUSH IT.
HUFF
HUFF
DON'T RUSH IT.
HUFF
DON'T RUSH IT.

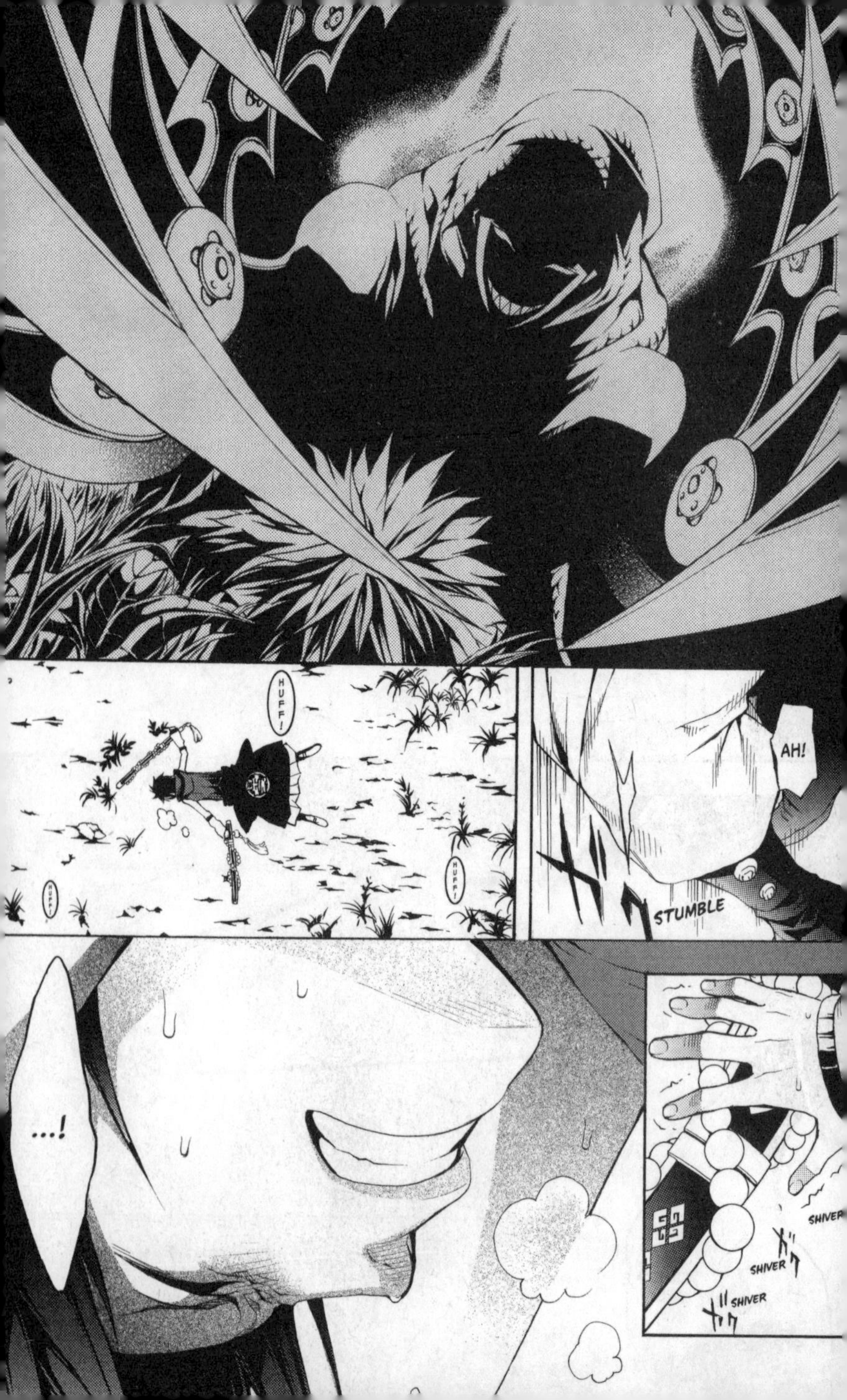
AH!
STUMBLE
HUFF!
HUFF!
HUFF!
SHIVER
SHIVER
SHIVER
...!

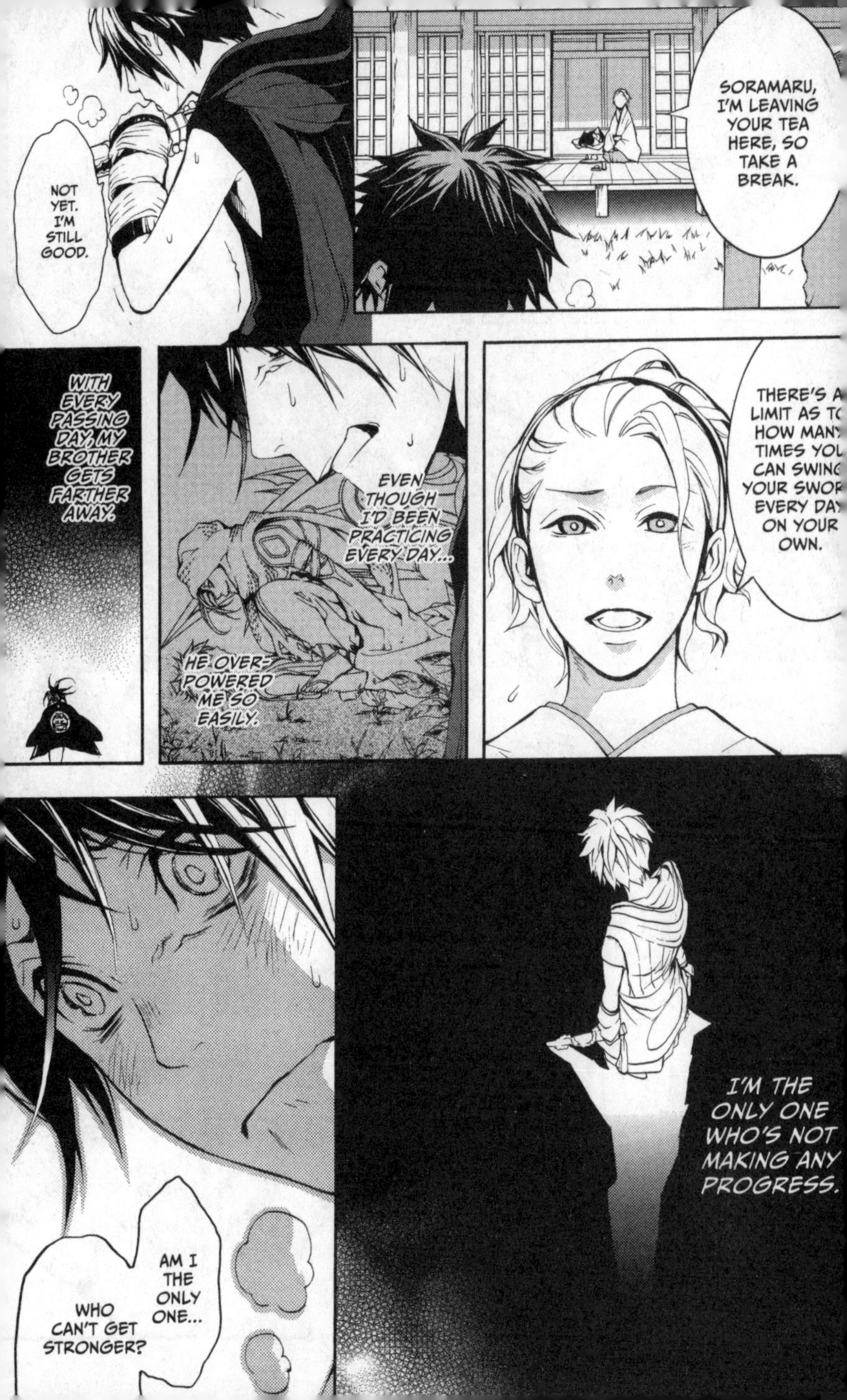
SORAMARU, I'M LEAVING YOUR TEA HERE, SO TAKE A BREAK.
NOT YET. I'M STILL GOOD.
THERE'S A LIMIT AS TO HOW MANY TIMES YOU CAN SWING YOUR SWOR EVERY DAY ON YOUR OWN.
EVEN THOUGH I'D BEEN PRACTICING EVERY DAY...
HE OVER-POWERED ME SO EASILY.
WITH EVERY PASSING DAY, MY BROTHER GETS FARTHER AWAY.
I'M THE ONLY ONE WHO'S NOT MAKING ANY PROGRESS.
AM I THE ONLY ONE...
WHO CAN'T GET STRONGER?

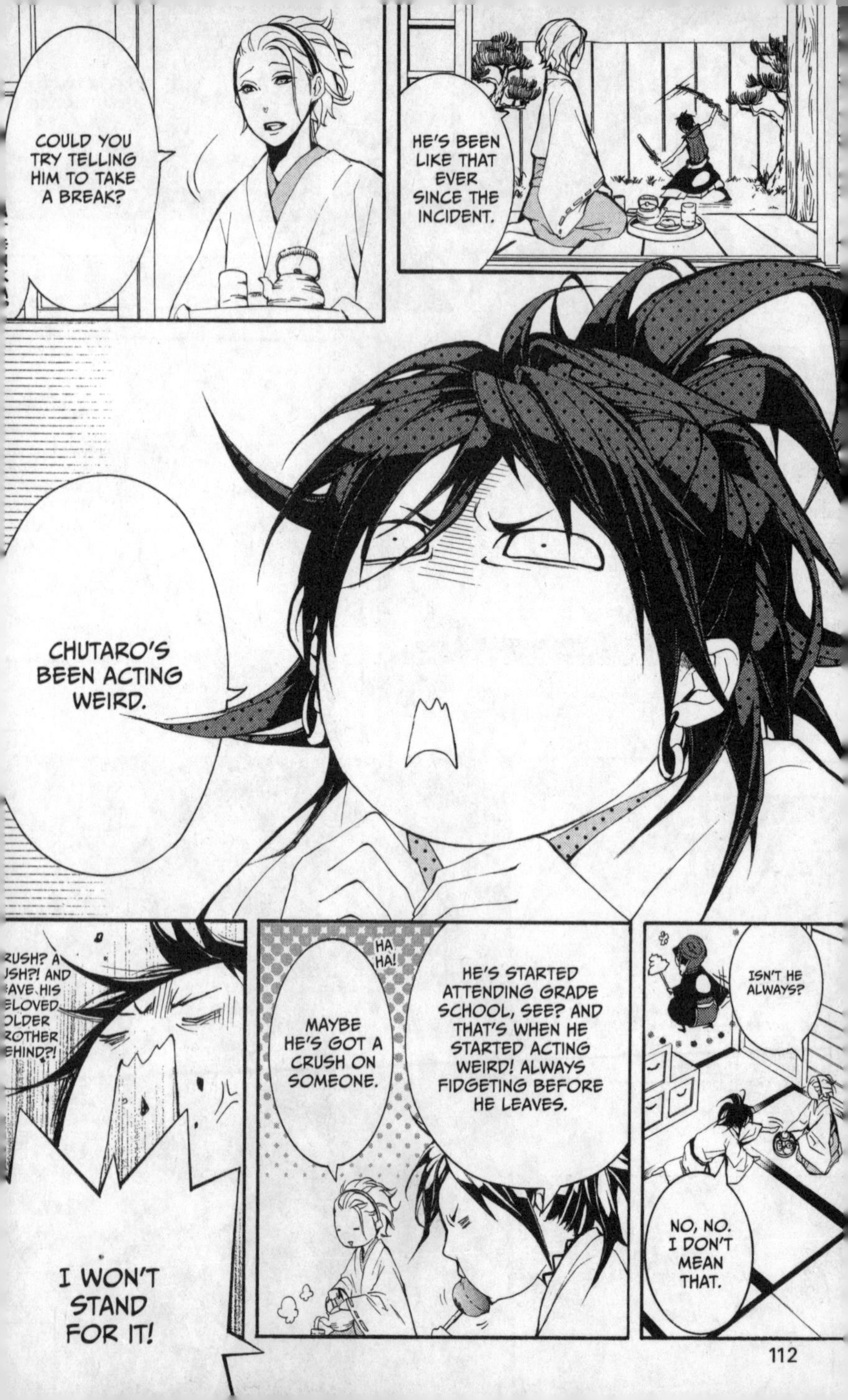
HE'S BEEN LIKE THAT EVER SINCE THE INCIDENT.
COULD YOU TRY TELLING HIM TO TAKE A BREAK?
CHUTARO'S BEEN ACTING WEIRD.
ISN'T HE ALWAYS?
NO, NO. I DON'T MEAN THAT.
HE'S STARTED ATTENDING GRADE SCHOOL, SEE? AND THAT'S WHEN HE STARTED ACTING WEIRD! ALWAYS FIDGETING BEFORE HE LEAVES.
HA HA!
MAYBE HE'S GOT A CRUSH ON SOMEONE.
RUSH? A USH?! AND AVE HIS ELOVED OLDER ROTHER EHIND?!
I WON'T STAND FOR IT!

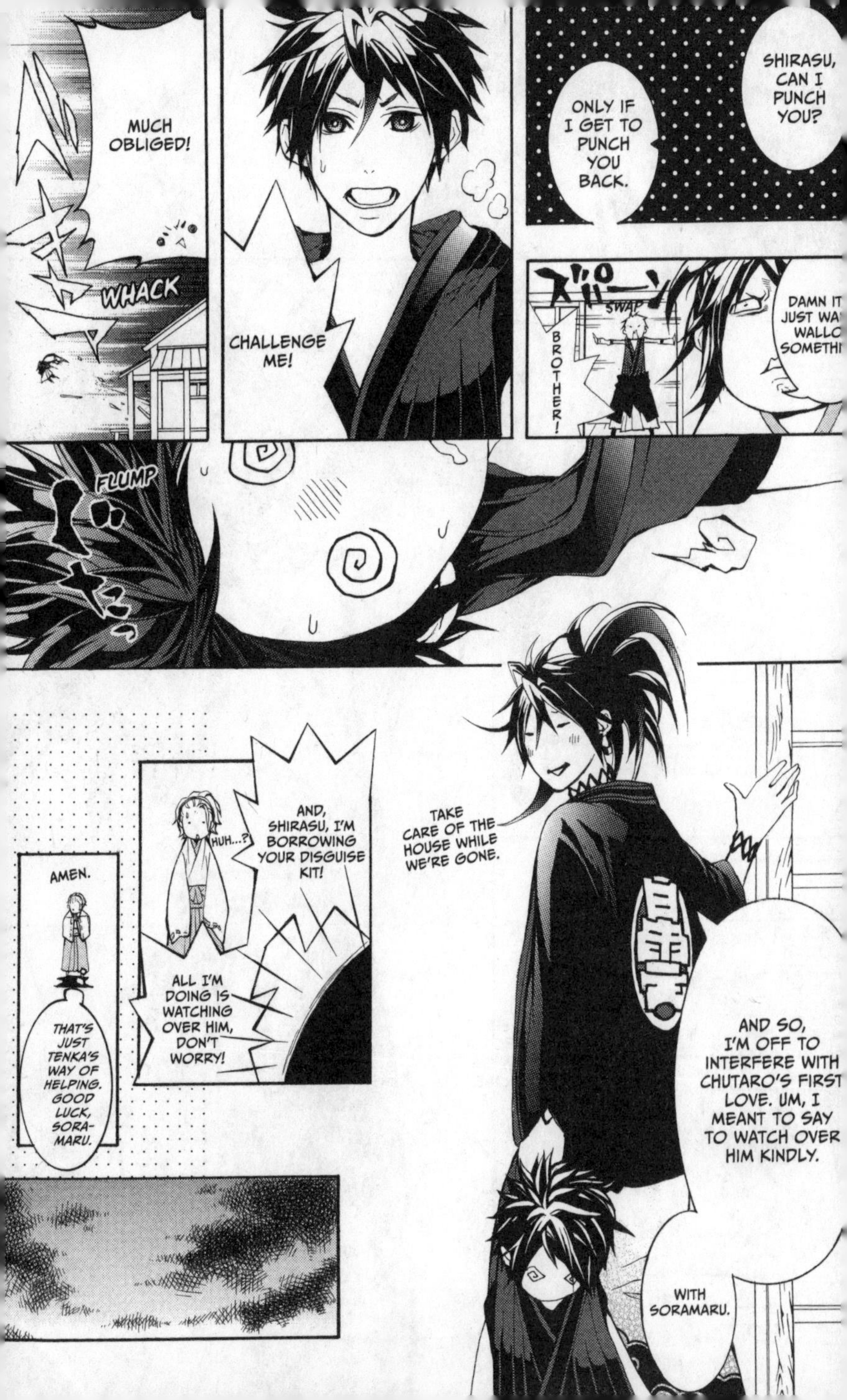
SHIRASU, CAN I PUNCH YOU?
ONLY IF I GET TO PUNCH YOU BACK.
DAMN IT JUST WA WALLO SOMETHI
SWAP
BROTHER!
CHALLENGE ME!
MUCH OBLIGED!
WHACK
FLUMP
TAKE CARE OF THE HOUSE WHILE WE'RE GONE.
AND SO, I'M OFF TO INTERFERE WITH CHUTARO'S FIRST LOVE. UM, I MEANT TO SAY TO WATCH OVER HIM KINDLY.
WITH SORAMARU.
AND, SHIRASU, I'M BORROWING YOUR DISGUISE KIT!
HUH...?
ALL I'M DOING IS WATCHING OVER HIM, DON'T WORRY!
AMEN.
THAT'S JUST TENKA'S WAY OF HELPING. GOOD LUCK, SORAMARU.

HM...?

WHAT [AR]E YOU [DO]ING?!

BROTH[ER]

QUIT STRUGGLING. YOU'RE SUPPOSED TO BE A BABY.

I'M TOO BIG TO BE A BABY!

JUST PUT UP WITH IT. WE HAVE TO BLEND IN ORDER NOT TO BE SPOTTED BY CHUTARO.

WE STAND OUT EVEN MORE THIS WAY!

PATIENCE, PATIENCE.

MURMUR

[Y]OU'RE [IM]AGING [T]HINGS.

[L]EAST [I]T ME [D]OWN!

BWA— HA HA HA HA!

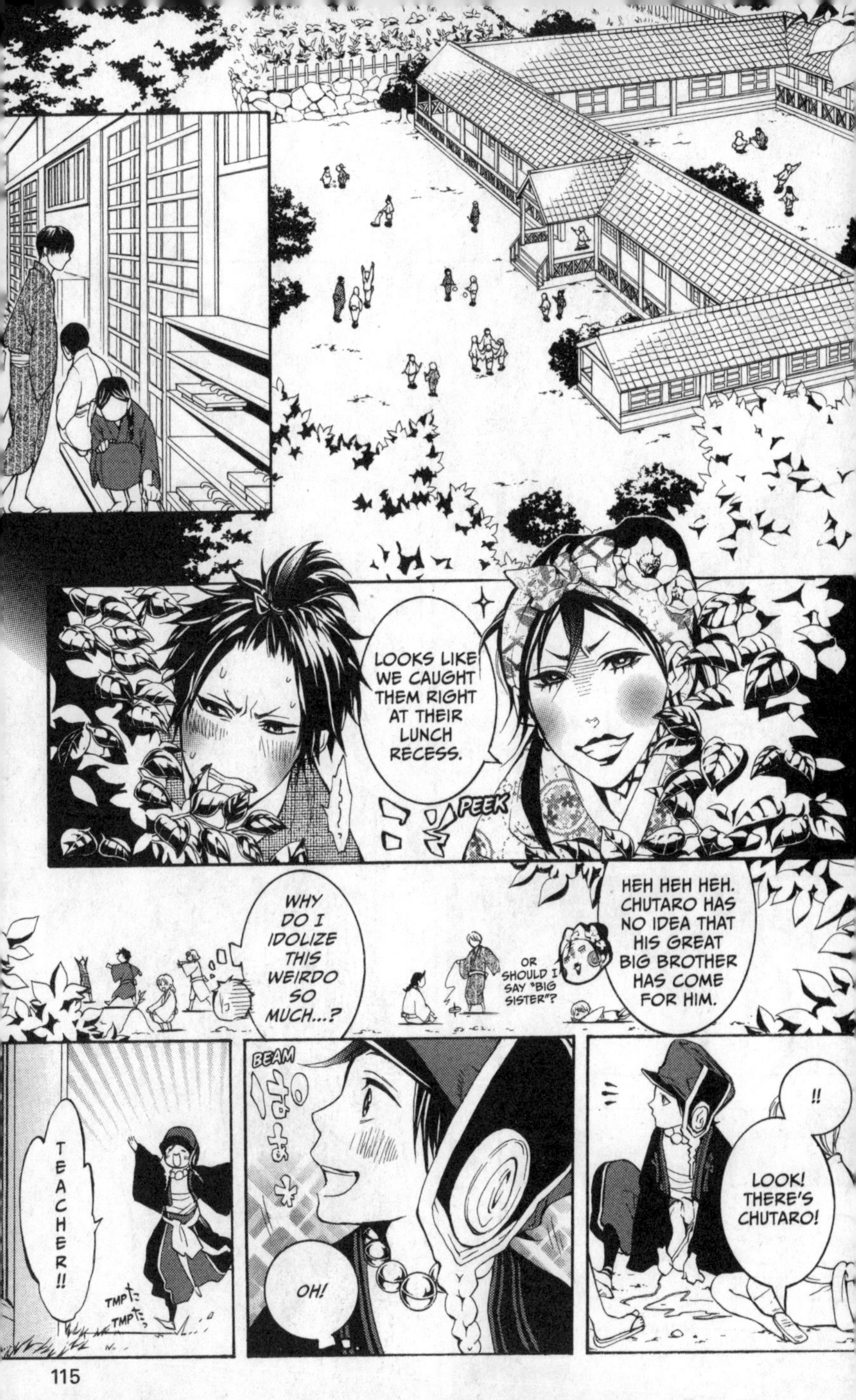
LOOKS LIKE WE CAUGHT THEM RIGHT AT THEIR LUNCH RECESS.
PEEK
HEH HEH HEH. CHUTARO HAS NO IDEA THAT HIS GREAT BIG BROTHER HAS COME FOR HIM.
OR SHOULD I SAY "BIG SISTER"?
WHY DO I IDOLIZE THIS WEIRDO SO MUCH...?
!!
LOOK! THERE'S CHUTARO!
BEAM
OH!
TEACHER!!
TMP
TMP

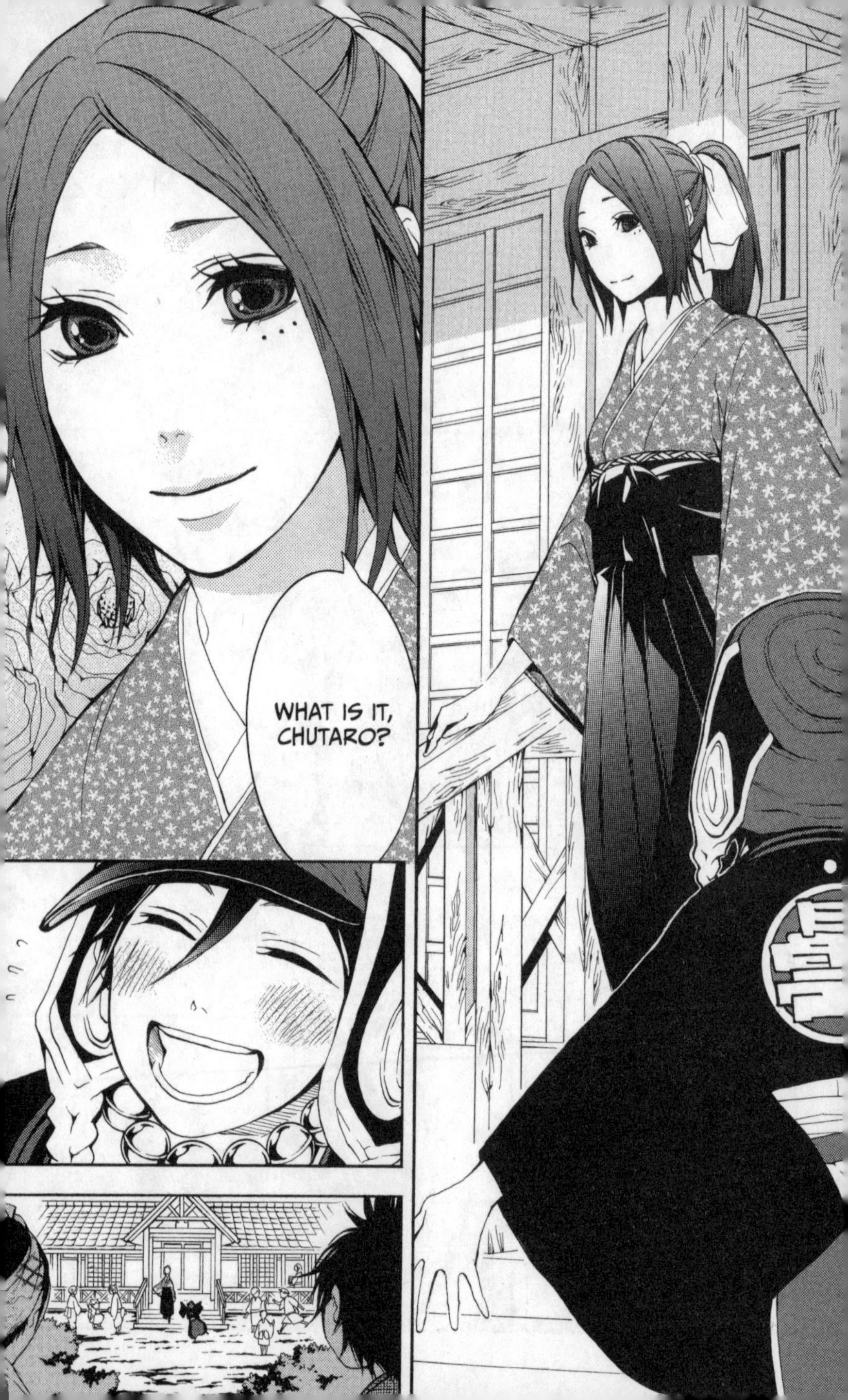
WHAT IS IT, CHUTARO?

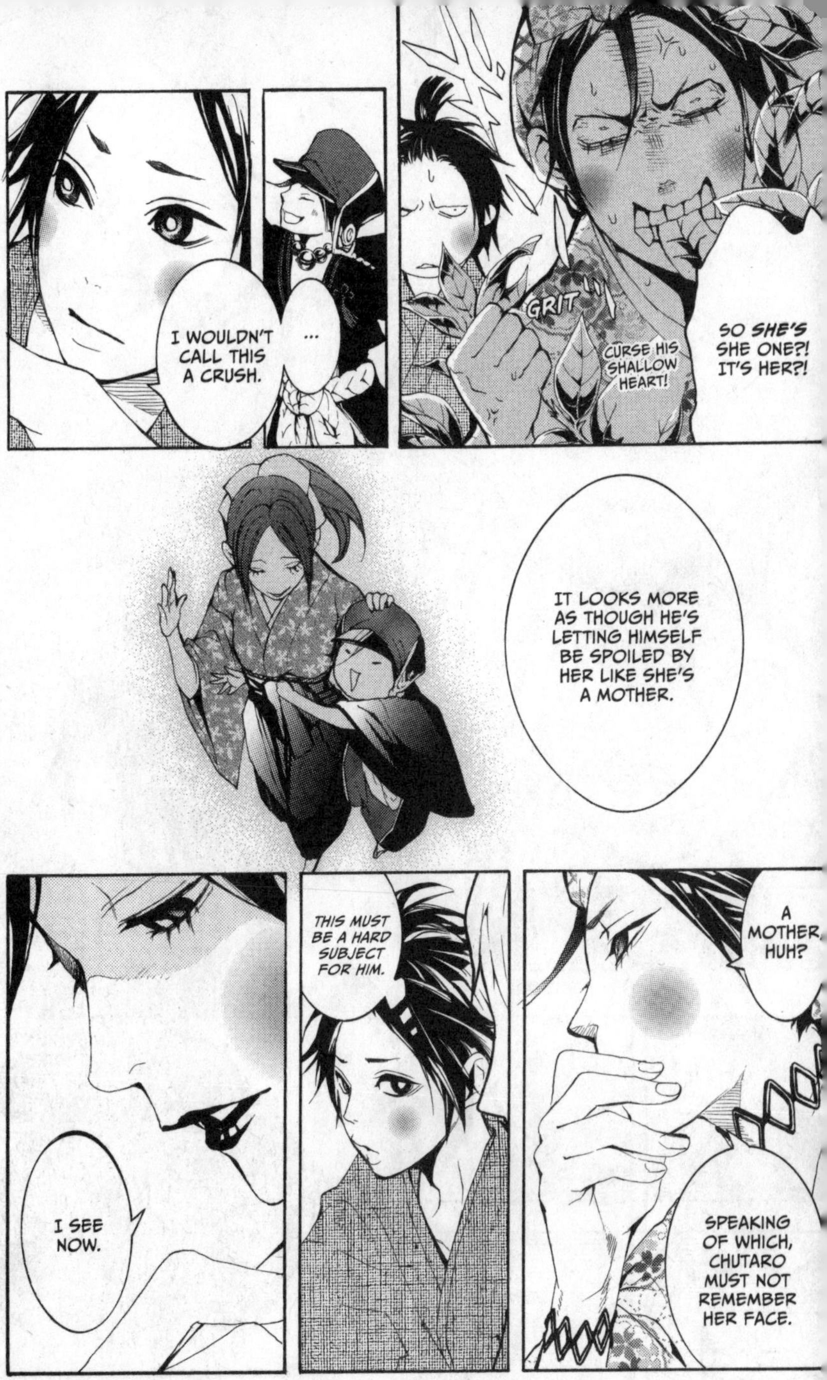
SO SHE'S SHE ONE?! IT'S HER?!
GRIT
CURSE HIS SHALLOW HEART!
...
I WOULDN'T CALL THIS A CRUSH.
IT LOOKS MORE AS THOUGH HE'S LETTING HIMSELF BE SPOILED BY HER LIKE SHE'S A MOTHER.
A MOTHER HUH?
SPEAKING OF WHICH, CHUTARO MUST NOT REMEMBER HER FACE.
THIS MUST BE A HARD SUBJECT FOR HIM.
I SEE NOW.

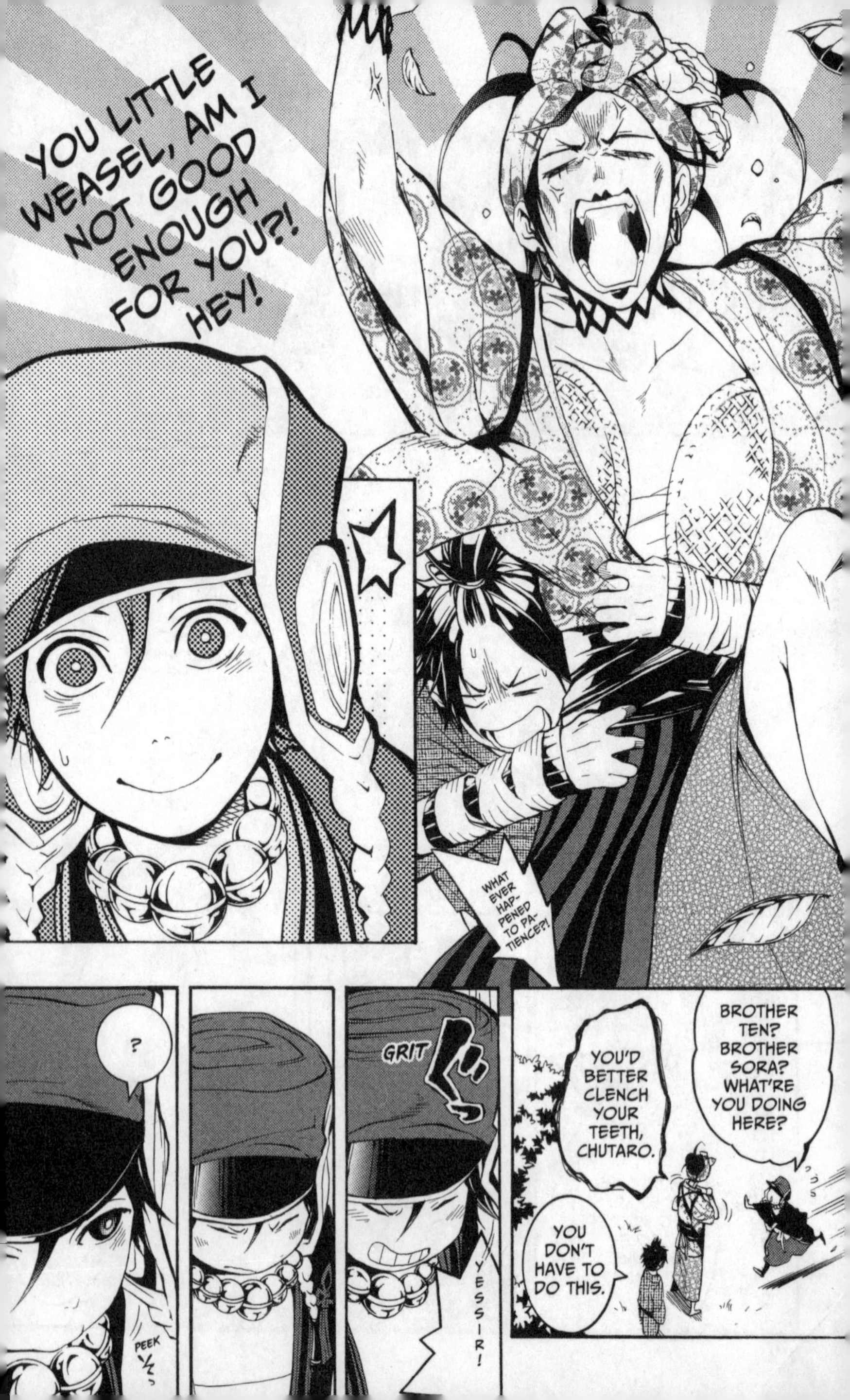
YOU LITTLE WEASEL, AM I NOT GOOD ENOUGH FOR YOU?! HEY!
WHAT EVER HAPPENED TO PATIENCE?!
BROTHER TEN? BROTHER SORA? WHAT'RE YOU DOING HERE?
YOU'D BETTER CLENCH YOUR TEETH, CHUTARO.
YOU DON'T HAVE TO DO THIS.
GRIT
YESSIR!
?
PEEK

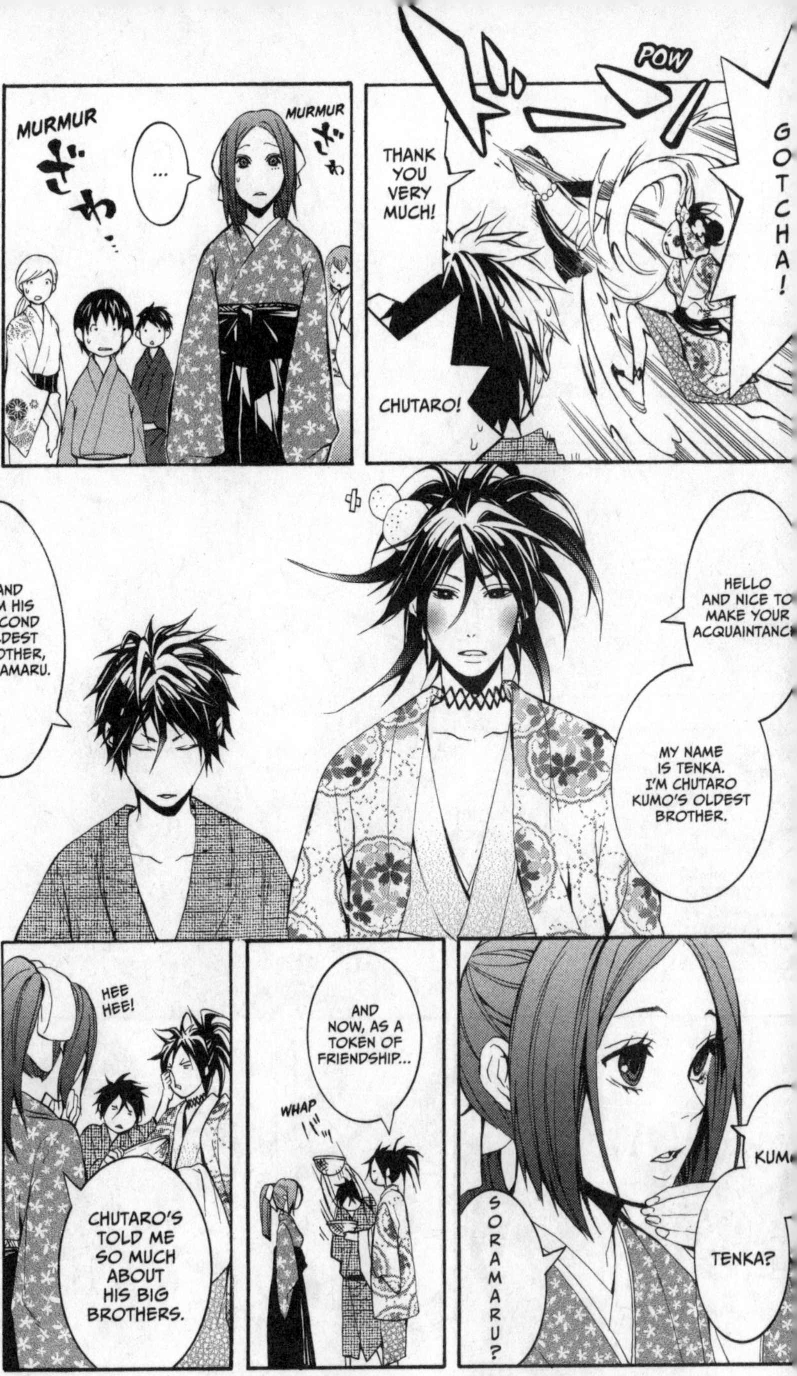
POW
GOTCHA!
THANK YOU VERY MUCH!
CHUTARO!
MURMUR
ざわ
...
MURMUR
ざわ
HELLO AND NICE TO MAKE YOUR ACQUAINTANC
MY NAME IS TENKA. I'M CHUTARO KUMO'S OLDEST BROTHER.
AND I'M HIS SECOND OLDEST BROTHER, SORAMARU.
KUM
TENKA?
SORAMARU?
AND NOW, AS A TOKEN OF FRIENDSHIP...
WHAP
バッ
HEE HEE!
CHUTARO'S TOLD ME SO MUCH ABOUT HIS BIG BROTHERS.

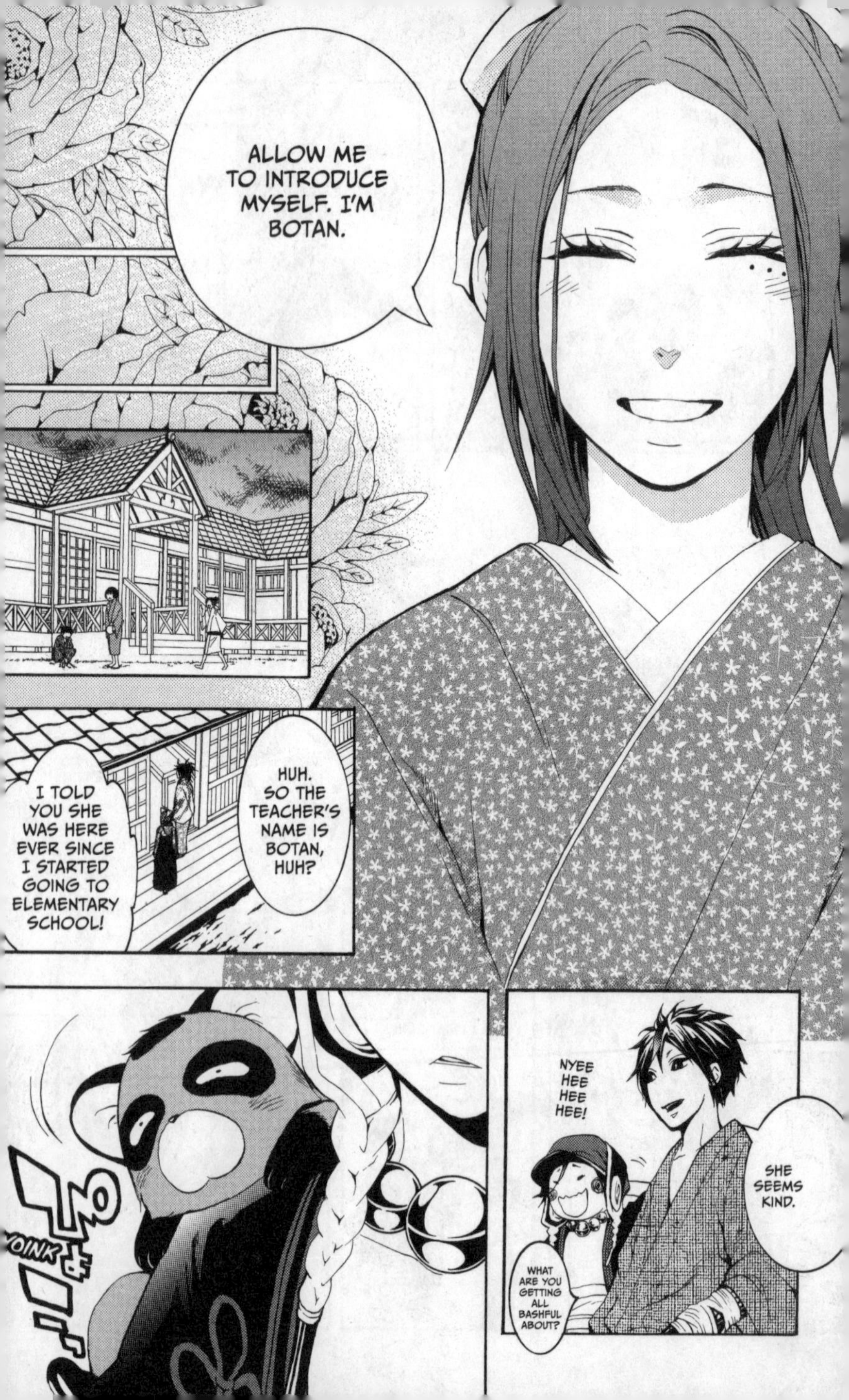
ALLOW ME TO INTRODUCE MYSELF. I'M BOTAN.
HUH. SO THE TEACHER'S NAME IS BOTAN, HUH?
I TOLD YOU SHE WAS HERE EVER SINCE I STARTED GOING TO ELEMENTARY SCHOOL!
SHE SEEMS KIND.
NYEE HEE HEE HEE!
WHAT ARE YOU GETTING ALL BASHFUL ABOUT?
YOINK

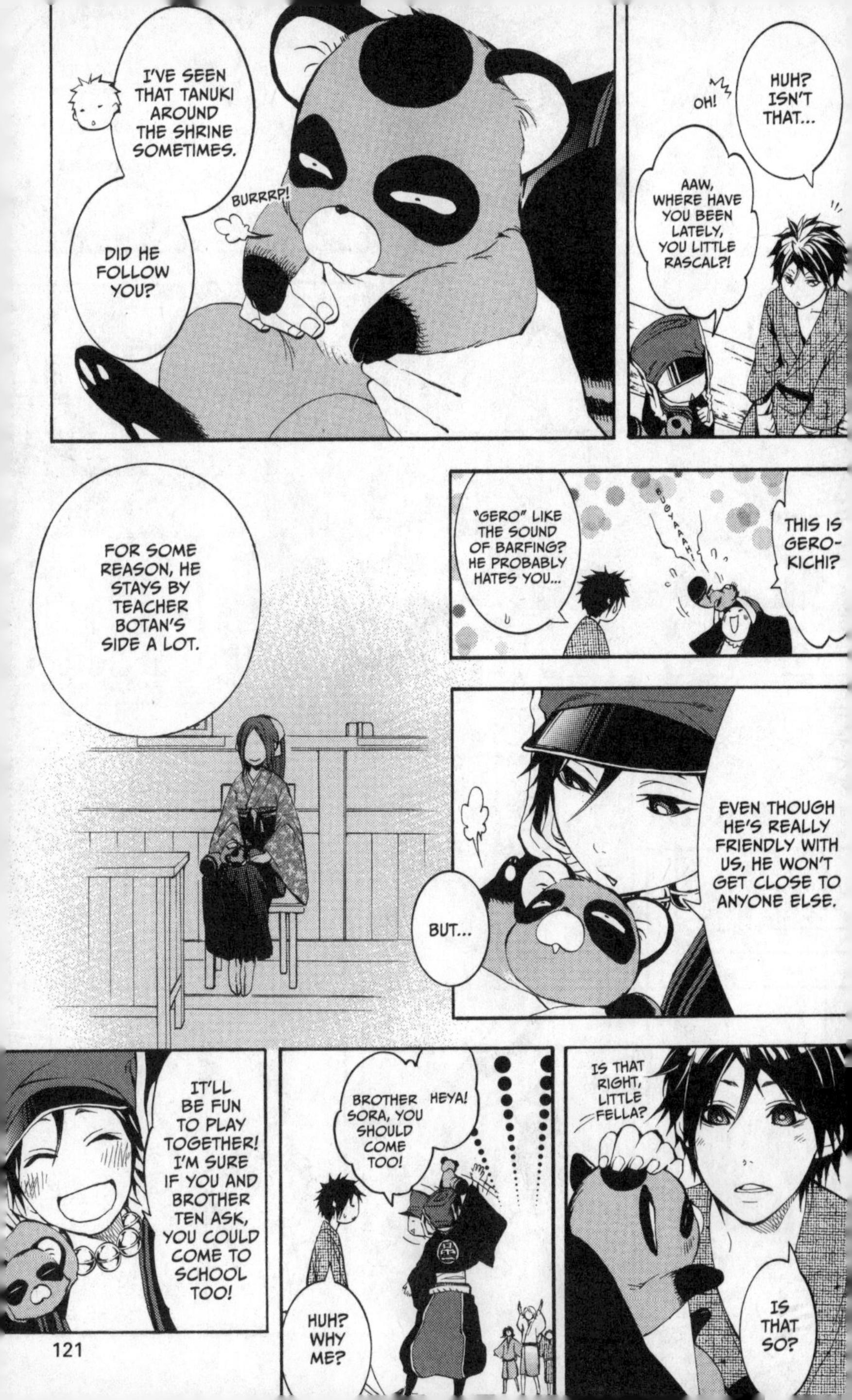
HUH? ISN'T THAT...
OH!
AAW, WHERE HAVE YOU BEEN LATELY, YOU LITTLE RASCAL?!
I'VE SEEN THAT TANUKI AROUND THE SHRINE SOMETIMES.
BURRRP!
DID HE FOLLOW YOU?
THIS IS GERO-KICHI?
"GERO" LIKE THE SOUND OF BARFING? HE PROBABLY HATES YOU...
EVEN THOUGH HE'S REALLY FRIENDLY WITH US, HE WON'T GET CLOSE TO ANYONE ELSE.
BUT...
FOR SOME REASON, HE STAYS BY TEACHER BOTAN'S SIDE A LOT.
IS THAT RIGHT, LITTLE FELLA?
IS THAT SO?
HEYA!
BROTHER SORA, YOU SHOULD COME TOO!
HUH? WHY ME?
IT'LL BE FUN TO PLAY TOGETHER! I'M SURE IF YOU AND BROTHER TEN ASK, YOU COULD COME TO SCHOOL TOO!

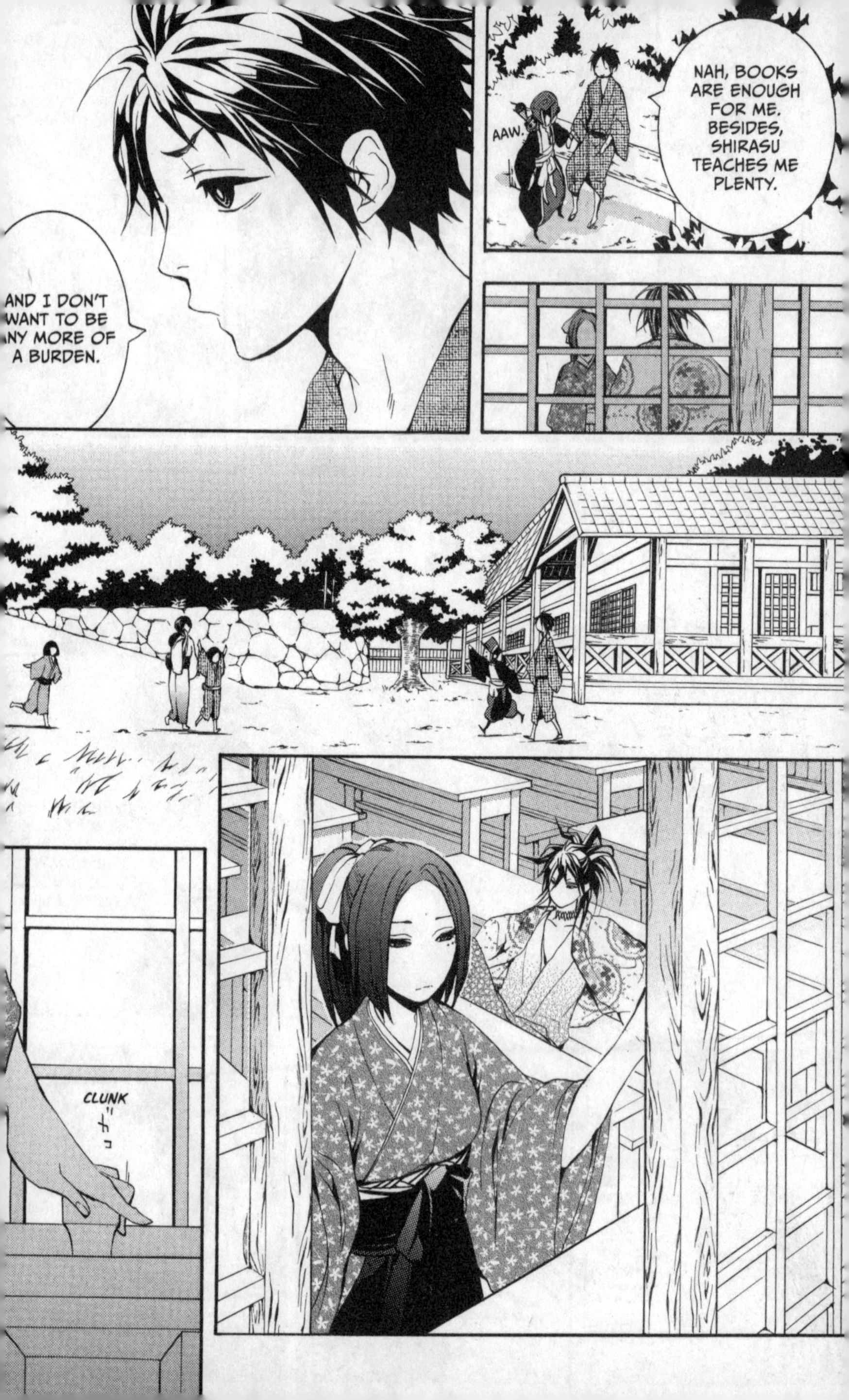
NAH, BOOKS ARE ENOUGH FOR ME. BESIDES, SHIRASU TEACHES ME PLENTY.
AAW.
AND I DON'T WANT TO BE ANY MORE OF A BURDEN.
CLUNK
ガコ

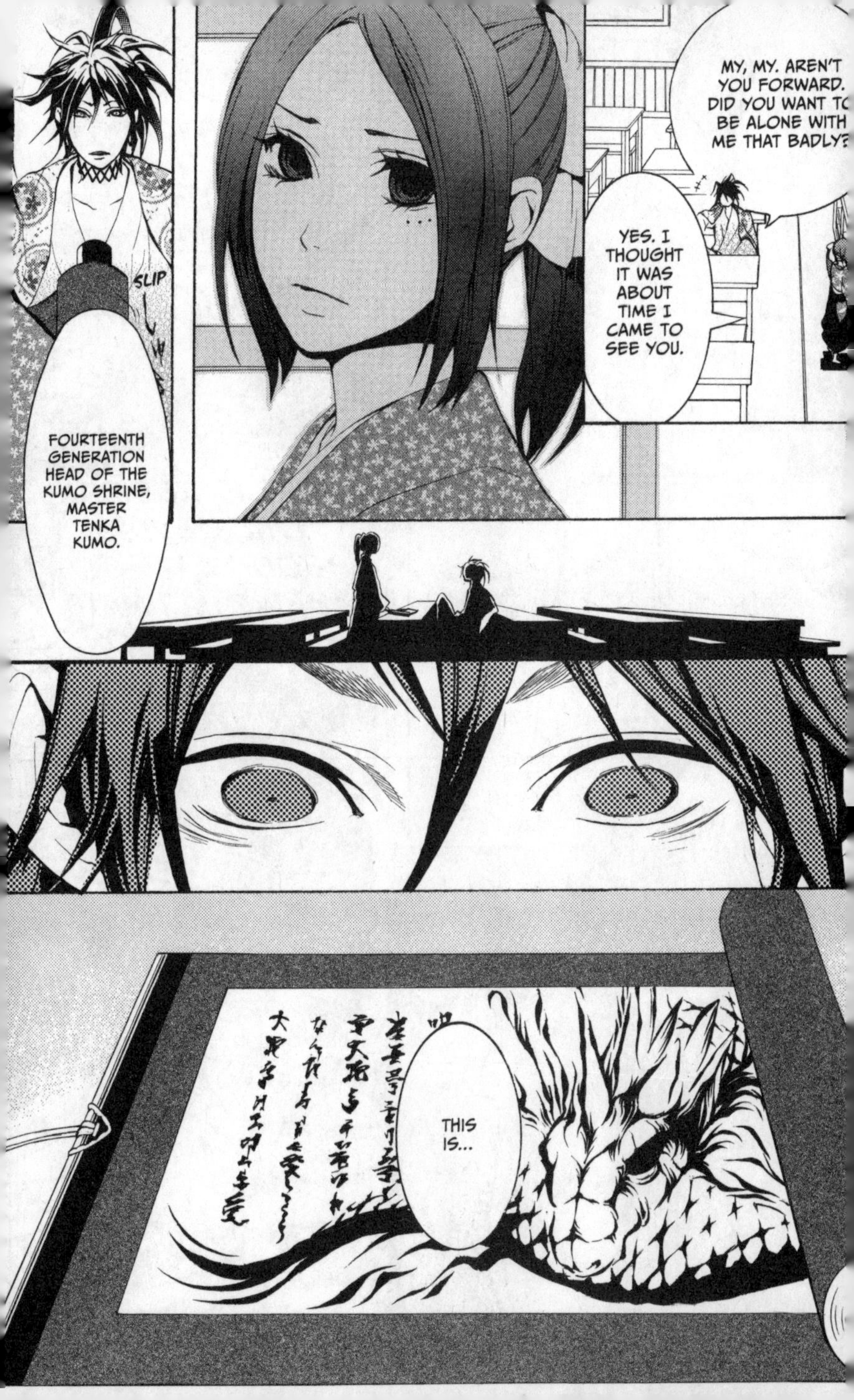
MY, MY. AREN'T YOU FORWARD. DID YOU WANT TO BE ALONE WITH ME THAT BADLY?
YES. I THOUGHT IT WAS ABOUT TIME I CAME TO SEE YOU.
SLIP
FOURTEENTH GENERATION HEAD OF THE KUMO SHRINE, MASTER TENKA KUMO.
THIS IS...

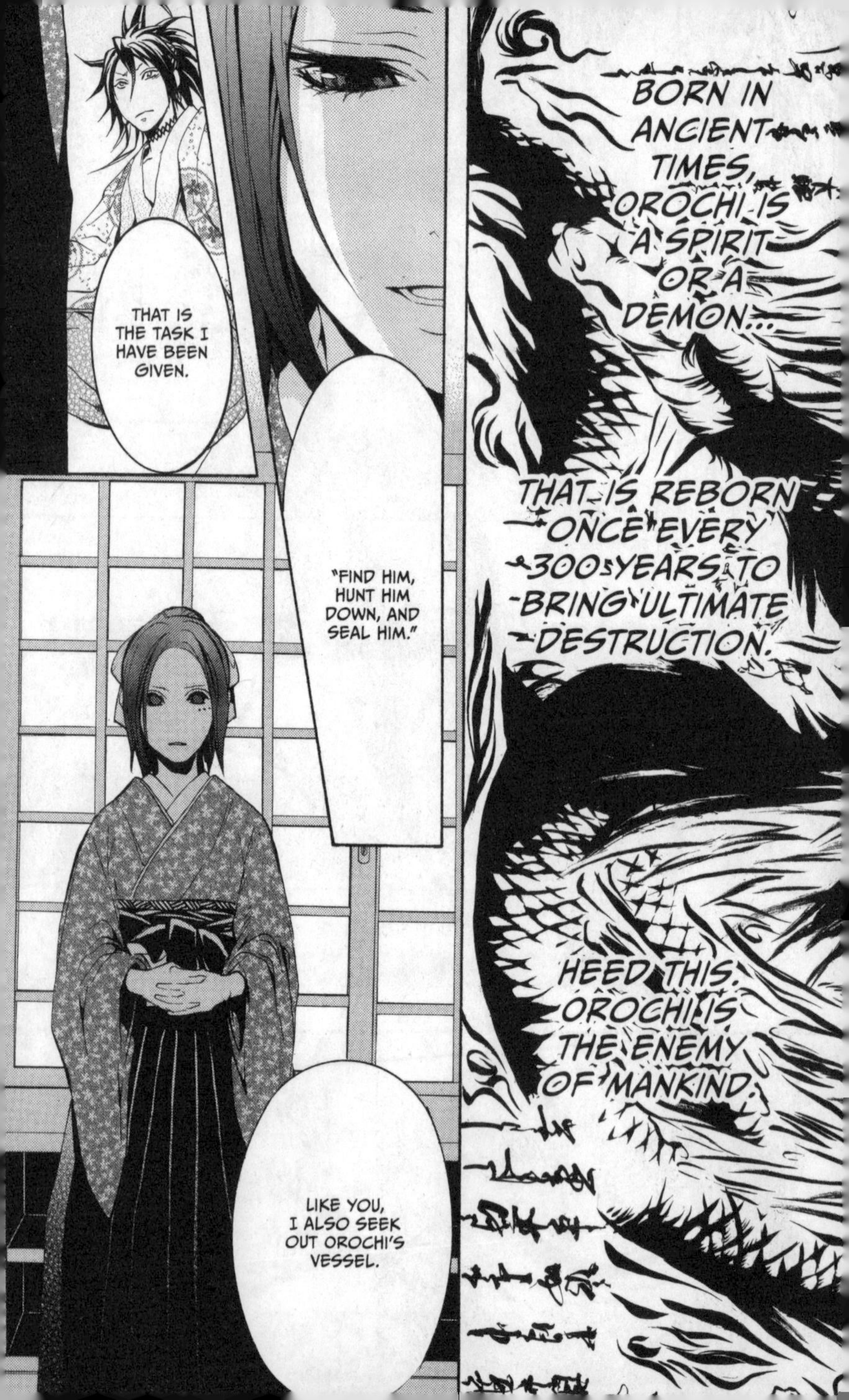
BORN IN ANCIENT TIMES, OROCHI IS A SPIRIT OR A DEMON...
THAT IS REBORN ONCE EVERY 300 YEARS TO BRING ULTIMATE DESTRUCTION.
HEED THIS. OROCHI IS THE ENEMY OF MANKIND.
"FIND HIM, HUNT HIM DOWN, AND SEAL HIM."
THAT IS THE TASK I HAVE BEEN GIVEN.
LIKE YOU, I ALSO SEEK OUT OROCHI'S VESSEL.

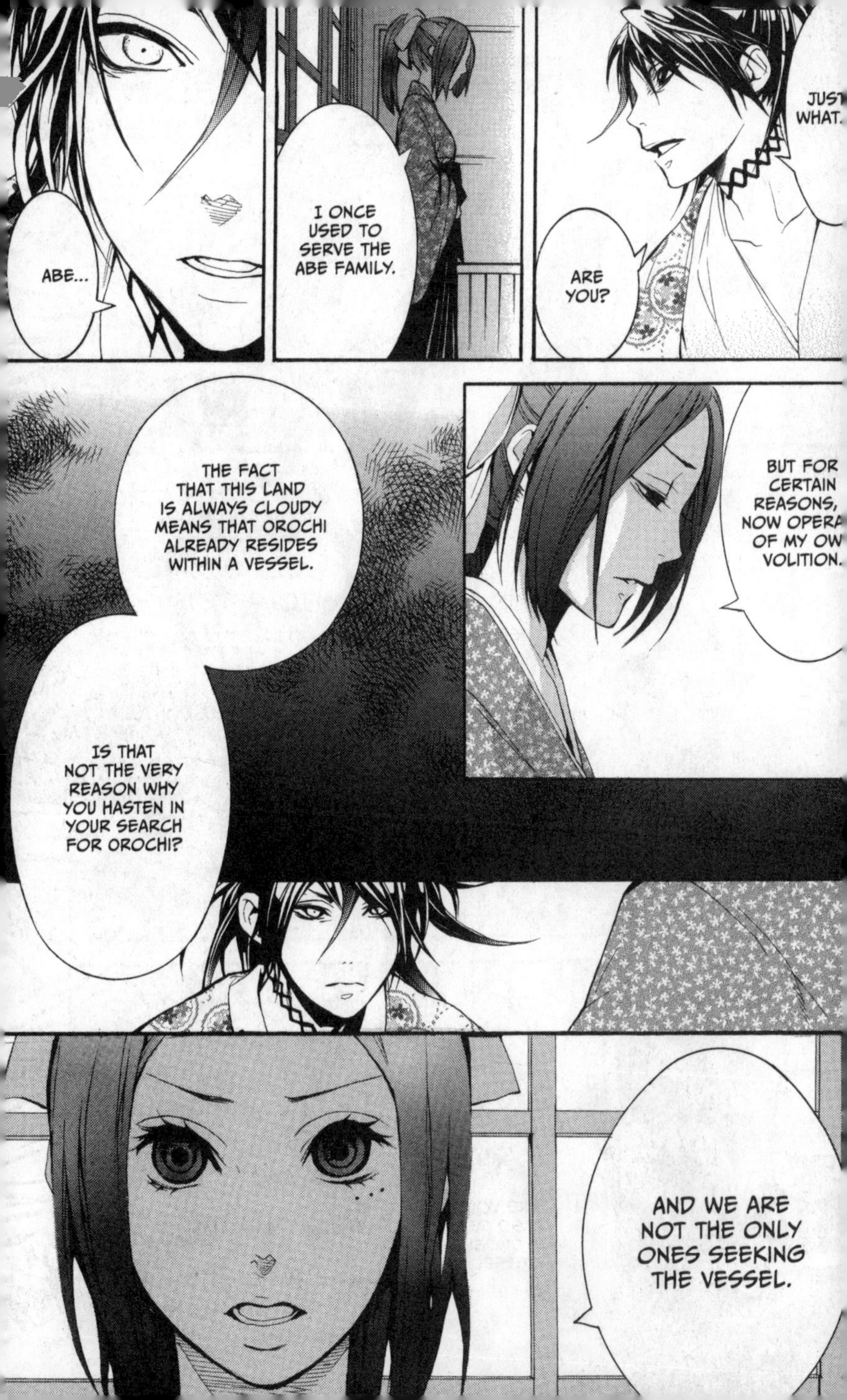
JUST WHAT.
ARE YOU?
I ONCE USED TO SERVE THE ABE FAMILY.
ABE...
BUT FOR CERTAIN REASONS, NOW OPERA OF MY OW VOLITION.
THE FACT THAT THIS LAND IS ALWAYS CLOUDY MEANS THAT OROCHI ALREADY RESIDES WITHIN A VESSEL.
IS THAT NOT THE VERY REASON WHY YOU HASTEN IN YOUR SEARCH FOR OROCHI?
AND WE ARE NOT THE ONLY ONES SEEKING THE VESSEL.

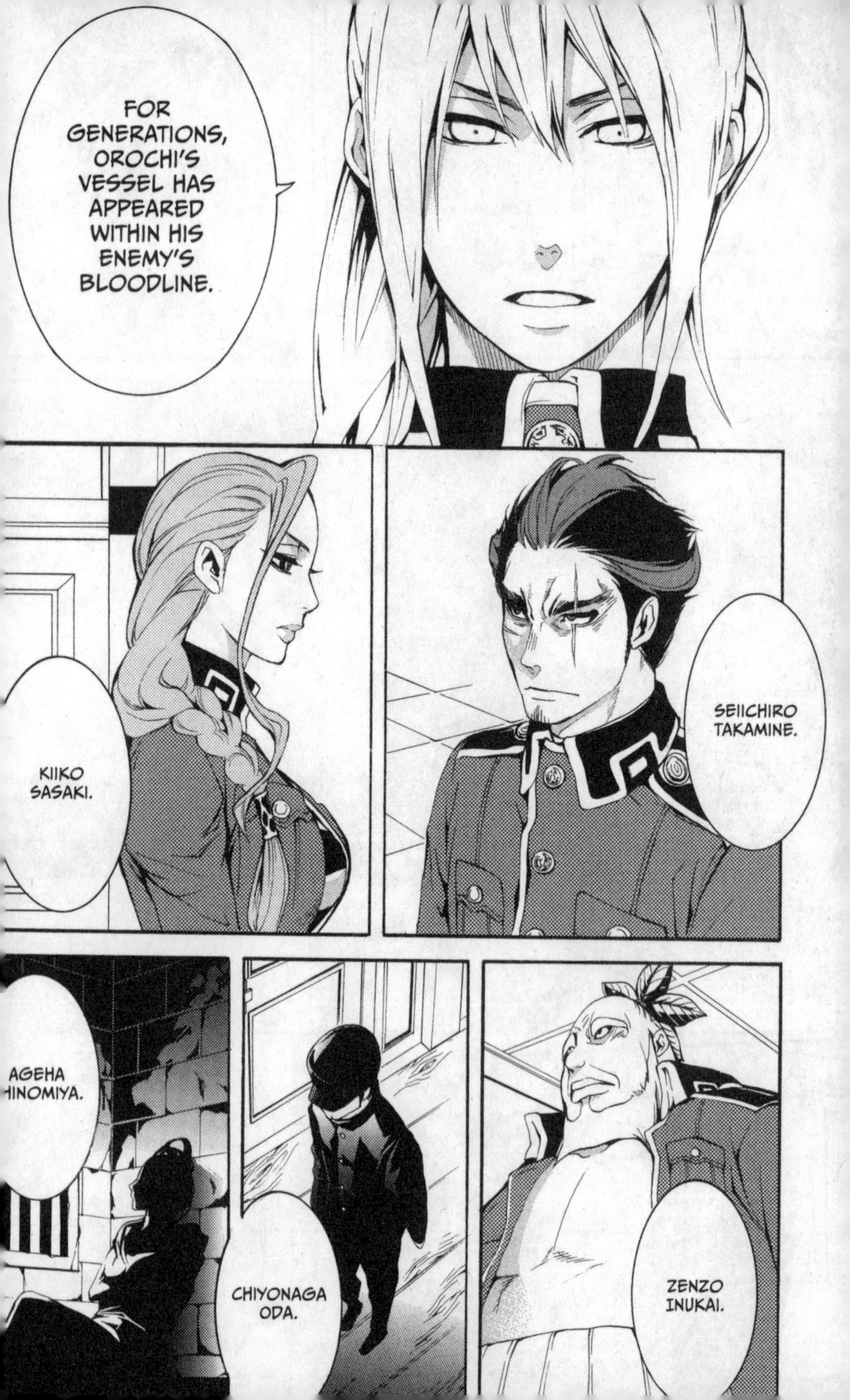
FOR GENERATIONS, OROCHI'S VESSEL HAS APPEARED WITHIN HIS ENEMY'S BLOODLINE.
SEIICHIRO TAKAMINE.
KIIKO SASAKI.
ZENZO INUKAI.
CHIYONAGA ODA.
AGEHA INOMIYA.

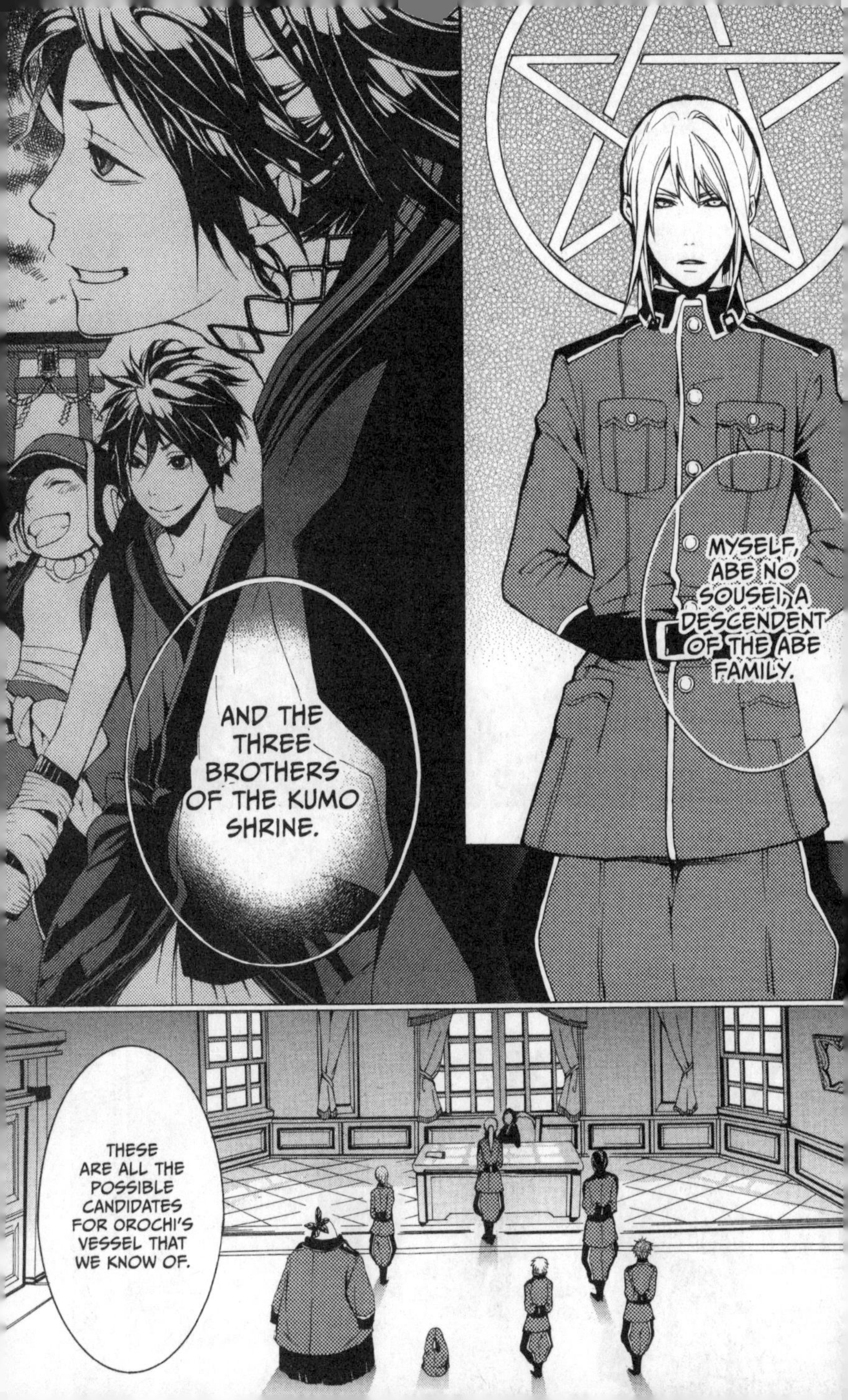
MYSELF, ABE NO SOUSEI, A DESCENDENT OF THE ABE FAMILY.
AND THE THREE BROTHERS OF THE KUMO SHRINE.
THESE ARE ALL THE POSSIBLE CANDIDATES FOR OROCHI'S VESSEL THAT WE KNOW OF.

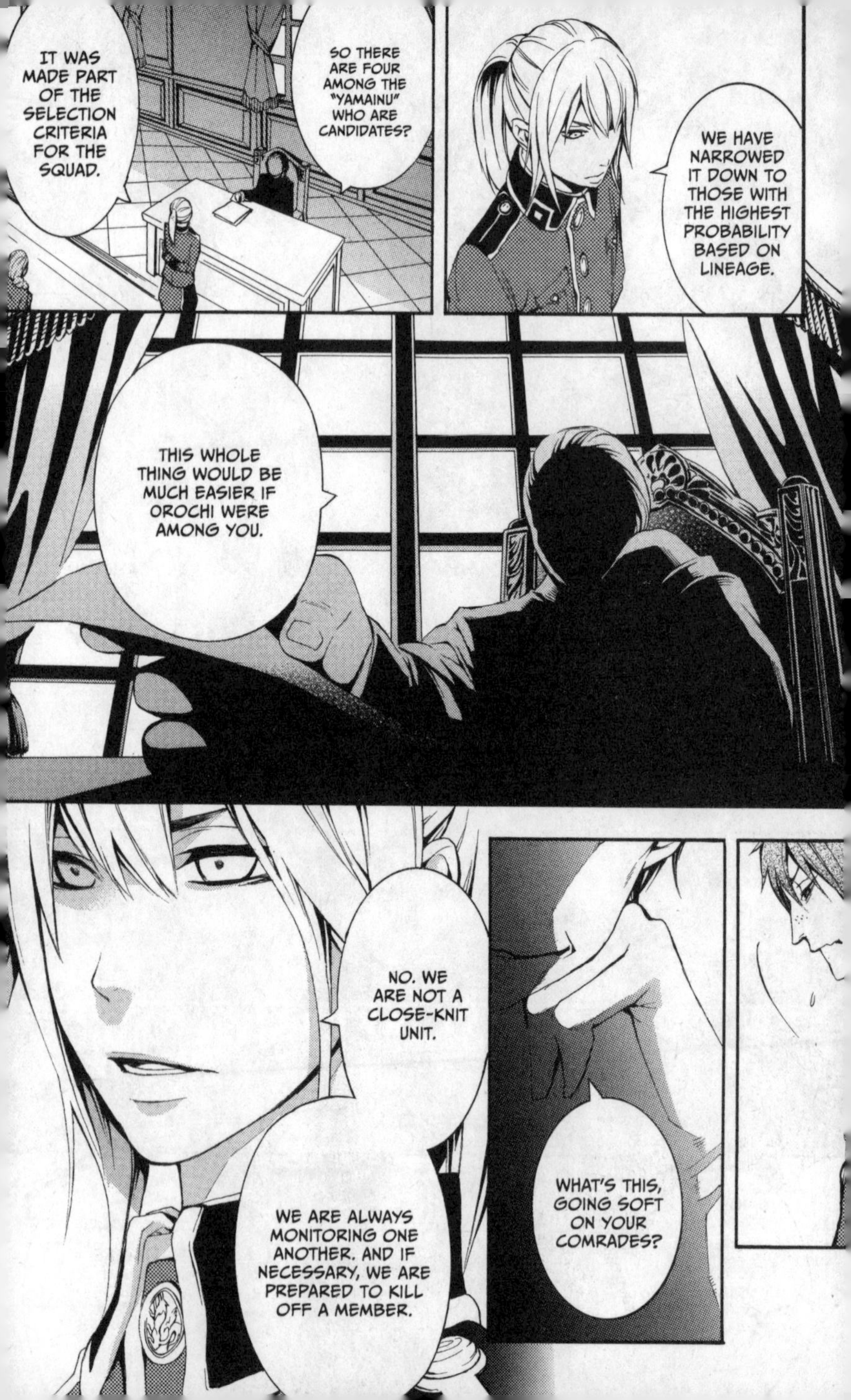
WE HAVE NARROWED IT DOWN TO THOSE WITH THE HIGHEST PROBABILITY BASED ON LINEAGE.
SO THERE ARE FOUR AMONG THE "YAMAINU" WHO ARE CANDIDATES?
IT WAS MADE PART OF THE SELECTION CRITERIA FOR THE SQUAD.
THIS WHOLE THING WOULD BE MUCH EASIER IF OROCHI WERE AMONG YOU.
WHAT'S THIS, GOING SOFT ON YOUR COMRADES?
NO. WE ARE NOT A CLOSE-KNIT UNIT.
WE ARE ALWAYS MONITORING ONE ANOTHER. AND IF NECESSARY, WE ARE PREPARED TO KILL OFF A MEMBER.

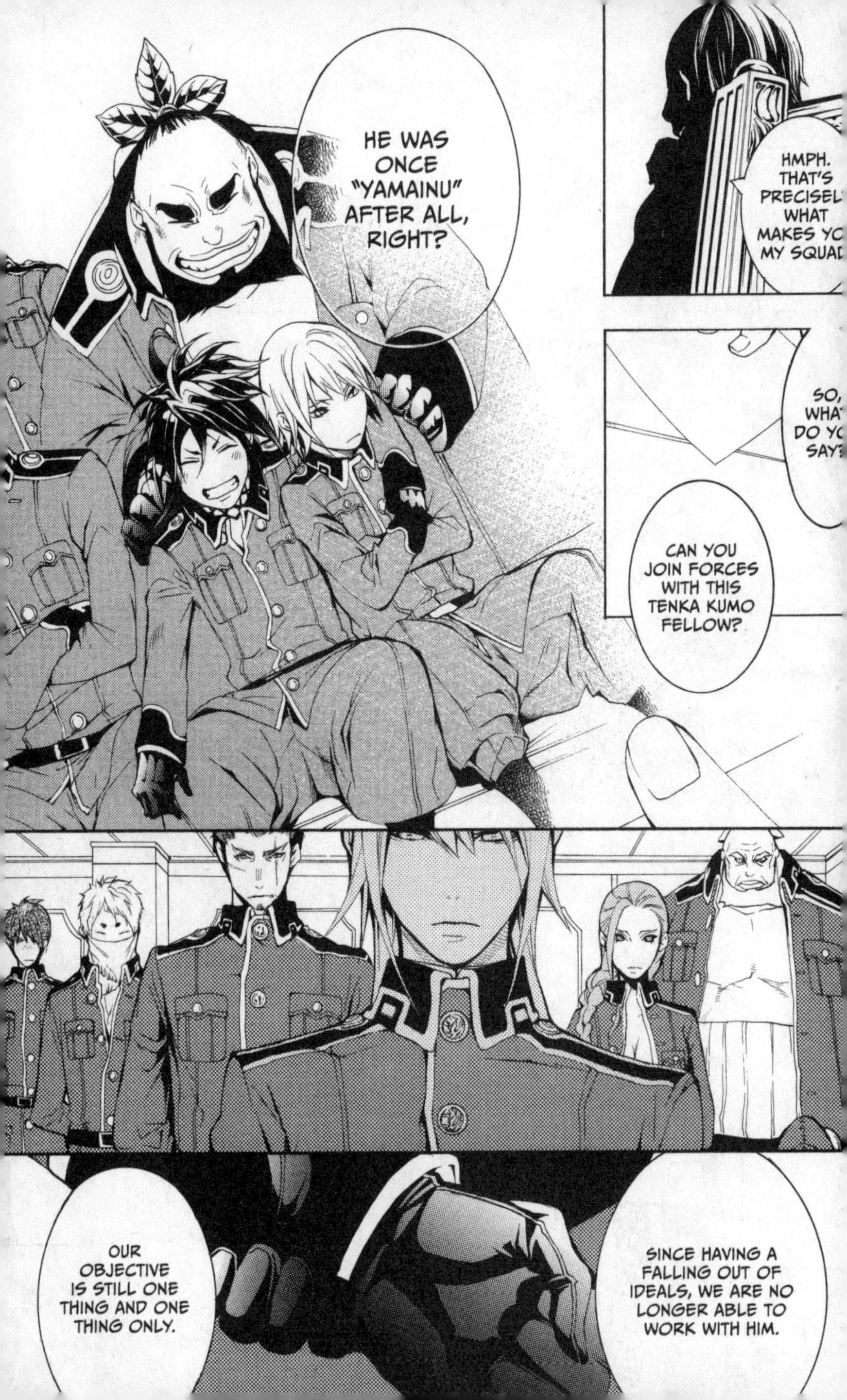
HMPH. THAT'S PRECISEL WHAT MAKES YO MY SQUAD
SO, WHA DO YO SAY?
CAN YOU JOIN FORCES WITH THIS TENKA KUMO FELLOW?
HE WAS ONCE "YAMAINU" AFTER ALL, RIGHT?
SINCE HAVING A FALLING OUT OF IDEALS, WE ARE NO LONGER ABLE TO WORK WITH HIM.
OUR OBJECTIVE IS STILL ONE THING AND ONE THING ONLY.

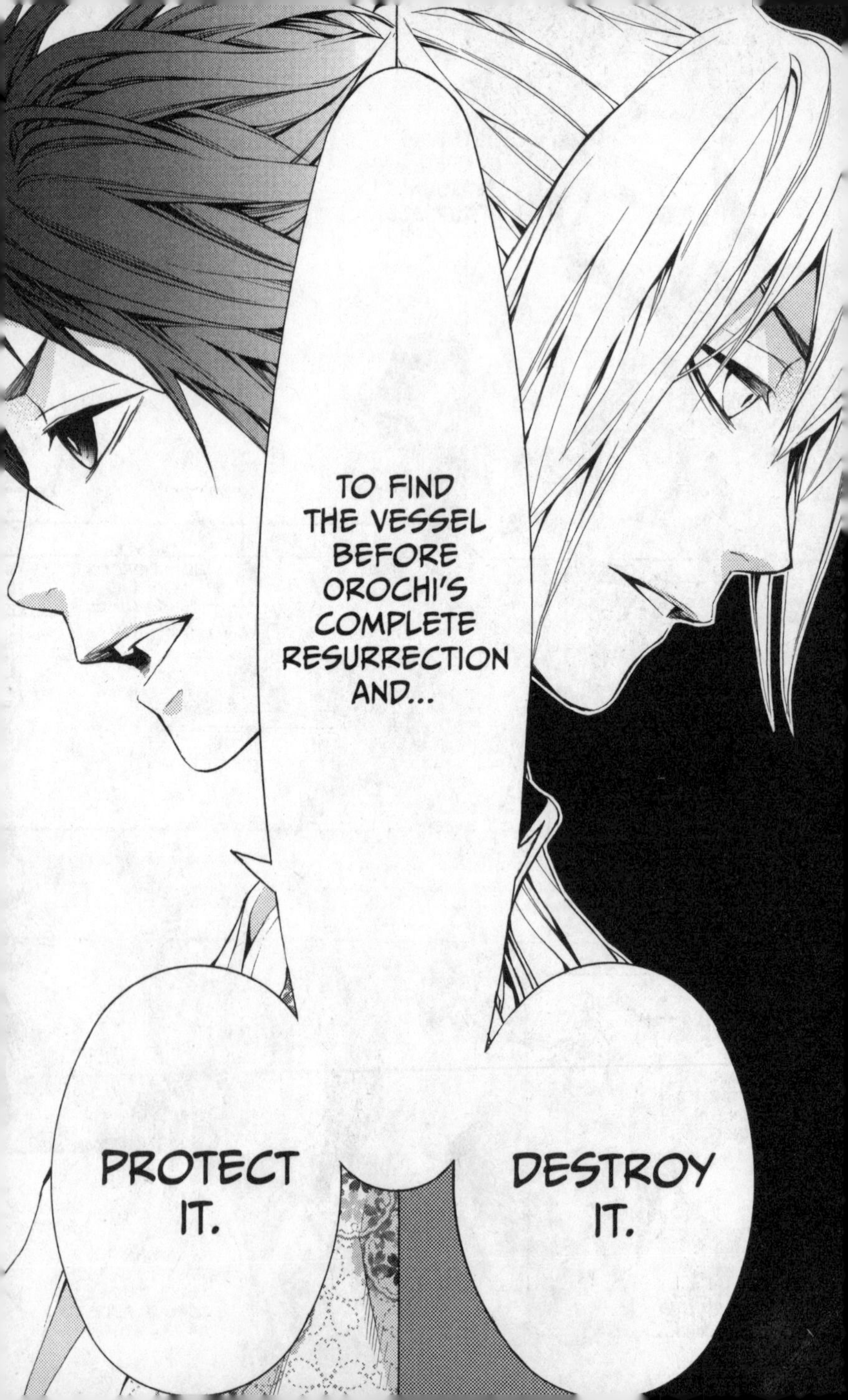
TO FIND THE VESSEL BEFORE OROCHI'S COMPLETE RESURRECTION AND...
DESTROY IT.
PROTECT IT.

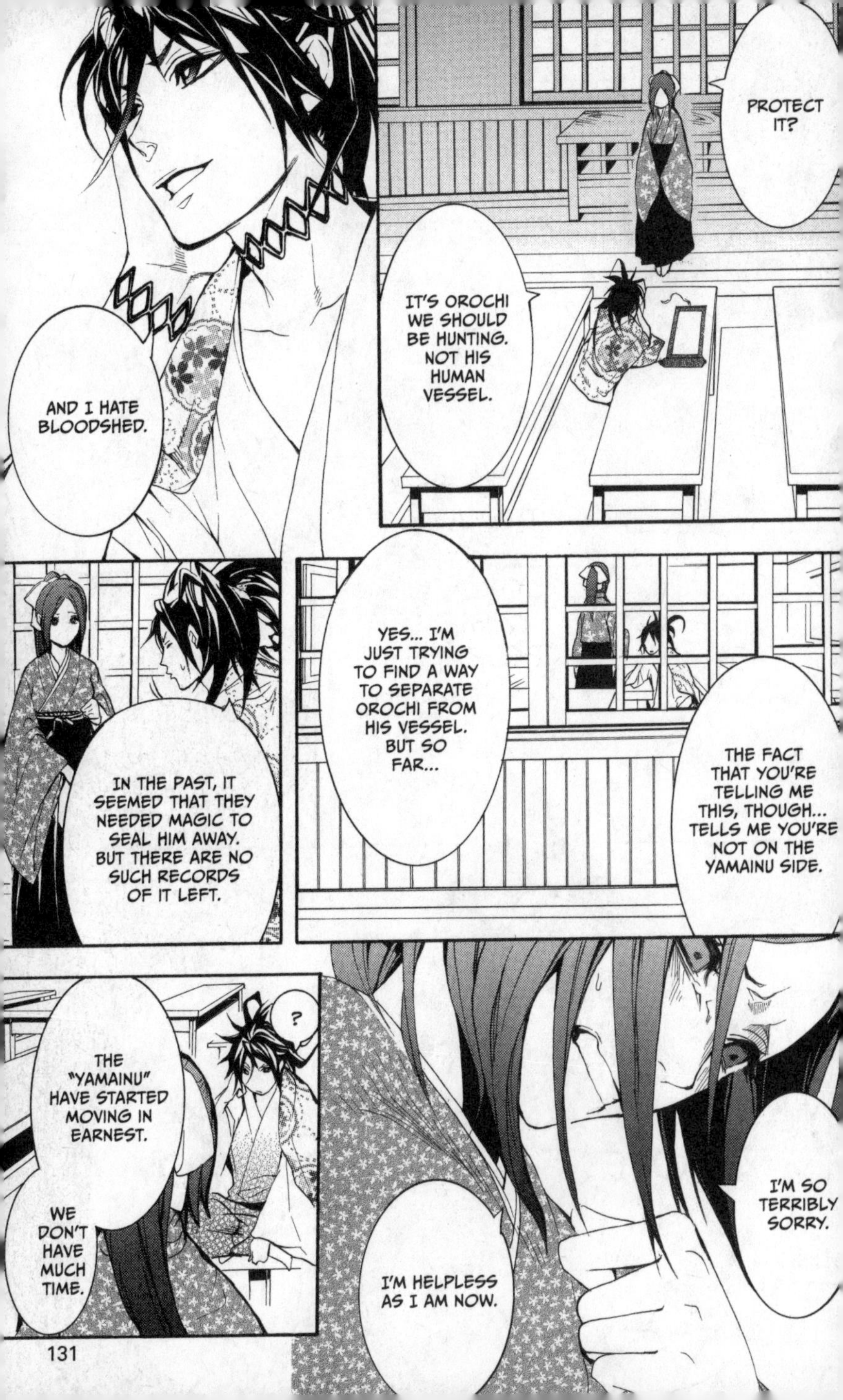
PROTECT IT?
IT'S OROCHI WE SHOULD BE HUNTING. NOT HIS HUMAN VESSEL.
AND I HATE BLOODSHED.
THE FACT THAT YOU'RE TELLING ME THIS, THOUGH... TELLS ME YOU'RE NOT ON THE YAMAINU SIDE.
YES... I'M JUST TRYING TO FIND A WAY TO SEPARATE OROCHI FROM HIS VESSEL. BUT SO FAR...
IN THE PAST, IT SEEMED THAT THEY NEEDED MAGIC TO SEAL HIM AWAY. BUT THERE ARE NO SUCH RECORDS OF IT LEFT.
I'M SO TERRIBLY SORRY.
I'M HELPLESS AS I AM NOW.
?
THE "YAMAINU" HAVE STARTED MOVING IN EARNEST.
WE DON'T HAVE MUCH TIME.

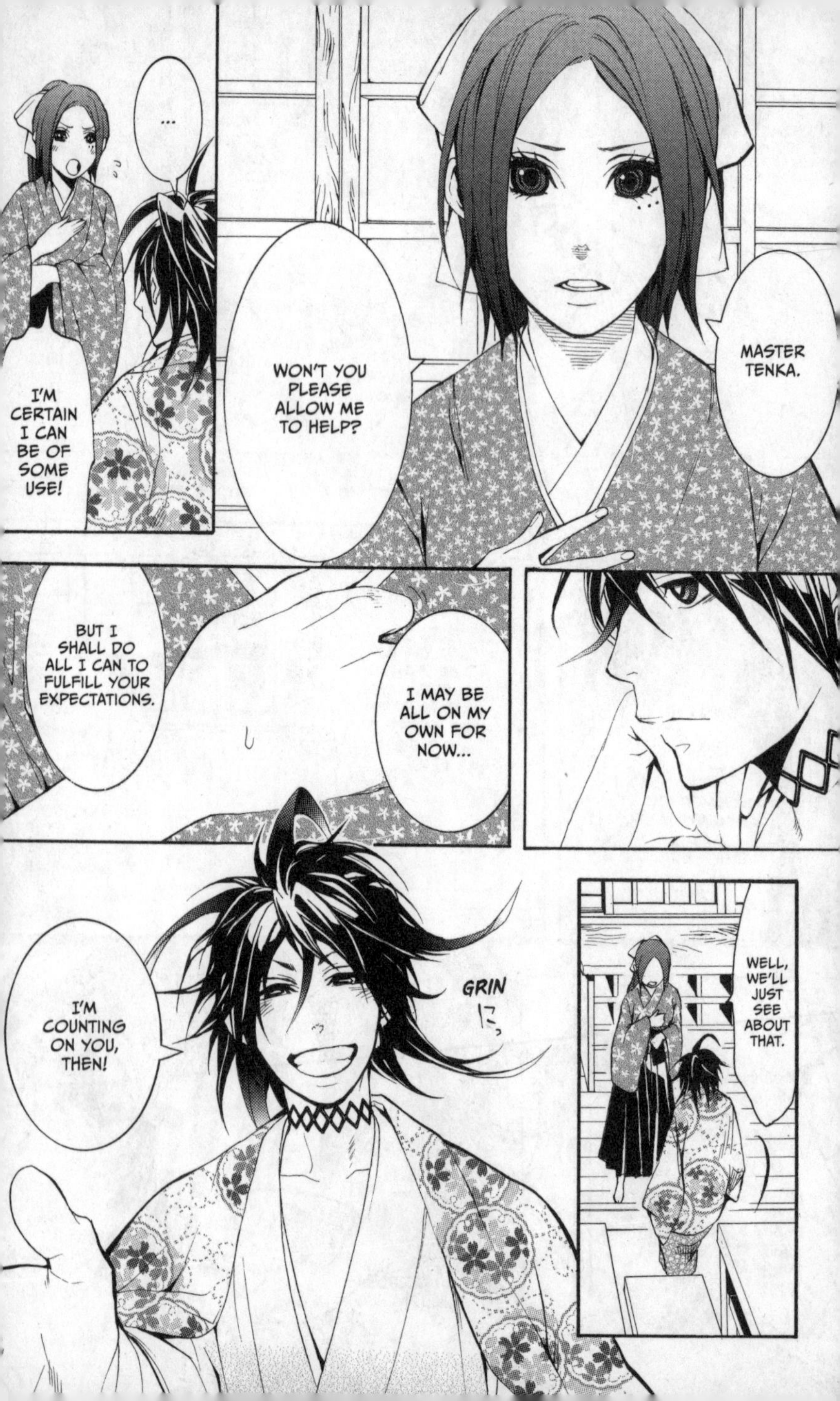
MASTER TENKA.
WON'T YOU PLEASE ALLOW ME TO HELP?
...
I'M CERTAIN I CAN BE OF SOME USE!
I MAY BE ALL ON MY OWN FOR NOW...
BUT I SHALL DO ALL I CAN TO FULFILL YOUR EXPECTATIONS.
WELL, WE'LL JUST SEE ABOUT THAT.
GRIN
I'M COUNTING ON YOU, THEN!

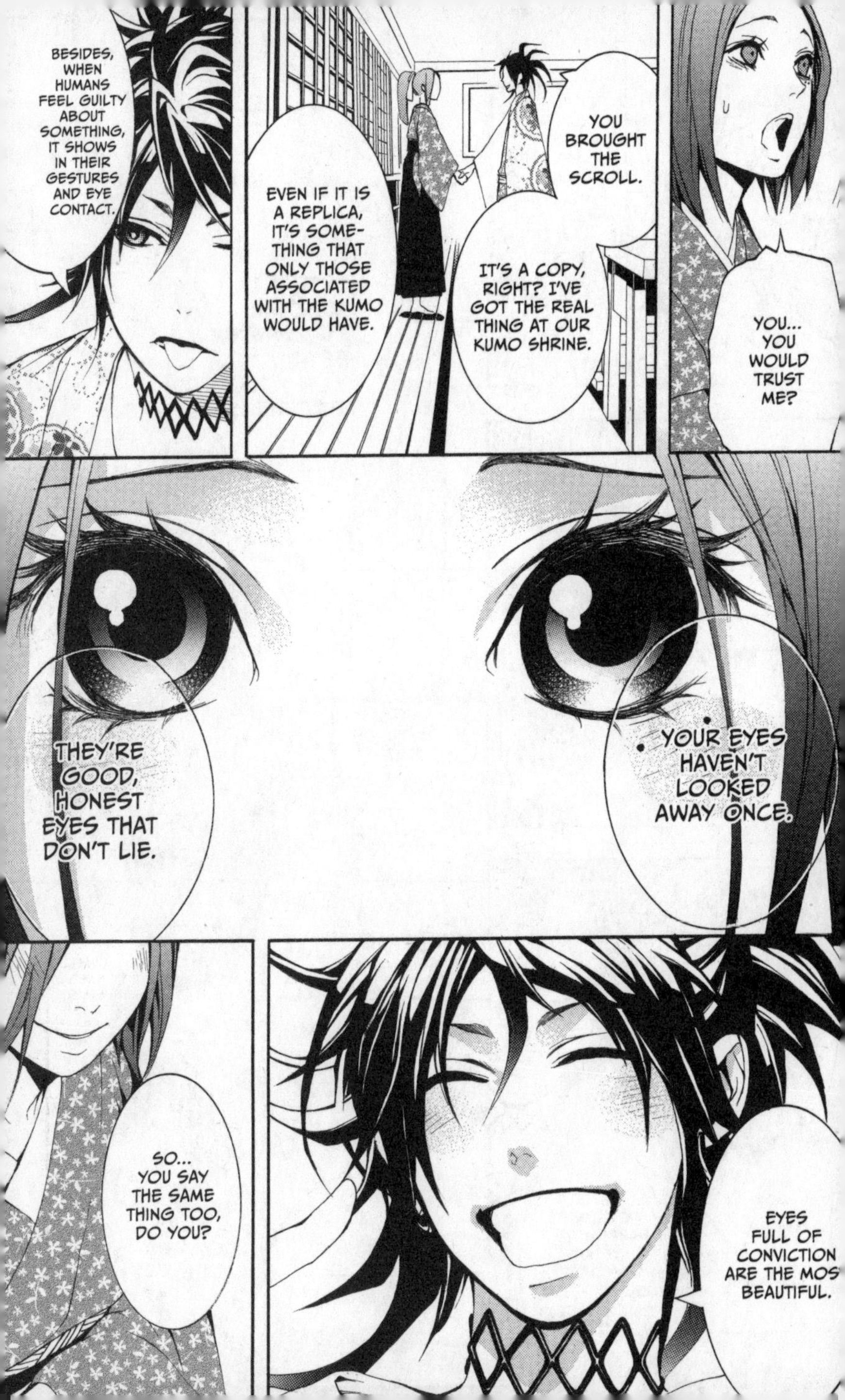
YOU... YOU WOULD TRUST ME?
YOU BROUGHT THE SCROLL.
IT'S A COPY, RIGHT? I'VE GOT THE REAL THING AT OUR KUMO SHRINE.
EVEN IF IT IS A REPLICA, IT'S SOMETHING THAT ONLY THOSE ASSOCIATED WITH THE KUMO WOULD HAVE.
BESIDES, WHEN HUMANS FEEL GUILTY ABOUT SOMETHING, IT SHOWS IN THEIR GESTURES AND EYE CONTACT.
YOUR EYES HAVEN'T LOOKED AWAY ONCE.
THEY'RE GOOD, HONEST EYES THAT DON'T LIE.
EYES FULL OF CONVICTION ARE THE MOS BEAUTIFUL.
SO... YOU SAY THE SAME THING TOO, DO YOU?

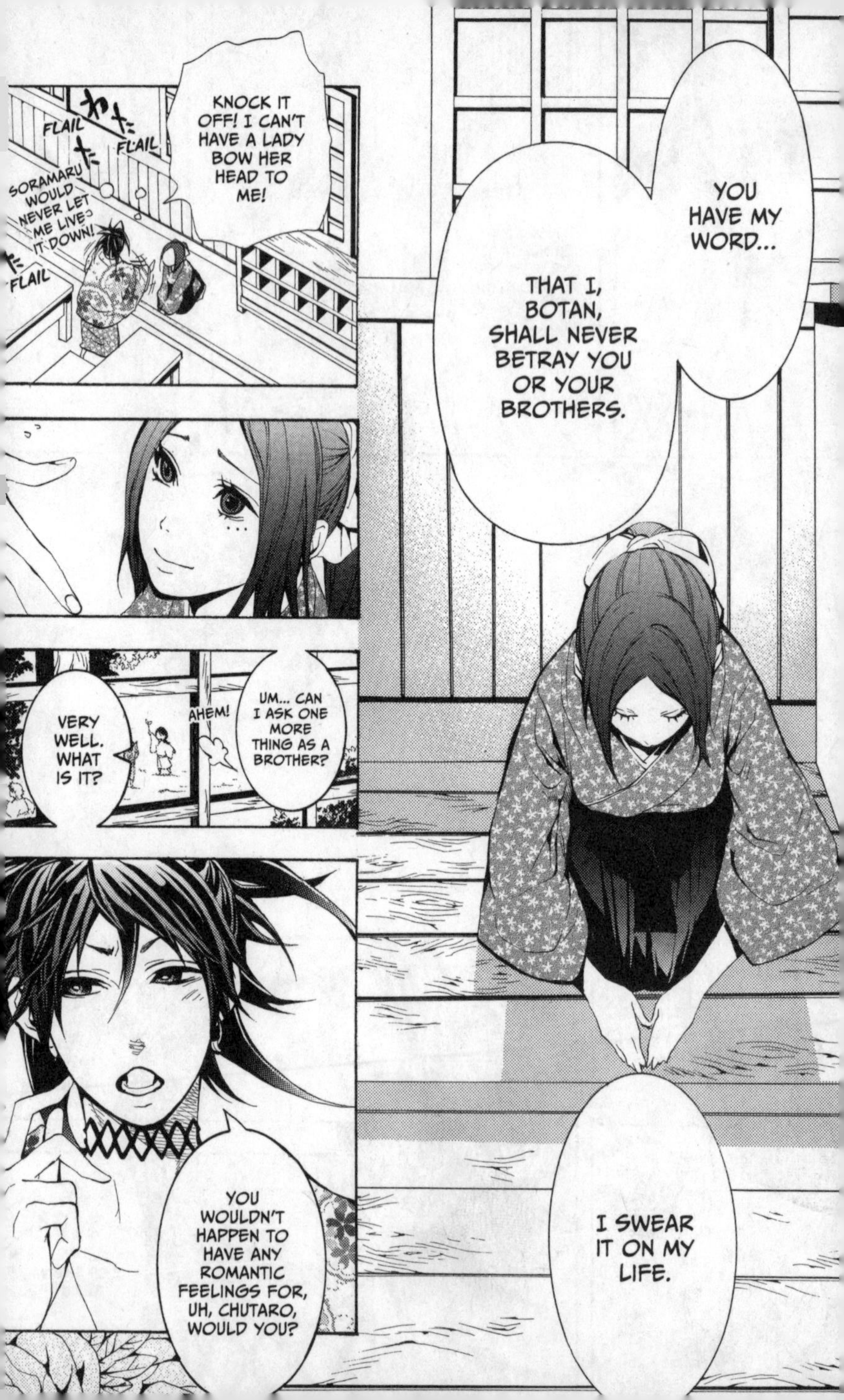
YOU HAVE MY WORD...
THAT I, BOTAN, SHALL NEVER BETRAY YOU OR YOUR BROTHERS.
I SWEAR IT ON MY LIFE.
KNOCK IT OFF! I CAN'T HAVE A LADY BOW HER HEAD TO ME!
FLAIL
FLAIL
SORAMARU WOULD NEVER LET ME LIVE IT DOWN!
FLAIL
UM... CAN I ASK ONE MORE THING AS A BROTHER?
AHEM!
VERY WELL. WHAT IS IT?
YOU WOULDN'T HAPPEN TO HAVE ANY ROMANTIC FEELINGS FOR, UH, CHUTARO, WOULD YOU?

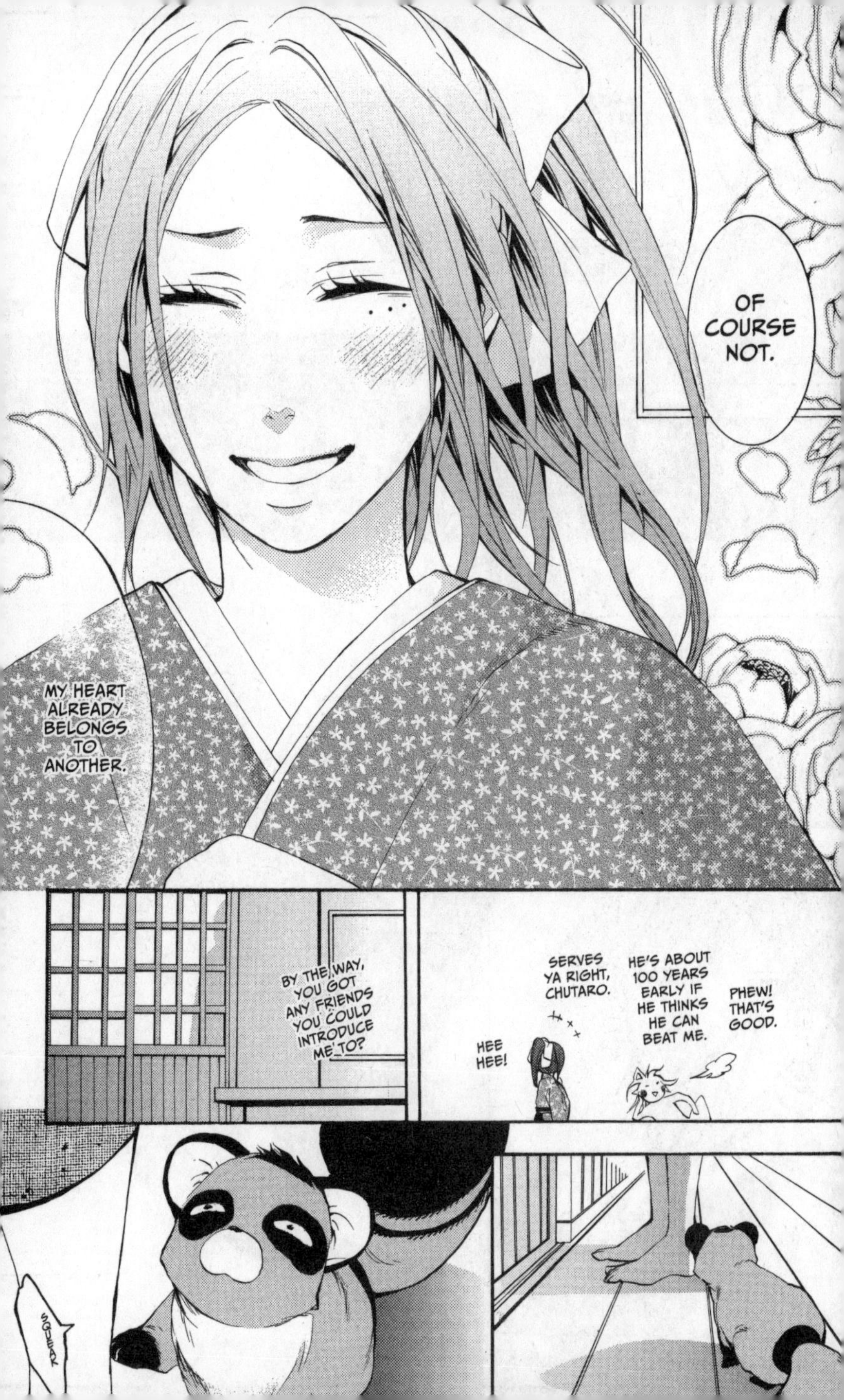
OF COURSE NOT.
MY HEART ALREADY BELONGS TO ANOTHER.
PHEW! THAT'S GOOD.
HE'S ABOUT 100 YEARS EARLY IF HE THINKS HE CAN BEAT ME.
SERVES YA RIGHT, CHUTARO.
HEE HEE!
BY THE WAY, YOU GOT ANY FRIENDS YOU COULD INTRODUCE ME TO?
SQUEAK

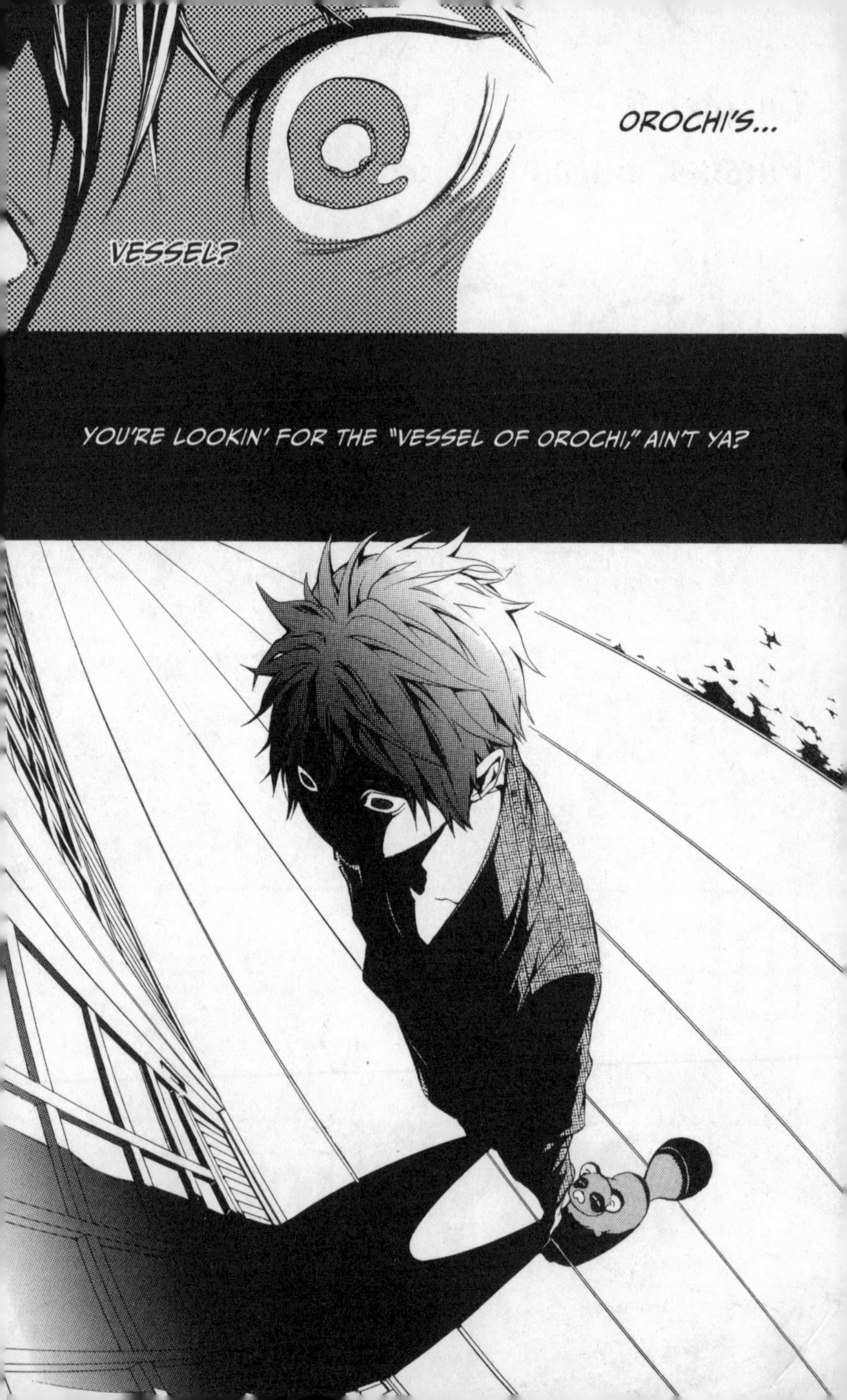
OROCHI'S...
VESSEL?
YOU'RE LOOKIN' FOR THE "VESSEL OF OROCHI," AIN'T YA?

Chapter 6
Pursuer, Burning Under the Clouds

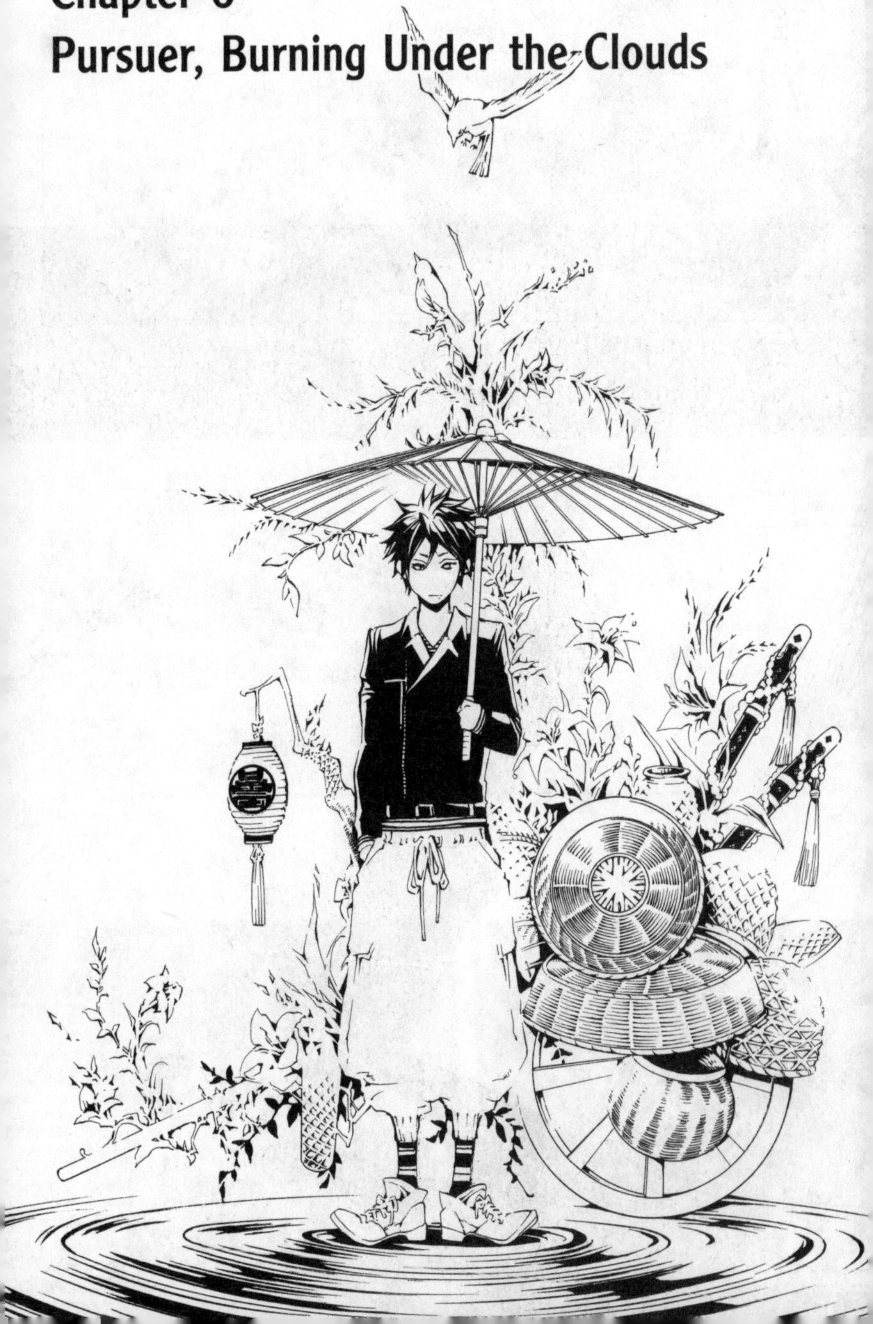

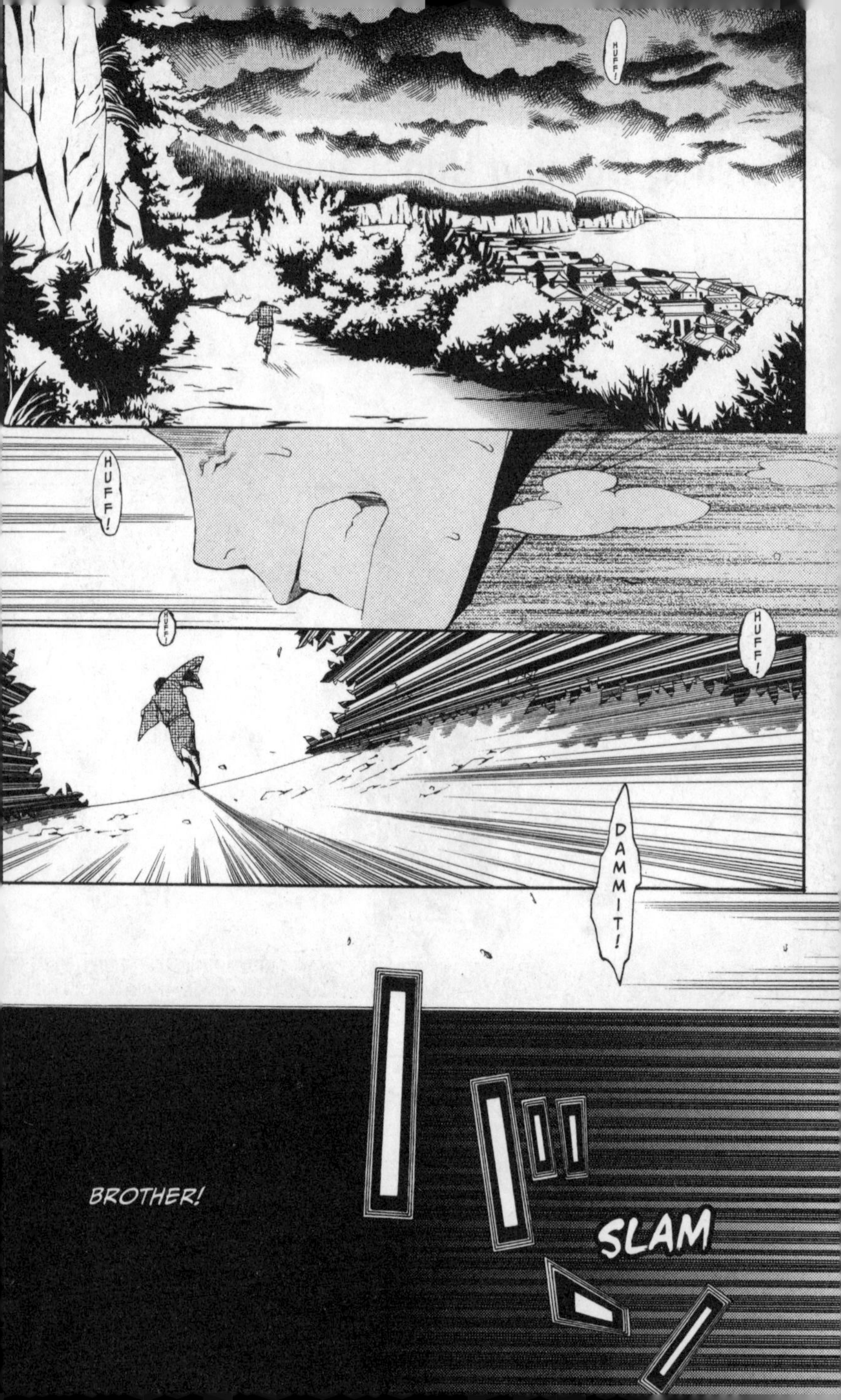
HUFF!
HUFF!
HUFF!
HUFF!
DAMMIT!
SLAM
BROTHER!

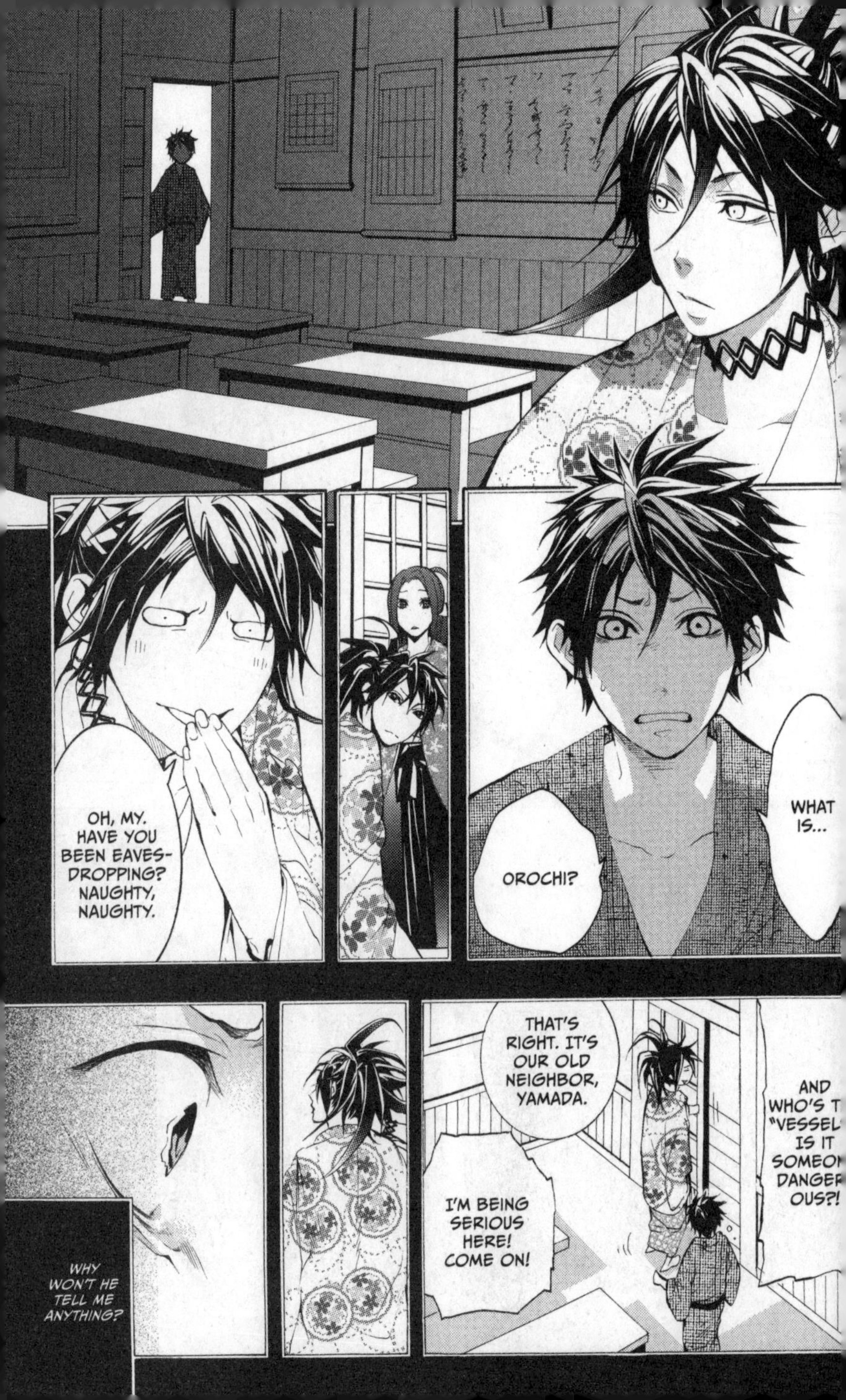
WHAT IS...
OROCHI?
OH, MY. HAVE YOU BEEN EAVES-DROPPING? NAUGHTY, NAUGHTY.
AND WHO'S T "VESSEL IS IT SOMEO DANGER OUS?!
THAT'S RIGHT. IT'S OUR OLD NEIGHBOR, YAMADA.
I'M BEING SERIOUS HERE! COME ON!
WHY WON'T HE TELL ME ANYTHING?

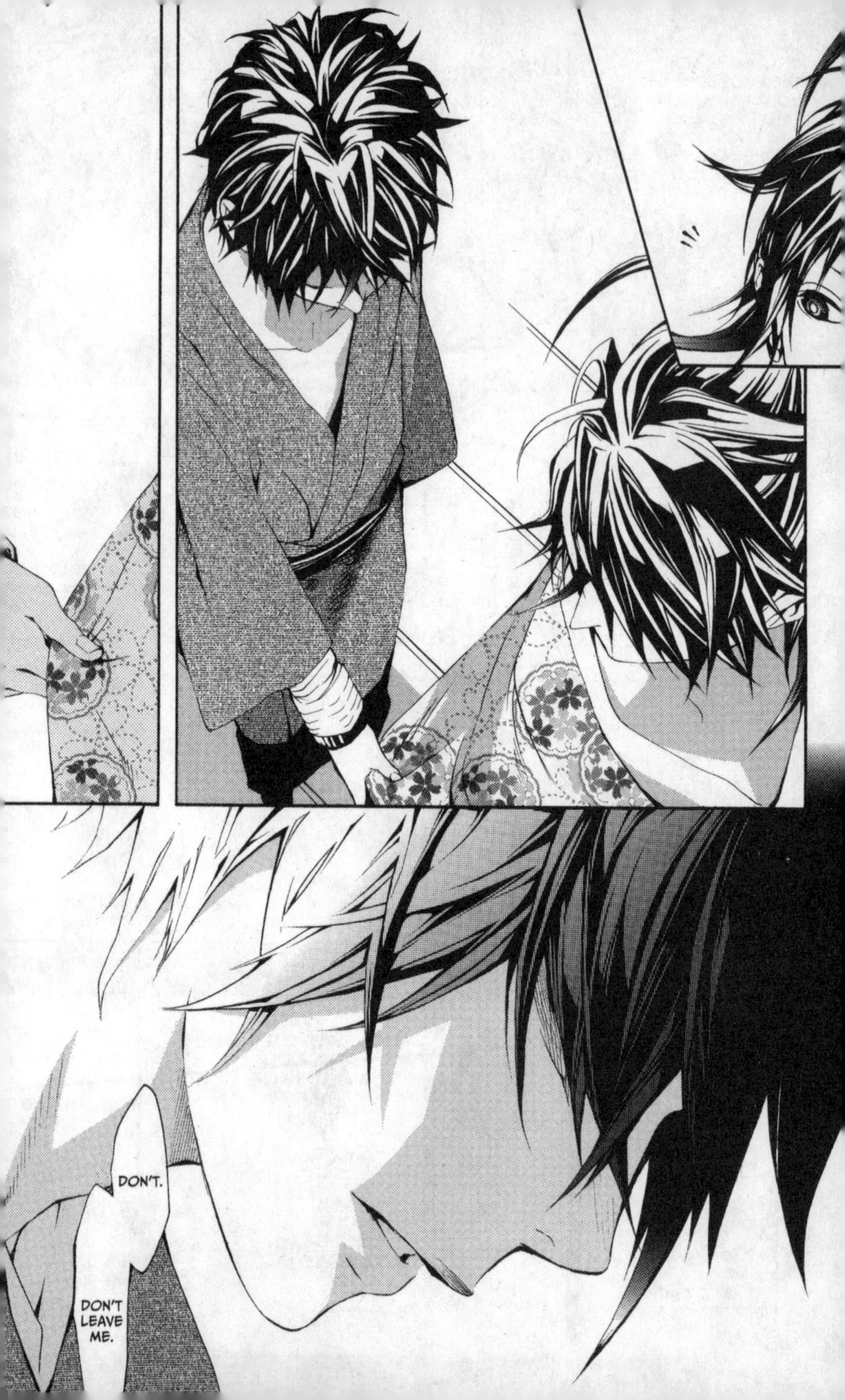
DON'T.
DON'T LEAVE ME.

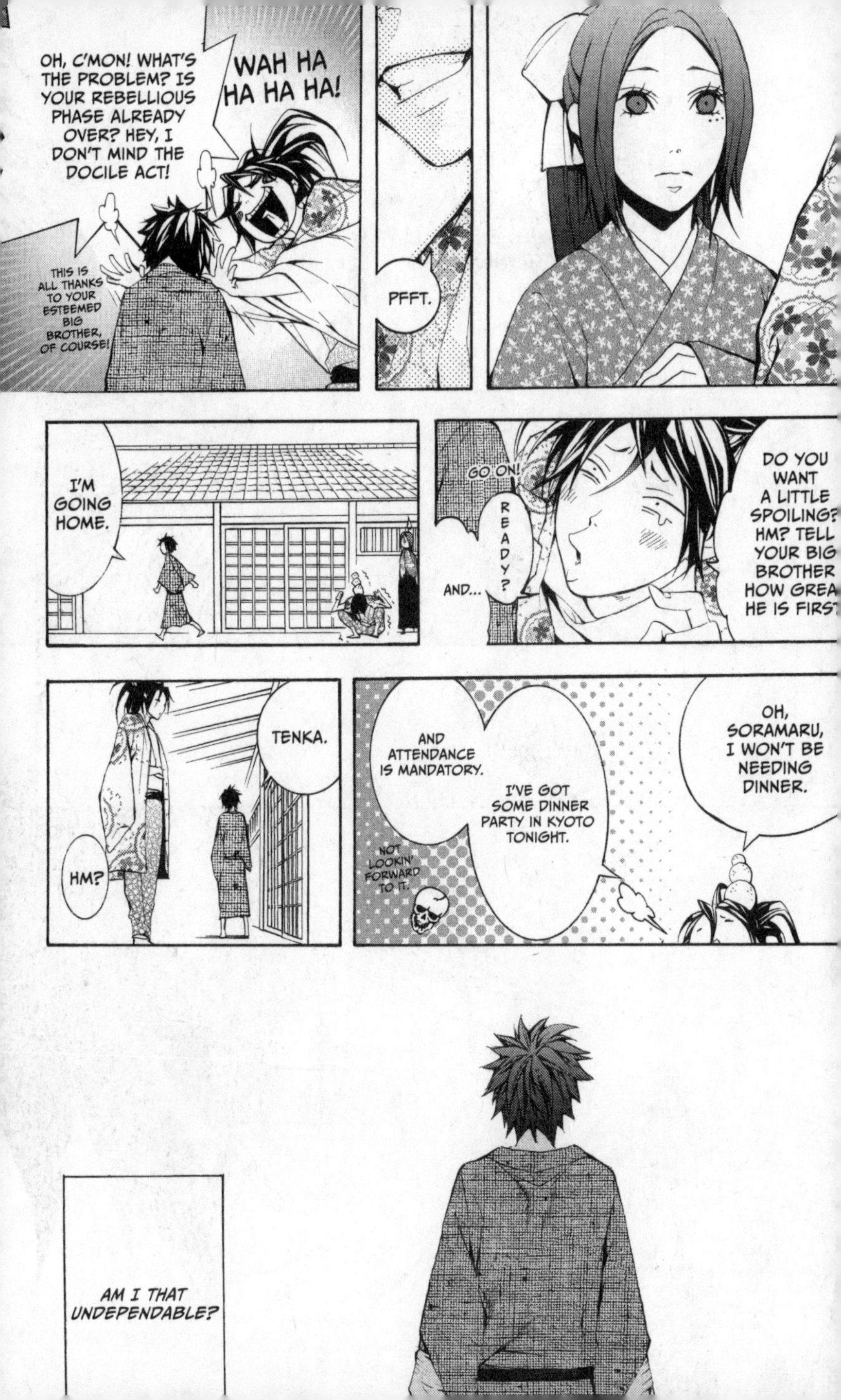
PFFT.
WAH HA HA HA HA!
OH, C'MON! WHAT'S THE PROBLEM? IS YOUR REBELLIOUS PHASE ALREADY OVER? HEY, I DON'T MIND THE DOCILE ACT!
THIS IS ALL THANKS TO YOUR ESTEEMED BIG BROTHER, OF COURSE!
DO YOU WANT A LITTLE SPOILING? HM? TELL YOUR BIG BROTHER HOW GREA HE IS FIRST
GO ON!
READY?
AND...
I'M GOING HOME.
OH, SORAMARU, I WON'T BE NEEDING DINNER.
I'VE GOT SOME DINNER PARTY IN KYOTO TONIGHT.
AND ATTENDANCE IS MANDATORY.
NOT LOOKIN' FORWARD TO IT.
TENKA.
HM?
AM I THAT UNDEPENDABLE?

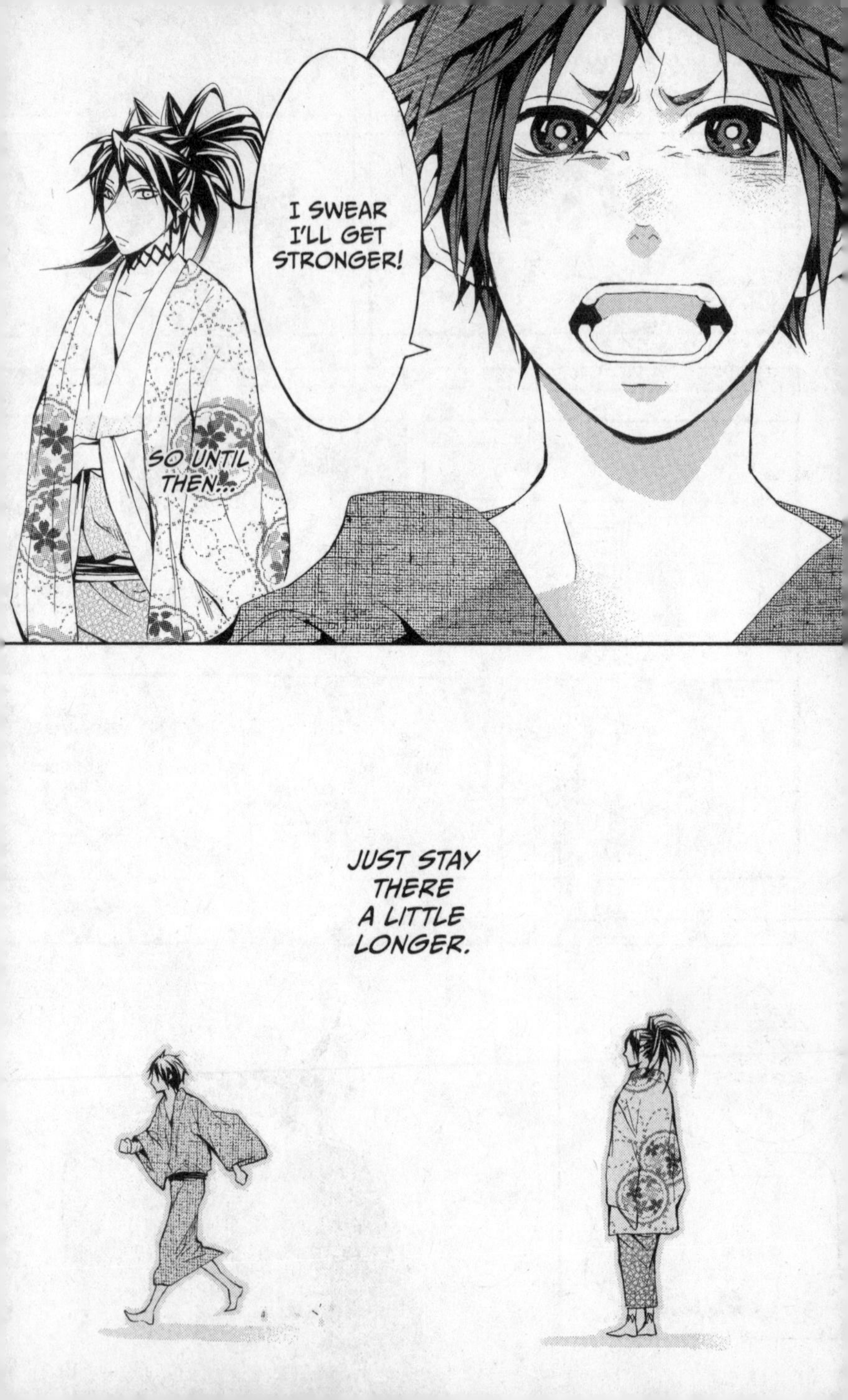
I SWEAR I'LL GET STRONGER!
SO UNTIL THEN...
JUST STAY THERE A LITTLE LONGER.

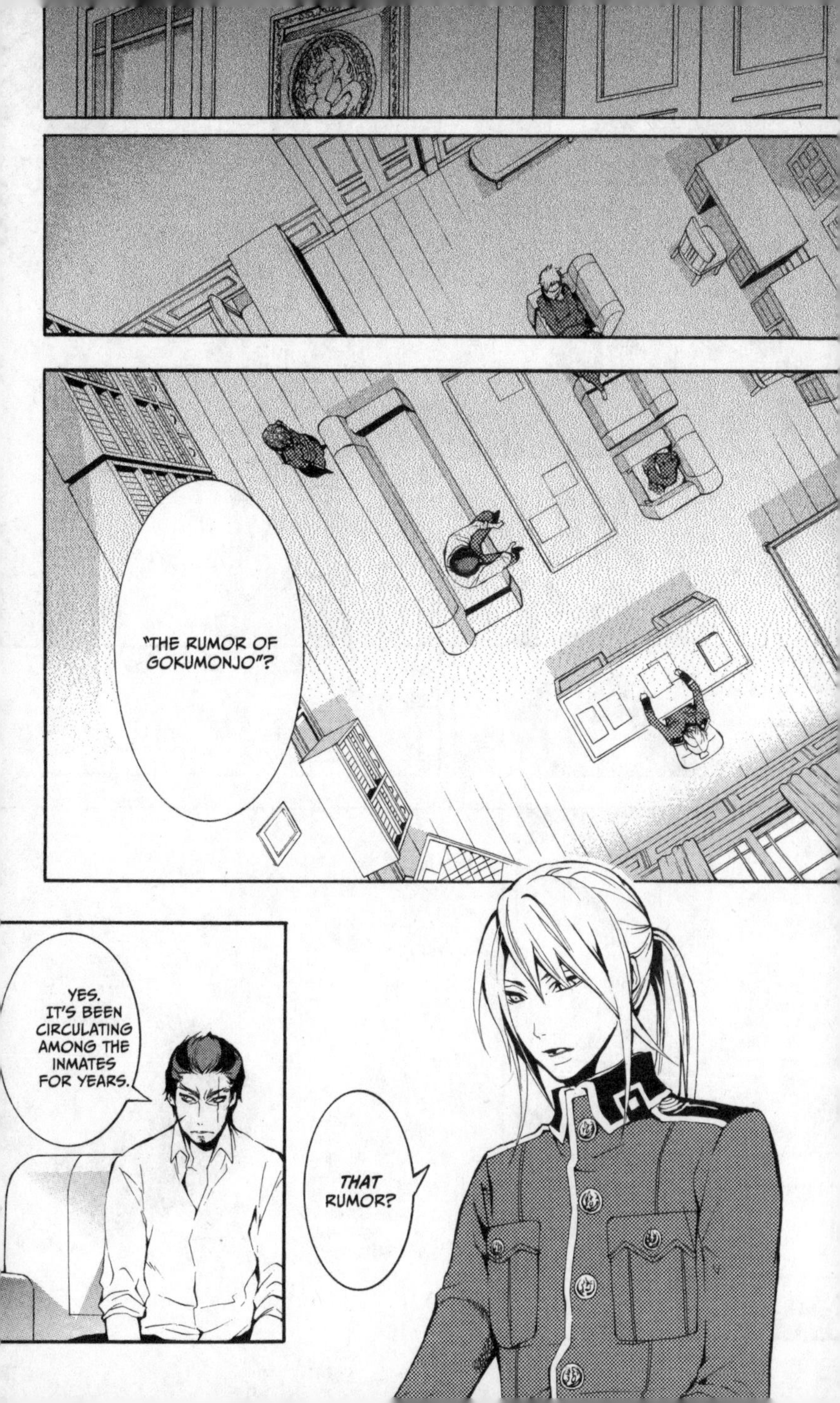
"THE RUMOR OF GOKUMONJO"?
THAT RUMOR?
YES. IT'S BEEN CIRCULATING AMONG THE INMATES FOR YEARS.

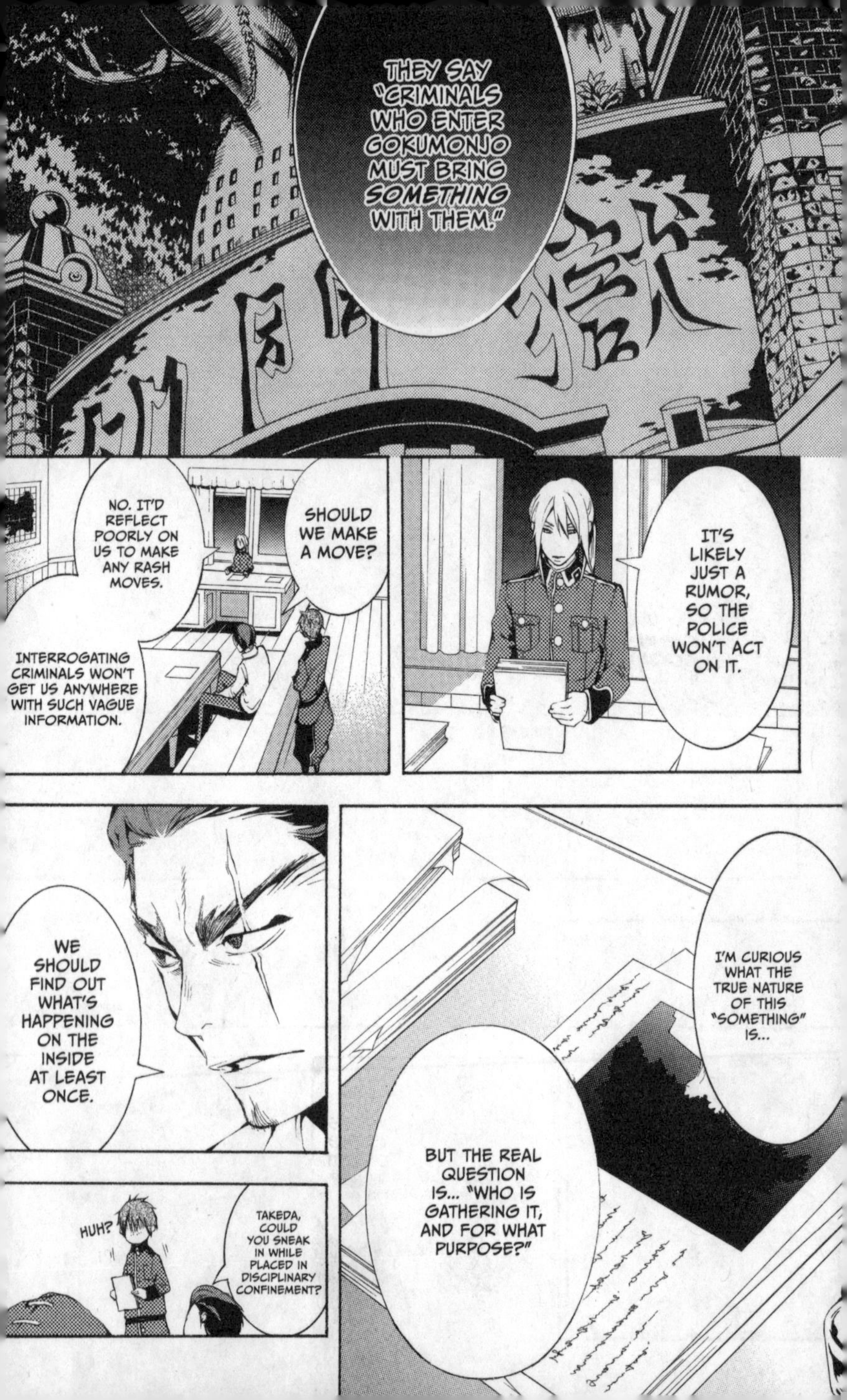
THEY SAY "CRIMINALS WHO ENTER GOKUMONJO MUST BRING *SOMETHING* WITH THEM."
IT'S LIKELY JUST A RUMOR, SO THE POLICE WON'T ACT ON IT.
SHOULD WE MAKE A MOVE?
NO. IT'D REFLECT POORLY ON US TO MAKE ANY RASH MOVES.
INTERROGATING CRIMINALS WON'T GET US ANYWHERE WITH SUCH VAGUE INFORMATION.
I'M CURIOUS WHAT THE TRUE NATURE OF THIS "SOMETHING" IS...
BUT THE REAL QUESTION IS... "WHO IS GATHERING IT, AND FOR WHAT PURPOSE?"
WE SHOULD FIND OUT WHAT'S HAPPENING ON THE INSIDE AT LEAST ONCE.
TAKEDA, COULD YOU SNEAK IN WHILE PLACED IN DISCIPLINARY CONFINEMENT?
HUH?

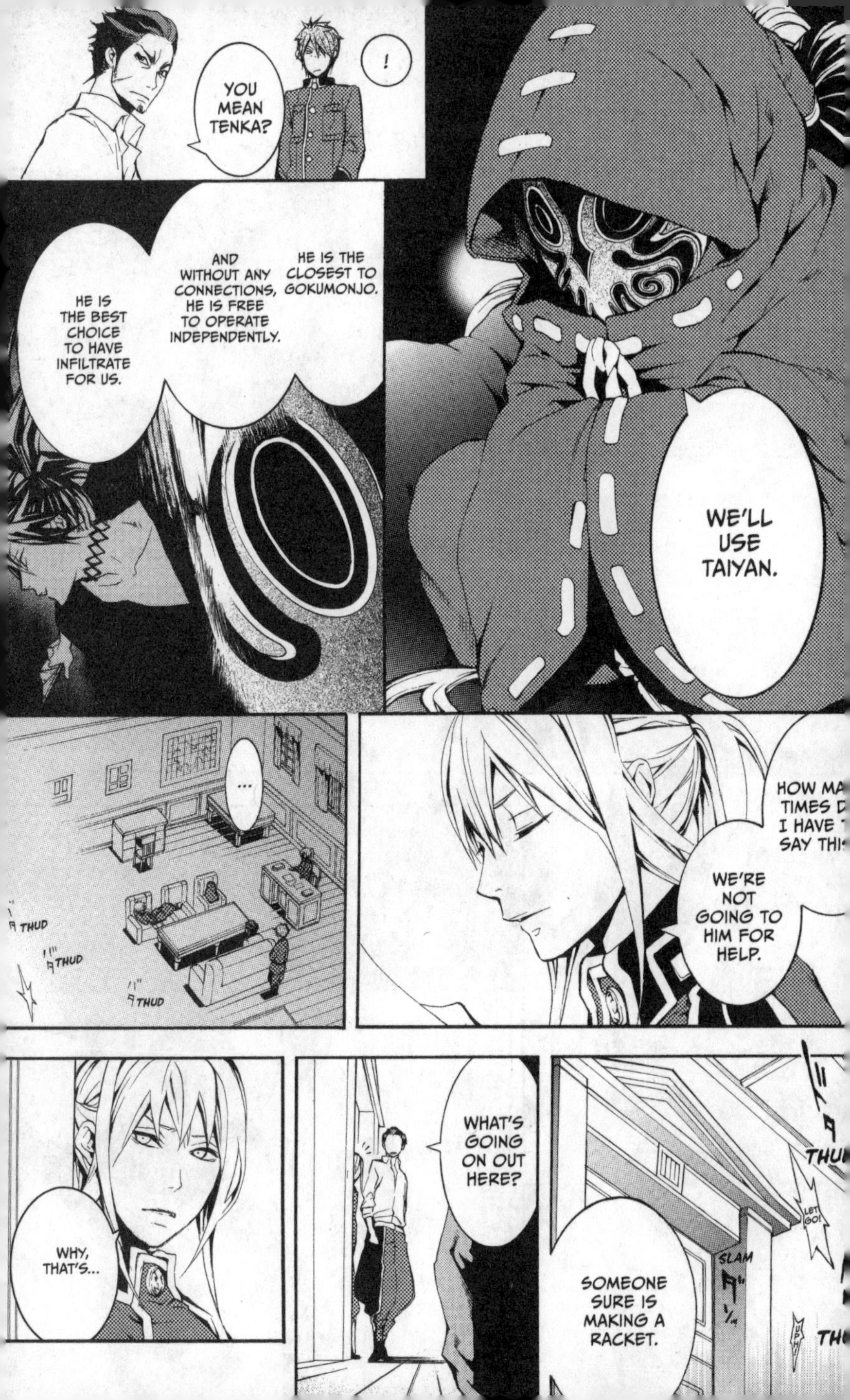
WE'LL USE TAIYAN.
!
YOU MEAN TENKA?
HE IS THE CLOSEST TO GOKUMONJO.
AND WITHOUT ANY CONNECTIONS, HE IS FREE TO OPERATE INDEPENDENTLY.
HE IS THE BEST CHOICE TO HAVE INFILTRATE FOR US.
HOW MA TIMES D I HAVE T SAY THI
WE'RE NOT GOING TO HIM FOR HELP.
...
THUD
THUD
THUD
THUD
LET GO!
SLAM
SOMEONE SURE IS MAKING A RACKET.
WHAT'S GOING ON OUT HERE?
WHY, THAT'S...

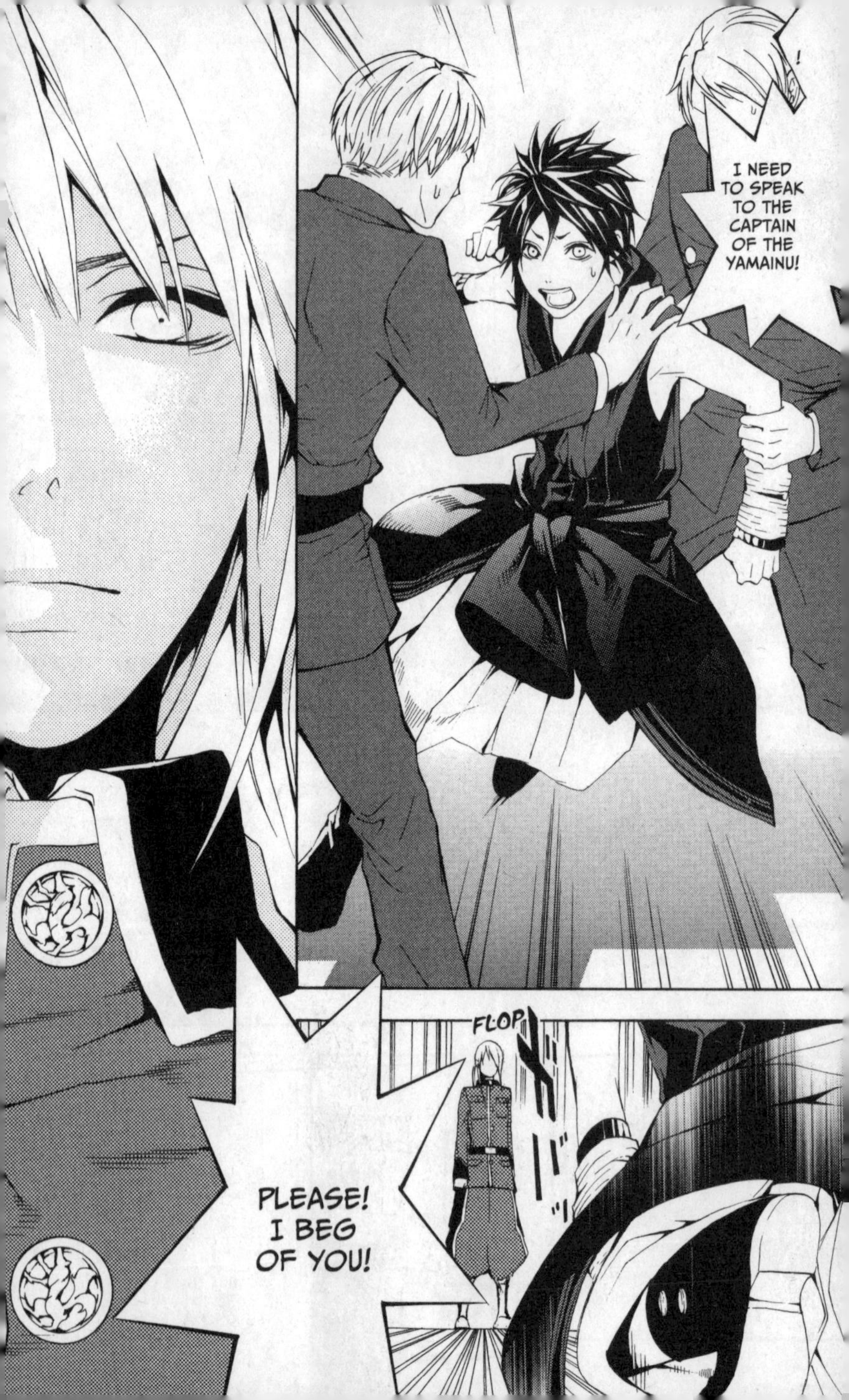
!
I NEED TO SPEAK TO THE CAPTAIN OF THE YAMAINU!
FLOP
PLEASE! I BEG OF YOU!

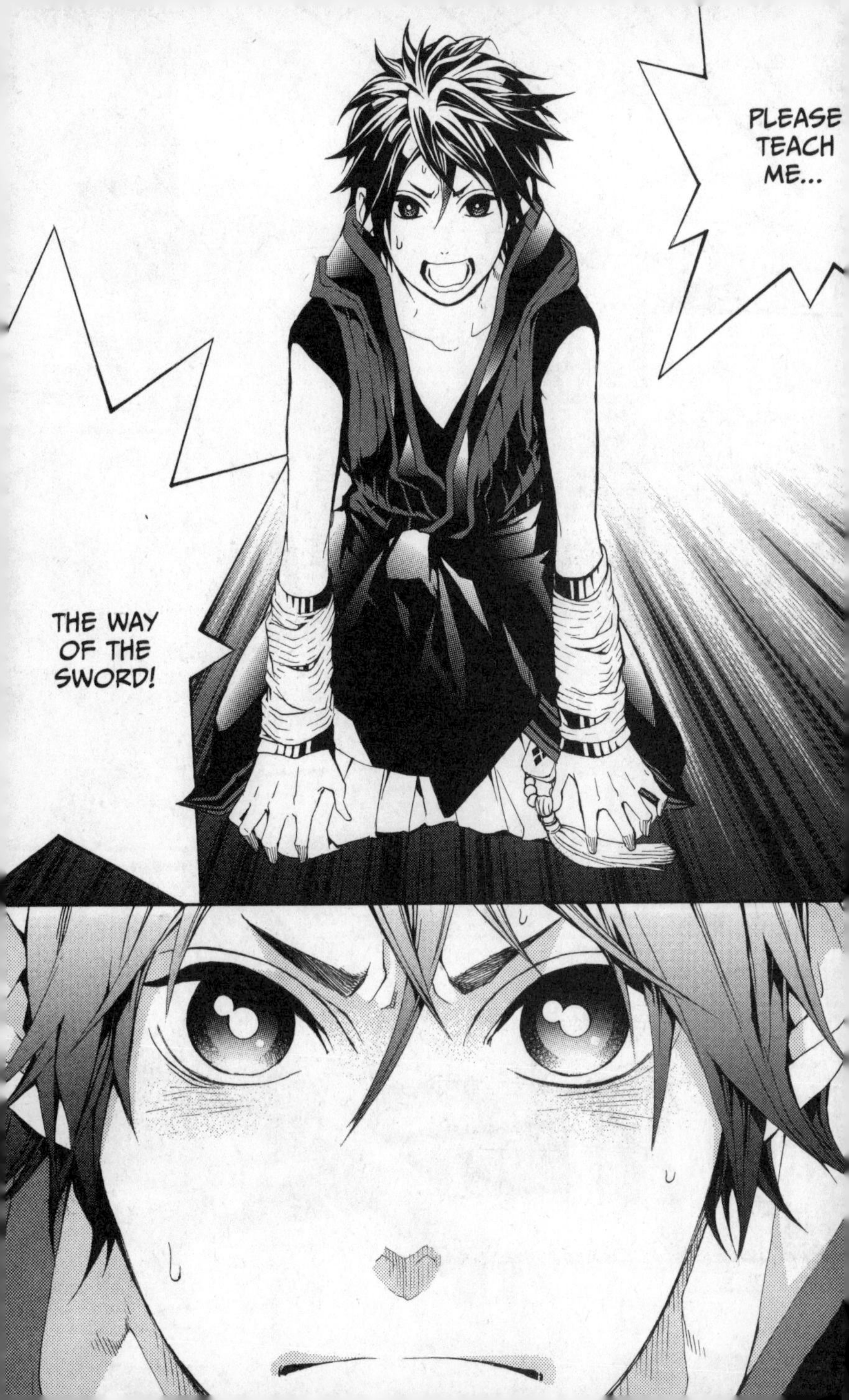
PLEASE TEACH ME...
THE WAY OF THE SWORD!

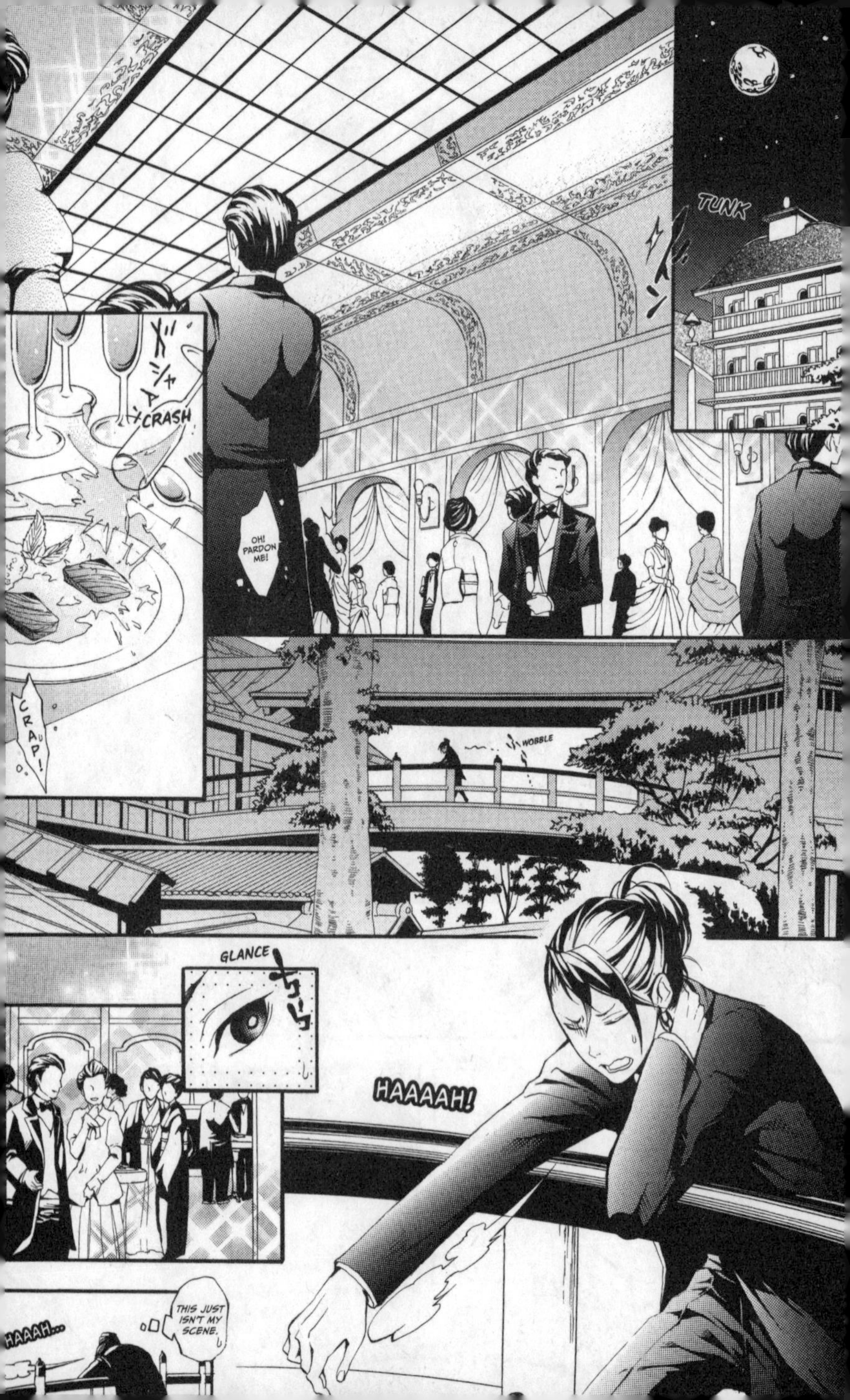
TUNK
OH! PARDON ME!
CRASH
CRAP!
WOBBLE
HAAAAH!
GLANCE
THIS JUST ISN'T MY SCENE.
HAAAH...

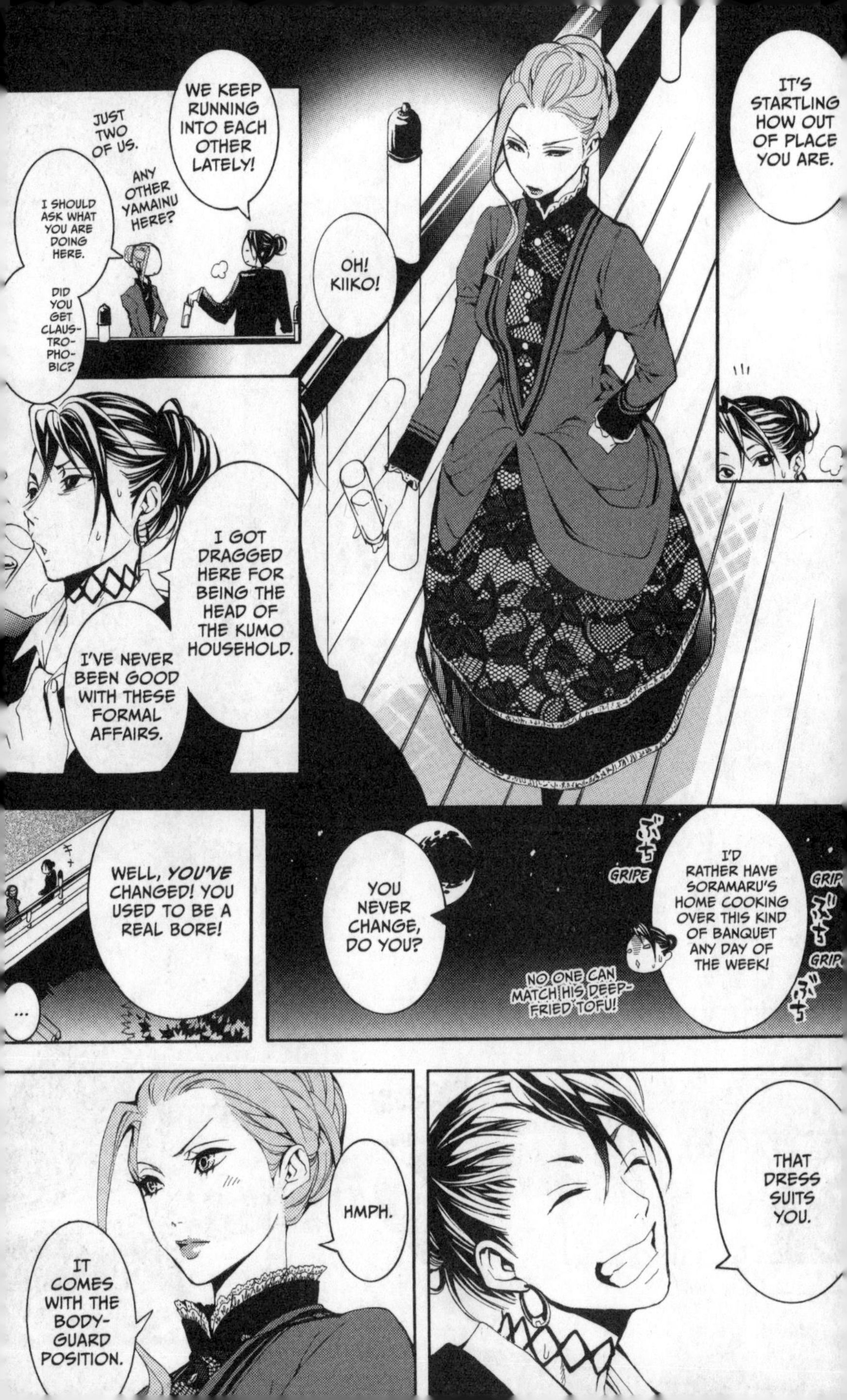
IT'S STARTLING HOW OUT OF PLACE YOU ARE.
OH! KIIKO!
WE KEEP RUNNING INTO EACH OTHER LATELY!
JUST TWO OF US.
ANY OTHER YAMAINU HERE?
I SHOULD ASK WHAT YOU ARE DOING HERE.
DID YOU GET CLAUS-TRO-PHO-BIC?
I GOT DRAGGED HERE FOR BEING THE HEAD OF THE KUMO HOUSEHOLD.
I'VE NEVER BEEN GOOD WITH THESE FORMAL AFFAIRS.
GRIPE
I'D RATHER HAVE SORAMARU'S HOME COOKING OVER THIS KIND OF BANQUET ANY DAY OF THE WEEK!
GRIPE
GRIPE
NO ONE CAN MATCH HIS DEEP-FRIED TOFU!
YOU NEVER CHANGE, DO YOU?
WELL, *YOU'VE* CHANGED! YOU USED TO BE A REAL BORE!
...
THAT DRESS SUITS YOU.
HMPH.
IT COMES WITH THE BODY-GUARD POSITION.

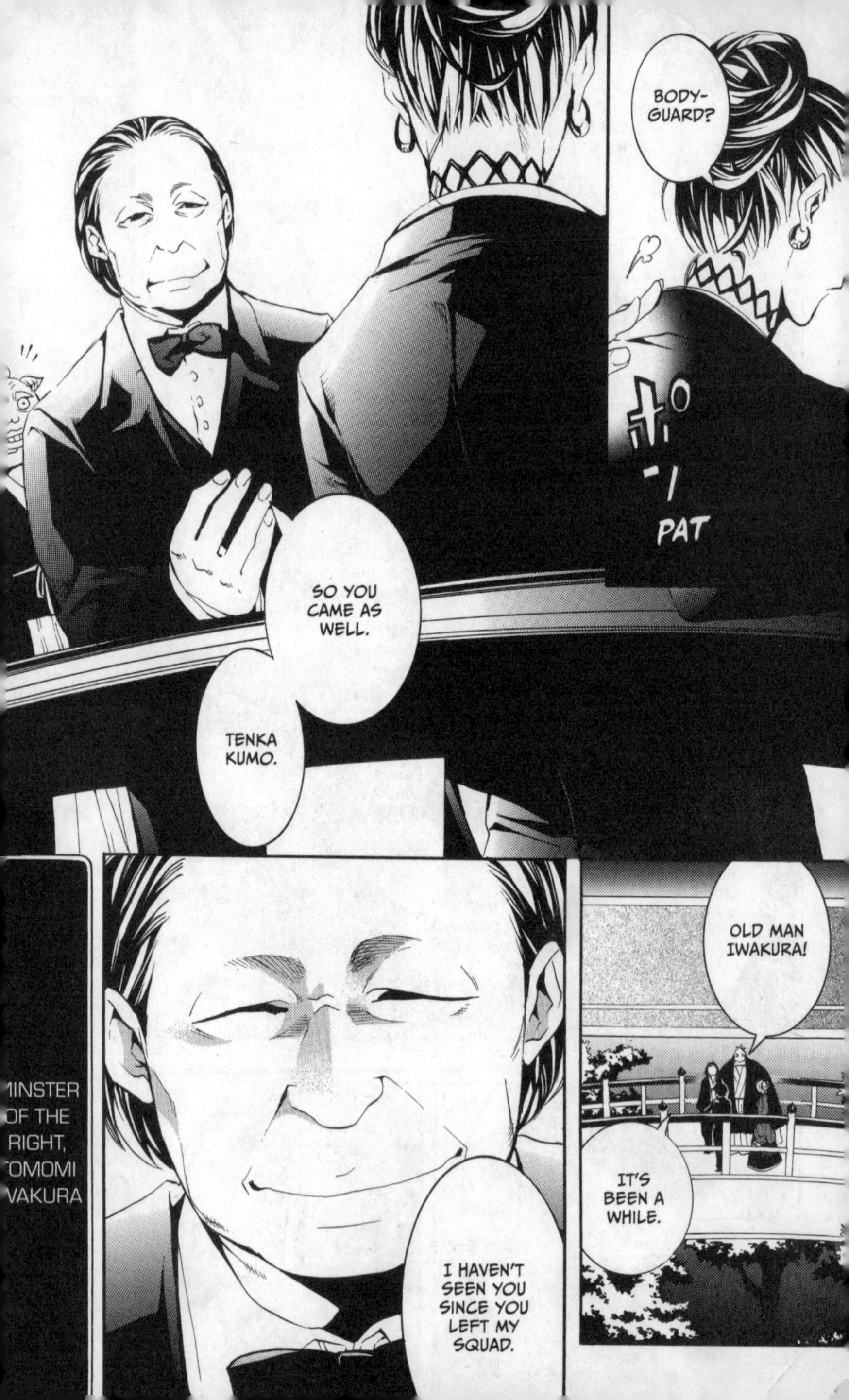
BODY-GUARD?
PAT
SO YOU CAME AS WELL.
TENKA KUMO.
OLD MAN IWAKURA!
IT'S BEEN A WHILE.
INSTER OF THE RIGHT, OMOMI VAKURA
I HAVEN'T SEEN YOU SINCE YOU LEFT MY SQUAD.

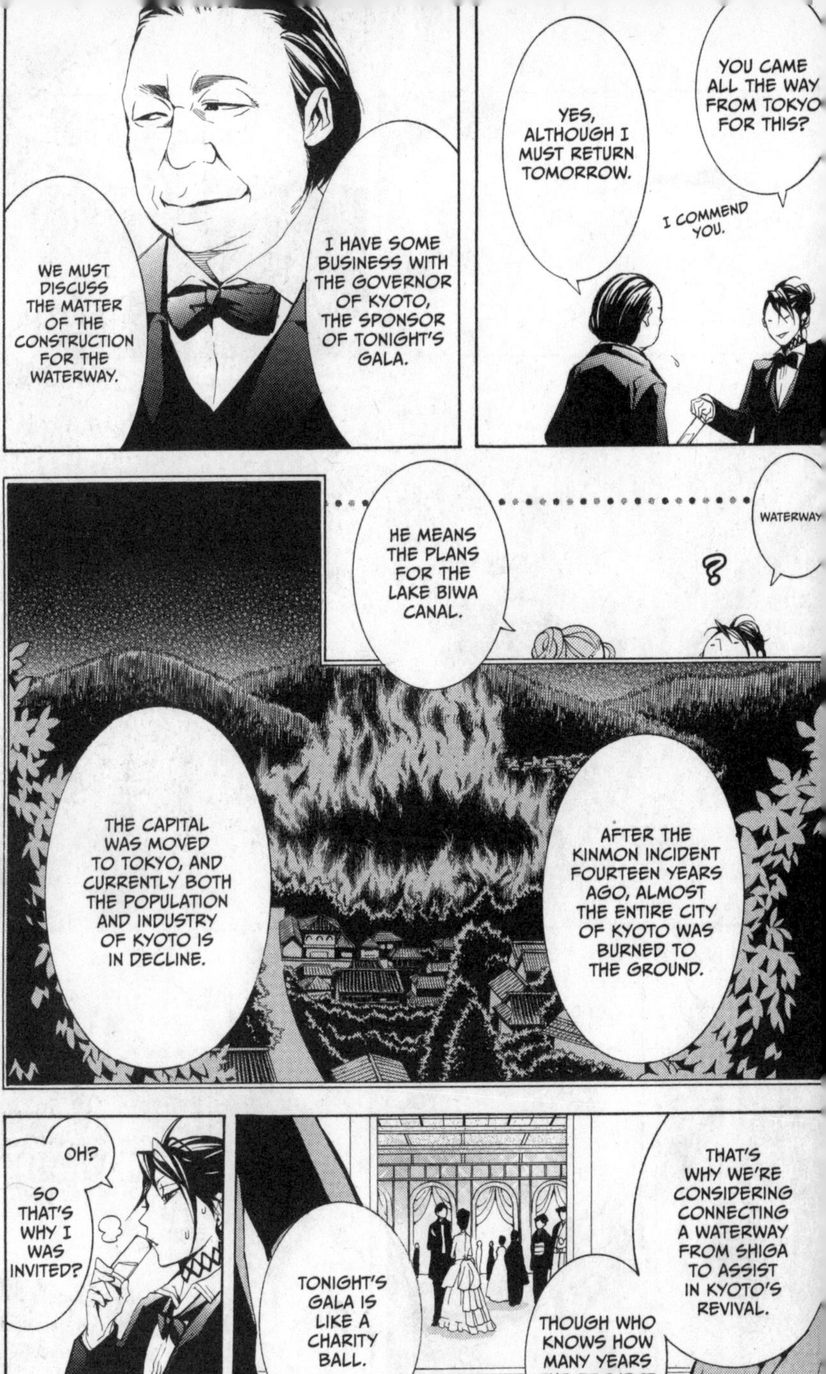
YOU CAME ALL THE WAY FROM TOKYO FOR THIS?
YES, ALTHOUGH I MUST RETURN TOMORROW.
I COMMEND YOU.
I HAVE SOME BUSINESS WITH THE GOVERNOR OF KYOTO, THE SPONSOR OF TONIGHT'S GALA.
WE MUST DISCUSS THE MATTER OF THE CONSTRUCTION FOR THE WATERWAY.
WATERWAY
HE MEANS THE PLANS FOR THE LAKE BIWA CANAL.
AFTER THE KINMON INCIDENT FOURTEEN YEARS AGO, ALMOST THE ENTIRE CITY OF KYOTO WAS BURNED TO THE GROUND.
THE CAPITAL WAS MOVED TO TOKYO, AND CURRENTLY BOTH THE POPULATION AND INDUSTRY OF KYOTO IS IN DECLINE.
THAT'S WHY WE'RE CONSIDERING CONNECTING A WATERWAY FROM SHIGA TO ASSIST IN KYOTO'S REVIVAL.
THOUGH WHO KNOWS HOW MANY YEARS THE PROJECT WILL TAKE.
TONIGHT'S GALA IS LIKE A CHARITY BALL.
OH?
SO THAT'S WHY I WAS INVITED?

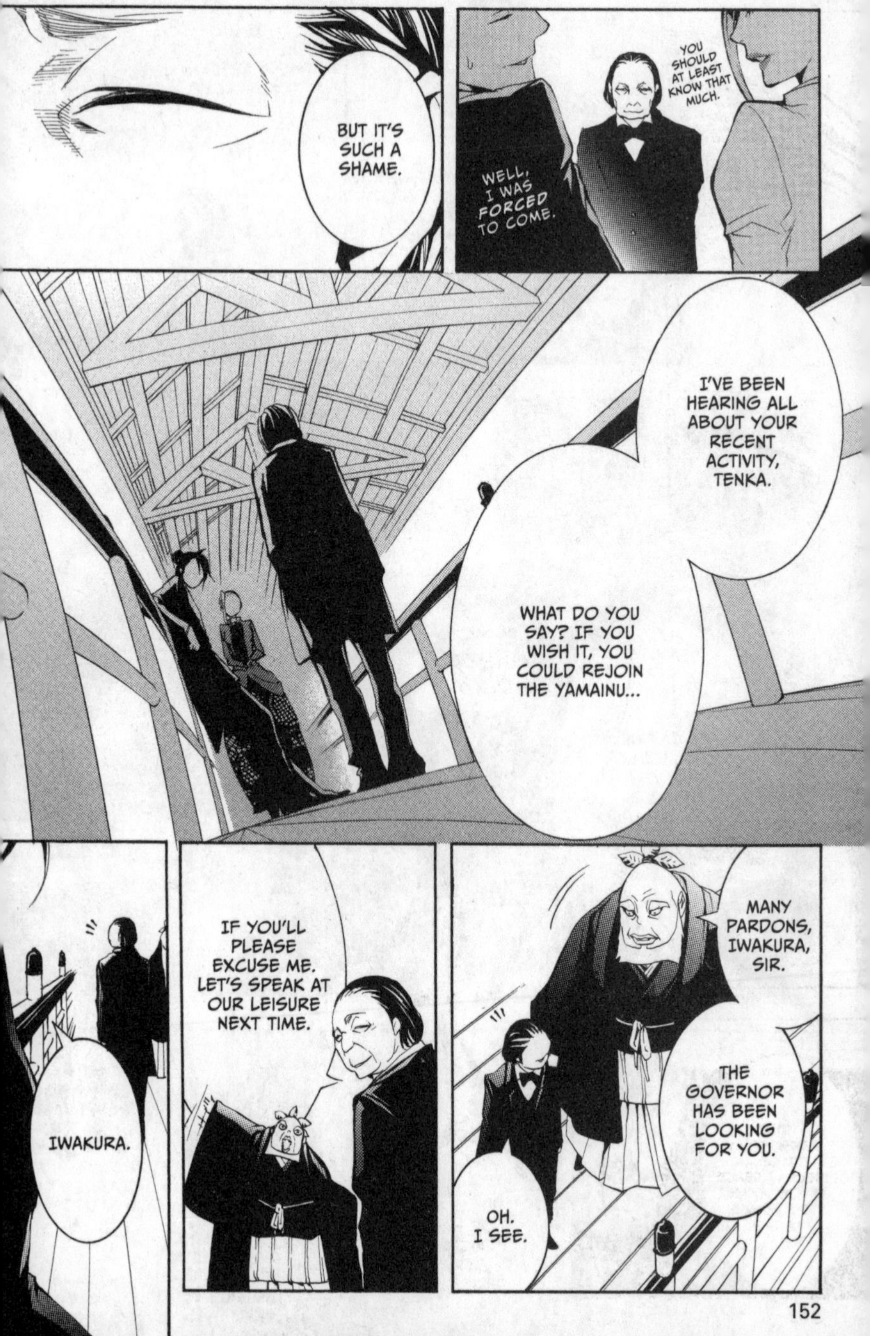
YOU SHOULD AT LEAST KNOW THAT MUCH.
WELL, I WAS FORCED TO COME.
BUT IT'S SUCH A SHAME.
I'VE BEEN HEARING ALL ABOUT YOUR RECENT ACTIVITY, TENKA.
WHAT DO YOU SAY? IF YOU WISH IT, YOU COULD REJOIN THE YAMAINU...
MANY PARDONS, IWAKURA, SIR.
THE GOVERNOR HAS BEEN LOOKING FOR YOU.
OH. I SEE.
IF YOU'LL PLEASE EXCUSE ME. LET'S SPEAK AT OUR LEISURE NEXT TIME.
IWAKURA.

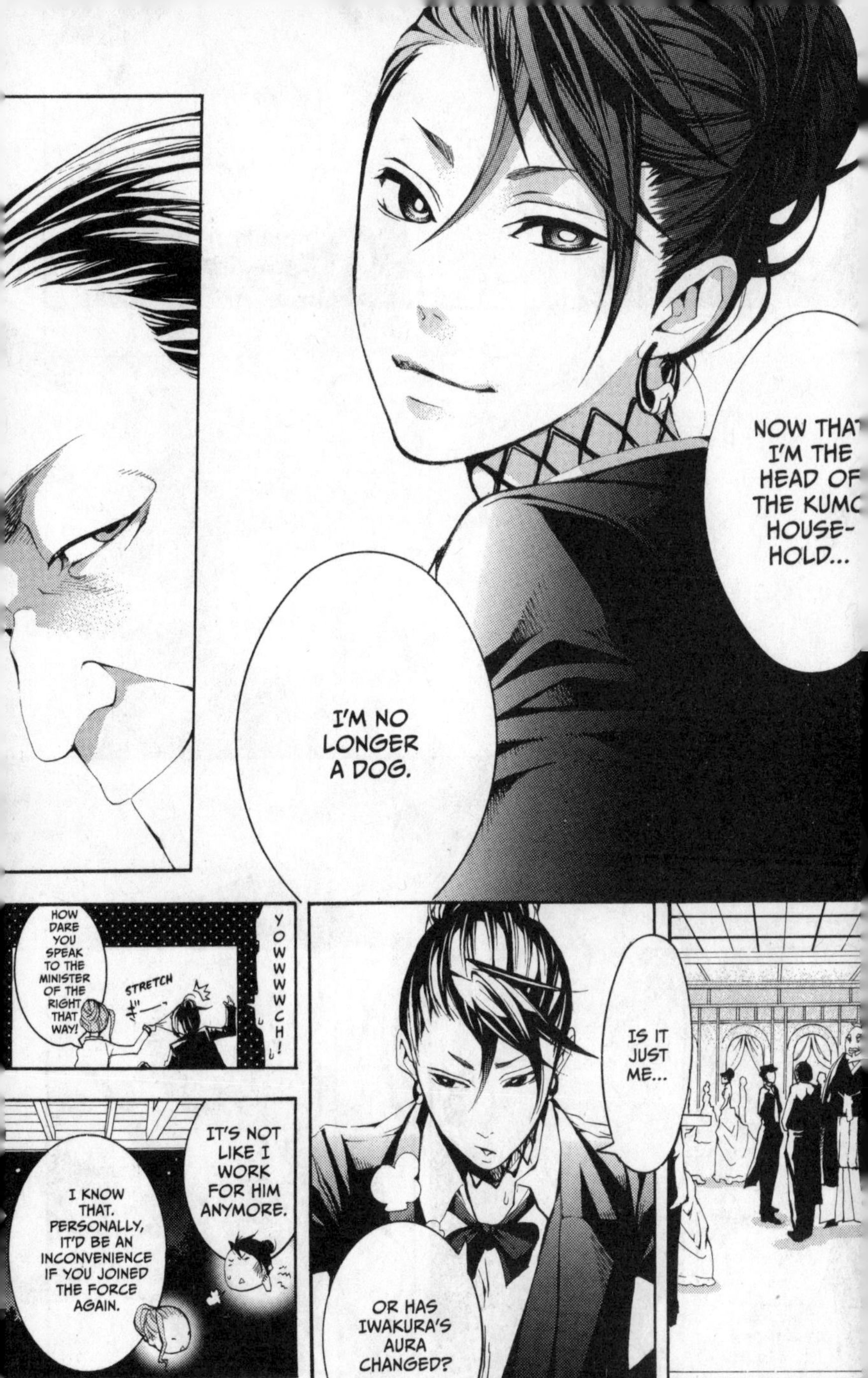
NOW THAT I'M THE HEAD OF THE KUMO HOUSE-HOLD...
I'M NO LONGER A DOG.
IS IT JUST ME...
OR HAS IWAKURA'S AURA CHANGED?
YOWWWWCH!
STRETCH
HOW DARE YOU SPEAK TO THE MINISTER OF THE RIGHT THAT WAY!
IT'S NOT LIKE I WORK FOR HIM ANYMORE.
I KNOW THAT. PERSONALLY, IT'D BE AN INCONVENIENCE IF YOU JOINED THE FORCE AGAIN.

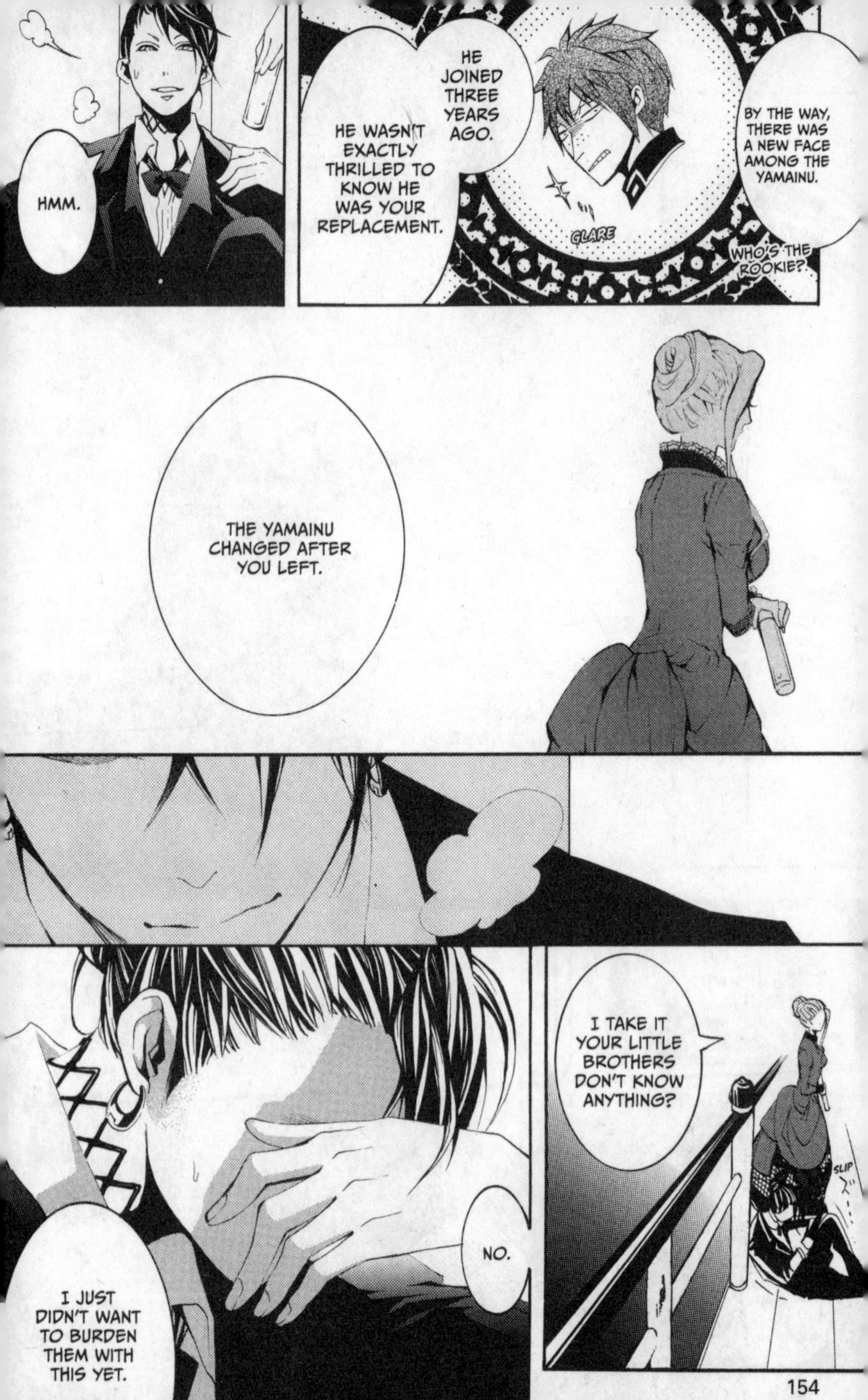
BY THE WAY, THERE WAS A NEW FACE AMONG THE YAMAINU.
WHO'S THE ROOKIE?
GLARE
HE JOINED THREE YEARS AGO.
HE WASN'T EXACTLY THRILLED TO KNOW HE WAS YOUR REPLACEMENT.
HMM.
THE YAMAINU CHANGED AFTER YOU LEFT.
I TAKE IT YOUR LITTLE BROTHERS DON'T KNOW ANYTHING?
SLIP
NO.
I JUST DIDN'T WANT TO BURDEN THEM WITH THIS YET.

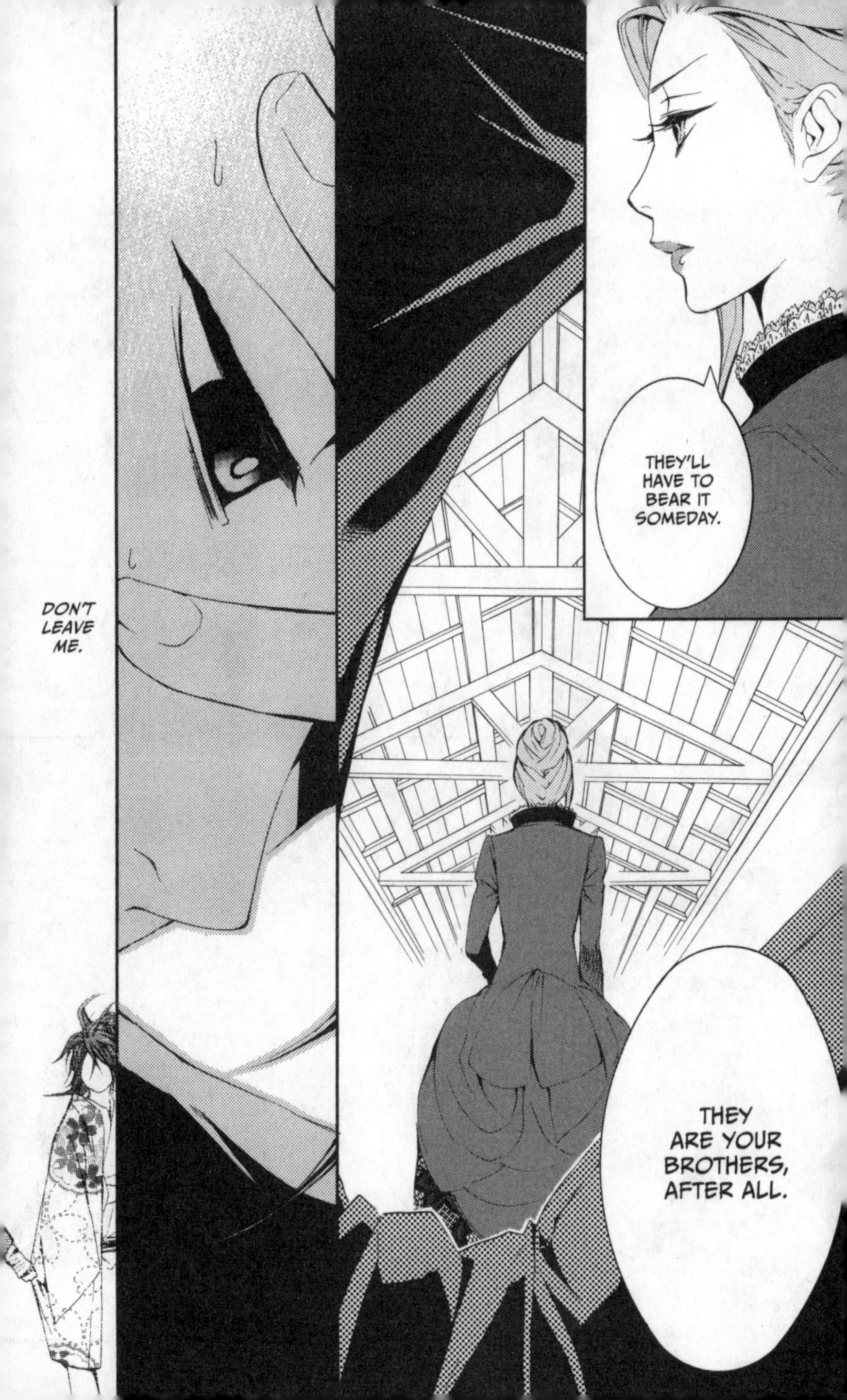
THEY'LL HAVE TO BEAR IT SOMEDAY.
THEY ARE YOUR BROTHERS, AFTER ALL.
DON'T LEAVE ME.

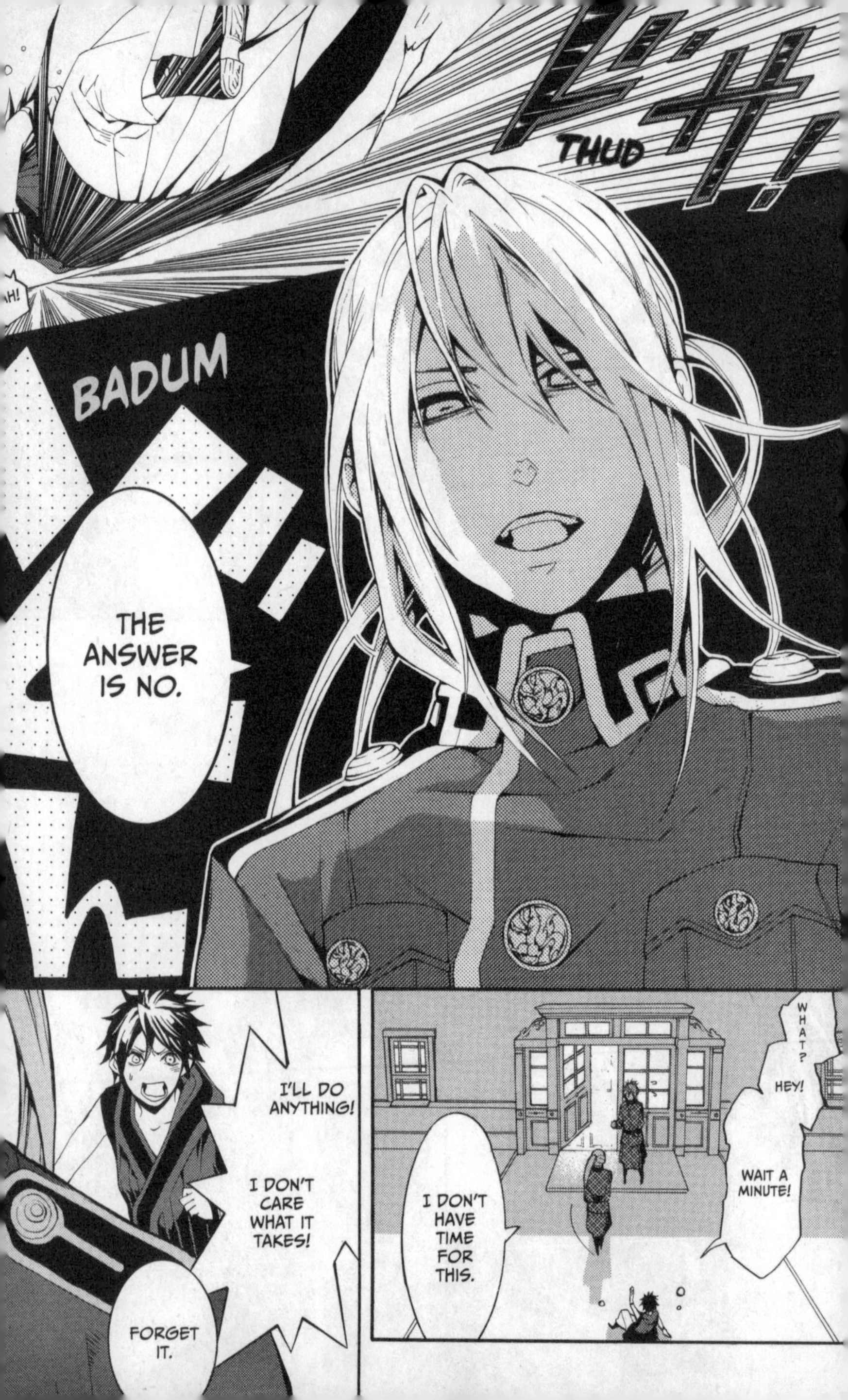
THUD
AH!
BADUM
THE ANSWER IS NO.
WHAT?
HEY!
WAIT A MINUTE!
I DON'T HAVE TIME FOR THIS.
I'LL DO ANYTHING!
I DON'T CARE WHAT IT TAKES!
FORGET IT.

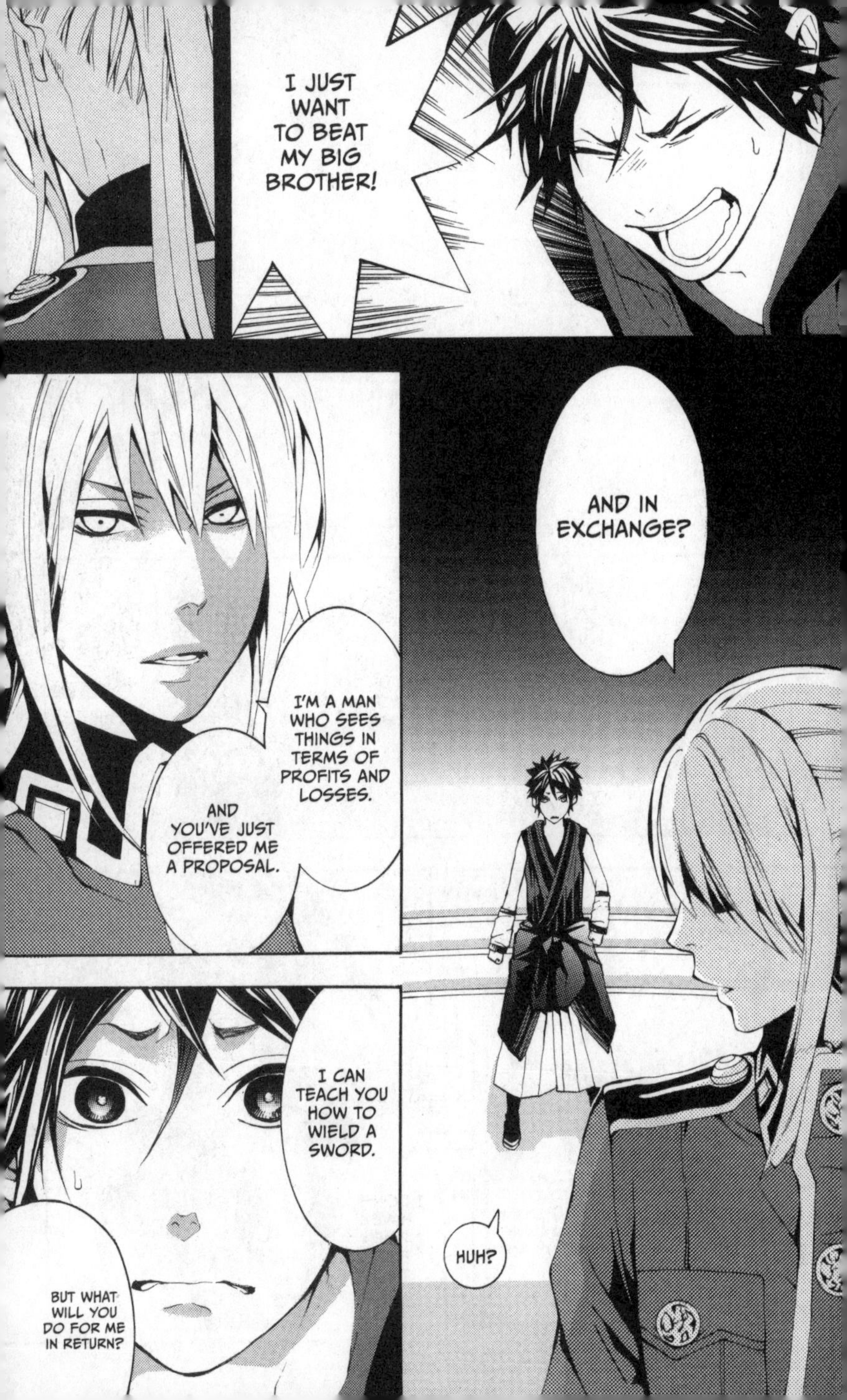
I JUST WANT TO BEAT MY BIG BROTHER!
AND IN EXCHANGE?
HUH?
I'M A MAN WHO SEES THINGS IN TERMS OF PROFITS AND LOSSES.
AND YOU'VE JUST OFFERED ME A PROPOSAL.
I CAN TEACH YOU HOW TO WIELD A SWORD.
BUT WHAT WILL YOU DO FOR ME IN RETURN?

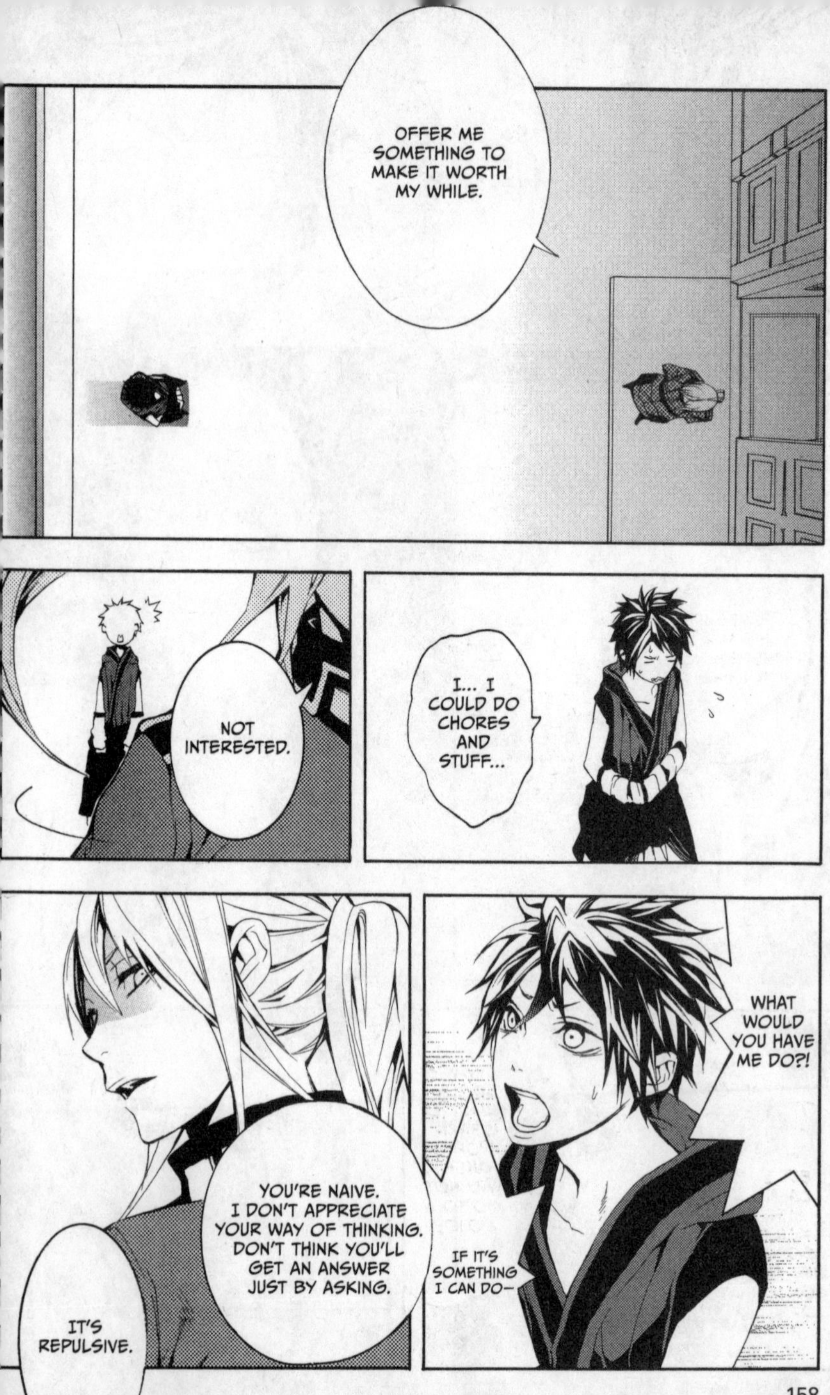
OFFER ME SOMETHING TO MAKE IT WORTH MY WHILE.
I... I COULD DO CHORES AND STUFF...
NOT INTERESTED.
WHAT WOULD YOU HAVE ME DO?!
IF IT'S SOMETHING I CAN DO—
YOU'RE NAIVE. I DON'T APPRECIATE YOUR WAY OF THINKING. DON'T THINK YOU'LL GET AN ANSWER JUST BY ASKING.
IT'S REPULSIVE.

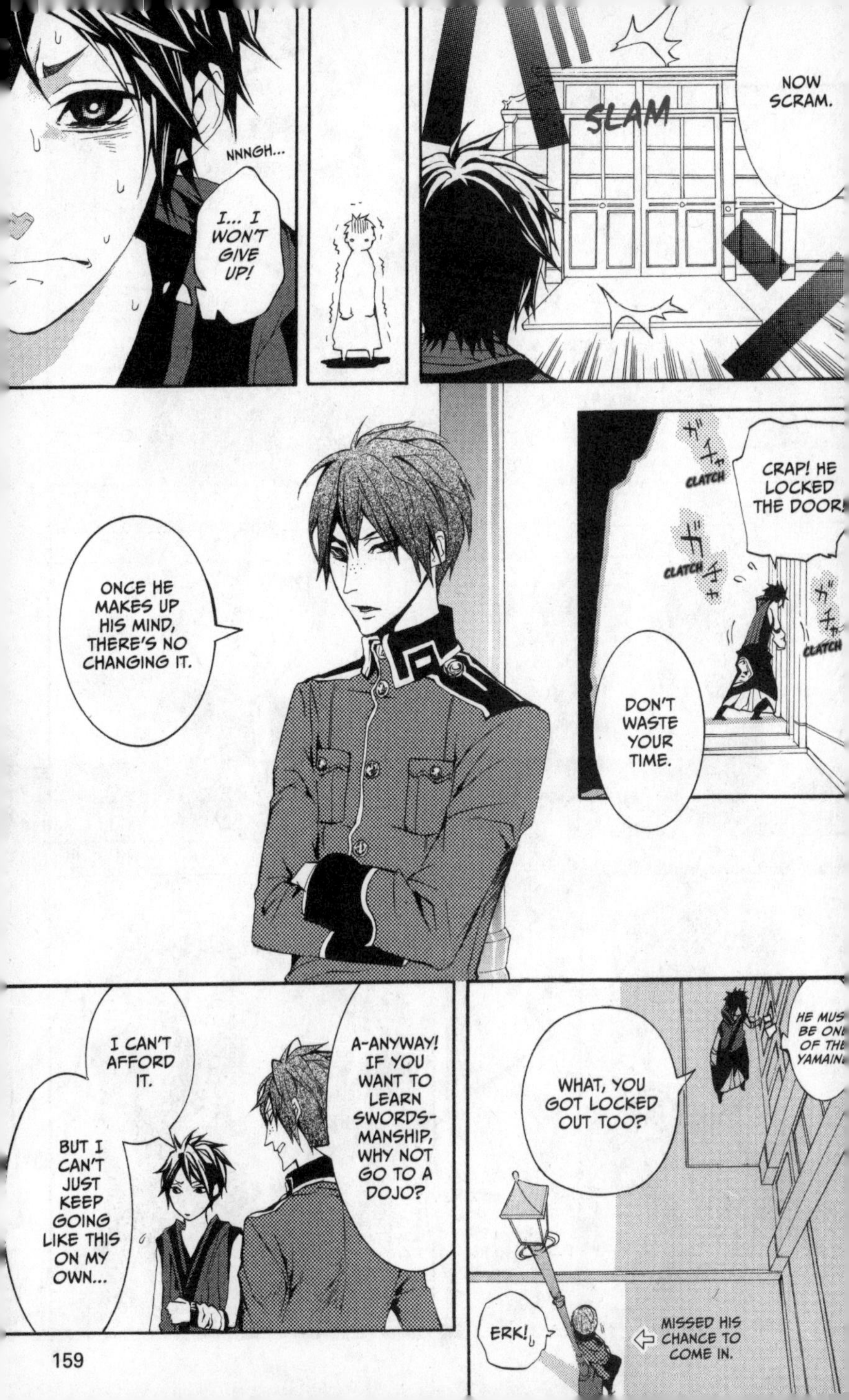
NOW SCRAM.
SLAM
NNNGH...
I... I WON'T GIVE UP!
CRAP! HE LOCKED THE DOOR!
CLATCH
CLATCH
CLATCH
DON'T WASTE YOUR TIME.
ONCE HE MAKES UP HIS MIND, THERE'S NO CHANGING IT.
HE MUS BE ON OF THE YAMAIN
WHAT, YOU GOT LOCKED OUT TOO?
ERK!
MISSED HIS CHANCE TO COME IN.
A-ANYWAY! IF YOU WANT TO LEARN SWORDS-MANSHIP, WHY NOT GO TO A DOJO?
I CAN'T AFFORD IT.
BUT I CAN'T JUST KEEP GOING LIKE THIS ON MY OWN...

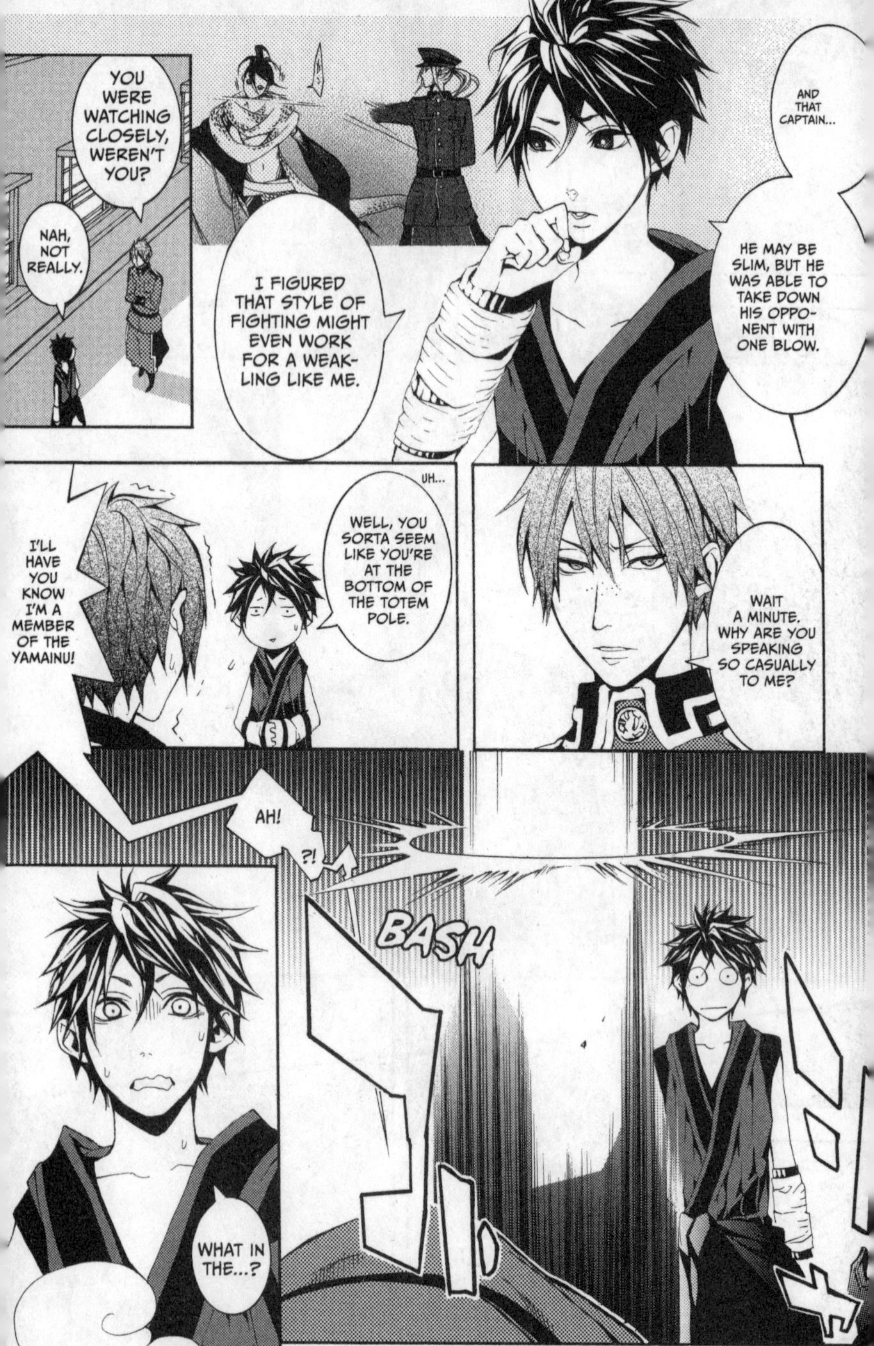
AND THAT CAPTAIN...
HE MAY BE SLIM, BUT HE WAS ABLE TO TAKE DOWN HIS OPPONENT WITH ONE BLOW.
I FIGURED THAT STYLE OF FIGHTING MIGHT EVEN WORK FOR A WEAKLING LIKE ME.
YOU WERE WATCHING CLOSELY, WEREN'T YOU?
NAH, NOT REALLY.
WAIT A MINUTE. WHY ARE YOU SPEAKING SO CASUALLY TO ME?
UH...
WELL, YOU SORTA SEEM LIKE YOU'RE AT THE BOTTOM OF THE TOTEM POLE.
I'LL HAVE YOU KNOW I'M A MEMBER OF THE YAMAINU!
AH!
?!
BASH
WHAT IN THE...?

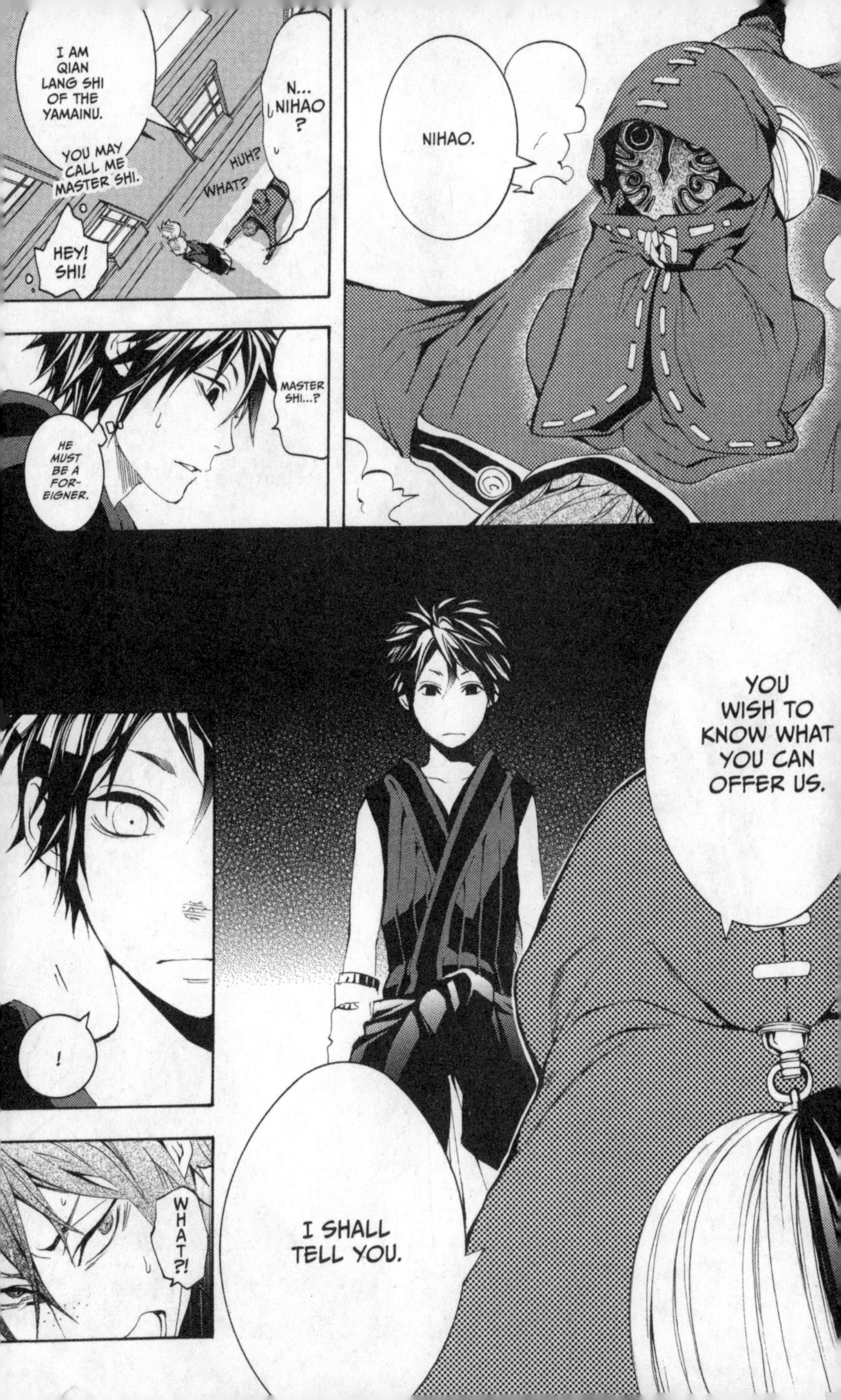
NIHAO.
N... NIHAO?
HUH? WHAT?
I AM QIAN LANG SHI OF THE YAMAINU.
YOU MAY CALL ME MASTER SHI.
HEY! SHI!
MASTER SHI...?
HE MUST BE A FOR-EIGNER.
YOU WISH TO KNOW WHAT YOU CAN OFFER US.
I SHALL TELL YOU.
!
WHAT?!

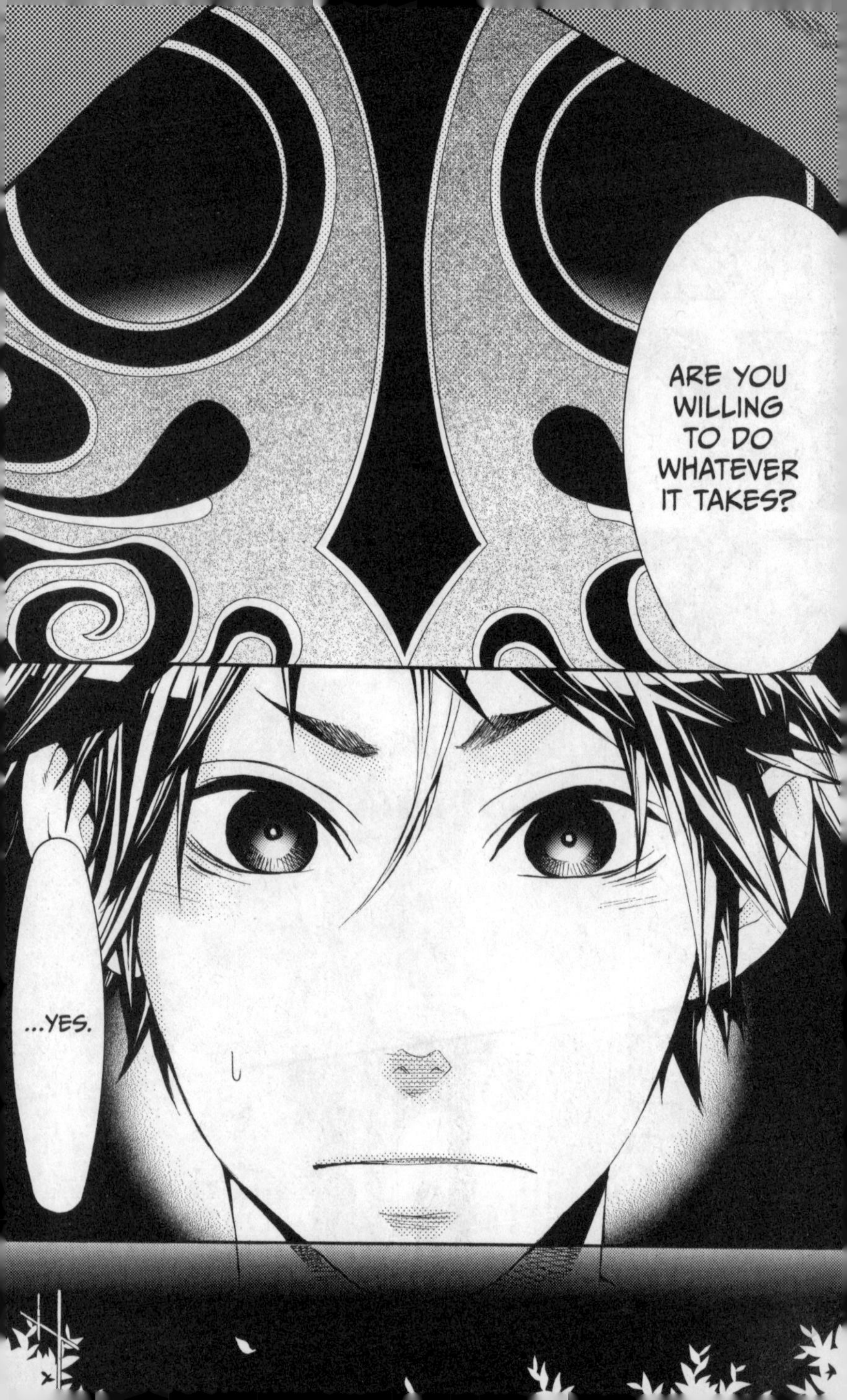
ARE YOU WILLING TO DO WHATEVER IT TAKES?
...YES.

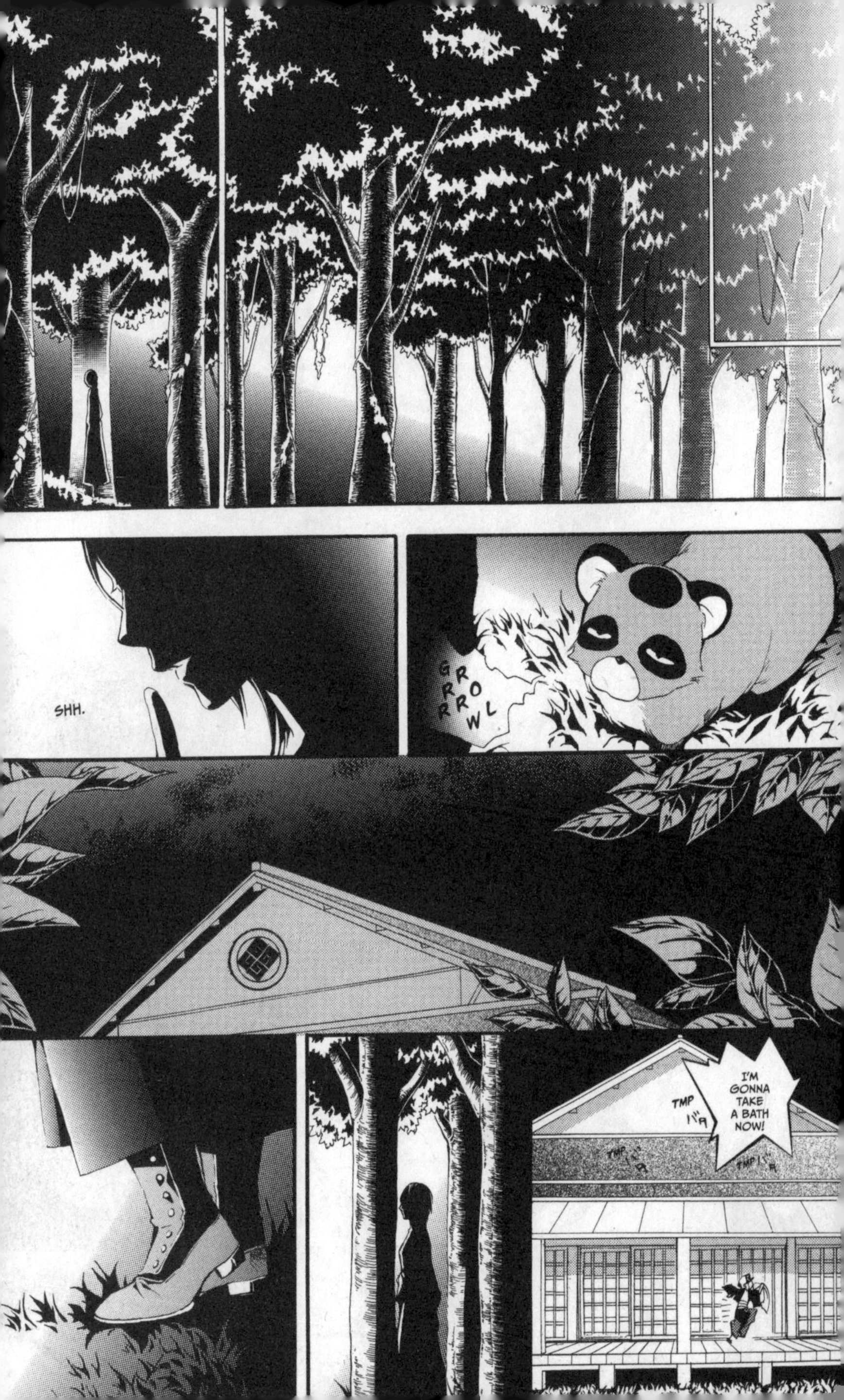
GRRRROWL
SHH.
TMP バタ
I'M GONNA TAKE A BATH NOW!
TMP バタ
TMP バタ

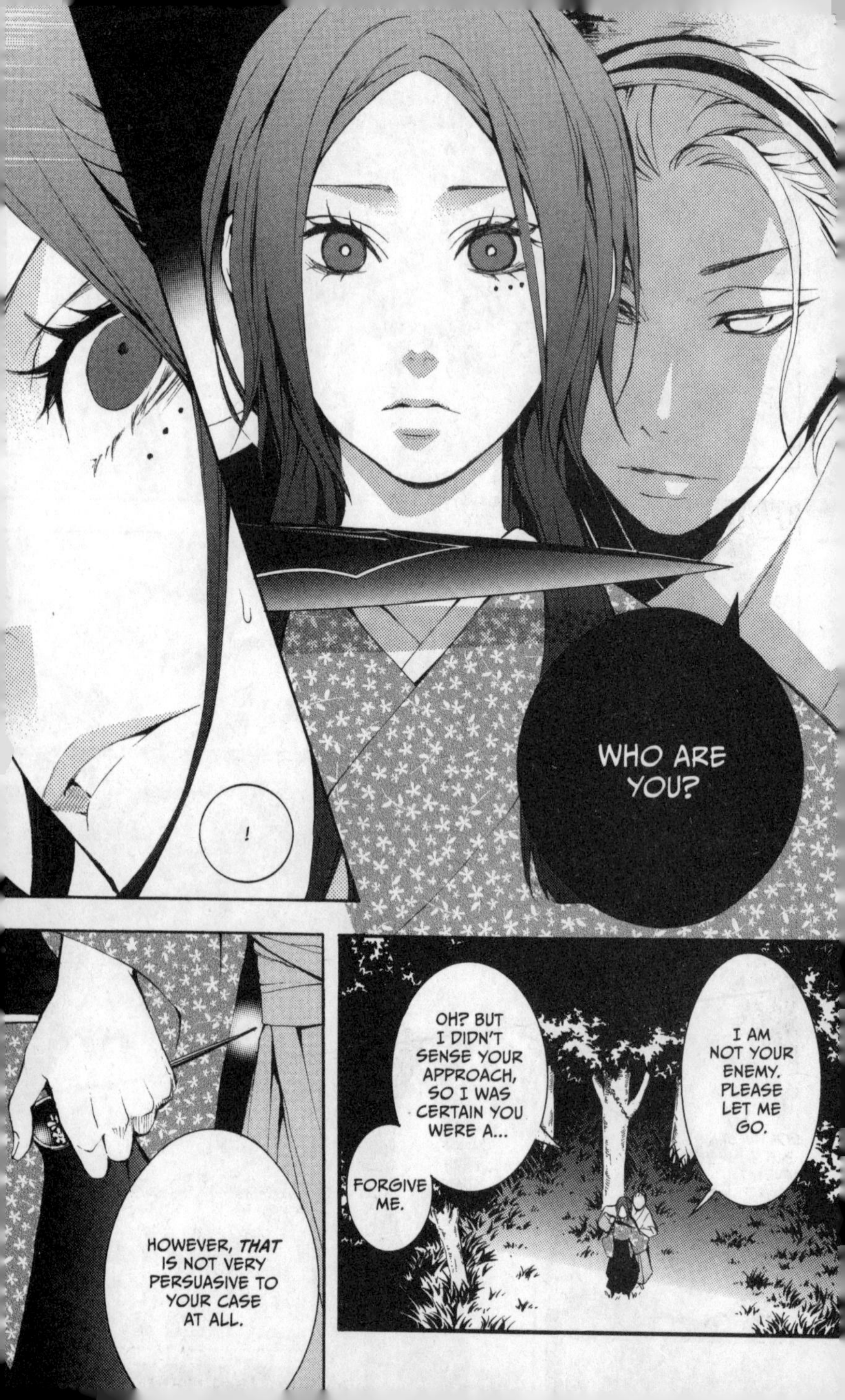
WHO ARE YOU?
!
I AM NOT YOUR ENEMY. PLEASE LET ME GO.
OH? BUT I DIDN'T SENSE YOUR APPROACH, SO I WAS CERTAIN YOU WERE A...
FORGIVE ME.
HOWEVER, *THAT* IS NOT VERY PERSUASIVE TO YOUR CASE AT ALL.

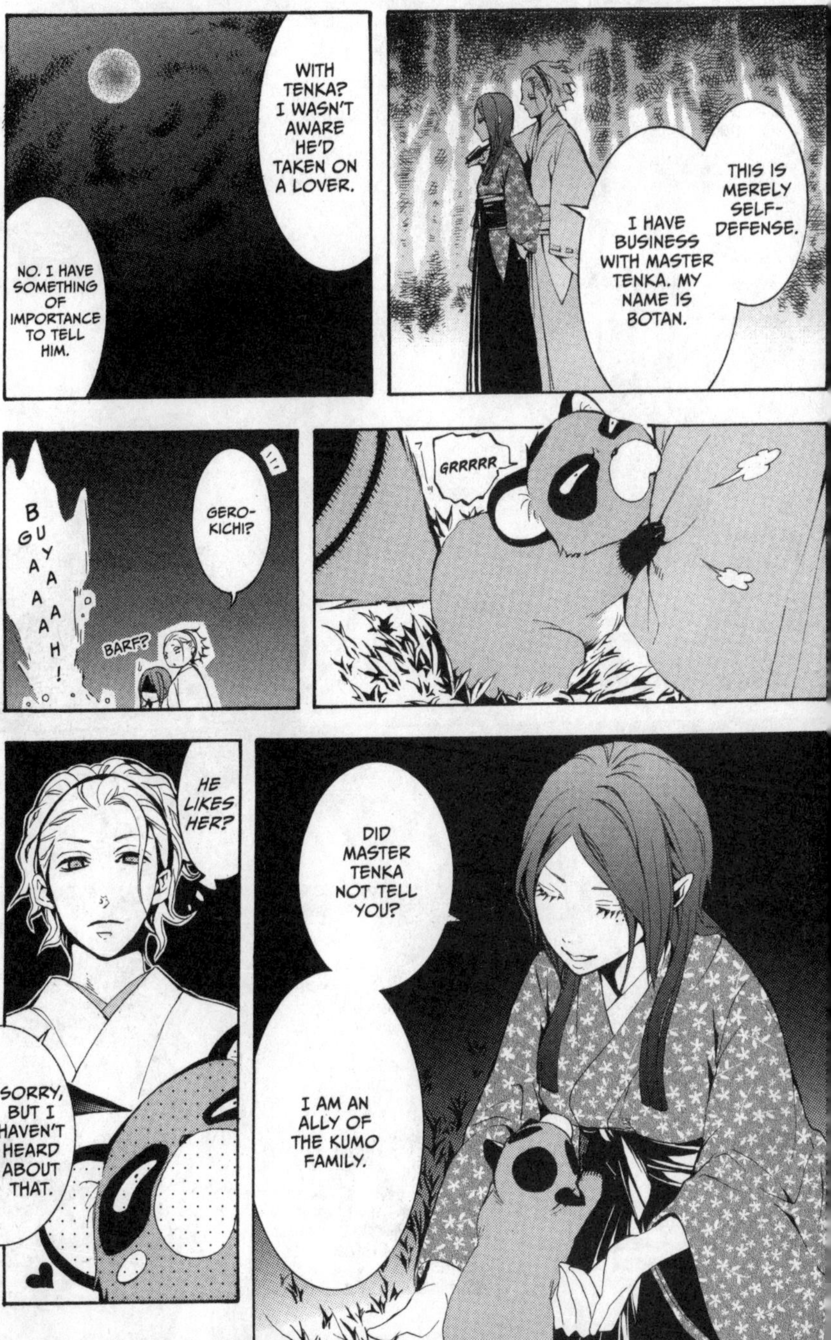
THIS IS MERELY SELF-DEFENSE.
I HAVE BUSINESS WITH MASTER TENKA. MY NAME IS BOTAN.
WITH TENKA? I WASN'T AWARE HE'D TAKEN ON A LOVER.
NO. I HAVE SOMETHING OF IMPORTANCE TO TELL HIM.
GRRRRR
...
GERO-KICHI?
BUGYAAAAAH!
BARF?
DID MASTER TENKA NOT TELL YOU?
I AM AN ALLY OF THE KUMO FAMILY.
HE LIKES HER?
SORRY, BUT I HAVEN'T HEARD ABOUT THAT.

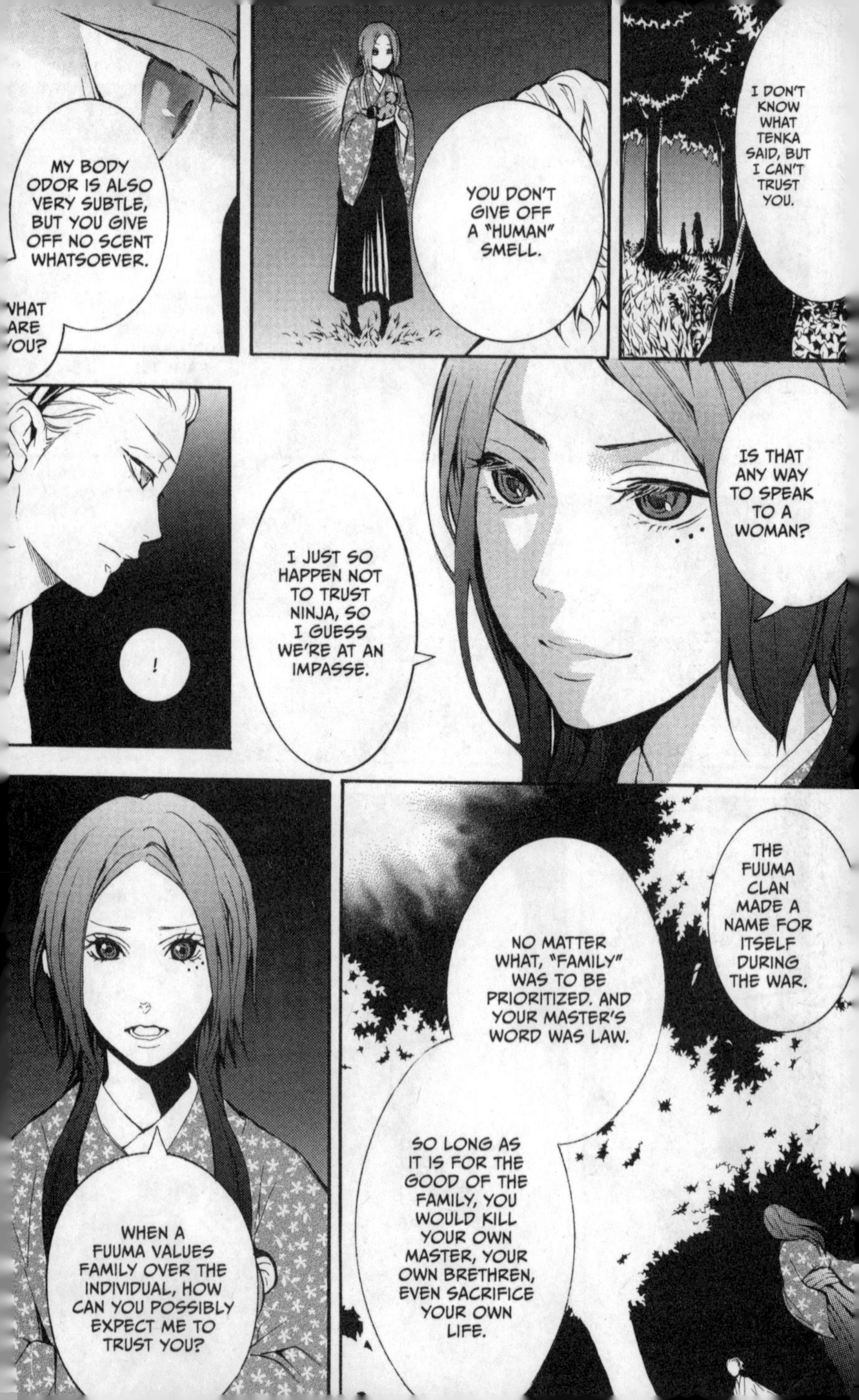
I DON'T KNOW WHAT TENKA SAID, BUT I CAN'T TRUST YOU.
YOU DON'T GIVE OFF A "HUMAN" SMELL.
MY BODY ODOR IS ALSO VERY SUBTLE, BUT YOU GIVE OFF NO SCENT WHATSOEVER.
WHAT ARE YOU?
IS THAT ANY WAY TO SPEAK TO A WOMAN?
I JUST SO HAPPEN NOT TO TRUST NINJA, SO I GUESS WE'RE AT AN IMPASSE.
!
THE FUUMA CLAN MADE A NAME FOR ITSELF DURING THE WAR.
NO MATTER WHAT, "FAMILY" WAS TO BE PRIORITIZED. AND YOUR MASTER'S WORD WAS LAW.
SO LONG AS IT IS FOR THE GOOD OF THE FAMILY, YOU WOULD KILL YOUR OWN MASTER, YOUR OWN BRETHREN, EVEN SACRIFICE YOUR OWN LIFE.
WHEN A FUUMA VALUES FAMILY OVER THE INDIVIDUAL, HOW CAN YOU POSSIBLY EXPECT ME TO TRUST YOU?

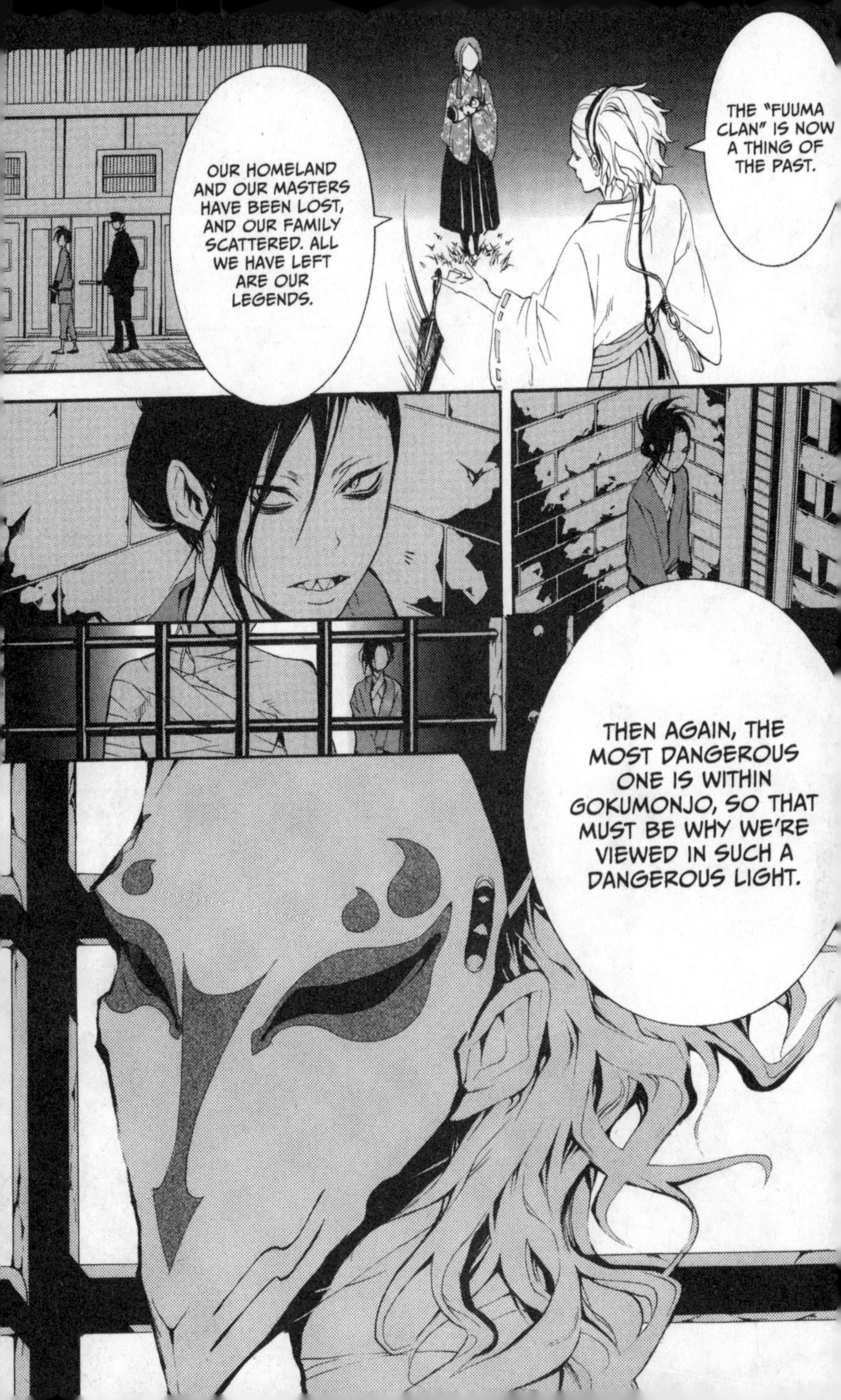
THE "FUUMA CLAN" IS NOW A THING OF THE PAST.
OUR HOMELAND AND OUR MASTERS HAVE BEEN LOST, AND OUR FAMILY SCATTERED. ALL WE HAVE LEFT ARE OUR LEGENDS.
THEN AGAIN, THE MOST DANGEROUS ONE IS WITHIN GOKUMONJO, SO THAT MUST BE WHY WE'RE VIEWED IN SUCH A DANGEROUS LIGHT.

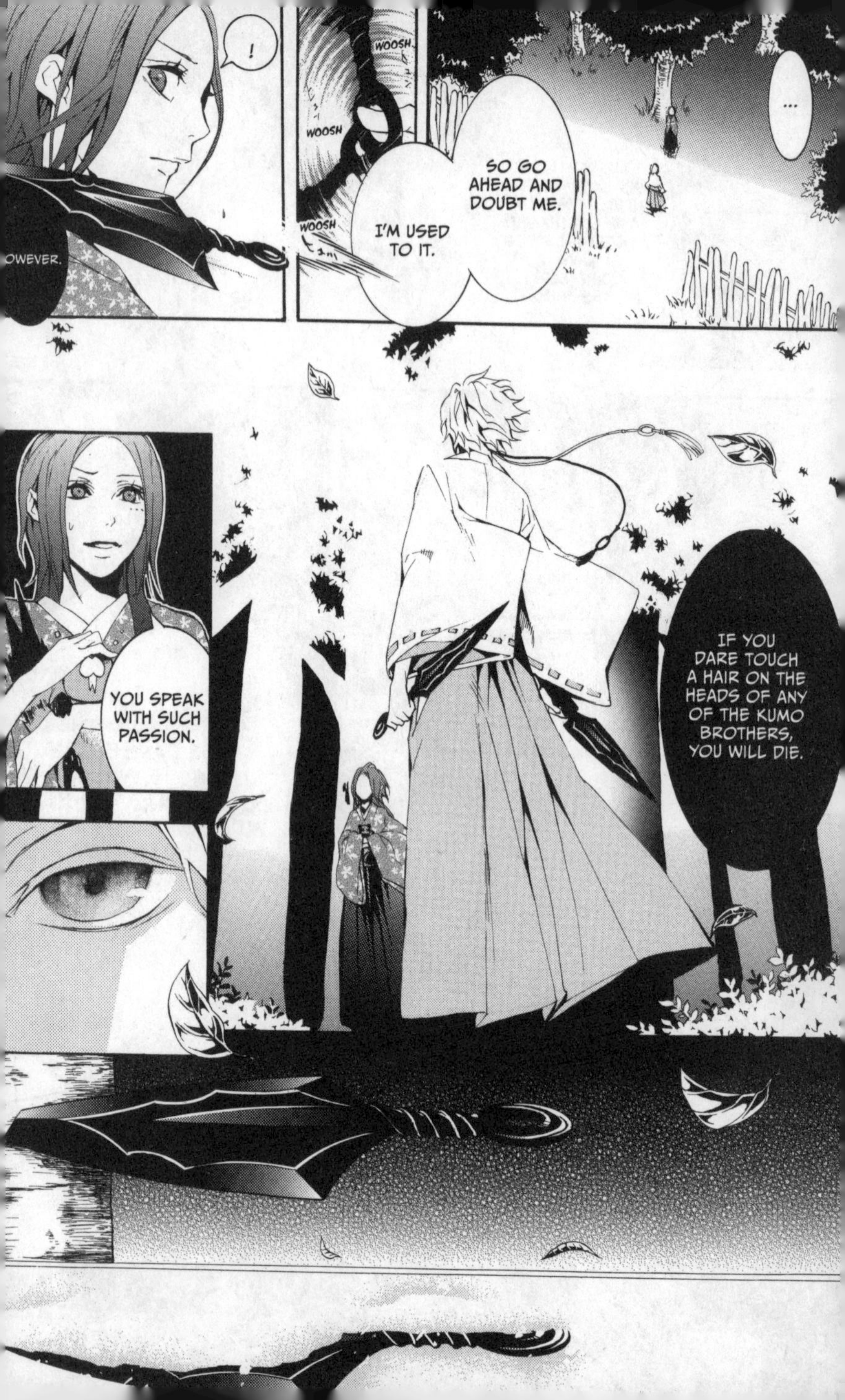
...
SO GO AHEAD AND DOUBT ME.
I'M USED TO IT.
WOOSH
WOOSH
WOOSH
!
OWEVER.
IF YOU DARE TOUCH A HAIR ON THE HEADS OF ANY OF THE KUMO BROTHERS, YOU WILL DIE.
YOU SPEAK WITH SUCH PASSION.

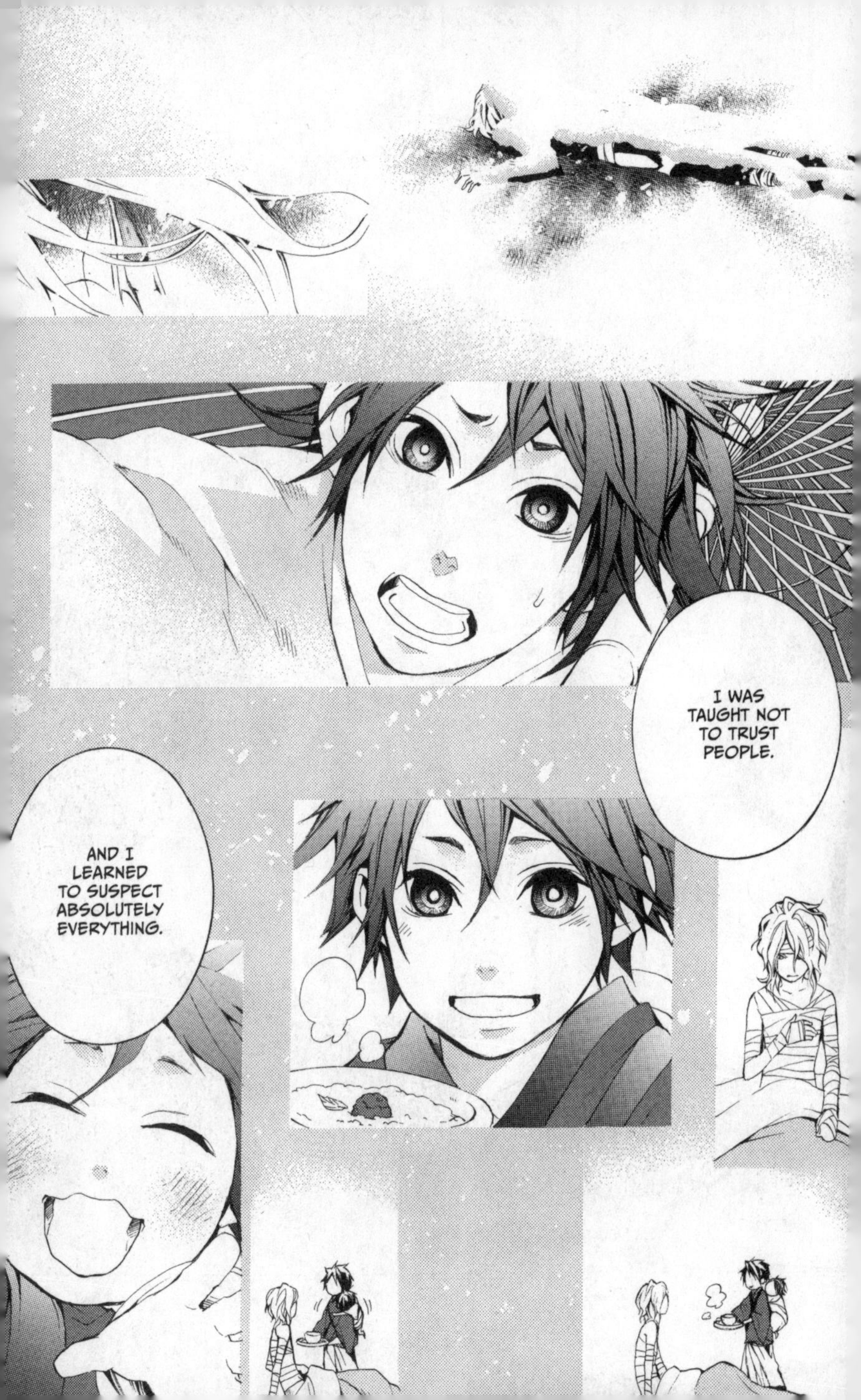
I WAS TAUGHT NOT TO TRUST PEOPLE.
AND I LEARNED TO SUSPECT ABSOLUTELY EVERYTHING.

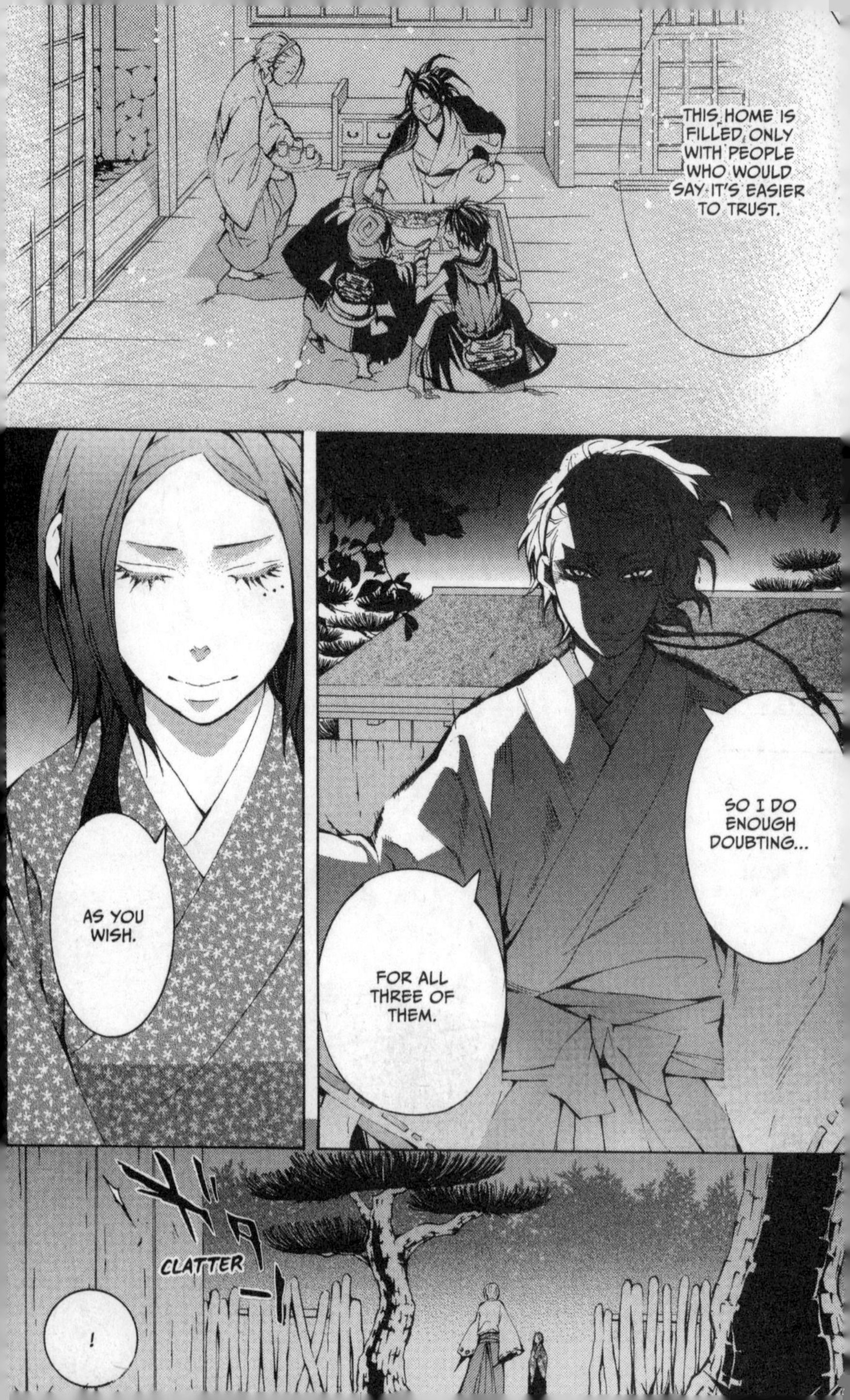
THIS HOME IS FILLED ONLY WITH PEOPLE WHO WOULD SAY IT'S EASIER TO TRUST.
SO I DO ENOUGH DOUBTING...
FOR ALL THREE OF THEM.
AS YOU WISH.
CLATTER
!

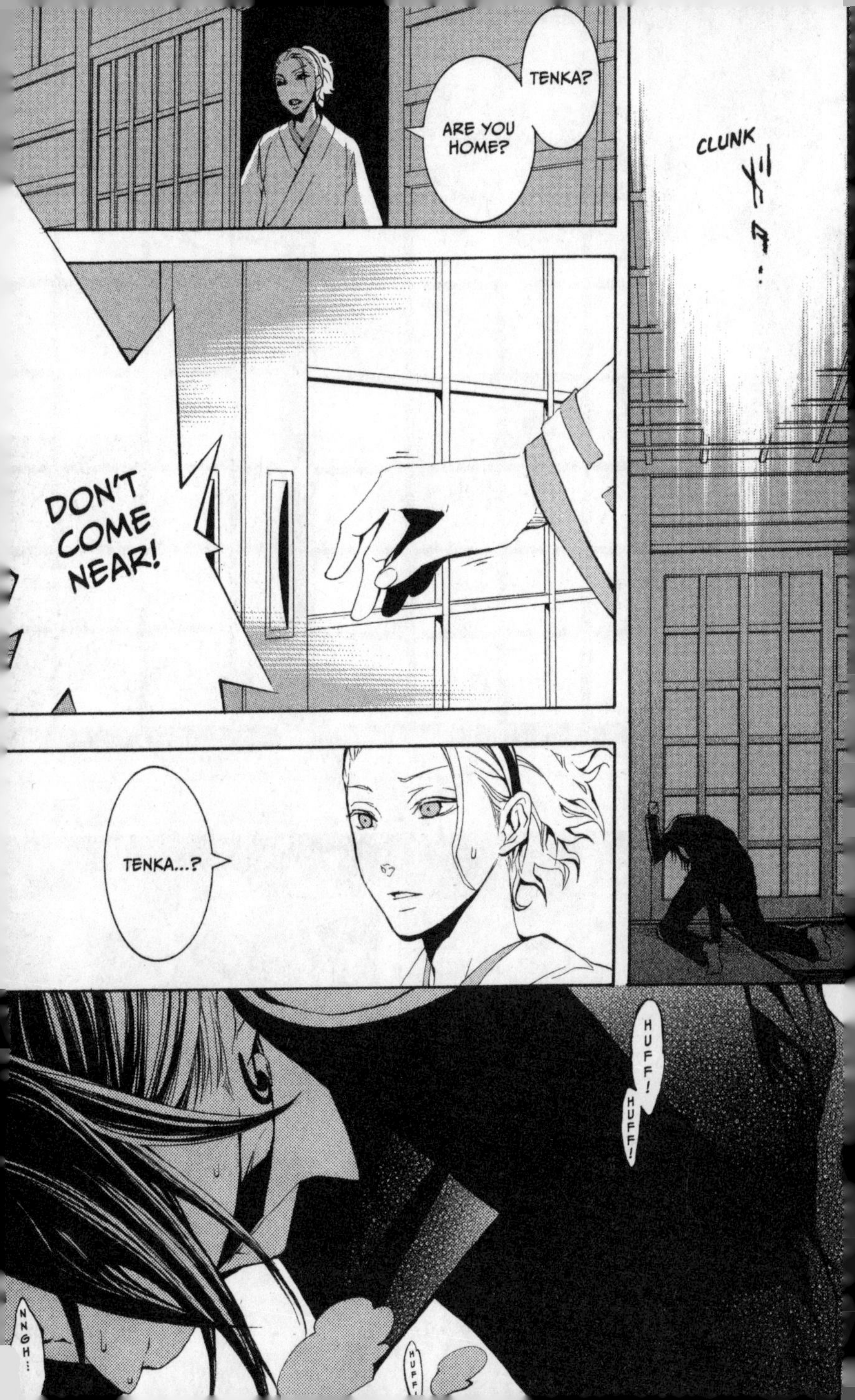
CLUNK
TENKA?
ARE YOU HOME?
DON'T COME NEAR!
TENKA...?
HUFF! HUFF!
NNGH..

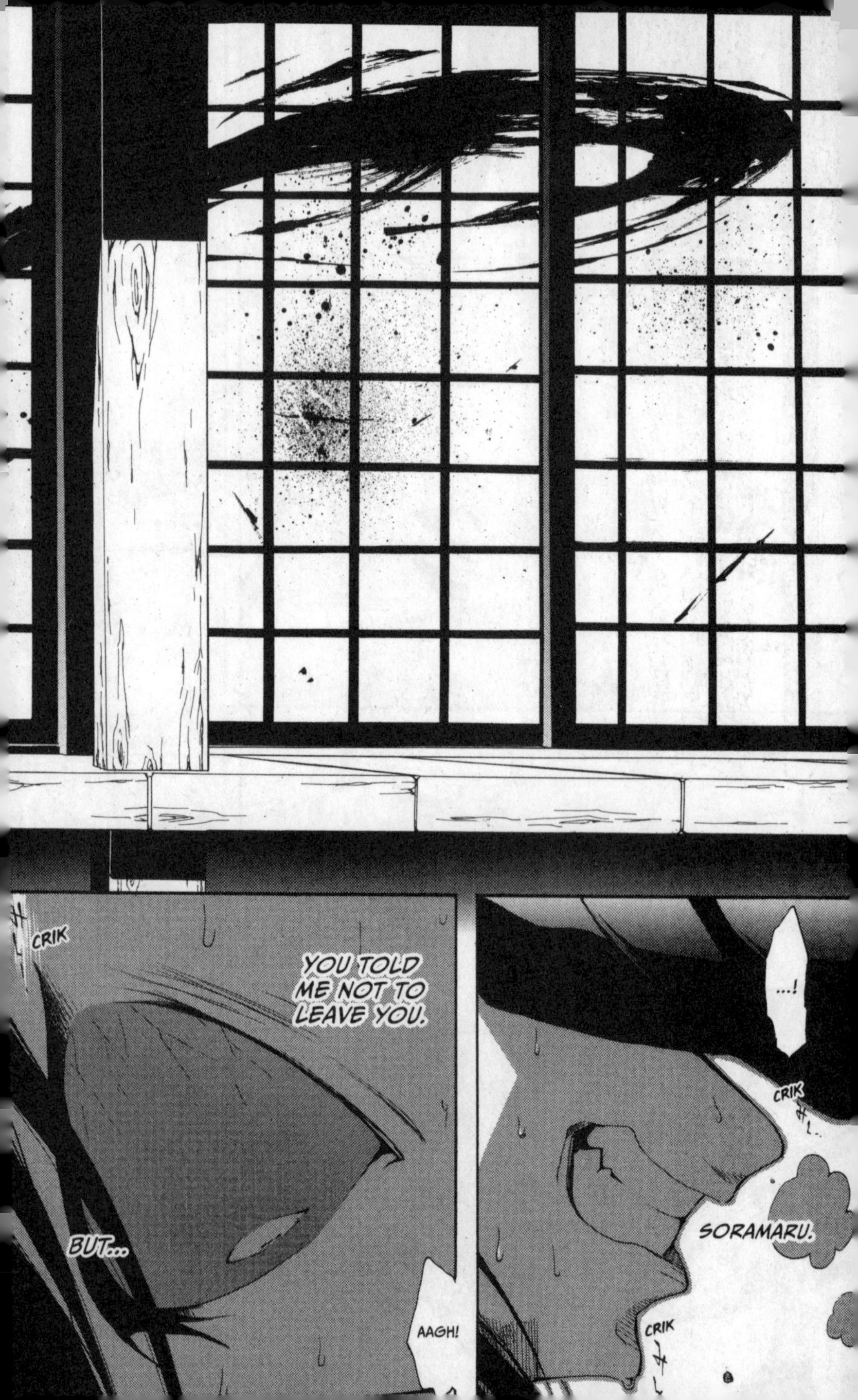
...!
CRIK
SORAMARU.
CRIK
YOU TOLD ME NOT TO LEAVE YOU.
CRIK
BUT...
AAGH!

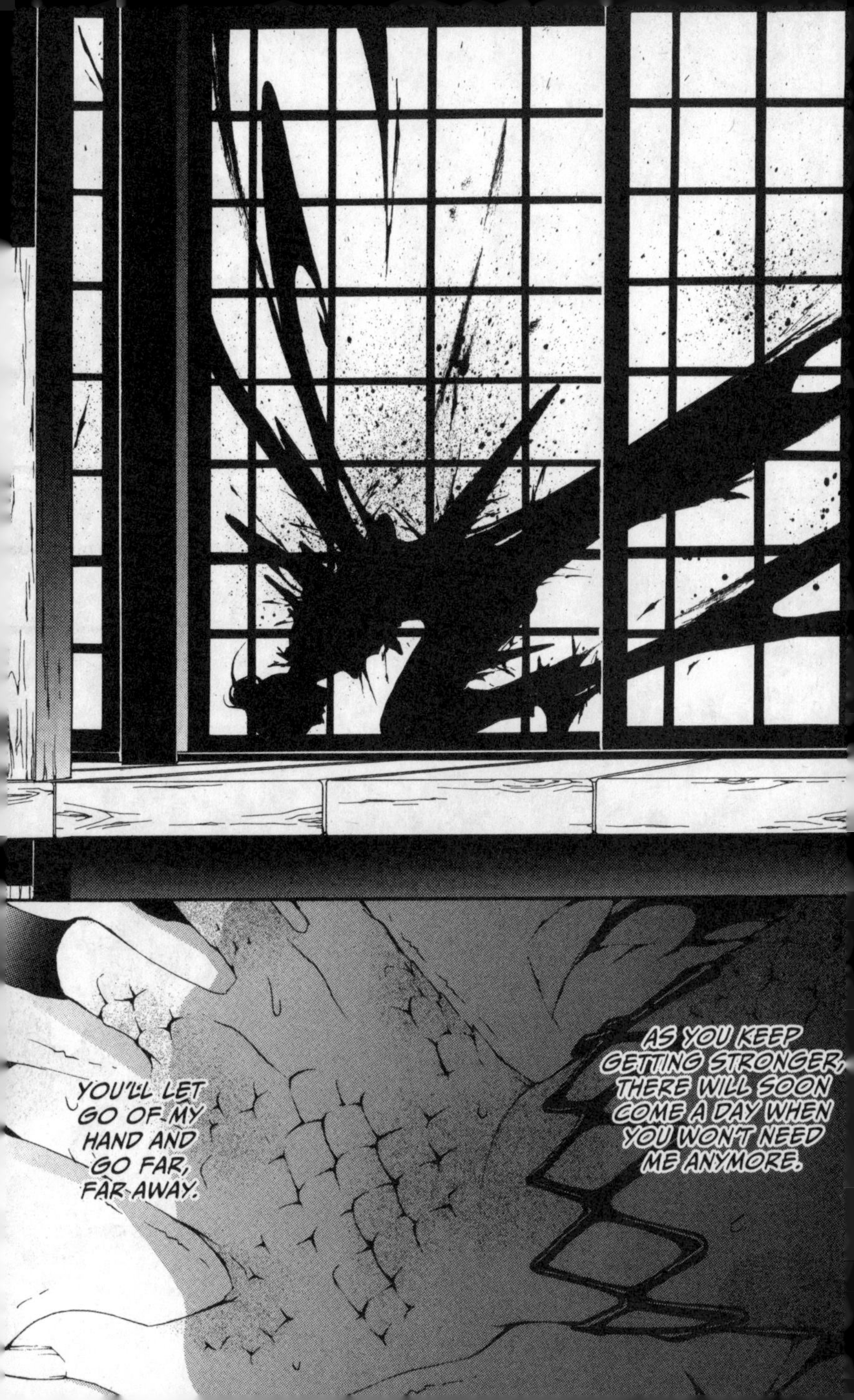
AS YOU KEEP GETTING STRONGER, THERE WILL SOON COME A DAY WHEN YOU WON'T NEED ME ANYMORE.
YOU'LL LET GO OF MY HAND AND GO FAR, FAR AWAY.

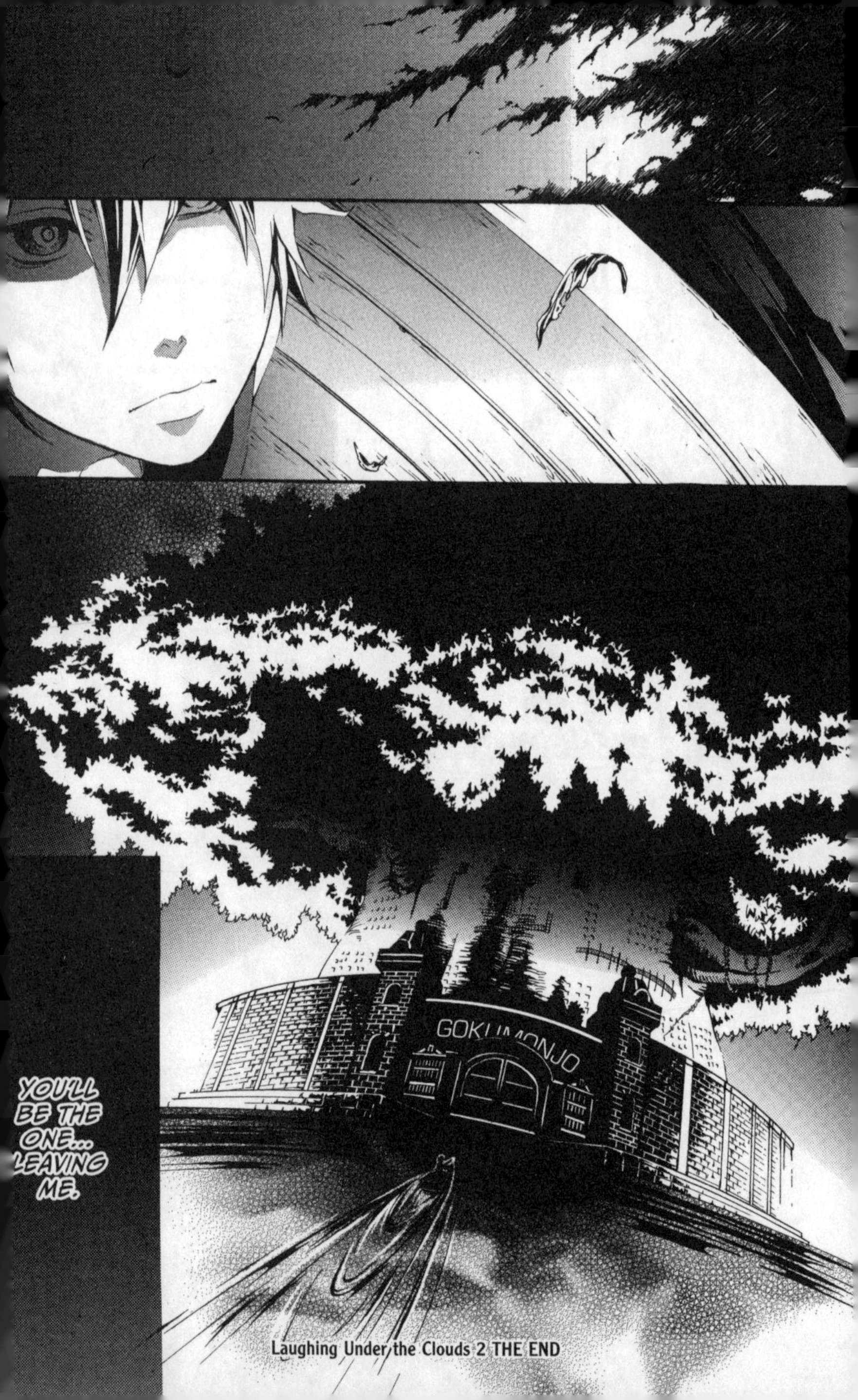
GOKUMONJO
YOU'LL BE THE ONE... LEAVING ME.
Laughing Under the Clouds 2 THE END

LAUGHING UNDER THE CLOUDS

THE CAT PROPOSED

Dento Hayane

The Cat Proposed

Dento Hayane

◊LOVE-x-LOVE◊

Matoi Souta is an overworked office worker tired of his life. Then, on his way home from a long day of work one day, he decides to watch a traditional Japanese play. But something strange happens. He could have sworn he saw one of the actors has cat ears. It turns out that the man is actually a bakeneko — a shapeshifting cat from Japanese folklore. And then, the cat speaks: "From now on, you will be my mate."

THE TREASURE OF THE KING AND THE CAT

You Kajika

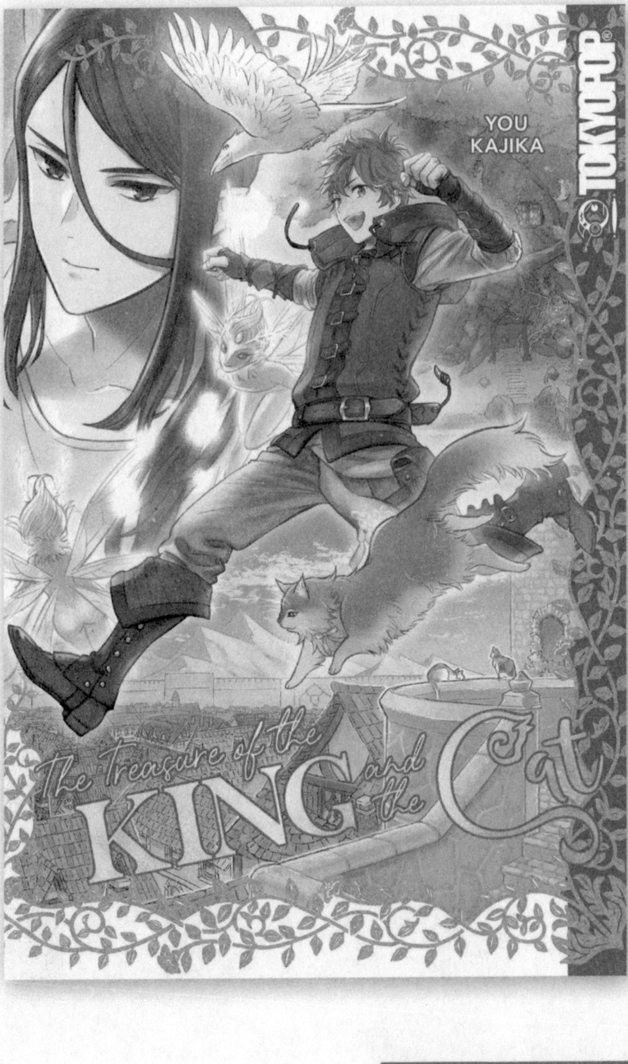
TOKYOPOP
YOU
KAJIKA
The Treasure of the
KING and the Cat

LOVE-x-LOVE

TOKYO POP

One day, a large number of people suddenly disappeared in the royal capital. When young King Castio goes out to investigate this occurrence, he comes across the culprit... but the criminal puts a spell on him! To help him out, the king calls the wizard O'Feuille to his castle, along with Prince Volks and his loyal retainer Nios. Together, they're determined to solve this strange, fluffy mystery full of cats, swords and magic!

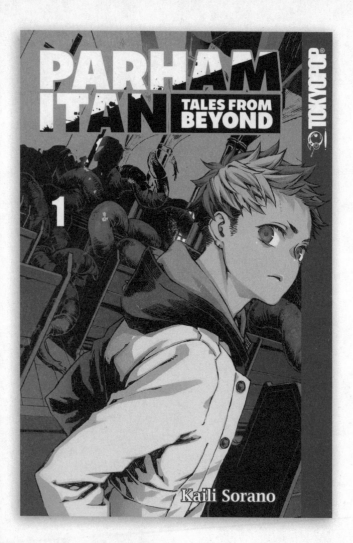

PARHAM ITAN: TALES FROM BEYOND, VOLUME 1

Kaili Sorano

SUPERNATURAL

Yamagishi and Sendo are schoolmates, but that's about all they have in common: one is a down-to-earth guy in the boxing club, while the other is a brainy, bookish conspiracy nut. But when they stumble across something weird and inexplicable after class one evening, it seems they'll have to set their differences aside in order to uncover the truth behind the mysterious creatures and strange figure prowling the school grounds.

HANGER, VOLUME 1

Hirotaka Kisaragi

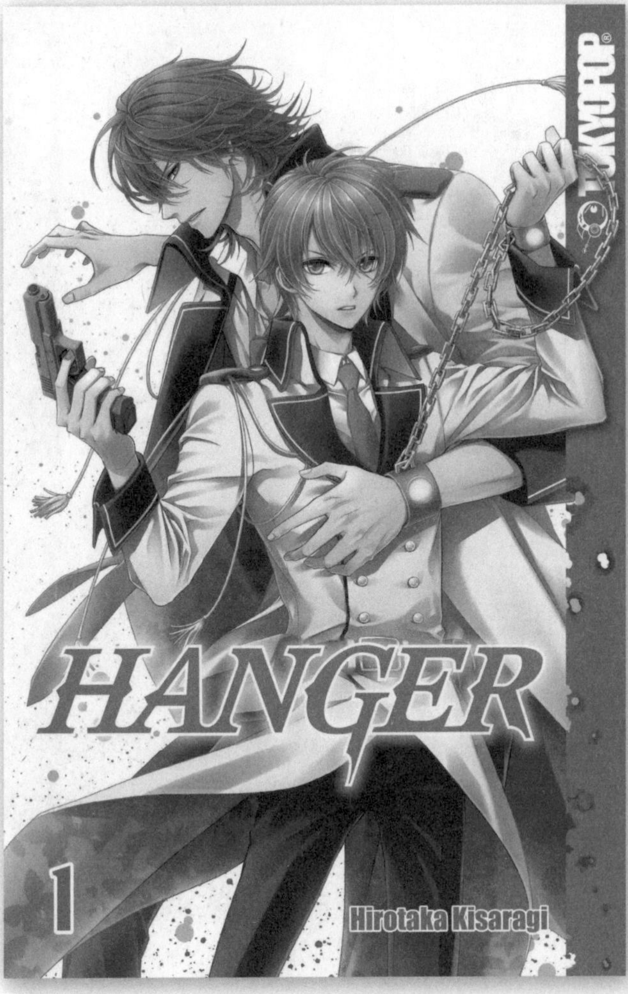
TOKYOPOP
HANGER
1
Hirotaka Kisaragi

ACTION

In a futuristic Neo-Tokyo, crime is rising rapidly in the wake of a new generation of super-drugs capable of enhancing the user's physical and mental abilities. Hajime Tsukomo is a new recruit on a federal task force trained to go after these powered-up criminals. Now he must team up with Zeroichi, a so-called Hanger looking to reduce his own jail sentence in exchange for helping to take down these chemically-boosted bad guys.

THE FOX & LITTLE TANUKI, VOLUME 1

Mi Tagawa

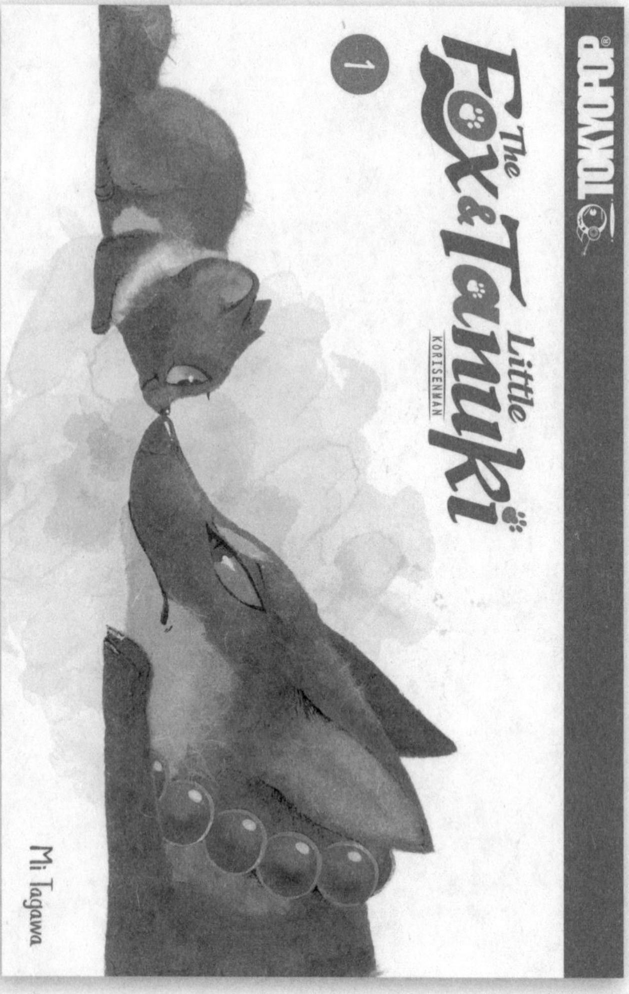

TOKYOPOP
The Fox & Little Tanuki
KORISENMAN
1
Mi Tagawa

FANTASY

It is said that there are some special animals occasionally born with great powers. Senzou the black fox is one of those... but instead of using his powers for good, he abused his strength until the Sun Goddess imprisoned him for his bad behavior. Three hundred years later, he's finally been released, but only on one condition — he can't have any of his abilities back until he successfully helps a tanuki cub named Manpachi become an assistant to the gods. Unfortunately for Senzou, there's no cheating when it comes to completing his task! The magic beads around his neck make sure he can't wander too far from his charge or ignore his duties, and so... Senzou the once-great Fox Spirit must figure out how to be an actually-great babysitter to a innocent little tanuki or risk being stuck without his powers forever!

TOKYO POP

DISNEY STITCH AND THE SAMURAI, VOLUME 1

Hiroto Wada

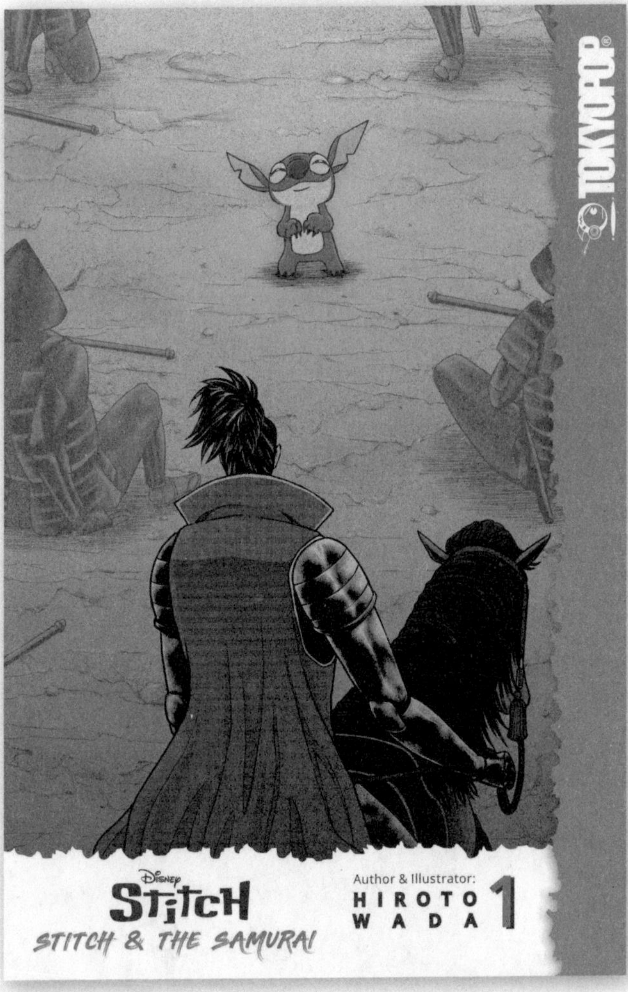
TOKYOPOP
Disney
Stitch
STITCH & THE SAMURAI
Author & Illustrator:
HIROTO WADA
1

DISNEY

While fleeing the Galactic Federation, Stitch's spaceship malfunctions and he makes an emergency landing... not in Hawaii, but in sengoku-era Japan! Discovered by the brutal warlord Lord Yamato and his clan, Stitch's incomparable cuteness is no match for the battle-weary samurai, who decides to bring the "blue tanuki" home with him. Will Stitch's love of chaos turn into a formidable advantage for the samurai's influence? Or will his cute and fluffy form disarm the noble lord's stern façade?

NO VAMPIRE, NO HAPPY ENDING, VOLUME 1

Shinya Shinya

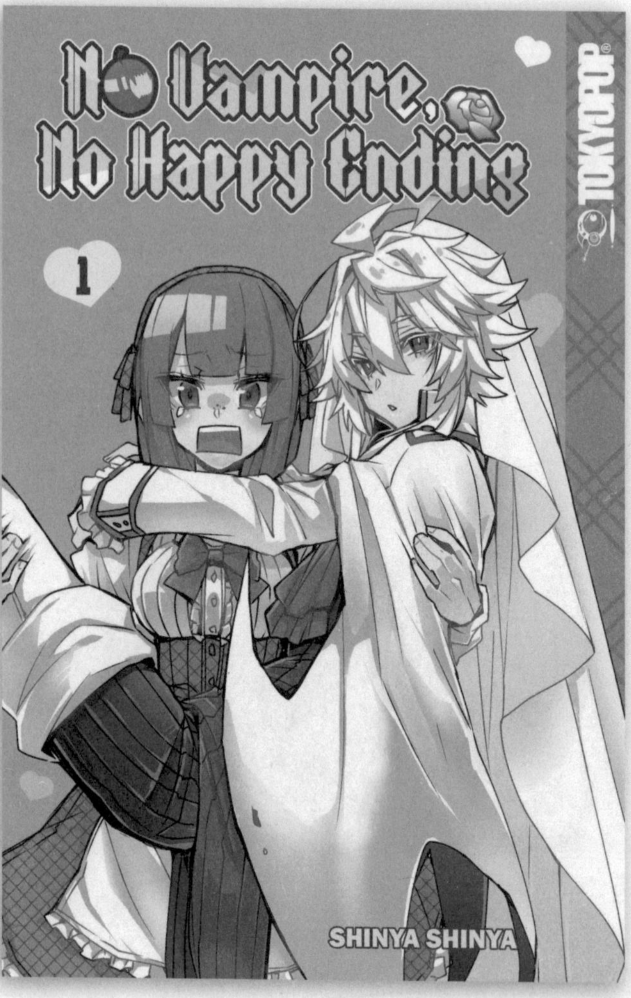
No Vampire, No Happy Ending
1
TOKYOPOP
SHINYA SHINYA

LOVE-x-LOVE

Arika is what you could charitably call a vampire "enthusiast." When she stumbles across the beautiful and mysterious vampire Divo however, her excitement quickly turns to disappointment as she discovers he's not exactly like the seductive, manipulative villains in her stories. His looks win first place, but his head's a space case. Armed with her extensive knowledge of vampire lore, Arika downgrades Divo to a beta vampire and begins their long, long... long journey to educate him in the ways of the undead.

TOKYO POP

KONOHANA KITAN VOLUME 1

Sakuya Amano

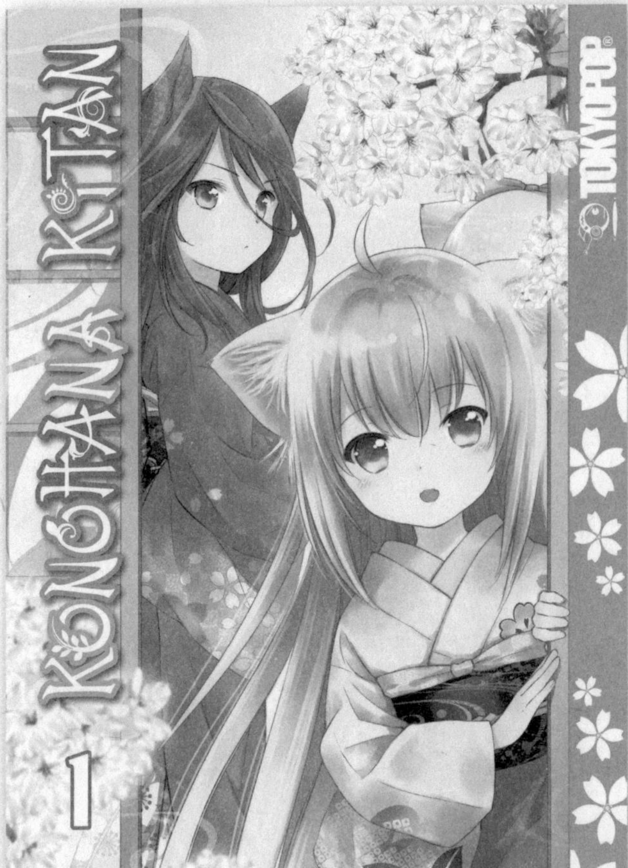
KONOHANA KITAN
1
Sakuya Amano
TOKYOPOP

FANTASY

Yuzu is a brand new employee at Konohanatei, the hot-springs inn that sits on the crossroads between worlds. A simple, clumsy but charmingly earnest girl, Yuzu must now figure out her new life working alongside all the other fox-spirits who run the inn under one cardinal rule - at Konohanatei, every guest is a god! Konohana Kitan follows Yuzu's day to day life working at the inn, meeting the other employees and ever-eclectic guests, and learning to appreciate the beauty of the world around her.

OSSAN IDOL! VOLUME 1

Mochiko Mochida

ICHIKA KINO • MOCHIKO MOCHIDA

IDOL

Miroku Osaki is 36 years old, unemployed, and unhappy. Having been bullied in his childhood and even into his adult life, he became a shut-in after being unfairly laid off. For a long time, the only thing that brought him joy was online gaming. Then, he tried the popular idol game called "Let's Try Dancing!" It was addicting... and transformative! Inspired by the game, Miroku decides to turn his life around. He begins singing karaoke and going to the gym, where he meets Yoichi, the director of an entertainment company who encourages Miroku to pursue his dreams. Miroku only wanted to be good at the game he loves, but when he accidentally uploads a clip of himself singing and dancing, it goes viral! Can he really become an idol, even at his age? Suddenly, it doesn't seem so impossible!

A Gentle Noble's
VACATION
RECOMMENDATION

MISAKI • MOMOCHI • SANDO

TOKYOPOP

1

ISEKAI

TOKYO POP

When Lizel mysteriously finds himself in a city that bears odd similarities to his own but clearly isn't, he quickly comes to terms with the unlikely truth: this is an entirely different world. Even so, laid-back Lizel isn't the type to panic. He immediately sets out to learn more about this strange place, and to help him do so, hires a seasoned adventurer named Gil as his tour guide and protector. Until he's able to find a way home, Lizel figures this is a perfect opportunity to explore a new way of life adventuring as part of a guild. After all, he's sure he'll go home eventually... might as well enjoy the otherworldly vacation for now!

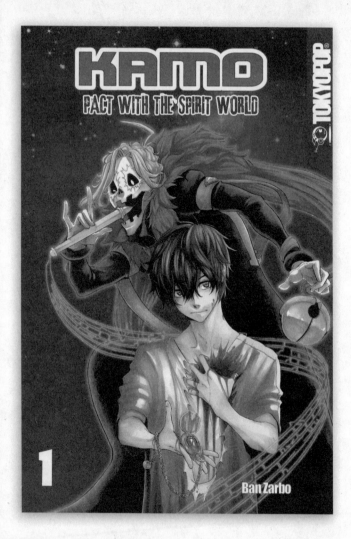

KAMO: PACT WITH THE SPIRIT WORLD, VOLUME 1

Ban Zarbo

Born with a failing heart, Kamo has fought death his whole life, but to no avail. As his body weakens and he readies to draw his final breath, he's visited by a powerful spirit named Crimson who offers him a deal: defeat and capture the souls of twelve spirits in exchange for a new heart. It seems too good to be true... and maybe it is. A pact with the spirit world; what could possibly go wrong?

UNDEAD MESSIAH, VOLUME 1

Gin Zarbo

TOKYOPOP
UNDEAD MESSIAH
1
Gin Zarbo

INTERNATIONAL
WOMEN of MANGA

TOKYO POP

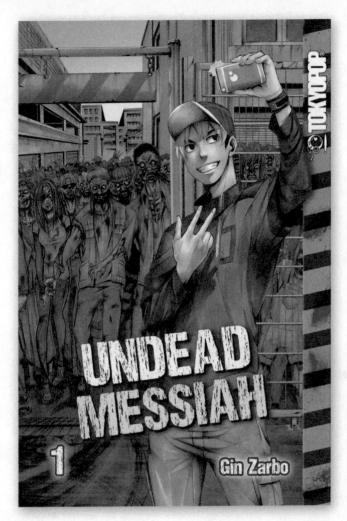

A pregnant woman is pursued by a supernatural creature. On the internet, videos of a bandaged hero surface. 15-year-old Tim Muley makes a terrible discovery in his neighbor's garden. Three seemingly unrelated events, all of which seem to point to an imminent zombie apocalypse! But this time the story's not about the end of mankind; it's about a new beginning...

Nana Yaa

GOLDFISCH, VOLUME 1

INTERNATIONAL
WOMEN of MANGA

Say hi to Morrey Gibbs! A fisher-boy in a flooded world overrun with dangerous mutated animals known as "anomals," he's got his own problems to worry about. Namely, how everything he touches turns to gold! Sure it sounds great, but gold underpants aren't exactly stylish -- or comfortable! Together with his otter buddy and new inventor friend Shelly, Morrey's on a quest to rid himself of his blessing-turned-curse and undo the tragedy it caused. That is of course, if they can dodge the treasure-hungry bounty hunters...

SCARLET SOUL VOLUME 1
Kira Yukishiro

SCARLET SOUL

KIRA YUKISHIRO

The kingdom of Nohmur has been a peaceful land for humans since the exorcist Eron Shirano repelled the demons and sealed the way to the underworld of Ruhmon. Generations later, sisters Lys and Rin are the heirs of the illustrious Shirano family, the most powerful exorcist clan charged with watching over the barrier and maintaining balance between the two worlds with the aid of Hikaten, the Sword of a Hundred Souls. Until one day, for unknown reasons, demons begin slipping through once more... and suddenly, Lys vanishes without a trace, leaving the sacred sword behind for her little sister to take up. As the underworld threat grows, Rin sets out alongside her companion, the mysterious Aghyr, to find her missing sister and figure out how to fortify the weakening barrier between her world and that of the monstrous creatures that threaten her kingdom once again.